The Greatest Traitor

The Greatest Traitor

The Secret Lives
of
Agent George Blake

ROGER HERMISTON

First published 2013 by
Aurum Press Limited
74–77 White Lion Street,
Islington N1 9PF
London
www.aurumpress.co.uk

A catalogue record for this book is available from the British Library.

ISBN 978 1 78131 046 5

1 3 5 7 9 10 8 6 4 2
2013 2015 2017 2016 2014

Typeset by SX Composing DTP, Rayleigh, Essex SS6 9HQ

Printed and bound in Great Britain by Clays Ltd, St Ives plc

To Eileen

Contents

Author's Note

For simplicity's sake, I have described the Soviet Union's security and intelligence organisation as the KGB throughout the whole of this book. It is the name, the acronym, most familiar to the general reader – and in any case, the *functions* of the organisation remained constant from 1917–1991. However, at various times in its history it has been called the Cheka, NKVD, OGPU, NKGB, MGB and MVD.

Likewise on the British side, I have opted to refer to SIS, the Secret Intelligence Service, as opposed to MI6, the title which is perhaps more familiar to twenty-first century readers. SIS was the name used from around 1920 onwards, and is enshrined in statute today. MI6 became a 'flag of convenience' for SIS in the late 1930s, and entered common parlance from the Second World War onwards.

Foreword and Acknowledgements

My interest in George Blake was first stirred on Friday, 17 September 1999, when I came into the offices of BBC Radio 4's *Today* to edit the following morning's programme.

Remarkably, I had not one but two spy stories on the running order that evening: it was as if the Cold War had never gone away. The breaking news concerned a lecturer from a northern university who had been exposed for his work as a recruiting agent for the Stasi – the East German secret police – in the late 1970s. My team started putting in the calls to mould the revelation into our 8.10 a.m. lead – the slot on the programme reserved for the most significant, compelling story. While they set to work calling the Foreign Office and assorted espionage watchers, I settled back to consider our other spy tale.

I had in my hands the tape of an interview our foreign affairs reporter in London had conducted over the telephone earlier that day, on the line to Moscow. It was an undoubted coup: apart from a brief flurry of activity around the time of his autobiography, a decade earlier, the Cold War traitor George Blake was not known for speaking to the Western media.

As I listened, I found myself completely absorbed by his voice, which was so redolent of the 1950s, a time when it seemed that educated men spoke in more assertive, rounded fashion. I knew little about Blake then beyond the bold headlines of his life – that he was a Soviet spy who had sold a nation's secrets and been sentenced to an incredible forty-two years in jail; that he had made a daring escape over the walls of Wormwood Scrubs and all the way to the Soviet capital.

That day we wanted to speak to Blake in his role as Cold War veteran, seeking his reaction to the unmasking, earlier that week, of 87-year-old Melita Norwood as a Soviet agent of some forty years standing. She had passed her KGB controller information about a top-secret project connected with the building of Britain's atomic bomb. In clipped, accented tones – those of a foreigner who has absorbed the English language well and can speak it almost too perfectly – Blake was effusive in his praise for the suburban pensioner, whom *The Times* had smartly dubbed 'The Spy Who Came in From the CO-OP'. Bracketing her with the 'atomic spies' – Donald Maclean, Klaus Fuchs, Morris Cohen, et al. – Blake told his interviewer: 'They were moved by higher considerations, because they firmly believed they were helping to save the world from an atomic holocaust, and so I think we all ought to be very grateful for what they had done.'

Asking his British audience to be 'grateful' to these characters was one thing; trying to persuade them that a member of the infamous Cambridge Five spy ring might be worthy of canonisation was quite another: 'I have known – and feel privileged to have known – a number of the atomic spies, and they're very good friends of mine, starting with Donald Maclean, and they are people of the highest character, indeed in some cases approaching saintliness; I don't hesitate to say that.'

Ten years after the Berlin Wall had been pulled down, Blake was still reluctant to budge from his ideological fastness. The failure of the Soviet Union, of Communism, was the fault of mankind not the system itself. 'Human beings are still too imperfect to build the perfect society,' was his assessment. It would arrive eventually, he maintained, but not for decades, even centuries.

Sure and unrepentant, the interview was certainly the most powerful item we had for the programme but, instead of giving it the hallowed 8.10 slot, I placed it at 8.40 a.m., separating it from the 'newsier' Stasi story. My editor Rod Liddle – whose instincts were invariably correct on these matters – rightly berated me afterwards for that decision.

In the coming years, I became fascinated with Blake and, as I learned more about him, I discovered an intriguing, flawed character, whose life had been played out against – and often at the heart of – some of the major events of the twentieth century. Twelve years later, once I had resolved to write about him, it was naturally incumbent on me to approach him for his version of the story. I telephoned him on the eve of his birthday in November 2011.

He had no warning of my call, despite a number of e-mails and letters which had all mysteriously gone astray. Most politely, he declined to be interviewed. He had written his own autobiography, and several other books, and said he had nothing more to add to what was already on record. He told me he felt in good health for his age, although his eyesight was steadily fading, to the point where he could no longer read or write, except to sign his name. For a man with a passion for literature and languages, this must be a bitter degeneration.

What he did agree to do was answer by e-mail, with his son acting as intermediary, some specific questions of fact about his life. The arrangement worked very smoothly for a number of months, until I began to probe the roles played by his various KGB handlers in the 1950s. Then the answers dried up.

This, then, is no authorised biography, but, through fresh interviews with those who knew Blake, previously unseen papers from his trial, and valuable material in British and German archives, I have been able to piece together what I hope is an authentic and revealing portrait of an astonishing life lived through remarkable times.

There has been no assistance from the present-day Secret Intelligence Service (SIS). Blake's file – like all the others – remains under lock and key, and the Service, unlike MI5, is not a participant in the regular Freedom of Information process. In 2010, it did commission Professor Keith Jeffery to write a history of its activities up to 1949, and it has released a limited amount of other material for 'biographies of important intelligence figures'. But by 'important', they mean, of course, heroic and worthy, and Blake is not considered either, hence the story of his treachery is something the Service would rather forget. One very senior former officer I contacted for assistance replied tersely that he had 'absolutely no enthusiasm for facilitating books about George Blake (of whatever type)'. I became used to this kind of response.

Despite that reaction, outside the intelligence community, there is an enduring fascination with Blake. Indeed, as I began to delve deeper into his life, I discovered that some of our leading film directors, novelists and playwrights had all trodden the path before me.

Blake inspired films by both John Huston and Alfred Hitchcock. The former's 1973 thriller *The Mackintosh Man* features the escape from prison of a KGB mole (played by Ian Bannen), alongside Paul Newman as a British intelligence officer. Hitchcock's *The Short Night*, had it ever been made, would have featured a British spy and traitor, Gavin Brand, escaping over the wall from Wormwood Scrubs prison. The screenplay had all the hallmarks of a classic Hitchcock thriller, even featuring a *Psycho*-like scene with an attempt to kill the heroine in a gas-filled sauna. Unfortunately, the director died just months after the script was completed and the project was cancelled.

Blake has also inspired several novels, notably Ted Allbeury's *Shadow of Shadows* (1983), in which the former secret agent meshes Blake's complete life story (thinly disguised) with the tale of SIS agent James Lawler's attempt to track down the missing Russian defector Colonel Petrov. A decade later, Ian McEwan gave a forbidding, suspicious Blake a substantial walk-on part in his 1990 novel *The Innocent*, the story of a twisted love affair set against the backdrop of spy-ridden Berlin in the 1950s.

Finally, there is the theatre: in his 1995 play *Cell Mates*, Simon Gray chronicles the volatile relationship between Blake (first played by Stephen Fry) and his co-conspirator Sean Bourke (Rik Mayall) in Wormwood Scrubs.

Blake's life could yet provide stories for many more films, novels and plays. Even before his defining years as spy and traitor, he performed a variety of roles: teenage courier with the Dutch Resistance; fugitive in occupied Europe; promising intelligence officer in Germany at the onset of the Cold War; and stoical captive at the hands of Communists in Korea.

His close confidante in jail, Kenneth de Courcy, assessed Blake's character in a way that is both troubling and difficult to dismiss: 'He was really three quite separate personalities. One was charming, witty, good natured and kind. The second was despairing, pessimistic, defeatist, while the third man was cruel, ruthless and without regard to personal or any other loyalty.'

How those different personalities manifested themselves, how they developed, and to what different ends Blake put them are the subjects this book seeks to examine. In his spy's 'wardrobe of disguises', how did the various cloaks Blake wore enable him to survive and prosper?

For survive he certainly did. Blake turned ninety in November 2012 and now lives out a comfortable retirement outside Moscow on a KGB pension, honoured as one of the major figures of Russian foreign intelligence, and held in high esteem by none other than President Vladimir Putin. Both men are products of an era in which Europe – indeed the entire world – was divided and carved up by two implacably opposed and warring ideologies. The Cold War required cold warriors – men and women who lurked in shadows, dealt in lies, half-truths and disinformation, and lived on the conflict's psychological and ideological frontline.

It also demanded belief. Blake, however deplorable his actions and choices might appear, remains a rare living specimen of a type that is almost lost to history: the principled traitor. Prime Minister Harold Macmillan had to delve back to the 1570s, to the young Catholic priests who plotted against Queen Elizabeth I, to find a satisfactory historical parallel to the intensity of faith and certainty of political ideology that he attributed to Blake.

And judged purely on the length of the sentence handed down to him at his trial, Blake might also lay claim to another title: the greatest traitor. Surely that unprecedented forty-two-year punishment, together with the Lord Chief Justice's conclusion that the spy had left the nation's intelligence service in tatters, is testament to a truly destructive betrayal?

Over in Moscow the 'honorific' certainly sits well. Recent years have seen a full-length dramatization of his life and a special documentary to celebrate his 90th birthday. In the pantheon of Soviet spies, he commands a seat at the top table, along with the likes of Second World War heroes Richard Sorge and Rudolph Abel.

It is true, of course, that Blake's nine years as a mole for the KGB never involved giving away the ultimate secret – the atomic bomb – as Klaus Fuchs did. It is arguable too that Kim Philby, in his more exalted position within SIS, caused greater quality of damage – if not quantity – than the middle-ranking Blake. Moreover, it has never been proven that his betrayal led to loss of life.

From this perspective then, his sentence might appear more a vindictive punishment than a carefully measured one; a late act of retribution borne out of the frustration of the political class at yet another in a long line of traitors who bedevilled British Intelligence in the 1950s and 1960s.

In that scenario Blake becomes something of a scapegoat. A confessed traitor, but also an outsider made to pay for the failings of a secretive establishment then in its death throes. As we shall see, there were certainly those who reached – and were prepared to act on – this interpretation at the time.

George Blake's life has touched many in the intelligence world and beyond it, for good or ill. Despite the passing of time I have managed to talk to a number of those who knew him, and there are two to whom I am especially indebted.

Lord Hutchinson of Lullington – then Jeremy Hutchinson – represented Blake at his trial in 1961, and details of his eloquent defence that day in May can be read for the first time in this book. He was most helpful in his recollections of Blake, and also described vividly to me the forces arraigned against him as a new QC fighting his client's case in the Old Bailey more than half a century ago.

Michael Randle, a longstanding peace campaigner, believed Blake's sentence to be inhumane, and the remarkable story of how he assisted his former prison companion is told in detail here. His own riveting book, *The Blake Escape*, was one of those that helped guide my chapters on Blake's time in prison, in hiding, and then of course on the dramatic journey across the Iron Curtain. Randle generously gave me access to some of his private papers and to a gripping chapter in another of his books, the as yet unpublished *Rebel Verdict*, an account of his 1991 trial on charges of helping Blake escape.

Michael's wife Anne was also most helpful, especially with memories of those days in the winter of 1966. The Randles may not share all my conclusions about their friend but I trust their own actions and views are faithfully represented here.

I also owe a special debt of gratitude to Tom Bower, acclaimed investigative journalist and writer, who was one of the first to interview Blake in depth back in 1990. The results were broadcast in an absorbing BBC *Inside Story* documentary, 'The Confession'. Not only did I watch the film, but buried away in a couple of boxes in Tom's garage were several hours of 'raw' tapes – a good deal of the interview with Blake, and others with his colleagues and friends, that had to be left on the cutting room floor. I have made full use of those recordings in this book, and they have provided invaluable insights into my subject and his times.

Ben Birnberg represented Blake for a while in his battle for his book royalties against the British Government. He was most generous in giving me access to all the legal documents associated with the case.

Leopold Van Ewijk talked to me very movingly and compellingly about the role his wife Greetje played in the Dutch underground and, in particular, the vital part she played in ushering young George Blake (then Behar) across the border and on the first leg of his journey across Europe.

Louis Wesseling learned Arabic alongside Blake on a course in Shemlan, Lebanon, in 1960–61, and his very clear memories of their association and their conversations are recorded in these pages.

There are also several former SIS officers who have been most helpful with their recollections of Blake and his times, but they have asked to remain anonymous.

While researching and writing this book, I regularly attended the stimulating seminars hosted by Professor Christopher Andrew, an authority on intelligence and espionage, at Corpus Christi College, Cambridge. I am most grateful to him. Through the wisdom of the guest speakers and the quality of the ensuing conversation, those sessions helped me build up a far deeper knowledge of the intelligence world.

Also from Cambridge University, I must thank Professor Jonathan Haslam, an expert on the Cold War – especially from the Soviet side – who has been a source of valuable suggestions and insights into some of the characters and events depicted in this book.

There are many other people who I must thank for advice and assistance and stories about Blake and his times, including Gordon Corera, Alan Judd, Tennent 'Pete' Bagley, Phillip Knightley, Ian McEwan, David Cornwell, Anthony Cavendish, Oliver Miles, Colin Cohen, Alain Gresh, Sylvie Braibant, Professor Keith Jeffery, Martin Coubert, Adri Wijnen, and 'Shorty' Eastabrook.

I am greatly indebted to Abby D'Arcy Hughes, who unearthed vital new information about Blake's time in Berlin. Elke Piron's researches into his early years in Holland were equally invaluable, while Nvard Chalikyan provided immaculate translations of Russian newspapers, books and films in which Blake featured. My friends Conny Loosen and Rita Cillessen contributed some important additional German and Dutch translation.

My agent Andrew Gordon has been a continuing source of encouragement and guidance. Ray Newman was a splendid copy editor, assiduous in locating errors in the text and equally creative when suggesting improvements. Finally, last but certainly not least, Sam Harrison has been the ideal editor, always full of the soundest advice on content and style, all done in the most constructive and helpful manner.

Roger Hermiston,
Cavendish,
January 2013.

'What do you think spies are: priests, saints and martyrs? They're a squalid procession of vain fools, traitors too, yes: pansies, sadists and drunkards, people who play Cowboys and Indians to brighten their rotten lives.'

Alec Leamas in *The Spy Who Came in from the Cold*
by John le Carré

'It is the spy who has been called upon to remedy the situation created by the deficiencies of ministers, diplomats, generals and priests . . . we do not have to develop, like the Parliamentarians conditioned by a lifetime, the ability to produce the ready phrase, the smart reply and the flashing smile. And so it is not surprising these days that the spy finds himself the main guardian of intellectual integrity.'

George Young, Vice-Chief of the British Secret Intelligence
Service, as reported by George Blake

'Blake asserted he had yielded to no material pressure or advantages but had been genuinely "converted to Communism while a prisoner of war in Korea". With the ideological spy, we were faced with a phenomenon such as had hardly appeared in these islands for some four hundred years.'

Harold Macmillan, *At the End of the Day: 1961–63*

Prologue

Central Criminal Court, London, 11.40 a.m., Wednesday, 3 May 1961

For more than half a century, No. 1 Court at the Old Bailey had been the Grand Theatre of Crime, the stage on which the worst of humanity took a bow. Few who stepped into the dock in this intimate oak-panelled room, representing the fearsome infallibility of English justice, could dare to contemplate freedom when the curtain came down at the end of their inquisition. Its many famous players had included the likes of patent medicine salesman Dr Harvey Crippen, who poisoned his wife and buried her in the coal cellar, and John Reginald Christie, the clerk who strangled at least eight women at 10 Rillington Place.

But in the Cold War, intelligence became the most dangerous weapon, and the court found itself dealing with a different kind of criminal – the betrayers of the nation's secrets. Klaus Fuchs, the theoretical physicist who gave the Soviets comprehensive plans for the atomic bomb, was one of the first of this new breed, convicted in March 1950 and sentenced to fourteen years imprisonment. Just two months previously, Court No. 1 had played host to the Portland Spy Ring – Gordon Lonsdale, Henry Houghton, Ethel Gee and Peter and Helen Kroger – who had all been handed substantial jail terms for passing details of Britain's nuclear submarine fleet across the Iron Curtain.

Never in anyone's memory, however, had such strict security measures been imposed on a criminal trial in peacetime as were put in place at the Old Bailey on 3 May 1961. Outside, dozens of police cordoned off the pavement, allowing no one near the building.

Inside, a 38-year-old 'Government official' who had already confessed to his crimes listened intently as the judge, Lord Chief

Justice Lord Parker, brought his summing-up to a conclusion and prepared to pass sentence. George Blake, a handsome man of dark complexion, with his brown hair fashionably long, was dressed smartly in a grey suit, checked shirt and blue silk tie with red dots. His hands gripped the ledge of the dock.

Little had been known about Blake before he entered the courtroom that May morning. A number of brief appearances in magistrates' court had disclosed something of the gravity of the charges facing him, but details of exactly who he was and what he had done remained scant and obscure. The newspaper reporters in court learned precious little more. The details of his profession were skirted around in open session, and the prosecuting counsel, Attorney-General Sir Reginald Manningham-Buller, merely referred to the fact that until his arrest Blake had been 'employed in the Government's service both in this country and overseas'. Fleeting mention was made of his five-year service in the Royal Navy. Although those present with sharp memories might have recalled that, back in April 1953, he had been one of the first prisoners set free by the Communists towards the end of the Korean War. They might also have remembered the sight of he and his fellow captives arriving to a heroes' welcome in front of the TV cameras at Brize Norton airfield.

At 10.40 a.m., the court had gone into closed session, and Lord Parker had ordered No. 1 Court to be locked and the shutters to be put up on the glass-panelled doors. What there was to know about George Blake – his life story, the details of his career – was laid out by his defence in private, only adding to the air of mystery surrounding him.

The court had been open for the prosecution speech and was re-opened for the Judge's summing-up. Of the detail of his offences, there was only the broadest outline but, in Blake's own words, the enormity of his crimes was made abundantly clear. Manningham-Buller had quoted the heart of Blake's confession back at him: 'I must freely admit there was not an official document of any importance to which I had access which was not passed to my Soviet contact.'

Lord Parker's opening remarks in his summing-up offered little comfort: 'It is clear your case is akin to treason. Indeed, it is one of the worst that can be envisaged other than in a time of war . . . your conduct in many other countries would undoubtedly carry the death penalty. In our law, however, I have no option but to sentence you to imprisonment, and for your traitorous conduct extending over so many years there must be a very heavy sentence.'

Blake feared the worst – fourteen years in prison, as had been handed down to Fuchs. He fervently hoped it might be ten, perhaps eleven, but he had few grounds for optimism. Throughout the trial to that point, he had felt more like a spectator, or a filmgoer, content to sit and watch as others played out another man's drama. Now, though, Parker's ominous words demanded his attention: 'The court cannot, even if so minded, give you a sentence of life imprisonment . . . there are, however, five counts to which you have pleaded guilty, each dealing with separate periods in your life during which you were betraying your country, and the court will impose upon you a sentence of four-teen years imprisonment on each of those counts.'

Even then, Blake and everyone else in No.1 Court had no reason to expect what was to come. In the natural order of these matters, surely the sentences would run *concurrently*, meaning he would serve four-teen years. Parker delivered the hammer blow: 'Those in respects of counts one, two and three being *consecutive*, those in respect of counts four and five concurrent. Accordingly, the total sentence upon you is one of forty-two years imprisonment.'

A communal gasp sounded from the spectators in the gallery, followed by a moment of shocked silence. As they glanced towards the prisoner in the dock for his reaction, they noticed a flicker of a smile play across his lips as he stood still, uncomprehending, gazing directly at Lord Parker. After some seven or eight seconds, Blake turned around slowly, taking in the faces around the court, first those on the press bench, then those on the solicitors' table, and finally those with a profes-sional interest who gazed down from the prime seats in the gallery.

Then, escorted by a warder, Blake hesitantly crossed the wooden floor of the dock. He leaned over and whispered courteously to his defence team: 'Thank you.' He then disappeared from view, descending to the cells below.

Forty-two years in jail: a record. The previous longest consecutive sentence in British criminal history dated from 1887 when a man was jailed for twenty-nine years for demanding money with menaces and robbery with violence. The severity of the punishment led Prime Minister Harold Macmillan to reflect in his diary: 'The Lord Chief Justice has passed a savage sentence – forty-two years in prison! Naturally, we can say nothing.'

Forty-two years, and almost no one knew exactly what Blake had done to deserve it.

Among the friends and colleagues with whom he had endured the miseries of the Korean prison camps, there was disbelief. To them, he had been the epitome of bravery and defiance; a man worthy of implicit trust. Commissioner Herbert Lord of the Salvation Army told the *Daily Mirror's* reporter: 'I find it almost impossible to believe that the George Blake I saw kneel nonchalantly in the snow as a North Korean guard beat him with a rifle butt could have turned into a traitor . . . For that was only one of many times the young vice-consul, who was my fellow prisoner for thirty-four months, showed contempt for the Communists.'

Yet as reporters began to uncover the other side of George Blake, the quietly brave, charming man beyond the headlines screaming 'TRAITOR', one or two of the testimonials hinted at something else. Philip Deane, the Greek-born *Observer* journalist, who, like Herbert Lord, had suffered side by side with Blake in North Korea, said his friend 'had Walter Mitty dreams, always seeing himself knighted or consecrated bishop for some service to the state or God'. Was this daydreaming merely a harmless, introspective habit, indulged during the long hours suffered in the hothouse psychology of the prison camp? Or had it developed into something more than a dream? A temptation to play the great spy in the secret power play of the Cold War?

Clues as to what had driven Blake's treachery could be found in Jeremy Hutchinson's eloquent speech of mitigation, though, at the time, neither the Press or the public were allowed to hear it. His client's life, the QC said, had been almost wholly forged in the conflicts and upheavals of the twentieth century. From the age of sixteen Blake had known little else but constant clandestine activity, since he immersed himself in 'war, deprivation, murder and suchlike'. Hutchinson had told the closed court Blake's extraordinary life story – a story that, to all intents and purposes, was now at an end.

Blake, however, had a final chapter in mind. As he left the Old Bailey that afternoon for Wormwood Scrubs, handcuffed to two prison officers in the back of a small van, he peered out of the window and saw the newspaper vendors carrying placards emblazoned with his photograph and sentence, and he made a vow to himself: he wouldn't stay in prison until 2003, when he would be 80 years old, whatever it took. Fourteen years he could have accepted, but forty-two appeared vengeful. To paraphrase Marx, he had nothing to lose but his chains.

He would escape.

1

A Question of Identity

George Blake was born George Behar, in Rotterdam, in the
Netherlands. His mother Catherine Gertrui (née Beijderwellen)
gave birth on 11 November 1922, at 3 p.m. In a life that would be
shaped by confused identity and shifting loyalty, what happened next
was surely a portent of things to come.

His mother and father discussed what to call their son and had
reached an easy decision: two grandfathers on either side of the family
were called Jacob, so the baby boy would carry that name in memory
of both. But, on leaving his wife and infant son that afternoon to walk
to the town hall in Rotterdam to declare the birth, Albert William
Behar had time to think, free of family constraints.

It was Armistice Day, just four years after the end of The Great
War in which he had fought. Despite his own rather mysterious
origins, Albert was then a patriotic Briton: he decided there could
be no more appropriate name on that auspicious day than George,
in honour of king (George V) and country. The registrar was duly
informed.

It was an uncommon name for a Dutch boy, and Albert quickly
discovered that his impulsive act was scorned by little George's

conservative and parodial relatives: instead, they would always prefer
to call him by his Dutch nickname, Poek.

A few years later as little George started to read, the first book with
which he was presented was the illustrated *Children's Bible*. Heroes like
Abraham and Isaac, David and Saul, and Samson stirred his imagination. But above all, the character he enjoyed most, and with whom he
most closely identified, was Jacob – the biblical source of his intended
name.

The Behar family home was at 104, Gedempte Botersloot, in
Rotterdam, one of the city's oldest and wealthiest streets. By the time
Albert and his family took up residence there it had undergone major
development, but without losing its air of affluence. The year after
George's birth the Behars moved into the vacant house next door,
No. 102, where there was more space. Their second child, Adele
Gertrud, was born there in June 1924, and the family moved soon
afterwards to an even bigger residence at 40c Spengensekade, an
equally respectable address. There, Catherine gave birth to their
second daughter, Elizabeth, in August 1925.

It seemed an entirely conventional middle-class life, but their road
to this destination had been a rocky one, and their union was anything
but commonplace.

Both sets of parents had frowned upon the relationship. The
Beijderwellens were very reluctant to see their daughter marrying a
somewhat exotic man whose past seemed cloaked in mystery, however
charming he might have been: a Dutchman with solid bourgeois
credentials would have been their preference. And the wealthy Behar
family, for reasons that would only become clear many years later,
warned Albert, quite straightforwardly, that if he married this Dutch
girl he would be cut off without a penny.

Catherine Beijderwellen was 26 at the time of her marriage – tall, fair-
haired, and vivacious. She came from a conventional, well-established
Rotterdam family with deep Protestant roots, although they were
actually members of the minority Remonstrant Church. She knew

little about her fiancée. She thought Behar was an English surname and understood that Albert was British, though she knew he had been born in Cairo, and that his family still lived there. His origins did not matter: she was under the spell of this dark, handsome man whose romantic image was only enhanced by shrapnel wounds on his face sustained in the First World War. An unreliable outsider in one light, he was undoubtedly a heroic figure in another.

Albert had constructed a stirring narrative of the life he had lived before meeting Catherine. He claimed to have studied at the Sorbonne in Paris, to have served in the French Foreign Legion, and then, in the First World War, to have won the Military Cross and the French Croix de Guerre. Other accounts of his life have even had him serving on Field Marshal Haig's Intelligence Staff.

Although a good deal of this story had the ring of truth, certain parts were undoubtedly embroidered, and one or two others would later fail to stand up to examination. It only becomes possible to clearly separate fact from fiction in Albert's life when looking at what he did in the First World War, where his full service record reveals the less glamorous, though no less heroic, experience of an 'ordinary' soldier.

Enlisting in France in 1915, he served as a driver and motorcycle despatch rider on the Western Front. He was, indeed, seriously wounded, sustaining a fractured back and skull and contusions to his face and hands. Such injuries certainly resemble the damage that might have been caused by an exploding shell, but his service notes include the word 'acc', suggesting that the words were accidentally incurred. Either way, he was evacuated to England for treatment on 25 May 1918. While recovering in hospital in London, he was awarded the Meritorious Service Medal for gallantry and commendable war service.

Albert's last posting with what was by then called the Royal Army Service Corps was to Rotterdam, in December 1918. It was early in the following year, as he helped the British Expeditionary Force wind down its wartime operations, that he met Catherine.

Despite unanswered questions about his background and her family's disapproval, the marriage went ahead. Given their strength of purpose, Albert and Catherine felt they had little choice but to elope and so headed for London, a city Albert knew well after spending time there recuperating after his wartime exploits. The wedding ceremony took place at Chelsea Registry Office on Monday, 16 January 1922. The certificate shows that they both listed 11 Markham Square – just 300 yards away – as their residence at the time of the marriage. Two men named G. Challis and A.J. Grimes – Army colleagues of Albert – were noted as the witnesses.

The Behars' opposition to that marriage would remain total. They would have little or no contact with their son and his growing family for the next thirteen years. The Beijderwellens, however, were gradually worn down. They were reconciled with Catherine and accepted Albert before George was born.

The new arrival quickly became the subject of great attention from his many aunts and uncles. His favourite companion was Aunt Truss, his mother's unmarried youngest sister, who held a good job with an established Dutch bank. On long weekend walks, she would regale him with interesting tales of her workplace, skilfully imitating the speech and mannerisms of her colleagues and keeping young George endlessly amused.

Albert, meanwhile, had a secret and meant to keep it. The battle he had fought to persuade Catherine's parents to accept him was difficult enough, and he felt – almost certainly correctly – that to disclose the nature of his true self to them would still have disastrous consequences. Having listed his religion as Roman Catholic for the British Army, he now promptly declared he was Evangelical Lutheran when registering for citizenship in Rotterdam.

Initially Albert relied on two sources of income to provide a comfortable life for his family. One was his Army pension, but the other – more significant – came from his Turkish railway bonds. Those were rendered worthless, however, when Kemal Atatürk's government nationalised the railway industry in 1927. For several years, Albert ran a store selling leather and sports goods down in the Leuvenhaven, one of Rotterdam's oldest harbours. Then, in 1928, he decided to open a small factory – from the ground floor of his house – making leather gloves for the longshoremen in the port. That venture was barely underway when it was hit hard by the Wall Street crash of 1929 and the subsequent worldwide recession. Little work was taking place in the shipyards, and the widespread laying off of workers had a perilous knock-on effect for small businesses like Albert's.

George's aunt's husband, who was a grain dealer, went bankrupt at this time. 'Like several other ruined and embittered middle-class people my aunt and uncle began to look towards National Socialism for salvation,' Blake recalled. 'At home the daily conversation centred around the ups and downs of business, the difficulties of paying creditors, how many people and who should be sacked and kept on, whether there were signs that things were getting better or, on the contrary, worse.'

Albert's business struggled on even as his health began to deteriorate. He was having difficulties with his lungs, perhaps related to the effects of mustard gas from the battlefields of the First World War. Whatever the reason, the family doctor advised that a move away from smoky, grimy Rotterdam to an environment with cleaner, fresher air might do the patient some good. When, in 1933, an opportunity arose to move to Scheveningen, a pleasant seaside resort not far from The Hague, the Behars eagerly grasped it, settling into a villa at No. 4 Maasstraat, close to the impressive Kurhaus, the luxury hotel and concert venue.

To sit down at the dinner table in the Behar home in the early 1930s would have been an entertaining yet puzzling experience. Albert was fluent in English and French, usually opting to speak the former as he continued to uphold the image he had created of himself as a British entrepreneur. He did not speak Dutch, however, and stubbornly refused to learn the mother tongue of his wife and children. Catherine knew a little English and could communicate well enough with her husband, but George and his sisters – although just starting to learn both French and English at school – did not share a common language with their father. Albert would effectively remain a stranger in a foreign land, an attitude no doubt partially responsible for the failure of his successive businesses.

To his children he seemed a remote, otherworldly figure. When he was working, he would set off early in the morning and not arrive home in the evenings until after 8 p.m. when they had gone to bed. On Sunday, his only day off, he would usually choose to stay at home and read while George and his sisters would be taken for a walk by their mother and aunt. He left most of the care of his children, material and spiritual, to Catherine, and retreated into the background. When he did turn his attention to them, he invariably spoiled them with spontaneous gifts and presents.

Nonetheless, the young Blake inherited his father's intellectual curiosity and sense of adventure. When growing up in Rotterdam, he was inspired by the famous statue of one of the city's notable sons, Erasmus, which he could see from his window. The philosopher is depicted holding a book, and George was assured he would turn a page each time the clock on the nearby church struck the hour. The little boy believed the story and spent much time pleasantly anticipating the event.

As well as reading – he particularly enjoyed stories from the Bible, and books on Dutch history – George's imagination was stirred by thoughts of life in foreign lands. He would spend many hours on his own wandering the quayside at the port of Rotterdam, watching the ships come in from all over the world and observing the diverse cargo being unloaded – timber from Russia, spices from India, coffee from Brazil.

Dina Regoort, a long-serving maid to the Behar family, remembered him as a quiet, polite, somewhat solitary boy. 'I always felt he was apart and rather sad,' she said. 'He had no friends of his own age, and he did not play with his schoolmates or other boys.'

Instead he preferred to act out games of fantasy in his own home, often persuading his reluctant sisters Adele and Elizabeth to join him. One family snapshot of the time shows him in Arab dress, another in the guise of an admiral. In one game, dressed in an old black gown belonging to his grandmother, he would be a minister of the church addressing his congregation (his sisters). In another, he would place an old black hat on his head and pretend to be the judge presiding over a courtroom. Dina would often be called upon to play the prisoner in the dock – more often than not accused of serious crimes.

In 1935, Albert Behar's failing health took a turn for the worse. Lung cancer was diagnosed and, after a period of many months confined to his bed at home, he was transferred to a hospital in The Hague. George, who was in his first year at the municipal Gymnasium, went to see his father every day after school. One particular visit left an abiding and disquieting memory.

> He was lying in a cubicle with curtains around it, which were usually open. One day, as I was sitting at his bedside, he asked me to close the curtain. Somehow I just could not make out exactly what it was he wanted, however much I tried. The more I tried, the less I understood. He got angry with me and I felt desperate and was almost in tears . . . Fortunately, the man in the next cubicle who, being ill himself probably understood him better, told me what he wanted and all was well. But I shall never forget this experience, especially as he died shortly afterwards.

Albert Behar died on 6 April 1936, aged 46, leaving his family in dire financial straits. His faltering business went bankrupt almost immediately, and after all the outstanding debts had been paid off, there was little money for his wife and her three children to live on. Catherine took on lodgers in the villa, and cooked meals for office girls in Scheveningen. The family just about kept their heads above water until help arrived from an unexpected quarter, accompanied by the truth about Albert's origins, which he had successfully concealed for so many years.

Albert had had little, if any, contact with his well-off relations in Egypt after he had defied their wishes in 1922. However, before he died, he told his wife that if she found herself unable to cope, and was worried about the welfare and education of the children, she should contact his sister Zephira in Cairo. Catherine duly did so, receiving a reply that astonished her, and placed her in something of a dilemma. Albert, it transpired, was Jewish.

The Behars could trace their Jewish ancestry back to the Iberian Peninsula in the fifteenth century. Their ancestors were among an estimated 200,000 who were forced to find new lives in North Africa and Europe when the Spanish monarchs Ferdinand and Isabella issued the Alhambra Decree – expelling all Jews who would not convert from Christianity – in 1492. Many of these Sephardic Jews (*Sefarad* is the Hebrew name for Spain) found a safe haven in the Ottoman Empire. In an atmosphere of tolerance for religious minorities for which the Sultans were renowned, the Behars and others quickly flourished, fashioning livelihoods as artisans, doctors and intellectuals.

The status of Jews in the Netherlands in the 1920s was very different, however. Though overt anti-Semitism was less prevalent than in other parts of Europe, there were few Jews (only around 1.4 per cent of the population) and little widespread interaction between Jewish people and others. Albert was not religious and kept his ethnicity secret, eschewing all contact with Jewish organisations and Jewish cultural life, rather than belong to a minority.

All this was surprising enough for Catherine, but Zephira's letter also offered assistance, with conditions. She and her husband, a wealthy banker blind since birth, would help, but not by offering money. Instead, they proposed to take George off his mother's hands for a few years and give him a home with them, along with a good education in Cairo.

Catherine was in a quandary. She did not want to lose her son but the financial pressures bearing down on her were great. She also recognised this as a unique opportunity for George to expand his horizons beyond provincial Holland. He was a gifted boy and Cairo, famed as a great classical city of learning, could be the making of him.

'I was torn. I was very much attached to my home, my Dutch relatives . . . and the thought of leaving them for the home of an unknown aunt and uncle, whose language I did not speak, frightened me,' Blake recalled. 'On the other hand, I was strongly attracted by the prospect of travelling to a far and exotic country and the entirely new life and adventures which awaited me there. It was this thirst for adventure and the unknown that proved the stronger and, after a few days of thought, I told my mother I would like to go.'

Two months later, on a bright September morning in 1936, 13-year-old George boarded a Norwegian cargo ship bound for Alexandria. There is a picture of him taken on that day on the quayside, smartly-dressed in his plus fours suit, flanked by his mother, grandmother and two sisters. Adele and Elizabeth are wreathed in smiles, while Catherine – a little nervous-looking – has an affectionate arm round her son's shoulder.

George himself looks confident enough, as if emboldened by his first trip abroad, a journey to one of the countries of his imagination. Indeed, in the fortnight's voyage that followed, he relished the company and the guidance of his shipmates and, by the time the boat docked in Egypt, he was more than ready to confront any challenges the world abroad might present.

For the next two years, George lived in conditions of great comfort at No. 42 Gabalaya Street – otherwise known in Cairo as 'Villa Curiel', after the family name of his aunt's husband, Daniel Curiel. This lavish mansion stood in the most fashionable suburb of the Egyptian capital, far removed from the earthy, dirty city streets. It was situated at the northern tip of the Island of Zamalek, between two branches of the

River Nile and right alongside the famous Gezira Sporting Club, sanctuary of the British occupation. Effectively, a small palace with seventeen rooms, it was surrounded by a large park planted with palms and bushes. Exquisite tapestries and rare paintings hung on the walls, and the floors were covered with oriental carpets and rugs. The view over the Nile from the second floor was among the very best in the city.

George's first year in Cairo was a miserable one. His uncle and aunt decided to send him to a French school so he could might become fluent in the language of choice for the Middle East's educated classes. At the Lycée he was alienated from his peers, surrounded by rich Egyptian boys, most of them older, who spoke Arabic outside the classroom.

Only when he was moved to the English School in 1937 did he begin to settle down in his new surroundings. This establishment resembled a traditional English public school, with prefects, morning prayers and corporal punishment, although most of the pupils were 'day boys' rather than boarders. George's first school report clearly demonstrated that he had now found his feet. 'His work has given satisfaction in all subjects,' wrote his form master, 'and promises well for the future'. His aptitude for languages and application in his lessons were praised fulsomely. With the benefit of hindsight, however, the school motto now seems singularly inappropriate for this particular alumnus from the Class of '37: *Ducit amor patriae* – Patriotism is our guide.

Once settled in the English School and getting to grips with the English language, George started going to the American Reformed Church, whose services were similar to those of the Dutch Church. Later he would visit the Anglican cathedral, much moved by the beauty of the liturgy. Back in the villa, he discovered a French Bible in his uncle's library and read a chapter of it, morning and night.

Surprisingly, perhaps, his Jewish relations never seriously attempted to convert him to their religion. At this stage, anyway, George had taken his newfound identity in his stride. 'The fact that I had Jewish blood did not worry me,' he later maintained. 'On the contrary I was rather proud of it. It seemed to me that I was now twice elect; once by birth through the promise made to Abraham and once by grace through redemption by the blood of Christ.'

Instead, any efforts to shape young George's views on life took political form. It was at Villa Curiel, a monument to wealth and privilege, that he received his first primer in the virtues of Communism. It came from his cousins, Daniel's two sons, Raoul, aged 24, and Henri, 23. Raoul had introduced his brother to the works of Marx and Lenin, and Henri had fast become a Communist in all but name. Tall, thin, with a serious, thoughtful look and an occasional dazzling smile, he took young George under his wing. They would have many long political and philosophical discussions in which Henri would try to persuade the teenage boy of the benefits of a Marxist society.

Blake has recognised the impact of those long conversations: 'Henri was a young man, very charming, very attractive and he held strong Communist views. They were a great influence on me, but I resisted them at that time because I was a very religious boy. But, with hindsight, many of Henri's views acted as a time-bomb.'

In the summer of 1939 George's academic progress was confirmed when he passed his end-of-term exams with flying colours, winning prizes for Latin and History. He was all set to sit for the London University matriculation examination the following spring and went home to Scheveningen for a holiday.

Then, just a week before he was due to return to Cairo, something happened which derailed not only George's future but that of the whole world: Hitler's troops marched into Poland.

George did return to Cairo, but the Beijderwellen family conferred in his absence. His uncle Anthony who lived in Gelderland, and with whom George had spent some time during recent vacations, advised his mother that, in these uncertain times, the boy should return home and be with them. George was brought back from Egypt in time for the autumn term. He enrolled as a pupil at the Dutch High School in Rotterdam, staying with his grandmother and aunt in a spacious, three-storey house, while his mother and sisters continued to live at the villa in Scheveningen.

He was greatly relieved to be back in the Netherlands, and his academic progress continued apace. His schoolmates admired him in particular for his skill at languages, appreciating the help he was prepared to give them with their homework. He seemed to keep himself a little apart from the rest of the crowd, though, appearing introspective if not unsociable. 'To us lads brought up in the strict tradition of Dutch middle-class respectability, he was a somewhat exotic figure. He had travelled widely and mixed with important people,' recalled a fellow pupil, Henrik Dentro. 'He told us sometimes about his visits to the Pyramids and the Sphinx, the marvels of Luxor, sailing on the Nile, but he never boasted about it or bragged about his rich uncle in Cairo, or anything like that . . . He never had a close friend. I sat next to him for a long time, but we never became very close. It wasn't in George's nature to open up.'

At 16, George was a confident, self-contained boy. He was of medium height, dark and handsome, but looked much younger than his years. Spurning team games, he was nonetheless very fit, a good swimmer and a capable all-round athlete, especially proficient in gymnastics. His experiences abroad had matured him and he was far more at ease with adults than any of his contemporaries.

Beneath the surface, however, George's peripatetic childhood had left him in a confused state of mind, as he acknowledged much later in life: 'Looking back now, I am sure that I lived through an identity crisis in those years. Where did I belong? A Jewish cosmopolitan home, an English school, which reflected the glory of British imperial power of which I also felt a part, and in my heart, all the time, a longing for Holland and all things Dutch.'

After Hitler's march into Poland, a general mobilisation was ordered but still no one wanted to believe that the Führer had designs on the Netherlands, despite the fact that, six months earlier, intelligence that their country was in peril had reached the Dutch Government. Some German officers were uncomfortable with Hitler's plan to invade the

Low Countries and decided to leak details of it. One of them, Colonel Hans Oster, an *Abwehr* intelligence officer, even gave the Dutch military attaché in Berlin, Major Gijsbertus J. Sas, a precise date for *Fall Gelb* (the codename for the future attack on Holland). Oster's information, given in March 1939, turned out to be completely accurate, but was ignored.

Throughout the winter of 1939 and into the early months of 1940, when 'The Phoney War' was underway, the Dutch nation retained its misplaced sense of security. The country had not experienced war on its territory since the days of Napoleon more than a century ago, and the people's view of the Nazis was far more positive than elsewhere in Europe.

As in the First World War, the Netherlands had declared itself neutral, even though in September 1939 the New Holland Water (Defence) Line was ready and could be flooded at any moment for the protection of the western part of the country It was arguably the only worthwhile defence, however, because the Netherlands boasted an army with no tanks and only eighteen armoured vehicles, while the artillery was still being pulled by horses. Most of the rifles were of 1890s vintage, and there were precious few hand grenades.

Operation Weserübung – the invasion of Denmark and Norway – on 9 April 1940 should have put the Dutch on alert, but nothing changed. Even their allies were by no means certain that the Nazis would invade. In his diary for 10 May 1940, Winston Churchill's Private Secretary, Jock Colville, recorded: 'Rab Butler tells me that the Secret Service told him yesterday that there was no chance of an invasion of the Netherlands: it was a feint.' But, even as he wrote that entry, at the end of a momentous day – one in which Churchill succeeded Neville Chamberlain as Britain's Prime Minister – the invasion was well underway. 'So much for our renowned foreign agents.'

The Luftwaffe destroyed much of the Dutch Air Force: airfields at De Kooy, Amsterdam-Schiphol and The Hague were hit hard, and just seventy Dutch aircraft remained. The Germans also dropped

paratroopers over Rotterdam to occupy the bridges across the River
Maas, which linked the Southern with the Northern Netherlands.
Dutch marines were holding out on several fronts but it already
appeared to be a hopeless task.

At 8 a.m., four hours after the invasion had begun, George and his
family, like everyone else in the country, gathered round their wireless
set to hear the distinctive voice of the principal radio newsreader read
out a proclamation from Queen Wilhelmina. It was a moving address,
expressing anger that the Gérman attack had not been preceded by
a proper Declaration of War, and fury that Hitler had betrayed his
'solemn undertakings' over Holland's neutrality. For the young Blake,
listening avidly to the Monarch's words, these were daunting yet
exciting moments. As he looked out of the window he saw aircraft
exchanging machine-gun fire, and could hear the sounds of explosions from the port. Everything in his life was about to change: he was
ready to do his duty, whatever that might be.

2

Resistance

By the morning of Tuesday, 14 May 1940, Adolf Hitler was growing frustrated by the stubborn defiance of the forces defending the Netherlands. Five days after the initial German invasion, he had failed to sweep aside the Dutch opposition in order to better concentrate efforts on the more important theatres of war in Belgium and France. So he issued an order to his generals, making it abundantly clear that he expected them to use all means at their disposal to crush the unexpectedly resilient opponent.

When the fifty-seven Heinkel planes from the Luftwaffe's *Kampfgeschwader* 54 squadron joined the assault at 1.20 p.m. that day, by raining down their 60-tonne payload of 110lb and 550lb bombs on the centre of Rotterdam, the terrified population had two unpalatable alternatives. They could either sit out the attack in their homes or underground shelters, and risk being trapped by the avalanche of falling wreckage, drowned when the water mains burst, or burned alive by the fires set off by the bombs. Or they could venture out into a veritable Dante's Inferno – the firestorm whipped up by a fierce easterly wind that was raging through every street in the heart of the medieval city – and try to dodge the falling debris and the leaping flames and make it to the beach, or nearby villages.

Tens of thousands chose to make a run for it, mothers pushing prams, husbands wheeling handcarts with the few belongings they had time to snatch on the way out of their collapsing homes, and children laden with backpacks. The sky was alternatively red with fire, and dark and grey from smoke, and all around the city people wandered around caked in dust, looking like ghosts.

Seventeen-year-old machinist Roos Molendijk, who had been hiding in a shelter near her home in Goudsesingel, fled through the streets with her mother and two young sisters when there was a brief lull in the bombardment: 'Everyone was focussed on leaving the city. We were holding our hands to our heads because of the heat of the fires. There was no conversation with anyone else, it was all about yourself. I remember the sound of people fleeing as a strange, incessant mumbling noise.' They found refuge in nearby Kralingen. The next day her father tried to return to the family home – only to find it had been completely destroyed. 'He came back with burned feet – the city was still burning,' Molendijk recalled.

George Behar was sitting down to lunch with his Aunt Truss and his grandmother when the German aircraft struck. All three crouched down under the dining-room table with kitchen pans over their heads, waiting for the raids to finish. When they finally emerged, less than half an hour later, their house on Burgemeester Meinesz Plein had sustained only minor damage – one of the few that had remained largely intact amid all the wreckage.

'The streets were full of people fleeing from the burning hell . . . many were injured, dazed or crying,' he remembers. 'In a nearby church an emergency hospital was immediately set up to deal with the casualties. I worked there all night, together with many other people from our neighbourhood. We felt both grateful and guilty that we should still have a roof over our heads.'

But on this day, when it felt as if Armageddon had truly arrived, around 80,000 citizens of a bustling, dynamic city of 600,000 no longer had homes to return to. In just twenty-five minutes, Göring's bombers had reduced Rotterdam to a smoking mass of rubble. Between 800 and 900 people died that day. For many months – indeed years – afterwards, Allied propaganda put the figure much, much higher, at around 25,000 to 30,000. In London, the bombardment dispelled any qualms the War Office and Bomber Command had over incurring civilian casualties in Britain's planned attacks on Germany's industrial centres.

Not only had Rotterdam fallen that afternoon, but by nightfall the nation as a whole – with the exception of the province of Zeeland – had capitulated. General Henri Winkelman, commander-in-chief of the Dutch forces, felt he had no alternative as the Germans were threatening to mete out similar treatment to other major cities like Utrecht and Amsterdam. He signed the official articles of surrender the next day in the village of Rijsoord.

Later that week, as some semblance of temporary order was being established in Rotterdam, George decided to travel to Scheveningen to find out how his mother and sisters were faring. He was taken aback when his knock on the door went unanswered and, on entering, he found the villa empty. All that remained were some unwashed teacups on the kitchen table, which was most unlike his tidy, meticulous mother. The story of their disappearance soon unfolded after conversations with neighbours. Catherine, Adele and Elizabeth had left in a hurry before the bombing. They were, in fact, one of the very last groups to board a ship and flee their country for England.

The evacuation of Holland's great and good had begun in earnest on Monday, 13 May. Queen Wilhelmina and her entourage left Dutch shores from the Hook of Holland at midday, aboard HMS *Hereward* and accompanied by the destroyer HMS *Vesper*. Not without a scare or two from nearby enemy planes, they docked at Harwich five hours later.

On that same day, Mrs Behar was phoned by a friend and told that she had until 5 p.m. to report to the British Consulate, if she wanted to take up a berth on board a Royal Navy ship with her family. Catherine was assured that this offer – and the time constraint that accompanied it – would also have been relayed to her son in Rotterdam. But there was no way of knowing whether he would join them as Grandmother Beijderwellen had no telephone, and it was too dangerous to make the trip to pick him up, even if there had been time. Catherine could only hope that he would be at the quayside at the Hook of Holland that evening.

In the mid-afternoon, the Behar family gathered up what belongings they could and made the ten-mile journey along the coast. It was an anxious, frightening experience for all those descending on the Dutch port. Of the six Royal Navy destroyers at the pier, HMS *Windsor* was the first to depart, carrying the most important cargo – Prime Minister Dirk Jan de Geer, his Cabinet and the rest of his Government. Then, in the following four to five hours, HMSs *Janus, Malcolm, Vivien, Mohawk, Janus* and *Versatile* lined up to take the remaining refugees. Disaster struck the last of these – *Versatile* was hit by a bomb and seven sailors were killed, thirteen injured. With her engine room out of action she could neither steer nor steam, but she was towed successfully out of the harbour and somehow managed to limp across to England by the following evening. Mrs Behar and her daughters docked safely at Southend early in the morning of Tuesday, 14 May.

When George was able to piece together what had happened after his visit to the empty villa, he was relatively unperturbed. 'In the frame of mind I was in, I would not have left even if I had received a warning,' he would later reflect. 'In my eyes that would have meant abandoning the sinking ship. Besides, I would not have left my grandmother alone in those dangerous times.'

While he waited and hoped for news from England, George was able to resume his education. His school had survived the blitz of Rotterdam virtually intact, and studies continued just a week after the invasion.

Summer exams were taken as usual, and he attained excellent marks in all subjects. Factories and offices reopened too, and, on the surface at least, life in the city went back to some semblance of normality.

On 15 May, the first handwritten Resistance paper, *Geuzenactie* (Beggars' Action), appeared. A month later, *Bulletin* – closer to a real newspaper as regards form and content – followed. In reality, though, in the early summer months of the occupation, there was little by way of serious resistance to the invaders. The people of the Netherlands were still stunned by events, struggling to understand what sort of country they were now living in and what the future might possibly hold.

For their part, the occupiers did not want to alienate the Dutch. Hitler and his associates considered them to be of 'superior' Germanic breeding, almost 100 per cent Aryan. Ultimately they had in mind the complete Nazification of Dutch society: the integration of the economy into the German financial system and the elimination of the Jewish population. But at this stage, as long as they were receiving reasonable co-operation from a demoralised and pliant people, they were in no immediate hurry to fulfil these objectives.

The remaining Beijderwellen family convened and decided it would be best if George spent the summer holidays far away from the horrors of the bombing with his Uncle Tom, a grain merchant who lived in the village of Warnsveld, not far from the town of Zutphen in the central province of Gelderland. Young George had always enjoyed his trips to this area, walking the hills and visiting the old castles and grand country houses. He also liked to accompany his uncle in his car when he made work calls on neighbouring millers and farmers.

A fortnight into his holiday, however, this idyllic interlude was brought to an abrupt end. An elderly village constable knocked on the door and informed Uncle Tom that he was taking the boy into custody: young George was a British subject and, following instructions from the German authorities, would have to be interned along with the other Britons trapped in the Netherlands following the invasion.

The shock was profound. George and his family had grown so accustomed to thinking of him as an ordinary Dutch schoolboy that they had long banished from their minds the inheritance of his father's nationality.

He was duly escorted on the train to the Rotterdam Police head-quarters, where he spent a night in a cell. Aunt Truss arrived the next day to protest on his behalf, furiously berating the Dutch officials for locking up a teenage boy on the say-so of the hated invaders. Her indignation was to no avail. The following day, George was taken by two detectives to a camp on the sand dunes at Schoorl, a small village on the coast just north of Amsterdam.

It was surely an alarming experience for a 17-year-old boy to be whisked away from his family and incarcerated in a detention centre overseen by the dreaded Waffen SS. At this time, however, life in *Kamp Schoorl* was a relatively benign experience. The commander, SS-Untersturmführer Arnold Schmidt, was well aware that thousands of his own countrymen had been interned by British authorities throughout the world and, at this early stage of the war, seemed content to observe the rules of international law. The food was prepared by a local cook who lived in the nearby village, and prisoners enjoyed the same menu as their prison guards from the German Ordnungspolizei. The inmates' days were spent exercising vigorously, scrubbing the huts and keeping the rest of the compound clean.

The camp consisted of French and British subjects, many of them young. On 22 June the morale of the former took a turn for the worse when the fall of France was announced. The German guards then lost no time in taunting George and his fellow Britons that they would be next, that the German army would be landing in England any time soon.

George's heightened sense of adventure and the self-reliance devel-oped on his travels to Egypt ensured that his time at *Kamp Schoorl* was not entirely miserable though, and he had mixed feelings when, two weeks after the French capitulation, he was informed he was free to go. He and four others were allowed to leave. All were told it was because they were not yet of age to undertake military service. The Germans clearly felt the war was almost over and there was little prospect of these teenagers ever donning uniform. 'I was by now accustomed to camp life and had begun to make good friends with my fellow prisoners. Though thrilled at the unexpected prospect of freedom and of seeing my family again, I felt sad to leave my new friends to an uncertain fate,' George recalled.

All the French were released a week later, but the remaining British prisoners were transferred to a German camp, Gleiwitz, in September, where they remained until liberated by the Russians in 1945.

Throughout the summer, the speeches of Winston Churchill on the BBC provided a source of comfort and inspiration to the beleaguered Dutch. George was as enthralled as any listener, and his resolve to resist the invaders was only strengthened by these words from the Prime Minister on 14 July:

> All depends now upon the whole life-strength of the British race in every part of the world and of all our associated peoples and of all our well-wishers in every land, doing their utmost night and day, giving all, daring all, enduring all, to the utmost, to the end.

Back in Rotterdam, young George was welcomed as a conquering hero. To be imprisoned by the hated Germans was something of a rarity in those early days of the war, and his schoolmates and neighbours wanted to hear every last detail.

But the prospect of re-internment in November, when he turned eighteen, was now very real. At the same time, he had no news of the whereabouts of his mother and sisters and, in fact, had learned that a British destroyer had been attacked at the Hook of Holland. In his bleaker moments, he feared the worst. He certainly felt there was little to lose in fleeing from Rotterdam and so headed back to Zutphen, arriving on 16 October, and stayed for a while with Uncle Tom.

Knowing that it was the first place the Germans would come looking for him, however, his uncle arranged for him to hide out with a farmer named Boer Weenink, who lived in a small hamlet called Hummelo, twenty miles from Zutphen, in the depths of the countryside. Another friend of Tom's provided George with a fake identity card in case he was being sought by the authorities.

In the meantime the boy helped out in the dairy and the cowsheds. He continued to go to church and, if he pondered his future after the war at all, it was to envisage himself as a minister of the Dutch Reformed Church. A religious calling had always attracted him from his early days in the thrall of the *Children's Bible*. But his mind was really on the horror of here and now – the humiliation his country had suffered and the certainty of darker days to come. He wanted to play his part in the fight-back and ironically, given his religious instincts at that time, it was a priest who would set George Behar on the path of resistance and, ultimately, to espionage.

Fifty-four-year-old Dominee Nicolaas Padt was a tall, slim, inspiring preacher with strong left-wing views, who belonged to an organisation called *Kerk en Verde* (Church and Peace), one of several active Christian pacifist organisations to emerge after the First World War. In 1938, he had felt America, France and Britain should take at least an equal share of the blame for the looming crisis in Europe and, though he still held that view eighteen months later, having observed the evils of Nazism, he was now preaching against it from his pulpit, week after week. On 28 June 1940, he was the first Reformed minister to be arrested, accused of criticism of the occupation on the basis of reports of his sermons. Reverend Padt spent six weeks in a cell in the German city of Emmerich before being released.

George attended his confirmation classes and, as their friendship grew, was invited to the minister's house for tea and to meet the family. It was widely known in the district that Dominee Padt had links to the underground movement, so in the spring of 1941 George asked his advice on joining a resistance group. The minister listened to his request, saying only at this stage that he would reflect on it and make contact later. A week passed by, then he asked George to join him on a visit to Deventer, a sizeable provincial town some thirty miles north of Zutphen.

It was there, at a café in the central square, that George was introduced to a friend of Dominee Padt's, a bearded, middle-aged man who gave his name as 'Max'. After listening carefully to the teenager's story, examining his British passport and analysing his motivations, Max said he needed an assistant to carry messages and parcels the length and breadth of the country. Would the youngster be interested? George needed little persuading, so there and then he was given his first assignment; he was to travel the following Monday to Heerde, a village some twenty miles north of Deventer, where he was to liaise with the local grocer. He was to say he had come from 'Piet' to collect the groceries and then wait for further instructions. The boy with a taste for adventure was about to take his first steps in a clandestine world that would become his life. He did so with some trepidation, but also with a sense of mission.

Geographically, topographically and demographically the Netherlands was utterly ill-suited to a war of resistance. The country is small (little more than 30,000 square kilometres), flat (no mountains and very little forest to provide cover for partisans) and densely populated (nine million people at that time, the highest recorded population density in the world). Even the excellent transport links militated against any effective underground movement: Holland had an extensive and efficient railway system and roads of excellent quality, which enabled the German garrison of three infantry divisions and several regiments of the *Ordnungspolizei* (Order Police) to move around the country swiftly and maintain maximum control.

Then, of course, there was the sheer isolation of the country in 1940. To all intents and purposes, Holland did not share a border with a neutral country. It was blocked off on its eastern border by Germany, faced occupied Belgium to the south, and had no links to the north, either, where Hitler's troops stood vigilant in his Scandinavian satellites. On its western border, Holland faced England across the North Sea, but this coastal area – mainly dunes and beaches – was closely guarded by the Germans, both on land and by patrol boats in the waters.

As a result, the organisation of any lasting resistance group along the lines of the French *Maquis* was a practical impossibility, even if the Dutch Resistance had possessed a stock of working weapons, which they did not until well into 1942.

Instead little acts of defiance marked the opening months of the occupation, mainly centred around the Queen, with the Dutch showing renewed nationalist spirit. This symbolic opposition was demonstrated through growing flowers in the national colours, naming newborn babies after living members of the Royal Family, and wearing pins made of coins bearing the picture of Queen Wilhelmina. On 29 June 1940, the birthday of Prince Bernhard, people all across the country flew the national flag in defiance of a German ban. They also stopped work and took to the streets wearing carnations, the Prince's favourite flower, in their buttonholes. The occasion would be remembered as *Anjerdag* (Carnation Day).

All this was merely irksome for the invaders. What was more serious, and brought the 'honeymoon' period well and truly to an end, was the nationwide strike in February 1941. The Communist Party of Holland (by now illegal) printed leaflets and put the word out for the capital's citizens and the rest of the nation to down tools in protest. Not only did Amsterdam workers join the strike, but also whole factories in Zaandam, Haarlem, Ijmuiden, Weesp, Bussum, Hilversum and Utrecht, with some 250,000 people taking part. It lasted a couple of days, during which occupying troops fired on unarmed crowds, killing nine people and wounding many more. Around 200 of the leading activists were arrested and locked up in Scheveningen prison, which came to be known popularly as the 'Orange Hotel'. They were the first of several thousand resistance fighters who would find themselves incarcerated there in the next five years. Most were tortured and twenty-two were sentenced to death.

As a result of the events of February 1941, attitudes hardened on both sides. In particular, the Germans intensified their campaign against the Jews, banning them from parks, cafés, swimming pools, stopping them from using public transport and even preventing them from riding their bikes.

On the other side, the Dutch resistance started to marshal itself more efficiently. It was still, ten months into the war, a very fragmented and ideologically diverse movement. But having witnessed the events of February, and becoming ever more disenchanted with the increasingly ruthless tactics of the country's puppet leader Arthur Seyss-Inquart, their opposition intensified.

George Behar had been recruited to work for the *Vrij Nederland* (Free Netherlands) organisation, best known for its underground newspaper whose first copy had been launched on 31 August 1940, the date of Queen Wilhelmina's first birthday in exile. That issue, of which just 130 copies were printed, called for 'combat to free our country'. Publishing and distributing illegal newspapers was not the only function of *Vrij Nederland,* however: the group also set up radio transmitters to supply British intelligence services and the Dutch Government-in-exile with information on German army operations; and arranged for hiding places for Allied airmen who had been shot down, setting up escape routes to enable them to return to England.

The principal task for 18-year-old 'Max de Vries' – George's *nom de guerre* – was to ensure that as many as possible of his countrymen and women were able to get hold of a copy of the paper and read it. He was very young in appearance, looking more like a 14-year-old schoolboy than a grown man, which meant the Gestapo rarely gave him a second glance. He was also fit and athletic, vital requirements when his work as a courier required him to cycle long distances – sometimes thirty to forty miles a day. As the organisation's confidence in him grew, in addition to parcels of illegal newspapers he was entrusted with the delivery of intelligence messages – usually about the German Army – which the underground collected to be sent to England. This was dangerous work. There was always the possibility that *Vrij Nederland* would be penetrated by the security police, and that one day he would knock on a door to make a delivery, only to walk straight into a trap.

Already, on the journeys he made across the length and breadth of the country, he was learning some rudimentary 'tradecraft' that would stand him in good stead. Baggage was constantly searched, particularly on trains. 'I had, therefore, to be constantly on my guard for sudden checks and ready to take evasive action. I usually put my parcel or briefcase in a luggage rack some distance from where I was sitting so that if there was a check, I could always pretend that it wasn't me,' he recalls.

On one mission, in the town of Assen, a moment of heedlessness nearly cost him dear. He had just taken delivery of a parcel of newspapers, and – with not enough room in his suitcase – had stuffed half a dozen under his pullover. As he ran to catch a tram, the illegal papers spilled out right in front of an elderly German officer. George gazed at the road in horror: 'As I knelt down in a frantic attempt to collect the newspapers before he could see what they were, he also stooped down and began to help me pick them up. He handed them to me without even looking at me. I thanked him profusely and boarded the tram. I didn't tell any of my friends about this adventure.'

As he travelled around his occupied country, George noted the rapidly deteriorating circumstances of the Jewish population. Jews found themselves harassed and isolated, excluded from very many towns and villages. Yet this did not prompt in him any great feeling about his own Jewish heritage because he considered himself a Christian, not a Jew, and, although dark in appearance, he had no fear of being recognised as Jewish by the Germans. 'The only way, therefore, that the persecution of the Jews affected me was that it increased my hatred for the Nazis and all they stood for even more.'

In this thoroughly bleak period, with growing repression at home and continued German expansion in Europe, George found further encouragement in the speeches of Winston Churchill. He was especially heartened when he listened to the Prime Minister's broadcast on 22 June 1941, after the news came of the advance of Hitler's armies into the Soviet Union. Churchill put aside ideological differences to welcome a new ally to the Allied cause, in characteristically robust fashion.

> If Hitler imagines that his attack on Soviet Russia will cause the slightest division of aims or slackening of effort in the great democracies, who are resolved upon his doom, he is woefully mistaken . . . the cause of any Russian fighting for his hearth and home is the cause of free men and free peoples in every quarter of the globe.

In the spring of 1942, George's grandmother, with whom he had been very close, died at home in Rotterdam at the age of 77. Even while mourning her death, he realised that freedom from domestic responsibilities now gave him the licence to plan his journey to England. This yearning to escape to the friendly neighbour across the North Sea was common in many young Dutchmen working in the resistance and they were known in Holland as *Engelandvaarders*. England was where their Queen and government now resided; where there was freedom, albeit under fire; and from where Churchill was leading the battle against Nazism. For George, there was the prospect of seeing his mother and sisters again. He also felt that there he would be able to receive proper training as a secret agent, and then return to his homeland to act as a link between the resistance movement and the British intelligence services.

A daring if foolhardy way of reaching English shores would have been to get hold of a boat and cross the North Sea. George considered but quickly discounted that idea because of the surveillance the

Germans kept on the coastline. The only real hope was to try and get a place on one of the established escape routes: through Belgium, France, into Spain, and then on to England by boat from Gibraltar.

George confided in Max, the agent who had introduced him into *Vrij Nederland*. While regretting his protégé's desire to leave the country, he set out to put him in touch with resistance workers in the south of the country who might be able to help. In a couple of weeks, he had established contact with a family who lived not far from Breda, close to the frontier with Belgium, whose sons and daughters were doing sterling service in the cause of the resistance, including running a successful 'escape line' across into Belgium. Max and George set out to meet them.

The remarkable de Bie family lived in a large town house on the main street – *Markt* – in the pleasant village of Zundert, just three miles from the Belgian border. Their home sat across the road from the town hall, and next door to the house where the post-Impressionist painter Vincent van Gogh was born and brought up. Viktor de Bie – together with his brother Walter – ran a tree nursery, one of the largest and most highly regarded in the whole of the country, and he and his wife Marie had raised a large Catholic family of eight girls and five boys.

The eldest son, Pieter – or Piet – was the man Max and George went to meet in the station restaurant in Breda one July afternoon. It was a dangerous assignment for Piet as the Germans had put a price on his head as a result of his work smuggling Allied pilots to safety, and if they were to find and arrest him, torture and almost certain death would follow. He told Max and George that an escape party was shortly due to leave for Switzerland, and that he would do his best to have George included.

George went back up north to wrap up his affairs with *Vrij Nederland* before returning south to Zundert. The de Bie family offered him a bed in their crowded house, so he stayed and enjoyed their warm hospitality, watching and waiting for his chance to get away.

Initially, there was disappointment. The group that was heading for

Switzerland were not prepared to include him in their number because they would only take RAF pilots, Dutch army officials and others with particular skills who were of immediate and vital use to the war effort.

Now it was the turn of two of the de Bie sisters to come to his aid. Margaretha Francisca Maria – everybody called her Greetje – and Wietske intimately knew the terrain around the border; where the foot-paths were, where the soldiers patrolled, and any other dangers that might lie in store. Greetje de Bie was then aged 23, and photographs of her from that time show a pretty woman with a serious, defiant expression on her face. She worked as a secretary in her brother Piet's office at the nursery, but was also fully involved in the work of the escape group. She and Wietske offered to take George to the frontier, and beyond to Antwerp, where their aunt could accommodate him for a few days before he started on his long trek South.

It was a beautiful morning on Sunday, 19 July when the sisters led George carefully and cautiously through the woods near their home. Greetje selected a trail she particularly liked where she went blueberry picking with her father. They had come through a clearing and were on farmland, just a few hundred yards from the border, when a German soldier appeared from behind a haystack and barred their way with a rifle. It was a tense situation for the party of three, but suddenly the soldier's frown turned to a smile as he recognised the two girls. 'What are you doing here?' he said, some Dutch mixed up with his German. 'This is a forbidden zone.'

Fortunately, he was not a complete stranger. A few days earlier, Greetje had helped him buy potatoes in the grocery, saving him from embarrassment, and then, a day or so later, they had a friendly encounter in the Church of Saint Trudo in the village where he, an Austrian Catholic, attended mass. Greetje explained hurriedly that George was a cousin of theirs, and they were merely on their way to visit an aunt who lived in a nunnery close to the border in Belgium. The soldier not only let them through without a word of admonish-ment, but said that, if they returned the same way in the evening, he would be at his post in the same place and would guide them back across.

Greetje, Wietske and George duly crossed the border and made their way to their destination without any further alarms. But Greetje had been angry with George, as the man she married after the war, Leopold van Ewijk, recalls: 'My wife afterwards was absolutely furious with this George Behar because he told her he had all his papers hidden in his shoe. That was a stupid thing to do, because if the Germans had found out they could have shot him there and then.'

George later acknowledged the enormous debt of gratitude he owed his companions: 'Once more I had to say goodbye that day and for the first time I experienced a feeling which was often to recur in later life – a feeling of the inadequacy of words to express gratitude and admiration to people who, by assuming very considerable risks, had ensured my safety and freedom.'

3

Flight to England

On that July weekend in 1942, as George Behar headed for Antwerp on the first leg of his dangerous thousand-mile journey across Europe, the Jews of Holland were desperately trying to find sanctuary as transportation to the concentration camps began in earnest.

Four days earlier, the first train had left the Westerbork transit camp for Auschwitz, with two thousand men, women and children on board – the majority of them German Jews who had found sanctuary in Holland between 1933 and 1939. Many Dutch Jews were now going deep underground, being given shelter by non-Jews in towns such as Winterswijk and Aaalten.

Then, that very Sunday, 19 July, the Nazi hierarchy gave another indication of its ultimate intent. Heinrich Himmler, *Reichsführer* of the SS, sent a directive to Lieutenant-General Friedrich-Wilhelm Krüger, head of the police force in German-occupied Poland, ordering 'the resettlement of the entire Jewish population of the General-gouvernement to be carried out and completed by 31 December . . . in the name of the New Order, security and cleanliness of the German Reich'. At the same time, in France, the round up had also started.

The following day, Monday, 20 July, George left Antwerp and

made for the University of Louvain in Brussels. Greetje de Bie's aunt had given him an introductory letter to take to a friend of hers, a Dominican monk. At their meeting, the priest told George he had a contact in Paris – another Dominican – whom he felt sure could put the young fugitive in touch with resistance workers, who would help him along the way.

George next boarded a train to the French capital, knowing that his first major test on his journey across the continent could well come at the frontier, although as Belgium and occupied France formed one German military district, he was hoping the customs officers there would only take a cursory glance at his luggage.

In fact, he faced trouble even before the border. Just as the train was approaching Mons station, George saw two German *Feldgendarmes* (military police) moving purposefully down the corridor, inspecting identity papers. He had concealed his British passport in a loaf of bread and instead presented the officers with his fake Belgian identity card. They did not appear satisfied and told him they would return to speak to him after they had been through the rest of the train. It seemed as if the game might be up even as it had just started. After a moment's thought, he waited until the train started to slow down as it entered Mons station – the last stop before the frontier – jumped out, ran down the platform and raced through the exit before it had stopped.

Disappearing into the narrow streets of a strange city, he walked into a church in a secluded square, and was steadying himself, assessing his options, when he was approached by the priest. George, sensing a sympathetic ear, claimed he was an English pilot and that he urgently needed to reach the unoccupied zone. The priest advised him that he could go most of the way to the border if he boarded a certain tram outside Mons, and promptly gave him directions out of the city.

When he eventually reached the frontier, he saw a German airman on a bicycle, leaning against the barrier, nonchalantly smoking and chatting to two Belgian customs officers. After a while, the airman put out his cigarette and left, and had no sooner turned the corner than George heard the Belgians talking about him with disdain. In what was to prove the first of many fortunate encounters, he decided to gamble on the customs men helping him rather than handing him over to the German authorities. He had calculated correctly because, upon hearing his story, they offered nothing but encouragement, one of them promising he would find George a bed for the night and then see him on his way in the morning.

As he settled down to eat in a nearby farmhouse he could hardly believe his luck. 'To this day I remember the homely scene round the table with the customs officer's two little girls and his plump, friendly wife,' he recalled. 'At the end of the meal my host produced a bottle of brandy which he kept for a special occasion. We drank to Allied victory.'

The co-operation from the Belgians did not end there. In the morning, the other officer arrived to fetch him and escort him to the border post at the town of Maubeuge, about an hour's walk away. From there he took a bus to Lille, and then the train to Paris; by the evening he was excited to be in *La Ville-Lumière*, the city where he believed his father had lived and studied some thirty years before.

That feeling of exhilaration turned to one of anxiety when it became clear that his contact – the Dominican monk recommended to him by the priest in Brussels – was unwilling to harbour him. The monk explained that, although sympathetic to his plight, he was under strict instructions from the Abbot of his order in Paris not to hide anyone from the Germans, as discovery could seriously hinder the work of the Dominicans in the country. Nonetheless, he told George to give him a few hours and he would find a solution. Later that night, he returned from a lecture in the company of a middle-aged couple who offered to shelter George in their nearby apartment. They were devout Catholics and also fervent patriots, supporters of General de Gaulle, with many contacts in the resistance movement. For the moment, George was safe.

* * *

The branch of the intelligence service charged with assisting the escapes of British prisoners of war, and securing the return to the United Kingdom of those who had succeeded in evading capture on enemy territory, was Military Intelligence Section 9, known as MI9. Working hand in glove with the Secret Intelligence Service (SIS, also known as MI6) and the Special Operations Executive (SOE), MI9 set out to establish 'escape lines' across Europe to help thousands of captured soldiers, downed airmen and important members of the resistance to flee across Holland, Belgium and France and into supposedly neutral territory of Spain before finding a passage home, usually via British-controlled Gibraltar.

The 'O'Leary line' (aka 'Pat') and the 'Comet line' were perhaps the two best-established routes. The former was created by a Belgian, Albert-Marie Guérisse, whose *nom de guerre* was Pat O'Leary, and tended to run from Paris to Dijon, through Lyons and Avignon to Marseille; then via Nîmes and Perpignan, on to Barcelona. The latter was the brainchild of a courageous young Belgian woman, Andrée de Jongh, known as 'Dedee', and started in Brussels or Lille before taking in Tours, Bordeaux and Bayonne, terminating over the Pyrenees at San Sebastian, Spain.

Both routes were 'staffed' by a network of helpers, some connected, formally or informally, to intelligence organisations, though many were not. They provided food, clothing and sanctuary for the escapers, as well as false identity documents. George's path would more closely follow the 'Pat' line, although as his journey unfolded, it took him on several detours.

At first, he had to contend with disappointment. Two weeks into his stay, a resistance leader who went under the pseudonym 'The Belgian' arrived at the home of George's new Paris hosts to assess his worth for a place on one of the lines. Having heard his story, 'The Belgian' told George that, being neither an airman or a key member of the resistance, he was of insufficient importance to the war effort to warrant special assistance. He did, however, furnish him with a false French identity card and an address in Salies-de-Béarn in south-western France, where there were people who could help him over the border into unoccupied French territory. He also gave him the name and address of a contact in Lyons.

The dividing line between the occupied and 'free' (Vichy) zones of France ran along the periphery of Salies-de-Béarn. When George arrived at the town after his train journey from Bordeaux, he headed for his contact at a small boarding house, where, after quoting the correct password, he was allowed in and told to prepare for the crossing that night.

It proved to be a nerve-wracking affair in the company of three Jewish women and their dog, which was there to alert them, by barking, to any German patrols. After navigating the back streets of the town, then crawling through ditches and scrambling over hedges in the fields, their two Basque guides saw them to their destination. 'We had arrived safely in unoccupied France,' Blake said. 'Reaching the crest of the hill, we suddenly saw lights twinkling everywhere like a promise of peace and security, while behind us the land lay dark. It was as if an immense burden of fear and gloom was lifted from me. I was out of the hands of the enemy.'

When dawn rose, he made his way towards the medieval town of Argagnon. There, in the market square, he boarded a bus for Lourdes and his identity card was put to the test for the first time. The gendarme returned it to him without comment and he was on his way. From Lourdes, he boarded a train for Lyon and he was in the city by nightfall.

In September 1942, this city in the so-called *Zone Libre* (Free Zone) was becoming an increasingly dangerous place in which to seek sanctuary. The Germans were frustrated by resistance activities, and were preparing to send in 280 police under SS Major Karl Bömelburg to hunt down the possessors of illegal radio transmitters. Lyon had always been an intellectual hotbed and was now the effective 'capital of the

resistance'. Leaflets and clandestine newspapers like *Vérités* had begun
to appear from the summer of 1940 onwards, and crucial figures like
Captain Henri Frenay, who helped form the *Mouvement de Libération
Nationale* and *Combat*, and Jean Moulin, de Gaulle's personal emissary, were based in the city or its suburbs. The network of dark, dingy
traboules (passageways) that snaked their way through apartment
blocks, under streets and into the courtyards of the Vieux Lyon district
provided the perfect terrain for those escaping or attempting to hide
from the Gestapo.

Young Behar's new contacts were a French colonel and his wife,
both active members of the resistance, who lived in one of the city's
better hotels. They were impressed by his credentials, especially by the
recommendation from 'The Belgian', and soon found him somewhere
to stay while the next leg of his journey was planned. His new refuge
proved to be a bedroom on the top floor of an old, medieval house
where two sisters ran a modest restaurant, which was open for lunch
and dinner for regular customers like the colonel, but also doubled as
a meeting place for resistance groups.

During his three-week stay, George was relieved to be put to work
and allowed to contribute to the work of the French underground.
He helped ferry a weekly Gaullist paper to distribution stores in wine
cellars or factories, with two or three others wheeling a handcart
through the streets with hundreds of copies hidden underneath its
canvas cover. All the while, however, he was anxious to move on.

British interests in the city were represented at the American consulate. Here George was fortunate enough to encounter a young English
diplomat (actually an SIS officer), who proved more than willing to
help. He listened to George's story and then examined his British passport before suggesting that the best way forward would be to issue him
instead with a travel document that would put his age at 16 rather
than 19. In that way, he would not be of military age, and the Vichy
authorities would grant him an exit visa. At the same time, the officer
said, he would apply for Spanish and Portuguese transit visas. Once all

these permits were gathered, George would be able to make his way to England legally.

After three weeks, word came back from the American consulate that permission had been received from London for George's onward journey to be arranged. He was issued with a travel document, given some money and was now able to report to the Vichy authorities and apply for an exit visa.

While he awaited all the necessary documentation, he was obliged by the Vichy authorities to live in a place chosen by them, which he could not leave without permission. It was called a *résidence forcée* (compulsory residence), and amounted to a form of internment. George was unperturbed. He was used to confinement of one sort or another and did not find life at his particular *résidence*, a small inn in a village outside Grenoble, unduly constricting. Throughout October he waited patiently, preparing himself for an arduous climb over the Pyrenees and then a lengthy journey across Spain before he finally boarded a ship at Gibraltar that would ferry him across the Atlantic Ocean.

His dreams turned to dust on 8 November 1942 with Operation Torch and the landing of British and American forces on the coast of French North Africa. The failure of the French forces to repel the Allies gave the Führer the excuse to revoke any assurances he may have given guaranteeing self-government in the southern half of France. On 10 and 11 November, German troops marched into Vichy, and soon afterwards strict surveillance was ordered over the activities of British and American citizens.

George knew that he could be trapped indefinitely inside France unless he acted swiftly. He gathered together his few possessions and slipped away from the inn, back to Lyon to seek the advice of the colonel. His newfound patron urged him to head for Toulouse, where a journalist in the resistance movement would give him money and instructions on how to contact the *passeurs*, the civilian guides familiar with the best crossing points over the Pyrenees.

That rendezvous successfully accomplished, George then took a train to the city of Pau, birthplace of Henry IV of France and the 'gateway to Spain'. There, he teamed up with another escapee, a middle-aged, portly Portuguese Jew, and the two of them embarked on a series of bus journeys in the company of a guide (another resistance member), edging further and further up the mountains.

Eventually, on the third day, as darkness fell, the party reached the small village of Seix, whose skyline was dominated by a stunning medieval castle, complete with twin turrets and a watchtower with a panoramic view out across the mountains. There, they made contact with their *passeurs,* two young local men set to accompany them on their hazardous journey.

Perilous it most certainly proved to be. On their journey so far, their primary concern had been avoiding the dreaded *Milice,* the French paramilitary force that gave over-zealous support to the invaders, but now came a gruelling physical test – mile after mile of forest trail, wading across rivers, inching along perilous ledges and clambering up sheer faces of rock. All this was tough enough for a fit, young man like George, but desperately difficult for his companion, who was middle-aged and overweight. They rested at a mountain hut overnight, and enjoyed a nourishing meal of roasted meat and fresh bread, washed down with a bottle of wine. Replenished and revitalised, the group made it to the top of the snowy peaks later that day, and then early the next began the descent towards Spain.

Abruptly, it seemed, once they had reached a meadow that sloped down to a mule track, the guides announced they were leaving. George and his friend were told they were now actually in Spain, and that if they kept to the track they would reach a farmhouse where they could stay the night.

After some mishaps – George's nervous companion deserted him at one point, insisting they had strayed from the correct path and misguid- edly striking out in search of another – they advanced on what they fervently hoped was the last leg of their journey. But their freedom was not yet assured. 'On the bank of the stream stood a large farmhouse from which the sound of voices reached us. The figures of soldiers and mules moved among the trees,' George recalled. 'We hastily withdrew behind a rock, but it was too late. We had been spotted. A warning shot rang out and the soldiers, who, to judge from their uniforms, were neither French nor German, motioned us to come down. When we got to the stream they surrounded us. We were in Spain, but no longer free.'

In the early days of the war Spain was inclined to send escaping resistance fighters, their associates and Allied servicemen straight back to the Nazis, returning a favour paid by Hitler when he had contributed Stuka bombers to the Nationalist war effort in the Civil War. By October 1940, however, the relationship between Hitler and General Franco had started to cool, with the Führer famously remarking after his meeting with the *Generalissimo* in Hendaye, France: 'I would rather have three or four of my own teeth pulled out than speak to that man again.' Subsequent diplomacy failed to shift Franco into more active support for the Axis powers so, in November 1942, when George was arrested at the frontier, Spain's 'non-belligerent' status was still intact, though that certainly didn't mean they could expect to be treated kindly.

Once he had proved his Portuguese identity, George's companion was allowed to go on his way. But Behar was taken by bus, along with another group of refugees, to Irun, a well-recognised crossing point on the French-Spanish border. This was one of the lowest moments in his journey. Through the windows of the vehicle, just fifty yards away, he could see German soldiers guarding the frontier – and the rumour circulating was that his group were going to be handed back to them. It was with an initial sense of relief, then, that after a night at a small hotel in Irun, George's party were driven on to Pamplona, capital city of Navarre. But what greeted them there was just a taste of what was to follow in the coming weeks.

They were led to the city's prison, crowded seven in a cell, and served some unpalatable brown, liquid gruel. The next morning their heads were shaved, and their afternoon meal was the same brown liquid, this time leavened with a few potato peelings. This grim regime continued for three weeks, until one morning they were taken out of their cells, handcuffed together, and marched through the streets of Pamplona. They were then put on a train bound for the notorious prison of Miranda del Ebro, forty miles south of Bilbao.

Franco had created 'Miranda' in 1937 in order to house thousands of Republican prisoners during Spain's civil war: now it was the place where most foreign refugees eventually ended up. It had all the trappings of a Nazi concentration camp. Built next to a railway for easy delivery of detainees, it was filled with rows of parallel blocks of basic huts, surrounded by barbed wire, floodlights and sentry boxes. Originally meant to house around 1,500 prisoners, by the time George arrived, the camp's population had swelled to well over 3,000. In the huts, inmates slept on two tiers of bunks with just a tattered blanket to keep warm. The first few days were entirely discouraging. The diet was invariably poor, there was a lack of water and decent sanitation – the latrines emptied into a stream that was also the wash place – and disease was prevalent.

Then George's luck turned: he found out that each nationality had a representative in the camp, and when he sought out the British envoy, to his great relief he discovered it was the young man from the British consulate in Lyon who had issued him with his travel document a month earlier. He was now eligible for a generous food ration, supplied by the British Embassy in Madrid – including tea, coffee, milk, sugar, tins of sardines, packets of biscuits and cigarettes. His fear of death by starvation disappeared.

But while the Britons in the camp were now in reasonable shape because of these food parcels, others fared less well. The Poles, who had been there the longest and who had formed a tightly-knit community of their own, decided they had had enough of the squalid conditions and lack of food. They determined to go on a hunger strike, which they hoped would alert the international community to their plight and they called on all the other nationalities to join them. The strike started on Wednesday, 6 January. The Polish contingent picketed the food queues and made sure no one accepted any food. The protest lasted a week and only ended when a diplomatic negotiating team from four nations persuaded the strikers that they had won assurance from the Spanish authorities that conditions would definitely improve.

'I cannot say that I felt the worse for this experience,' was George's recollection. 'In the beginning I suffered from headaches, but after a few days my body seemed to get used to doing without food. The feeling of hunger disappeared and gave way to a strange feeling of elation, lightness and energy.'

Meanwhile, his bona fides were being checked out by MI9 and its sister organisations. Their operations were coordinated from the British Embassy in Madrid, led by attaché Michael Creswell (code-named 'Monday') who performed heroics to secure the freedom of stranded Britons, negotiating with the Spanish authorities while ferrying British evaders and escapers around the country.

These diplomatic efforts worked and a week after the strike, George and a group of about fifteen other inmates were released. He and a young Dutchman were met at the camp by an official from the British Embassy and taken to Madrid. There, they were put up in a hotel for a couple of nights before boarding a train for Gibraltar, accompanied by two embassy officials.

The following afternoon the party arrived at La Linea, the coastal town that formed the boundary between Spain and the British territory of Gibraltar. George was escorted to the Spanish customs post, where, after his papers were formally checked, he walked through.

At last, after a journey lasting 185 days and covering well over a thousand miles, he had reached his destination. He was now on British soil.

With barely any time to savour the moment, he was taken to a waiting bus that transferred him and a large group of others to the quayside. A naval launch saw them on to the RMS *Empress of Australia*, a stately ocean liner then functioning as a troopship. She was due to leave in convoy with a host of other ships, great and small, in a few hours' time.

When asked years later about the dangers of his epic journey, of the apprehension and fear he must have felt, George replied: 'Scared? You had the pressure of the Germans all around you, but I'd been used to that for more than two years. You get used to being scared – it's a part of your life and you stop thinking about it. And when you're young, you are far less scared than you are later in your life.'

While the *Empress of Australia* was ploughing its way towards Britain, Franklin Roosevelt and Winston Churchill sat down in the comfort of the Anfa Hotel in Casablanca to consider ways of combating the ruthlessly effective U-boat attacks on Allied shipping. In January 1943 German submarines, backed up by the Luftwaffe's Focke-Wulf Fw 200 Condor bomber aircraft, could still lay claim to hold the upper hand in the Battle of the North Atlantic. The President and Prime Minister discussed when and where to introduce better technical equipment and increase aircraft cover, in order to begin to turn the tables. In the meantime, George and his companions would endure that mid-winter voyage in a state of perpetual tension, with more than a few nerve-wracking moments before they eventually sailed up the River Clyde and moored safely in the Scottish port of Greenock.

This was George's second sight of his father's adopted country. His first had come in the summer of 1937 as he returned home from Cairo to Rotterdam for the school holidays. Then, on a brief stop at the East India Dock, London, he had taken his first walk on British soil, wandering the length of Commercial Road, noting that the people looked 'just that little bit grimier and shabbier than in my home town'.

If this time he had been hoping for a welcoming reception party to greet his arrival, then he was to be disappointed. No sooner had the *Empress of Australia* docked than he and his travelling companions – the official description for them was 'aliens' – were lined up and questioned, their travel documents closely scrutinised. Then, with an escort of soldiers, they were put on trains and whisked down south to London.

Once there, they were taken on buses to a 'monstrous building – built in the style of a Burgundian château and set in the midst of a bald and sooty park'. They had arrived at the grandly named Royal Victoria Patriotic School in Trinity Road, Wandsworth, the forbidding first port-of-call for all male foreigners coming from occupied Europe. Behind a neo-Gothic façade that hid detention and interrogation rooms, and even some cells in the basement, the RVPS hosted officers from MI5's B Division, who were busy working to separate what they called the 'sheep' (genuine refugees) from the 'goats' (suspected enemy agents). Although there were few of the latter, all those who passed through the gates of the RVPS could expect rigorous questioning from intelligence officials before their credentials were accepted and their freedom finally granted.

As the war went on, these cross-examinations proved immensely valuable. Knowledge about Gestapo interrogation techniques, safe houses, couriers and enemy penetrations of escape organisations was carefully indexed and cross-referenced in a central Information Index of intelligence, then made available to Whitehall departments.

But those interviews also served another purpose – one that was ultimately to benefit 20-year-old George. The intelligence agencies represented at RVPS were on the lookout for prospective recruits, and this regular influx of resourceful individuals from the continent provided them with a rich pool of talent.

The RVPS first opened its doors on 8 January 1941 and it quickly acquired a reputation as an inhospitable detention centre. Such was its oppressive atmosphere that on 21 February, Major W.H. Churchill-Longman, Commandant of the School, wrote a letter to Colonel Tommy 'Tar' Robertson of MI5, saying that the longer-term inmates would 'become lazy or crazy, or both' unless they were granted some diversionary activities. In response, officials at the RVPS endeavoured to create a more relaxed, informal environment. Outside of the interviews – usually conducted one-to-one – entertainment included dance bands, a croquet lawn and a football pitch. Eventually, MI5 allowed a wireless set into the camp. For some detainees, however, the whole experience still remained demeaning and depressing. To be treated with suspicion and, occasionally, a certain animosity after all they had endured to get to a country they admired and for which they hoped to fight, was a bitter blow.

George, although irritated at having his actions and motives pored over, confronted the situation with relative equanimity. He spent three days answering detailed questions from a young Army intelligence officer, who was particularly interested in the minutiae of his escape from enemy territory. On the fourth day, he was interrupted while watching a showing of *The Great Dictator* starring Charlie Chaplin and told there was someone on the telephone for him. When he picked it up, he heard his mother's voice for the first time in over two and a half years. He was to be released.

With half a crown for his train fare, he set off for the London suburb of Northwood, where Catherine now lived along with his sisters, Adele and Elizabeth. An hour later, in the rain and the dark of a winter's night, mother and son were overjoyed, finally, to be reunited.

4

Secret Intelligence Service

After the heady adventure of the preceding three years, George settled into a very different rhythm of life. While his mother worked as housekeeper and companion to an elderly lady in Northwood, and his sisters were usefully employed as nurses in central London hospitals, he took time to explore his new environment.

He was impressed by what he observed of England at war. In his eyes, the virtues of duty, solidarity, forbearance and courage under enemy attack were all clearly visible. He watched and admired the 'quiet discipline' of his neighbours, evident in their uncomplaining attitude when queuing for scarce foodstuffs, and also their strict observance of blackout regulations and civil defence measures.

Such stoicism no doubt reaffirmed his own desire to return to the fray and re-join Holland's war effort, but that proved far from easy. No letter arrived on his doorstep inviting him to enlist – notwithstanding the role he had performed in the Resistance, and despite all the connections he had made along his escape route – and he was extremely disappointed.

Onto the scene stepped Commander Douglas William Child, Secret Intelligence Service (SIS) officer and a family friend of the Behars from Holland days. He was to play a vital part in George's life during the war years and beyond.

Child was an unlikely recruit to British intelligence, simply because of his humble origins. A fisherman's son from Deal, in Kent, he left home at fifteen to join the Merchant Navy, eventually winning his master's certificate in his twenties. In the early 1930s, as the worldwide Depression took hold, he nonetheless managed to make a decent living as the skipper of private yachts, transporting the wealthy owners up and down the Rhine and along the Dutch water-ways. In 1936, as the threat of war loomed larger, he decided to join the Royal Navy Volunteer Supplementary Reserve, but his obvious potential as an intelligence officer, together with his experience of Germany and the Low Countries, saw him installed in SIS's station at The Hague at the beginning of the war. His cover was that of a lieu-tenant commander in the Naval Attaché's office.

When the invasion came Child stayed on, but was captured and badly wounded when German parachutists attacked his car. He had a leg amputated, and after his recovery he was imprisoned along with other British diplomats in a hotel in the Harz Mountains in northern Germany. There, he remained for more than two years before an exchange deal was struck to bring him and his colleagues back to England. Various German diplomats had been stranded in different parts of the British Empire at the start of the war and then interned; they were returned to Berlin, and Child and his colleagues to London.

When George met up with his old friend in the spring of 1943, Child was back at Broadway working in the P8 (Dutch Section) of SIS. Whatever his experience and his connections, he was not yet able to engineer a Secret Service position for George. Instead, he suggested that he should join the Royal Navy Volunteer Reserve and qualify to be an officer, just as he himself had done seven years earlier. George duly did so, successfully passing written examinations and then impressing in an interview. Not long afterwards he received a letter welcoming him into the Royal Navy, and informing him that in 'due course' he would be given instructions on where to report for duty.

While he waited, through connections his mother had with the Government-in-exile, he found a temporary clerical post at the Dutch Ministry of Economic Affairs, based at Arlington House, St James's. But he didn't relish the life of a commuting civil servant, and soon realised he was ill-suited to a regular nine-to-five job.

In the autumn the exiled Behar family decided to change their name by deed poll. 'It was my mother's decision – I took no part in the consultations as I was away from home by then,' George recalled. 'She lived with an old lady whose name was Drake, and had thoughts of taking that name. But she eventually decided it would be better to take the fresh name, Blake.'

By then, George had received his navy call-up papers and had reported to HMS *Collingwood* – not a ship but the Navy's principal shore-based training centre. For a fit, adaptable man, the ten weeks of mainly physical work were tiring but not over-demanding. From there, it was on to the Firth of Forth in Rosyth, Scotland, for a more gruelling six weeks aboard the cruiser *Diomede*, the aim being to give the new recruits as realistic an introduction to life at sea as possible.

Finally, in March, the enlisted men made the fifteen-mile journey to their last training institution, HMS *King Alfred* in Hove. Named after the ninth-century King of Wessex – considered the 'father' of the Royal Navy as the first monarch to use ships in the defence of the realm – HMS *King Alfred*'s aim when it opened its doors in September 1939 was to promote a new kind of officer to enlarge the ranks of the expanding Navy. These HO ('Hostilities Only') officers, such as George Blake, would be bright, assertive young men, commissioned into the RNVR as temporary appointments; at the end of the war they would return to their civilian lives. In fact, by the end of hostilities, nearly 80 per cent of the officers on active duty with the Royal Navy were from the RNVR.

Once more Blake applied himself well to the complicated system of weekly tests and examinations. Failure in any one of them would have meant immediate dismissal from the course, but he consistently achieved impressive marks and, in April 1943, 'passed out' successfully as a sub-lieutenant.

It was an achievement of which he could feel proud, but he still hankered after a Secret Intelligence role. The opportunity appeared to present itself when, after a few day's leave back in Northwood to celebrate his commission, he returned to HMS *King Alfred* for a further two weeks for postgraduate training. 'A man came down from the Admiralty to lecture to us on the various branches of naval service open to us,' recalled Blake. 'Right at the end of his talk, he added: "There is one other branch which I should mention. It is called 'Special Service', and I cannot tell you very much about it because it is secret and, as far as we are concerned, the people who join it vanish."' This was music to Blake's ears: 'Special Service, secret, people not heard of again. It must be intelligence work, the landing of agents on the enemy coast . . . I wanted to be a real member of the Dutch underground, I wanted to be dropped into Holland to do secret, important work and I thought the Special Service would provide this opportunity.'

He was to be sadly disabused of that notion when he received a letter a month later requesting him to report to HMS *Dolphin*, headquarters of the Royal Navy Submarine Service at Fort Blockhouse in Gosport. What the 'secret' work actually entailed was training to be a diver for midget (two-man) submarines. Though disconcerted by this turn of events, he had signed up to the course and felt duty-bound to see it through. It turned out to be even more of a disaster than he had anticipated.

Physically fit he may have been, but he didn't relish the long hours spent under water and the particular kind of stamina needed to cope with those conditions. More seriously, he soon discovered he had an allergy to the altered oxygen containers the divers carried. So much so that, when put to the test on one of the midgets off an island on the West Coast of Scotland, he actually fell unconscious in the water and had to be swiftly dragged back to the surface. His ears suffered severe, albeit temporary, damage.

While his superiors pondered what to do with him, Blake was taken off the course and given the job of officer of the watch on HMS *Dolphin*. A few weeks later, the captain of the establishment, who had taken a liking to the young man and had made some enquiries on his behalf, summoned Blake to his office: 'He asked me if I would be interested in fast boats and plenty of action. This was just the sort of thing that appealed to me. I was therefore told I was to go to London early the next day and report to an address in Palace Street, just off Victoria Street.' What Blake was about to discover was that 'fast boats' and 'plenty of action' was euphemistic language. He was, in fact, about to take the first steps towards realising his dream of becoming a Secret Intelligence Officer.

Arriving in the City of Westminster the following morning, Blake was introduced to a Royal Navy captain who questioned him about his background, his resistance work and his escape from Holland. He was then told to write down his life story, including as much detail as possible. What he didn't immediately realise was that, in spite of the presence of the naval officer, he was now within the precincts of the British Secret Intelligence Service. The office in Palace Street was one of SIS's many London outposts, habitually used for training in 'tradecraft'.

After lunch the captain escorted him on a ten-minute walk to a scruffy-looking place just opposite the entrance to St James's Park underground station. One of its occupants, a counter-intelligence officer about to take charge of a new anti-Soviet unit (Section IX), would later describe the interior and its most important inhabitant:

> Broadway was a dingy building, a warren of wooden partitions and frosted-glass windows. It had eight floors serviced by an ancient lift.

> On one of my early visits, I got in to the lift with a colleague whom the liftman treated with obtrusive deference. The stranger gave me a swift glance and looked away. He was well-built and well-dressed,

but what struck me most was his pallor: pale face, pale eyes, silvery blond hair thinning on top – the whole an impression of pepper-and-salt.

When I got out at the fourth floor, I asked the liftman who he was. 'Why, sir, that's the Chief,' he answered in some surprise.

Blake had arrived at 54 Broadway, also known as Broadway Buildings, the headquarters of SIS. The writer providing the description of its somewhat dilapidated state was Kim Philby. The 'Chief' – or 'C', as he was known in government circles – was the then head of SIS, Major-General Sir Stewart Menzies.

In Broadway, the staff worked in 'gloomy rooms where the floors were covered in worn lino, quite dangerous in places, [where] walls were a mucky grey/white/cream, and the rooms were lit with bare light bulbs; only senior personnel were allowed to have desk lamps'. Pigeons were housed in a loft in the roof; no one quite knew why, or who looked after them. Perhaps they would be vital messengers in the event of a calamity. Down in the basement there was an inhospitable bar, effectively a club for Service 'insiders', and those who stumbled into it unknowingly would be met by quizzical glances or frosty stares.

The fourth floor was clearly a cut above the rest of the building. One corridor, near the Chief's office and the main boardroom, was covered in thick red carpet, with Chippendale armchairs sat alongside a slim mahogany table. Those who had a personal appointment with the Chief would sit and gaze up at two lamps above his office door as they waited: one red and one green. Once the red light went off and the green one came on, they could then advance into the inner sanctum, provided they could get beyond the praetorian guard of secretaries.

On that day in August 1944, however, Blake did not move in such exalted circles, but was ushered up to a much smaller room with an attic window on the top floor. There, he was introduced to a man who remained anonymous then, but whom he would later know as Major Charles Seymour, head of SIS's Dutch Section. Blake was interviewed by Seymour, in Dutch, mainly about his work in the Resistance, before being led down to the first floor, sat at a desk and asked to fill in another questionnaire.

At this stage he remained unclear about what sort of job he was being considered for. Given his background in the RNVR, he wondered whether he was going to be offered employment on Motor Torpedo Boats, which were used by the Secret Services to land agents on the enemy coast. Or perhaps he might be being tested for a post in Naval Intelligence, or for liaison work with other allied navies? He left 54 Broadway no clearer.

A week later he was called back, and this time, in the boardroom on the fourth floor, he was interviewed in front of a five-man committee. Calmly and methodically, he answered all the questions fired at him, seemingly at random, by the different members of the board, still unable to fathom what role they might have in mind. A few minutes after he had been sent out of the room, the naval captain came out and tapped him on the shoulder. The news was good: he had been accepted into the Service and should report back at 10 a.m. the following Monday.

On 14 August, the mystery was finally solved. Blake returned to the eighth floor at Broadway Buildings, was greeted once more by Major Seymour and, after formal introductions, was led down the corridor to a large room. There, he met a 'short thick-set man, with pale blue eyes and a bristle moustache', who walked with a limp and addressed him in a brusque, military manner.

Colonel John 'Bill' Cordeaux's bark was worse than his bite. He was Major Seymour's superior, Controller of the Northern Areas (CNA), with the Low Countries and Scandinavia making up his sphere of influence. He gave Blake the momentous news that he was now on attachment as an officer of the British Secret Service and that he would be working there, at headquarters, in the organisation's Dutch

Section. While Cordeaux impressed upon him what an honour it was to be chosen, and outlined his future responsibilities, the young recruit's mind whirled with excitement.

> In fact, I could hardly believe it was true. I had of late suspected and hoped that job for which I was being interviewed had something to do with 'Intelligence'. But that I would actually become an officer in the British Secret Service, this legendary centre of hidden power, commonly believed to have a decisive influence on the great events of this world, was something that far exceeded my wildest expectations.

Two days later, Blake formally signed the Official Secrets Act. In his buoyant mood, he would have cast his eyes only fleetingly over its characteristically bureaucratic, understated language, including Paragraph 1(a), which read: '[If any person] communicates the code word, pass word, sketch, plan, model, article, note, document or information to any person, other than a person to whom he is authorised to communicate it, or a person to whom it is in the interest of the state his duty to communicate it . . . that person shall be guilty of a misdemeanour.'

All he could think of was getting straight down to work, serving his new country and, through that, helping the country of his birth to turn the tide against its German invaders.

Still highly collegiate in its structure and elitist in both its membership and attitude, SIS could be an intimidating organisation, especially for those who hadn't come from Eton, Winchester, Oxbridge, the Guards or the Royal Navy. It was staffed by very many fair-minded men and women with a strong sense of patriotism and a keen work ethic, but snobbish and patronising behaviour undoubtedly persisted in certain quarters. In wartime, however, this club (or tribe, perhaps?) opened its doors and loosened its attitudes just a little. Exceptional circumstances forced it to bring in useful outsiders like Blake. Even so, those beyond the Dutch Section who took notice of him often referred to Blake as 'some Dutch fellow' or 'that funny foreigner'.

Not that it mattered much. SIS's hermetically sealed departments meant that he generally mixed only with colleagues in P8. Blake had, in fact, started his career in Intelligence in exactly the right place. The Dutch Section wasn't a typical SIS department, and he fitted in well with a mixed bunch of characters under the considerate leadership of Charles Seymour. Though very much the office junior, Seymour valued him greatly for a number of reasons: 'He brought us a lot of useful addresses for safe houses in Holland, from his time in the underground. He was very good at decoding messages, scrambled or badly sent, as we were getting more and more information from our agents . . . But he'd also been a brave young man, from his experiences fleeing through Europe, and he was a good influence on the young agents we were sending over there. He was of great value in helping prepare them for their missions.'

For Blake, it was a seamless progression from the clandestine life he had been leading for the last four years. 'I came very naturally into this atmosphere of illegality,' he later observed. 'I liked being an Intelligence Officer – I loved the romantic side of the job.'

Colonel Cordeaux and Major Seymour had worked skilfully and effectively to repair the damage to SIS's operations in the Netherlands, which originated with the disastrous Venlo incident. Soon after the start of the war, on 9 November 1939, at a town on the Dutch-German border, two SIS officers and a Dutch intelligence agent were captured by the counter-espionage section of the *Sicherheitsdienst* (SD) in a clever sting which led to the destruction of much of the agent network in the Netherlands, and quite possibly damaged SIS's entire espionage operation in Western Europe. From mid-1942 onwards, Cordeaux and Seymour had an intelligence operation in Holland up and running once again, with SIS and the newly-created Dutch Secret Service, *Bureau Inlichtingen* (BI), working effectively together – the Dutch supplying the agents, and the British training and equipping them. By the time Blake joined P8 in 1944, the section was running five networks reporting through thirty wireless sets.

The famed Dutch secret agent, Pierre Louis Baron d'Aulnis de Bourouill, one of those dropped over Netherlands in 1943, testified to the work of P8: 'I for one have always felt that the spirit of co-operation and personal friendship from Charles Seymour, sitting there, with his crew of Dutch section, were of very great importance to our success.'

Blake worked hand in glove with his mentor Douglas Child, who had overall responsibility for the training of agents. The two men shared a flat in Petty France, a short walk away from the office. Child provided the technical, wireless training for the new recruits, after which Blake would accompany them to the Parachute Training Centre at RAF Ringway, near Manchester.

Blake had come to realise that his ambition to return undercover to his native land would never be fulfilled. An agreement between SIS and BI meant that no British nationals were to be dropped into Holland as agents. Nonetheless, while at RAF Ringway, he took the opportunity to undertake the training alongside his charges, and experienced a taste of the adventure awaiting them when he joined them for a trial jump. It was exhilarating: 'I felt myself gently rocking in the air. The relief that the parachute had opened, the light, floating feeling as if I was without weight . . . I thought this is what angels must feel like when they fly through the heavens.'

Blake's real role, however, was to add psychological comfort, accompanying the nervous agents to the airfield on the night of a dropping operation. He found this a difficult but rewarding experience.

On the way we would stop, first for tea and then for drinks in some cosy old pub. Myself, a girl from the Women's Services and the agent did our best to keep the mood carefree and usually succeeded in this . . . Just before departure the agent changed into clothes of Dutch origin and I had to check carefully that he had no English coins, letters, bus or cinema tickets, or anything else on his

person, which might give him away . . . Then I gave him his false
Dutch identity documents, his money, his codes and his transmitting schedules and – if he wished – a lethal pill.

But Blake's major asset was his facility with languages. By now the
Allies were pushing on through Europe following the D-Day landings,
and had reached the estuary of the Rhine and Meuse, which separates
the Northern from the Southern Netherlands. P8 had taken advantage of this advance to set up a field station in the liberated part of
Holland, and a vast amount of material came pouring in from agents,
often about German troop dispositions, the locations of headquarters
and all manner of other military information. These telegrams were
sent in code, and even when they had been deciphered at Bletchley
Park, the text was often still badly mangled, with whole strings of words
missing. With his thorough knowledge of Dutch, Blake's task was to go
through and 'stitch' them together.

SIS and BI continued to develop agent networks and began working
effectively with the Dutch Resistance. But Holland's liberation efforts
still faced major setbacks along the way, none more so than 'Operation
Market Garden', the bold Allied plan to drop 30,000 British and
American airborne troops behind enemy lines to capture the eight
bridges spanning the Dutch-German border, and from there to drive
on into the industrial heartland of Germany.

Blake played a minor role in that fateful operation. He was on
duty in the office at Broadway on the first day, Sunday, 17 September,
waiting on tenterhooks for a telephone call from SHAEF (Supreme
Headquarters Allied Expeditionary Force). Once it came, he was able
to successfully despatch a series of telegrams to SIS's underground
organisations in the Arnhem-Nijmegen area, which enabled them to
give assistance to the troops of the British 1st Airborne Division, who
were about to land. As he recalled: 'It was a tense afternoon . . . I
realised an important operation was afoot, which, if successful, would
bring about the liberation of Holland within a matter of days. Then

the call came and I at once sent off the telegrams. I felt as if a spring had been released inside me.' But it wasn't to be the decisive moment in this campaign. Indeed, it ended up a catastrophe. Thousands of lives were lost, and as a consequence the people of the Netherlands faced their harshest winter yet at the hands of an occupier bent on retribution.

Those who worked with Blake in this period were still unsure if this capable, serious-minded young man had all the required qualities to make a good intelligence officer. 'I think he was a bit of a dreamer. He was certainly not technically equipped to be a spy – he couldn't even drive a car properly,' was the opinion of Hazel Seymour, Charles's wife, who worked in another section of the Service. 'But with his intellectual skills, he would have made a brilliant codist – he had that sort of brain. He also wrote very good, very intelligible reports.'

The Seymours took Blake under their wing. Hazel Seymour was only a couple of years older than him, but was married and expecting a baby, and he felt comfortable in her presence: 'I had lots of conversations with him. He was fatherless, and he'd been missing his mother; he seemed a little bit lost. He was a very good listener, and always interested in other people . . . He was just a very pleasant, unassuming, quiet, gentle young man. He was someone we liked to have around. I didn't think he would stay in SIS after the war – I thought perhaps he might have settled down to become a very respectable family man, with a job as a lecturer, perhaps.'

Although he didn't know it at the time, in April 1945 Blake accompanied to the airfield the last agent to be dropped over Holland. It was a mission that had an unhappy ending: 'He was a nice, fair boy, just turned eighteen, who was going to one of our groups in the Amsterdam area as a wireless operator. Just before take-off there was a last-minute hitch. But, after a longish wait, the aircraft took off after all . . . Two days later we received a telegram from the group to which the young man had been dropped. He was dead.' The agent had been unable to free his harness as he came down over a large lake, close to the dropping site. There was a strong wind that night and his para-chute dragged him under. His body was discovered the following day.

As events moved rapidly in the spring of 1945, P8's office gradually emptied. Major Seymour headed off to The Hague, to re-open the SIS station there, while Commander Child, with no more agents to train, was given a new intelligence job at Naval Headquarters in Germany. When VE Day came on 8 May, Blake was the sole officer on duty.

With little left to do, he wandered out into the excited crowds to soak up the atmosphere of that momentous day: 'I found myself pushed in the direction of Buckingham Palace, where a surging mass of people kept on chanting: "We want the King! We want the King!" And then, when he and the Royal Family came out on the balcony, started singing "For He's a Jolly Good Fellow". The war was over, we had won.'

5

Cold War

In the week after the unalloyed excitement and relief of the VE-Day celebrations, the reality of the austere future stretching ahead for many years to come began to dawn on the British people. Widespread wartime restrictions remained and would only get harsher as American wartime aid dried up. Meat, butter, sugar, tea, jam, eggs – there were severe shortages of them all. Clothes were also rationed, and the salutary advice continued to be 'make do and mend'.

The national hangover was duly reflected in the corridors of power. Jock Colville, Churchill's Private Secretary, recorded in his diary for Monday, 14 May: 'At No. 10 I found everybody rather strained after a week of violent rejoicing and tumult . . . Victory has brought no respite. The PM looks tired and has to fight for the energy to deal with the problems confronting him. These include the settlement of Europe, the last round of war in the East, an election on the way, and the dark cloud of Russian imponderability.'

A couple of days later George Blake escaped the bleak mood of an exhausted nation when he set out to join Major Seymour and his team in The Hague, to assist with the task of winding down wartime affairs and reconstituting the SIS station. He would be engaged in delicate work, well suited to his ability to listen patiently and sympathetically to the problems of others. Agents had to be paid off; the fate of those who had disappeared must be investigated; and their widows and orphans taken care of. In collaboration with officers from the *Bureau Inlichtingen,* the Dutch Secret Service, he also had to make tricky decisions about who should be recommended for awards and decorations, and then write citations.

Blake himself, and the rest of his colleagues in the Dutch Section, all received the Order of Orange-Nassau (equivalent to Britain's OBE) for their work during the war.

In all, the SIS team in The Hague comprised five officers and three secretaries, all of whom lived and worked in a couple of large villas in Wassenaar, an affluent garden suburb of the Dutch city. The larger of the two houses had previously belonged to a Dutch Nazi. Just a fortnight earlier, he had been arrested and taken to a prison camp awaiting trial. The smaller building was used as an office.

Away from Wassenaar, in the wider Dutch population, the privations of war had been far worse than for the British, as George discovered when he went to visit his Aunt Truss in Rotterdam. He borrowed a bicycle with wooden wheels and cycled out to her home, which was some distance from the port: 'She had become very thin, but otherwise was well. It was a tearful reunion and we talked deep into the night when I had to get back to my ship . . . The next time I came, I drove up in my requisitioned car and brought with me ample supplies of food. My aunt needed these badly after the winter of famine she had just lived through.'

There was really not enough work to do at The Hague to keep the group of SIS officers busy. As Major Seymour recalled: 'I didn't really need him [Blake], but I brought him over with me to give him something to do.' George's light duties left him with plenty of free time. Still only twenty-two, for the last six years his day-to-day existence had been fraught and highly pressured. Now he was cast into a hectic social scene with a seemingly never-ending diet of high living. From the largesse of the military powers flowed the best accommodation in luxury hotels and picturesque country houses, rich food in expensive restaurants, and apparently never-ending stocks of champagne and brandy once greedily hoarded by the German Army.

In this bacchanalian-like setting even the quiet, serious-minded Blake threw off his shackles: 'I too found myself irresistibly drawn into this maelstrom of pleasure. In the words of the well-known hymn, "the world, the flesh and Satan dwelt around the path I trod" . . . It seemed to me that the whole of Europe went mad in that first summer after the war. We had cars, we went to parties, nightclubs, drinking sessions – we were young and we enjoyed life to the full.'

One of the SIS secretaries was a tall, fair-haired, attractive 21-year-old former debutante named Iris Irene Adele Peake, the daughter of Conservative MP Osbert Peake, then Financial Secretary to the Cabinet in Churchill's post-war caretaker government. Iris had previously worked in a different section of SIS to George but now the two were thrown together and, in the more intimate environment of the villa in Wassenaar, began to develop a close relationship.

Hazel Seymour, who was in The Hague with her husband Charles, observed the couple at close quarters: 'The two of them were very fond of each other. Despite their very different backgrounds, they seemed to find something in each other that just clicked.'

Blake observed that SIS secretaries in those days more often than not belonged to the higher echelons of the Establishment. 'Though often scatter-brained, they worked hard because they were very conscious of their patriotic duty, instinctively equating the interests of England with their own class,' he noted a little disdainfully. 'They were very pretty, some very beautiful, but inclined to be vague and incompetent in varying degrees, though to this there were exceptions.' Clearly Iris was in the latter category, combining both good looks and intelligence.

She was also decidedly upper-class. Her mother was Lady Joan Capell, daughter of the Earl of Essex. Her father had travelled along the well-established route of Eton, Sandhurst, the Coldstream Guards in the First World War, and Christ Church College, Oxford. The Peakes also had many connections at Court and, in 1945, Iris was actually living in St James's Palace, sharing an apartment with her best friend, Diana Legh, also a secretary at SIS, whose father – Sir Piers – was Master of the King's Household.

George and Iris were, then, 'from different sides of the tracks'. She moved effortlessly in the highest social circles and, while he may have worked in an Establishment organisation, he was clearly a 'foreigner' – an outsider effectively, in his own words, 'a man of no class'. Though The Hague, away from the constraints of English society, offered an opportunity for this unconventional relationship to flourish, it was not to last. When the relationship petered out – under what circumstances remains unclear – those close to Blake later wondered whether it had lasting consequences.

'They were quite inseparable in Holland. But in those days, given their place in the social hierarchy, the Peakes wouldn't have approved of their daughter marrying somebody like George Blake,' recalled Hazel Seymour. 'It ended some time after they returned to England. We all thought he wanted to marry her. All we know is that he went to visit the family, and after that the romance was over. I don't think Iris would ever have married him – and she certainly wasn't the type to stand out against her parents. He was a sensitive sort of bloke, and to be told – or for it to be indicated to him – that he wasn't good enough, would have hurt him.'

Years later, in 1961, two days before her husband's trial at the Old Bailey, Blake's first wife Gillian referred to his friendship with Iris in a letter sent to his solicitor, Albert Cox. 'There is only one point which I have thought of since our talk,' she wrote, 'which is probably of no importance and which my husband may have mentioned to you. It is his friendship with Iris Peake, who he first met in about 1944. He was in love with her, but could not possibly marry her because of his circumstances, and the relationship ended when he went to Korea. I was thinking how this might have added to his restless state of mind.'

Nearly seventy years on, Iris Peake's recollection is that she continued to meet George from time to time in London on their return from The Hague, before they eventually lost touch after he was posted to Hamburg in the spring of 1946. She maintains that he never met her father and remembers George as highly intelligent, good company and a popular colleague. She also recalls that in those days he was still considering an alternative career in the Church. She was never aware of his Jewish heritage.

The theory that Blake was so scarred by Iris's rejection that it stored up feelings of resentment against the British 'Establishment' and helped sow some of the seeds of his later betrayal is one he himself has emphatically rejected:

> That's just thought up. I had several girlfriends in my younger years, and it's true she was one of them. But I never went to her home, or met her father, or any other member of her family . . . It was a friendship which was normal at that time of life – and it came to a natural end. I don't think she ever wanted to marry me and I don't think I ever wanted to marry her. I just wasn't the [right] age . . . She had plenty of money, I suppose – I don't know how much exactly – but I had no money and couldn't keep a family and wasn't in a position to marry at all.

On 19 October 1945, George Orwell contributed a typically perceptive essay to *Tribune* magazine. Entitled 'You and the Atomic Bomb', it presented his analysis of the state of the post-war world. He argued that the new nuclear age had brought a 'peace that is no peace', in which the United States and the Soviet Union would be both 'unconquerable and in a permanent state of *cold war* with each other' (author's emphasis). Orwell's phrase describing the ideological clash between East and West would quickly enter the political lexicon as the Cold War.

There were several key moments in late 1945 and early 1946 that helped crystallise this dangerous, new, bi-polar world of warring power blocs. The first occurred in George Blake's own world of espionage in September 1945, when he returned to Broadway from The Hague to resume his work in the Dutch Section of SIS. It concerned the defection of Igor Gouzenko in Canada, an event that first alerted the West to the scale of a Soviet spying offensive that had, up until then, gone unnoticed. Gouzenko, a cipher clerk in the Soviet Embassy in Ottawa, decided to defect with his family rather than return to Moscow to face complaints about his conduct. After initial scepticism, the Royal Canadian Mounted Police started to examine over a hundred documents that Gouzenko had brought with him, spirited away from the Embassy hidden in his briefcase. Very quickly the FBI and Britain's internal Security Service (MI5) were called in to look at this treasure trove, which revealed the existence of extensive networks run by the KGB (the all-powerful Soviet State Security agency, at home and abroad) and the GRU (Soviet foreign military intelligence). These networks spanned Canada, stretched into the United States, and had strong links to Europe. The secret frontlines of the Cold War were now being established.

On the political and ideological front, the rhetoric was also ratcheting up. On Saturday, 9 February 1946, Stalin made an imposing appearance in the Bolshoi Theatre before an audience of voters in the Soviet 'elections'. Part of his speech was a characteristic appeal for yet more effort from his people as new five-year plans for heavy industry were put in place. But the passage that sent a shudder of anxiety through Western policy-makers appeared to suggest that the mere existence of capitalism and imperialism made future wars inevitable. Some in Washington even went so far as to read his words as a delayed Declaration of War against the United States.

The White House sought clarification from those best qualified to read the Soviet leader's intentions. It duly arrived two weeks later, from George Kennan, US Ambassador to Moscow and an old Soviet hand. Kennan's 'Long Telegram', as it would become known, was dictated to his secretary Dorothy Hessman while he was laid up in

a

bed after a painful attack of sinusitis. His foul mood almost certainly
contributed to the vehemence of his language, in what was one of the
most influential documents in the long history of the Cold War. In a
remarkably cogent and prescient eight thousand word essay, he set out
to explain to President Harry Truman why he believed conflict with
the Soviet Union was inevitable:

> We have here a political force committed fanatically to the belief
> that with US there can be no permanent *modus vivendi*, that it is
> desirable and necessary that the internal harmony of our society
> be disrupted, our traditional way of life be destroyed, the inter-
> national authority of our state be broken, if Soviet power is to
> be secure . . .

Beware the attempts of Stalin and his cohorts to expand their
influence throughout the world, he advised President Truman, while
maintaining that those ambitions could be effectively countered by a
policy of containment (the Cold War in practice) rather than military
engagement. The latter would, in any case, be likely to result in the
most horrific outcome – nuclear war.

Less than a month after Keenan's telegram, Winston Churchill
picked up on the Ambassador's theme of the Soviets' seemingly relentless desire to expand their power and dogma. The occasion was his
'Sinews of Peace' speech on 5 March, in the Missouri town of Fulton,
before a crowd of 40,000. With an approving President Truman alongside him, he delivered a classical but chilling oration. In one particular
passage, he defined forever the state of affairs now building between
West and East – and effectively sounded the official starting gun on
the Cold War:

> From Stettin in the Baltic to Trieste in the Adriatic an iron curtain
> has descended across the continent. Behind that line lie all the
> capitals of the ancient states of Central and Eastern Europe.

Warsaw, Berlin, Prague, Vienna, Budapest, Belgrade, Bucharest
and Sofia, all these famous cities and the populations around them
lie in what I must call the Soviet sphere, and all are subject in one
form or another, not only to Soviet influence but to a very high,
and in some cases, increasing measure of control from Moscow.

The presence of this 'iron curtain' meant of course that intelligence gathering on the Soviet threat – now firmly re-established as
SIS's number one priority – was severely restricted.

All manner of operations were now being considered in an effort
to build up information on the new enemy and, to that end, George
Blake was given his own role in this new type of war when he was posted
to Hamburg in April 1946. With no German government yet formed,
the British ruled an area half the size of their own country, with direct
responsibility for a population of more than 20 million. The British
'zone' consisted of Schleswig-Holstein, Hamburg, Lower Saxony, the
present-day state of North Rhine-Westphalia and the western sector of
Greater Berlin. It was anticipated that the occupation could last for a
decade or more.

The Royal Navy – to which Blake was still nominally attached – was
involved in the development of British 'denazification' policy. German
admirals and submarine commanders were considered to need particular attention as likely sources of opposition to military occupation.
These men were not to be placed in the same category of danger as SS
or Gestapo war criminals but their militaristic instincts, combined with
staunch patriotism, meant they required close interrogation to ensure
they were not considering rebellion of any sort.

Commander Douglas Child, whose influence had led to Blake
finding a place in SIS, now saw another opportunity for his young
protégé. A naval intelligence body called the Forward Interrogation
Unit, stationed in Hamburg, was about to be wound up. Child
suggested that it should be continued, but that Blake should take
over its running. He envisaged that Blake, still a sub-lieutenant in the

Navy, would now have the perfect cover for any Secret Intelligence activities. Conveniently, there was also a large SIS station for support in Hamburg. It was a great responsibility for an intelligence officer aged just twenty-three, and barely two years into his career, but Blake spoke good German and exuded an air of calm and maturity that belied his years.

On 7 April, he arrived in a city brought to its knees. Hamburg, a once proud mercantile and cultural centre, had lain in ruins ever since the Allies launched a fearsome bombing campaign, codenamed 'Operation Gomorrah', in July 1943. More than 40,000 civilians had been killed and 37,000 wounded over eight days of raids by the RAF and the United States Army Air Force, and the city's infrastructure was to all intents and purposes completely destroyed. Almost three years later, the population were still suffering a lack of food and housing, and had just endured a lethally cold winter. Cases of death by malnutrition were still being recorded, and in the first five months of 1946, 4,732 fresh cases of tuberculosis were reported.

The unit Blake inherited had been formed in January 1944 and latterly had links to a colourful, highly secret intelligence group created by Commander Ian Fleming RNVR. The man who would later create SIS's most famous fictional spy, James Bond, had spent the war as personal assistant to Rear Admiral John Godfrey, Director of Naval Intelligence for the Royal Navy. Following success with a number of quixotic deception schemes, in 1942, Fleming decided to form 30 Assault Unit, a tightly-knit commando group operating in conjunction with forward troops, with its brainpower drawn from the Royal Navy, and its brawn supplied by the Royal Marines. Its primary task was to steal German naval intelligence, be it codes, documents, equipment or personnel – and carry out interrogation of the latter, if necessary.

The Forward Interrogation Unit had worked closely with 30 Assault Unit in intelligence gathering and translation in 1945, but its particular remit had been to extract vital information from prisoners, together with their papers, and send it all back to the Admiralty. By April 1946, that work was all but complete, and its leader, Lieutenant Commander Ralph Izzard, had left for home along with five other members of staff. Only Captain Charles Wheeler remained in the unit's HQ, a house with a fine view of the River Elbe, two cars, and a resident black spaniel dog.

Wheeler spent a month briefing Blake and handing over the work of the Unit to him, which included passing on his impressive collection of German naval contacts and some useful social connections, too. Later an outstanding foreign correspondent for the BBC, Wheeler had enough time to form a clear impression of Blake's character and motivations. 'He was a curious person. He was very charming. People liked him. Smiled a lot . . . smiled rather too much. Smiled at breakfast,' he would later reflect. 'He was affable, he was sociable, he was likeable – but I can't say I liked George particularly. He was very secretive. George would never tell you what he was doing. We knew, of course, that he was a spook, that his naval uniform was just cover. And it was clear to me that he was looking ahead to a career as an intelligence officer.'

Some of Blake's behaviour and methods, according to Wheeler's description, could almost be lifted from the pages of an Ian Fleming novel:

> He used to play around with invisible ink. And his particular friend, a Major Ramsbotham, would arrive carrying a small wind-up gramophone and a single 78 record.

> Major R always made straight for the telephone; he would dial a number, play the 'Blue Danube' waltz into the mouthpiece and replace the receiver. The purpose of this brief communication neither Blake nor the Major ever explained.

> This was all slightly childish to my mind, but he obviously got a kick out of playing around with these toys. He seemed to enjoy the conspiracy of the job – and I would have thought he was very good at it.

As far as the substance of Blake's job went, Wheeler did not believe there was much left for him to do with the German submarine officers: 'I don't really know what George did in Hamburg – unless the whole operation became an anti-Russian exercise.' Wheeler guessed correctly. His SIS masters had instructed Blake to take over the most promising of the FIU's naval contacts and use them to help develop intelligence networks in the Soviet zone. This was the real stuff of the intelligence trade – running agents and gathering crucial information on the enemy. The U-boat officers recruited were briefed to attempt to collect information on the Soviet armed forces, and on political and economic developments in the Soviet zone.

Personally interrogating some of the cream of the German Navy, plotting operations against the Communists . . . for a time, it went to Blake's head. To his credit, he had thrown himself into his work with ferocious enthusiasm, immersing himself in huge amounts of technical, military and political detail, and writing reports of interminable length. Some of his colleagues, however, and especially the Royal Navy officers, disliked the way this boyish-looking commanding officer seemed to lord it over them. He could be 'rude, fussy, vain and voluble, and he often struck them as a little mad'. He consistently urged his sceptical colleagues to be on their guard lest a Soviet agent should penetrate their work, and he introduced special security measures to that end.

Years later, Blake would concede that his newfound status had made him a little arrogant: 'The life I was leading in Hamburg was very much a continuation of life in the first few months after the war in liberated Holland . . . The large villas, requisitioned cars, luxury hotels and country clubs . . . All this gave me a feeling of importance and did nothing for my humility.'

In attempting to establish networks inside the Soviet Zone, he was helped by the deep loathing the German naval officers felt for the Soviet military and, at a time of hunger, money and copious supplies of food, drink and cigarettes also proved powerful incentives in recruiting agents.

Blake himself relished the reconnaissance side of his intelligence work. He would leave the office for several days at a time and travel to Lübeck, just a few miles from the Soviet border, in the guise of a 'displaced person'. There, he would meet contacts and get a feel for the level of useful clandestine activity in the city.

In those days, it was also straightforward enough to send agents into the Soviet Zone through Berlin, where movement between the Eastern and Western sector was still virtually free: 'I used to dress them up in a Royal Marine uniform, issue them with a movement order in a fictitious English name and service number and then take them myself in my station wagon through the Soviet control posts at Helmstedt and Berlin,' Blake recalled. 'Once in Berlin, they made their own way across the boundary into the Eastern sector and from there to various towns in the Soviet Zone.'

The 'intense Dutchman' may have alienated some of his naval colleagues but his superiors in SIS, while acknowledging his eccentricity, were also highly impressed by the results he produced: Blake reckoned that by the spring of 1947, he had succeeded in building up two intelligence networks in East Germany, the members of which were nearly all former naval and Wehrmacht officers.

He returned to Broadway at the end of March, exhilarated by this experience, and satisfied he had played some part in the early moves in the Cold War. However, another year of relentless socialising in the country homes of the German aristocracy, and in less salubrious surroundings, had forced him to reconsider his earlier, alternative calling. 'My Calvinistic side strongly disapproved and thought it all rather dissolute,' he said. 'The inner battle which ensued had one important consequence. I felt that I was no longer worthy of becoming a minister of the Church as I feared I might not be able to live up to the high standards that calling demanded. I abandoned therefore all thought of going on to a theological college after my return to civilian life.'

There was, however, a different kind of career open to him. His old friend Commander Child, also demobilised from the Navy, decided to set up a company offering pleasure cruises on the Rhine and the Dutch canals. He offered his apprentice the opportunity to join him in this new venture. Blake declined. Indications from senior SIS officers were that his progress thus far had been duly noted, and that a promising full-time career in intelligence awaited.

In the final months of his time in Hamburg, Blake had been invited to dinner with Child and several other senior members of SIS's European operation, including Andrew King, shortly to become Controller Eastern Area (covering Germany, Austria and Switzerland). Before the war he had made his name as a member of Colonel Claude Dansey's Z organisation – a parallel spy network to SIS, using legitimate and front businesses rather than embassies to collect intelligence on the build-up to war. Impressed by what he had seen and heard about Blake, the dinner merely reinforced King's views: 'We were attracted by his foreign languages and cosmopolitan background. So few Britons spoke foreign languages.' His impressions were duly logged back at Broadway, where an old colleague from Z organisation, Kenneth Cohen, was Director of Production (D/P) – effectively 'global controller' in charge of intelligence gathering. This highly respected senior officer also noted Blake's potential: 'A gallant past, numerous languages and an ingenious mind.'

The upshot was that in April 1947 Blake was offered a permanent post in SIS and accepted 'without hesitation': 'I found intelligence work fascinating and liked travelling. The thought of having to serve perhaps in far-flung and wild countries did not worry me and, indeed, attracted me. I knew the direction of the work and was happy with that. Opposing any further Russian advance in Europe was a worthwhile task; I looked upon the Soviet Union as a menace to Western civilisation and our way of life.'

Even before being sent to Hamburg Blake had been fluent in Dutch, English, German and French. Once there, he started to learn Russian. Blake recalls a senior SIS officer paying a visit to his Hamburg apartment and noticing a worn-out textbook on his bedside table.

'Are you studying Russian? That's praiseworthy, but amateurism is not yet an art,' was the encouraging if oblique observation. Once back at Head Office, it was suggested to him that he might like to attend Cambridge University for six months to develop his Russian on a special course designed for officers of the Armed Services. Blake jumped at the idea. He took great delight in the pure intellectual pleasure of learning a new language and, of course, he could see the obvious advantages of it for him in the changing world order.

After a brief return to Hamburg to hand over the agent networks to his SIS colleagues, he travelled up to Cambridge in October, eagerly anticipating the opportunity to study at one of the world's oldest and grandest academic institutions.

Equally, in such congenial and relaxing surroundings, he now had the chance to reflect upon and take stock of his life. The previous seven years – resistance, escape and SIS – had been a constant whirl of exciting, but demanding activity. Now, amid the ancient spires and towers, he could plot the course ahead.

6

Cambridge

By the time George Blake arrived to take up his place at Cambridge in October 1947, the politicians' ardour for all things Russian was starting to cool a little. Enthusiastic talk about future intellectual contacts, or the teaching of Russian in British schools, was heard less as the regime of 'Uncle' Joe Stalin proved a very different proposition in peacetime from the redoubtable ally of the war. There were, nonetheless, political, trade and cultural links to maintain, despite the gradual lowering of the Iron Curtain, and, for spies like Blake, understanding the new foe meant a good grasp of the Russian language was invaluable.

Dr Elizabeth Hill was the charismatic, exuberant lecturer at Cambridge University who was to guide his academic progress over the course of the next eight months. It was a period he would describe as 'one of the watersheds in my life'. Dr Hill liked to regale her new students with the history of Russian studies in Great Britain, tracing it all the way back to Queen Elizabeth I, and even claiming that the Monarch herself had learned the language.

Certainly the start of close Russo-English relations can be plotted back to the sixteenth century, with Richard Chancellor's voyage to the White Sea and extraordinary journey to Moscow, the subsequent formation of the Muscovy Company, and then the correspondence over many years between Elizabeth and Ivan the Terrible, who offered at one point to marry the 'Virgin Queen'.

Short and stocky with broad features, her hair usually tied back in a severe bun, Elizabeth Hill was indubitably a woman of great personal magnetism and warmth of spirit. She was an outstanding if exacting language instructor, urging her pupils to '*rabotat, rabotat, rabotat* – work, work, work', and thus 'fall in love with themselves'. She also stirred them with her passion for the classical Russian writers of the nineteenth century like Tolstoy, Dostoyevsky, Turgenev and Gogol.

Born Yelizaveta Fyodorovna in St Petersburg in 1900, she came from a well-off Scots-Russian family who were forced to flee the Bolshevik regime in 1917. Her father Frederick eked out a meagre living as a door-to-door chocolate salesman in London – and won a few shillings from time to time playing bridge – while her mother was forced to knit to raise money for the household.

The barriers against women academics at Cambridge were substantial in those days but Liza – as she was known – persevered, and through a mixture of talent, charm and sheer doggedness finally secured a coveted post as lecturer in the Slavonic Studies department in 1936.

Among Dr Hill's eccentricities was a firm belief in the influence of the stars on people's lives. Her more cerebral friends and colleagues would joke about it with her, but she was not to be deterred. 'I consider that the character of a person, his or her personality, indeed the whole structure of a person are very influenced by the stars,' she maintained. She would listen attentively to new students, drawing them out into conversation, all the while trying to assess which astrological type they were. 'Very often I was right, and so it was with George Blake. He turned out to be a Scorpion, which is what I am myself. We are either great eagles, or awful devils, so I would say, well George, you can attain great heights, and I'll help you when you're flagging.'

She would take him and other favourite pupils in her rickety Renault car to London to attend services at the Russian Orthodox Church. Trips like this, along with her inspiring lectures and tutorials on the history, literature and art of her homeland, began to work a change on Blake. By Christmas he had read Tolstoy's *Anna Karenina* in the original Russian and, after that, moved swiftly on to *Resurrection*. He felt he was now developing a real understanding of the Russian people, their customs and traditions:

> Until then I had made little distinction between the notions 'Russian' and 'Soviet', and regarded the Russians as semi-barbarians, oppressed by a ruthless, atheistic dictatorship which relentlessly persecuted all Christians . . . During the war I had, of course, looked towards the Soviet Union with hope, admired its fighting spirit and welcomed its victories . . . but these sentiments were mixed with fear and dislike for Communism and devoid of any particular affection for the Russian people. Now I began to admire their courage, their patience, their generosity and their piety.

With his interest in philosophy and theology, Blake was increasingly attracted, through books like Gogol's *Dead Souls,* to the mysterious, poetic idea of the *Russkaya dusha* ('Russian soul'), a kind of national consciousness that, for its adherents, developed from the sum of personal and spiritual experiences. This romantic ethos, appealing to feeling rather than fact, reflecting a sense of connectedness rather than competition, contrasted the purity of traditional Russian values against the encroachment of Western enlightenment, rationalism and secularism.

Blake would later maintain that his change in attitude to all things Russian in this period was not accompanied by any switch in his political outlook. He continued to be as resolutely hostile to Communism as before, and that feeling was shared by his teacher. Having been forced to flee her homeland in 1917, Elizabeth Hill remained a fierce critic of the regime and its ideology, which attracted so many converts at Cambridge in the 1930s.

The infamous Cambridge spies – Guy Burgess, Anthony Blunt, Kim Philby and Donald Maclean – had all been before her time at the University, although she did have fleeting encounters with two of them. She had given Burgess a Russian lesson in 1935 while at London University, and afterwards Burgess's case officer Alexander Orlov, the KGB *rezident* in London, reported back to Moscow: 'The University luckily sent him to Hill, who gave him one lesson privately. The next step will be for him to ask her to put him in a group or pair him with other pupils so he may get a better ear for pronunciation and to make lessons livelier. Thus we count on approaching other pupils, since MÄDCHEN [Burgess's codename] knows how to make friends.' The hope – unfulfilled – was that Burgess would be able to befriend and then 'turn' other SIS officers also thought (almost certainly incorrectly) to be learning Russian in the Slavonic Studies department.

As for Blunt, Hill recalled attending a lecture at Cambridge: 'Blunt seemed to me very tall, elegant, effete really, and he gave a beautiful talk on some art subject which everybody applauded vigorously.'

Blunt and Burgess were not the only ones to have lost faith in capitalism in the 1930s and, at Cambridge, such was the disillusionment that nearly everyone with intellectual pretensions was gravitating to the left – or, increasingly, the extreme left. 'Aside from the politics lecturers, there were the economics people who were much more left-wing, then there were people like Roy Pascal, in the German literature department, who were absolutely bright red in their beliefs,' Hill remembered. 'Then there were the concealed Communists, who we only found out about later. I was invited to dinner by all these various people – and then dropped by them very quickly.'

One of Blake's fellow students was Major G.W.A. ('Darby') Courtice, who during the war had led a heroic effort by the 85 Royal Marines to try and defend the ancient citadel in the centre of Calais. He was eventually captured and imprisoned at Colditz. 'I'm not sure anybody had quite made their minds up about Russia in 1947,' he recalled. 'There was, though, a feeling that the Russian language was going to be terribly important and anyone who didn't speak Russian would be left in the sidings, as it were.'

When he arrived in Cambridge in October 1947, Blake was attached to Downing College and, in his first term, he took rooms in the town. This was to be no clandestine education: the service officers were expected to live the life of the undergraduate, wear the gown and follow the curriculum of the faculty of Slavonic Studies, albeit with extra tuition. Consumed by his studies, Blake found the busy social scene around the University distracting, eventually choosing to move out to the rural community of Madingley, about four miles away.

Madingley was an attractive village set amid farm and woodland, with a splendid church, St Mary Magdalene, dating back to Norman times. Madingley Hall, the stylish country house built in 1543, had gardens designed by Capability Brown, and was rented by Queen Victoria in 1860 for her son – the future Edward VII – while he was an undergraduate at Trinity College, Cambridge.

In the heart of the village Blake found spacious accommodation in a wing of a large house owned by an elderly lady, the widow of a vicar. She cooked him good meals, and so he spent much of his time studying in his sitting room, venturing out only to cycle into college to attend lectures, and receive extra coaching from Dr Hill.

'I would say to him, why do you live in Madingley, away from the other officers? It seems very odd to me. He'd merely say that he liked the exercise,' she recalled. 'I would spend many hours – two hours of a free afternoon, or when there was a window in the timetable – practising his verbs with him. I was happy to spend a lot of time with him because I thought he was extremely diligent, very shrewd and very intelligent.'

Like so many others, Dr Hill was unaware of Blake's somewhat exotic background: 'Now I never, for one single moment, thought that he was anything but British – though there was a slight greasy look about him, which gave me the idea that he might perhaps have some Jewish blood in him, or perhaps Oriental . . . But it just passed over because we are great mixtures in the world and these types appear. Besides, he had such an English name, George Blake, and I was fool enough not to realise that Blake is the name of an Admiral, you see, and it was his pseudonym.'

At Easter 1948, Blake's group sat their final exams, overseen by Dr Hill and a gifted young academic from Trinity College called Dimitri Oblensky, who hailed from an ancient aristocratic Russian family and was an acclaimed expert in the poetry of Pushkin. Blake passed both oral and written exams comfortably enough, although he was not among the three students who earned a distinction in the former category. He had enjoyed the intellectual challenge and poured his energies into his work, but had also found time to reflect further on his own political and religious views, which were now starting to change quite markedly.

It took five kings of England, from the austere and pious Plantagenet Henry VI in 1446 to the indulgent and ostentatious Henry VIII of the House of Tudor in 1515, to build King's College Chapel in Cambridge, but what a majestic achievement it was. Once inside the huge Gothic structure, the visitor steps into a gravity-defying hall of light, truly entering the realms of the celestial. High above the head is the largest single span of medieval arched roof anywhere in Christendom, two thousand tons of remarkable fan vaulting, a huge forest of carving and tracery. To the side lies a spectacular picture gallery of twenty-six Renaissance-painted stained glass windows, animating stories from the Old to the New Testament from East to West. All around on the walls are the giant coats-of-arms and beautiful fleurs-de-lis, highlighting the power and majesty of the Tudors.

George Blake was drawn to this place. 'I used to stay behind after the service when the candles were extinguished, but the organ went on playing, the sound filling every space . . . Sitting there in the darkness it was as if I no longer existed but had become one with the sound of the music. It was a mystical experience.' Despite these moving moments in an extraordinary spiritual house, he was by now starting to seriously question his religious beliefs. With time to meditate in quiet surroundings like King's College Chapel and his sitting room at Madingley, he had – he would later say – worked out from his own theological standpoint that he no longer believed in the central tenet of the Christian faith.

He believed in the doctrine of predestination, in which all good and evil proceed from God and every person is allocated a place in heaven and hell, and nothing they can do will affect this destiny.

> From this it follows that He being just, cannot hold us responsible and require our punishment for sins of which He himself is the author . . . If there is no sin and no punishment then there is also no need for atonement and justification through Christ's sacrifice. Would God play an elaborate game with Himself and having implanted sin in man and using it to work out His eternal purposes, find it necessary to come into the world Himself and be crucified to atone for this sin?

> From this reasoning, I was led to the inescapable conclusion, however reluctant I was to face it, that Christ was not God, that he had not by his sacrifice atoned for our sins and, indeed, there was no need for any atonement . . .

> However much I might continue to respect and admire the person of Christ as a human being . . . I found I had argued myself out of the Christian religion and could no longer call myself a Christian.

Was he perhaps now a deist, or simply a fatalist? Or was there a yawning chasm in his belief system waiting to be filled by something else, religious or political? Years later, his wife, Gillian, would observe:

'He always does like to strive after something. He liked, I think, to have an ideal. And once inspired by an ideal, was utterly dedicated to it.'

Blake had been back at his desk in Broadway no more than a couple of weeks when the first major crisis of the developing Cold War broke out.

The 'Berlin Blockade' had its immediate origins at the end of March 1948 when the Soviet Union began putting restrictions on traffic to the city from the Western Zones. This included making US personnel travelling through the Soviet Zone present evidence of identity, dictating that shipments from Berlin to Western Zones had to be cleared through Soviet check points and insisting on baggage inspections.

The Western powers responded by restricting vital exports to the Soviet Zone, and then declaring their own common currency, the Deutschmark. Two days later, in an immediate tit-for-tat, the Soviet Union announced it too had launched a currency.

Then, just before midnight on 23 June, the Soviets cut the power to West Berlin and began a full-scale blockade of the city. All rail, road and water access from the Western Zones to Berlin was halted. The Berlin Airlift – or 'Operation Plainfare', as the British called it – began two days later, with eighty tons of provisions delivered to Tempelhof airport by American C-47 aircraft.

In both rhetoric and action Stalin and his puppets were adopting an increasingly hard line. Early in July, the Cominform (Communist Information Bureau, the international organisation of Communist parties) urged the people of Yugoslavia to overthrow their defiantly independent leader, Josef Tito. He was accused of 'Trotskyism, leanings towards capitalist states, inordinate ambition and grandeeism'.

Meanwhile, a second front in the Cold War was developing in Asia, brought about by the rapid turn of events in the Chinese Civil War. By June 1948, Chiang Kai-shek's Nationalist armies were in retreat, while Mao Zedong's Communists had three million troops and were in control of 168 million inhabitants.

Perceptive policy-makers in the Foreign Office and in SIS realised that the impending Communist triumph in China would have weighty strategic implications in the region, and could also signal a fundamental change in the whole nature and positioning of the Cold War. A Joint Intelligence Committee report at the time, 'Communism in the Far East', was in no doubt which way the wind was blowing: 'The end of the war in 1945 found the Far East more vulnerable to communist influence than ever before'. The JIC observed that, during 1947, there was clear evidence of Russia's increasing interest in the region, noting that 'large quantities of Marxist literature were exported from Moscow at heavy discount rates and the Chinese Communist propaganda organisation was expanded'.

SIS sought to make changes to its operations in the region to meet the demands of this changing world order. In China, there were stations at Hong Kong, Tientsin, Shanghai, Nanking and Urumchi, but SIS had been reliant on the Nationalist Chinese Kuomintang in these areas for its intelligence and, with the rapid advance of Mao's armies, information became extremely scarce, and life increasingly restricted for both Foreign Office and SIS staff.

Blake was originally told he would be sent to Urumchi, near the border with Soviet Kazakhstan, but in light of transformed circumstances, SIS's Chief Controller Pacific, Dick Ellis, changed his mind. Instead, it was decided Blake should open a new outpost in Seoul, the capital of South Korea, along with an assistant, Norman Owen. His cover for the mission would be as vice-consul at the legation.

Still only 25 years old, to be chosen to head up a new SIS station – albeit a small one – was quite an achievement. Blake, however, was disappointed. He had been hoping to win a posting in Central Asia, preferably Afghanistan, a country he had always wanted to visit after hearing so many colourful stories from his cousin Raoul, who travelled there frequently.

As he moved into the Far Eastern Department in London in the summer of 1948, Blake began to realise the crucial importance of his task. After Washington and Moscow had divided Korea along the line of the 38th parallel in 1945, the stated hope was that this was merely a pause in the nation's history, pending the creation of a single Korean government and the consequent withdrawal of the respective occupying forces. The American and Soviet armies did pull out during 1948 and 1949, but with no agreement about who would run the country, South and North effectively remained client states of the two superpowers.

On 15 August 1948, elections sanctioned by the United Nations were held in the American-supported South, and Syngman Rhee was proclaimed the first president of the new Republic in Korea. Very quickly, on 9 September, the Soviet-backed North responded by declaring the Democratic People's Republic of Korea, with Kim Il-Sung as leader.

During July and August, Blake prepared for his mission to Seoul. He sat down with the outgoing consul-general, Derwent Kermode, for an up-to-date briefing on the politics of Korea, and was given books and papers to read. Among them was one that would have a profound effect on his political sympathies. It was *The Theory and Practice of Communism* by Robert Nigel Carew Hunt – more familiarly 'Bob' to his colleagues in the Foreign Office and SIS. Carew Hunt was the son of a priest, Oxford-educated, and a veteran of the First World War. By 1948 he had established himself as the senior SIS scholar on Marxism. In characteristically dry, caustic fashion, Kim Philby said of him: 'He had the advantage of being literate, if not articulate . . . at a later date, he told me that he had intended dedicating to me his first book on the subject, *The Theory and Practice of Communism*, but he had decided that such a tribute might embarrass me. Indeed, it would have given me grave embarrassment for a number of reasons.'

For Blake, the book was a revelation. Until then, he had been little exposed to Marxism itself, and what he had read was largely critical. His conclusion on turning the final page of Carew-Hunt's book was a dramatic one: 'I was left with the feeling that the theory of Communism sounded convincing, that its explanation of history made sense and that its objectives seemed wholly desirable and did not differ all that much from Christian ideals – even though the methods to attain them did . . . I began to ask myself whether Communism was really the terrible evil it was made out to be.'

SIS issued the book on the principle, espoused by the Chinese military strategist Sun Tzu in *The Art of War.* 'If you know your enemies and yourself, you will not be imperilled in a hundred battles.' The irony was the book revealed to Blake that he had not, up until then, actually known himself. In clear, objective language, Carew Hunt's text set out to explain to the reader the philosophical, political and economic underpinnings of Marxism. For Blake there was nothing off-putting or dangerous about this ideology. Quite the opposite, in fact: it seemed to marry snugly with his own system of values and beliefs.

As he read the general introduction to the book, Blake might have paused and reflected on Carew-Hunt's premise that, in the last analysis, Communism was a 'body of ideas which has filled the vacuum created by the breakdown of organised religion'. He would certainly have been attracted to his comparison of religion and Marxism in the following paragraph: 'For its devotees communism has the *value* of a religion in so far as it is felt to provide a complete explanation of reality and of man as part of reality, and at the same time to give to life, as does religion, a sense of purpose'. Blake had just lost his 'explanation of reality' with his rejection of Christianity. Here was something to replace it.

Carew-Hunt's view was that 'the only intelligible attitude towards the riddle of existence is agnosticism . . . there is nothing outside ourselves and the products of our mind by which the final truth can ever be tested', but he went on:

> As neither communism nor religion is content to rest in this position, each is ultimately driven to appeal to certain propositions

which have to be accepted by faith, but from which, once accepted, whatever else it is desired to prove logically follows.

Only while religion frankly accepts this, communism maintains that its fundamental dogmas are guaranteed by science, which they are certainly not, since one and all are very disputable.

Carew-Hunt used religious terms and analogies throughout, describing Marx, Engels, Lenin and Stalin as the 'four apostles' of Communism. Discussing one of Marx's most famous dictums – that 'All philosophies have sought to explain the world; the point, however, is to change it' – he said: 'Marxists have always insisted that theory and action are one. A theory of which the truth is not confirmed by action is sterile, while action which is divorced from theory is purposeless. The two stand in much the same relation to one another as do faith and works in Christian theology.'

Dick White, Chief of SIS at the time when Blake's treachery was eventually unmasked, would later observe: 'Christianity is an extremist movement, Marxism is another. It's perhaps not so difficult to move from one to another, to make the journey between these two worlds . . . Marxist theory accounts for everything, and you can subordinate the interests of life for it, and believe yourself to be on the side of history.'

In his questioning state, Blake started to equate the early Christians' struggle for acceptance with the battles fought by Marxism, a young 'faith', in the twentieth century. He began to believe that there was no real difference in the social and economic ends that Communists professed and Christians sought. When he now considered the words from Chapter Two of 'Acts of the Apostles', he read them as merely an early version of the Communist creed: 'And all who believed were together and had all things in common. And they were selling their possessions and belongings and distributing the proceeds to all, as any had need'.

Put simply, if God is replaced by the State, Communism aligns neatly with Calvinism. Just as God plans everything beforehand, so the State under Communism is all-knowing, all-powerful, all-controlling. Comparisons continued beyond theology: dissent in Calvin's Geneva often led to humiliation and public abasement and, four centuries later, in Stalin's Russia, serious opposition to the regime meant a show trial and a forced 'confession'.

So, it was in a somewhat restless mood that Blake departed for Seoul at the end of October. He was not allowed the luxury of a leisurely journey, and the voyage by seaplane, via Japan, took just a week. He did, however, manage a stopover in Cairo, where he visited his Uncle Daniel and Aunt Zephira.

The creation of the state of Israel in May had destroyed the previous harmony between Jews and Arabs in the city, and Blake found the Curiels had fallen on hard times and were in poor health. Their telephone had been cut off and they were burdened by all manner of restriction and degradation. As for Henri and Raoul, the former was in prison as a Communist and the latter was living abroad. 'They were glad to see me,' he recalled, 'but it was a sad reunion. I left at midnight as I had to resume my journey early in the morning. With a heavy heart I said goodbye to these aged and lonely people who had done so much for me.'

Blake finally arrived in Seoul on Saturday, 6 November. On that same day, the largest operation of the Chinese Civil War, the Huaihi Campaign, commenced. Under General Su Yu, the People's Liberation Army was heading towards Xuzhou with the intention of killing or capturing over half a million Kuomingtang soldiers.

The new vice-consul had arrived in the region at a turbulent time. Just how turbulent, would soon become apparent.

7

Captive in Korea

George Blake began his intelligence mission in Seoul in a discontented frame of mind. Not only had he abandoned his Christian faith and was now harbouring serious, unsettling thoughts about the merits of Communism, but he also felt dismayed at the scale of the tasks SIS had set him in Korea.

His assignments were three-fold. The main undertaking was to establish agent networks in the Soviet Far Eastern 'Maritime' Provinces, the principal city of which was Vladivostok, naval base of the Soviet Pacific Fleet. Secondly, given the onward march of Mao's Red Army, he was asked to try and build contacts of any kind in China's north-eastern provinces, chiefly Manchuria.

The third part of Blake's brief was never made explicit. He was given to understand that his superiors at Broadway thought war in Korea was more likely than not, with the chief scenario being an invasion of the South by the North, backed by Chinese troops. If such an occupation took place, Britain would retain 'non-belligerent' status and its consulate-general would be allowed to remain. Blake and his colleague, Norman Owen, would then be able to act as an effective covert 'listening post', monitoring and reporting back on any new Communist regime.

Blake felt that to ask him to spy on the Russians in Vladivostok, some 450 miles away from Seoul with no worthwhile communications of any sort – no political links, no trade links, nothing – was utterly impractical: 'As the crow flies, Seoul was the nearest place to build an SIS station. But I thought that giving me such unrealistic tasks, which were based not on any real assessments but merely a look at a map, was just not very professional . . . I just had to put up with it – but my attitude towards SIS was less enthusiastic than it had been before.'

After staying in the legation compound for a few weeks, he found much more spacious living quarters – a Japanese-style house in the commercial district of Seoul. There, he was joined by Norman Owen and a newfound friend, Jean Meadmore, the French Vice-Consul.

Aged thirty-two, Owen was 'an easy-going young Englishman with an equable temper and warm friendliness'. He had served in the RAF in an intelligence unit in Iraq during the Second World War before joining Marconi when civilian life resumed. Having then moved back to the intelligence world, and SIS, Korea was his first overseas appointment.

Meadmore, aged thirty-four, struck up a particularly close friendship with Blake. The Frenchman had already gained diplomatic experience in Asia, having served in China before being assigned to Seoul. Like Blake, he was a natural linguist and had mastered the Chinese language as well as eagerly absorbing its culture. A courteous, likeable man, he was also something of a *bon viveur*. His handsome looks meant he didn't want for female company. 'We were both bachelors, so of course we enjoyed the friendship of women. George too had some relationships with some very charming Korean girls,' he recalled.

Gradually Blake's mood began to lift and as he travelled in and around the capital, he found himself entranced by the country's wild landscape. Together with Meadmore and others he would journey by jeep for a picnic in some secluded spot, more often than not by the banks of a stream on the Bukhansan Mountain, or near the site of an old Buddhist temple.

The other person who helped ease his path into Korean life was his diplomatic superior at the legation, the Minister Captain Vyvyan Holt. At first, their relationship was remote, with Holt displaying the innate Foreign Office distrust of SIS and its officers. Behind his reserved and rather taciturn manner lay a generous spirit, however, and he was definitely a man after Blake's heart – multilingual, an Arabist, traveller and a lover of the desert. Soon the suspicion evaporated and Holt took Blake under his wing, leading him on long walks through the city, introducing him all the while to the customs and culture of the local people.

The tall, thin, bald, slightly stooping and weather-beaten Holt had 'rather sharp bird-like features' that gave him the appearance of a taller Mahatma Gandhi. The resemblance only increased when he wore the rimless glasses needed for long periods of reading. He was a man of great charm and possessed of a dry sense of humour, but also unconventional behaviour and habits. His ascetic tastes included a preference for boiled vegetables, fruit and curds over hot meals – a difficult diet to maintain with the obligations of diplomatic dinners, something he loathed.

Holt's cultural and political instincts were entirely antithetical to America. Nonetheless, in his annual review of Korea for Foreign Secretary Ernest Bevin in January 1950, he was under no illusion about the ideological influence Washington exerted – even after the withdrawal of all American troops by the end of June 1949: 'The cinemas for the most part show American films, the "Voice of America" is picked up on radio sets in thousands of homes, and the children everywhere play volleyball, basketball and baseball . . . it is not surprising that Korean Government and its people (other than the Communists) should regard the United States as the most prosperous, the most democratic and the most glorious country in the world.'

If Holt reluctantly accepted the onward march of the American way of life, Blake saw little but ill in it. In the case of South Korea, he believed it was having an unhealthy effect on the character, morals and manners of the people: 'Close and prolonged contact with the American way of life causes Orientals, to lose entirely their inborn dignity and refinement, which often distinguishes them favourably from the white man, and turns [them] into loud-mouthed go-getters.'

Worst of all, as far as he was concerned, were the Korean former émigrés who had returned to administer the country. He witnessed a small community of rich businessmen lining their pockets with aid the Americans poured into the country, while the majority of the population remained extremely poor. As swanky American cars pulled up in front of large, plush Chinese restaurants, the nearby streets and alleyways of Seoul played host to desperate poverty, crammed full of thousands of vagrants in filthy clothes with festering sores and maimed limbs.

One particular incident lodged vividly in Blake's memory, and he described it in the style of one of those Old Testament stories he had read as a boy:

> I had wined and dined in the overheated house of an American friend and I decided to walk home. It was a very cold night. As I passed the doorway of a building I heard a whimpering cry and saw a figure huddled under a rice sack. It was one of the many home-less beggar boys who filled the streets of Seoul.

> Like the priest and the Levite in the Bible I passed on, but that pitiful whimper remained on my conscience for a long time. If I had taken him to my house, as perhaps I should have done, I would still have come across others, and if I had taken them in until my house was full and my resources exhausted, there would still be others huddling in doorways and whimpering from cold and pain.

> I realised then that private charity could never solve this problem but only a system which resolutely tackled poverty and eradicated it.

That system, to Blake's mind, was Communism.

His views were further coloured by observing the manifest corruption of the American-backed Syngman Rhee government, which ruled by dictatorial methods and brooked no opposition. Elections were rigged and political opponents – whose views might be equated to no more than that of a moderate liberal in Britain – were branded Communists and frequently tortured, even murdered. From time to time, Blake would have to call on the education minister in the Rhee government, An Ho Sang. Educated at Oxford, Sang was at one time a Professor at Seoul University. He had a photograph of Hitler on the wall of his office and was eager to copy Nazi ideas about youth organisations.

Captain Holt made sure Bevin was under no illusion about the nature of the Rhee regime. In his annual review of 1950, he noted that the regular use of torture was 'disgusting and antagonising many elements of the public, constantly making new converts to the Communist cause'. Holt observed that bands of Communist guerrillas – most of them trained in the North – were active in many parts of South Korea. The mountainous and thickly wooded terrain offered them ideal cover in the countryside, but they were also present in the towns and the police repeatedly claimed to have unmasked subversive plots.

Given his increasing loathing for the Rhee regime and the unhealthy influence he felt the Americans wielded over it, Blake had begun to admire the efforts of these bands of Communist partisans. He likened them to the resistance fighters in Holland and the rest of Europe during the Second World War, and considered they were stirred 'by the same noble motives'.

As for his espionage mission, he was making little headway. One of his duties in his cover role as vice-consul was to issue visas for Hong Kong, and this enabled him to meet prominent members of the South Korean business community, but this proved of little use as they rarely ventured into areas of Soviet influence. Nor were hopes that his links with the missionary community might yield useful contacts and intelligence ever fulfilled.

It was an increasingly frustrated Blake who prepared to report to the head of the Singapore Station (the regional hub for SIS) in the spring of 1950, eighteen months into his posting. Maurice Murrowood Firth was the officer who came to Seoul to receive his briefing, and for Blake it proved to be a deeply unpleasant encounter. He received the 'mother of all dressing-downs' for his failure to establish any worthwhile agent networks around Vladivostok, or in North Korea. Moreover, Firth told Blake's colleagues: 'He doesn't belong in the Service.'

Such criticism can only have added to Blake's mutinous mood. Already contemptuous of the demands placed upon him, appalled at the nature of the Rhee regime, and increasingly sympathetic to Communism, the allegiances he had sworn to the Service and his country were starting to wear thin.

He pondered on his situation throughout the spring and early summer of 1950, while at the same time in Pyongyang, the young, energetic North Korean leader Kim Il-Sung was busy laying the groundwork for an invasion of the South.

As the Americans had continued to render vital assistance to the government of Syngman Rhee throughout 1949 and 1950, so Stalin and his cohorts proved equally attentive to Kim's North Korea, building up its army and organising its economy. Throughout 1949, Stalin remained extremely wary as Kim relentlessly pressed him for his backing for an invasion. The Soviet leader was preoccupied with the crisis in Berlin, and in any case he didn't believe the North Koreans yet possessed the required military strength; he also fretted about a possible attack from the South.

Mao's victories in China in the latter months of the year encouraged Kim to increase the pressure on Russia and, by January 1950, Stalin was slowly, reluctantly, prepared to offer his support, at least in principle. Mao himself, in the early months of 1950, was still extinguishing the remnants of Chiang Kai-shek's resistance, and his energies were focused on reshaping China according to his own particular vision of Communism. Nevertheless, when Kim visited him in Beijing on 13

May for secret talks, Mao said he would give his support provided the war was quick and decisive. He promised too that China would send troops if the United States entered the war to defend the South.

When the telephone rang at his home in Independence, Missouri, just after 9.15 p.m. on the evening of Saturday, 24 June 1950, President Harry Truman had been enjoying a rare weekend's rest. On the other end of the line was Dean Acheson, his Secretary of State. 'Mr President, I have some very serious news,' Acheson informed him. 'The North Koreans have invaded South Korea.' There was a fourteen-hour time difference between Seoul and Washington, so the armies of North Korea had actually swept across the 38th parallel shortly before dawn on Sunday, 25 June.

Truman set off for Kansas City airport to return to Washington and take charge of the crisis. There was little doubt as to how he would react, with his personal physician, General Wallace Graham, telling reporters: 'Northern or Communist China is marching on South Korea and we are going to fight. The boss is going to hit these fellows hard.'

If the strategists and politicians were caught unawares, so too were the citizens of South Korea. Despite warning signs in recent months, they had developed a certain sense of complacency over any impending conflict.

That morning, Larry Zellers, a young, newly married Methodist minister from Texas, was sleeping soundly alone in his bed at 292 Man Wul Dong in the border town of Kaesong. He was woken by the sound of small arms and artillery fire soon after 4.30 a.m.: 'I then did something foolish: I decided that it was simply another border skirmish between North and South. I even turned over in bed and tried to go back to sleep. In my two years in Kaesong, I had learned that most such outbreaks of fighting across the 38th parallel took place during the early morning hours, and like many people all over the world who live with danger, I got used to it.'

In fact, some time during the night, just two miles from where he lay, the North Korean Army had slipped across the 38th parallel and re-laid the torn-up section of railway running north out of Kaesong. Then, in a brilliant manoeuvre, they had packed a train full of soldiers and driven it boldly into the town's station. Effectively, this was the start of the war.

Some fifty miles south, in the capital of Seoul, George Blake was clearing up after a party at his house to celebrate the 'name day' of his friend Jean Meadmore – the feast of St John the Baptist. He grabbed a few hours sleep before waking at around 9 a.m., then made the short walk to the Anglican Cathedral where it was his custom to attend morning service in the crypt. Before the service began, a hasty, whispered conversation between an American officer and some members of his Embassy alerted him to the fact that something out of the ordinary had happened, but Blake ignored the chatter and took his place in the pews, remaining there throughout the ceremony alongside Captain Holt. Afterwards, the wife of an American colonel excitedly informed the congregation that her husband had been called away because North Korean troops had crossed the 38th parallel and heavy fighting had broken out all along the line.

It was clear by late afternoon that the North Koreans were advancing rapidly towards the capital. The crisis required Blake to perform consular duties and he jumped into his jeep, criss-crossing the city to warn British families of the impending danger, urging them if at all possible to leave.

The diplomats, and a group of missionaries who had stayed behind hunkered down in the legation compound and waited for the invaders to arrive. On the following morning, their numbers were bolstered by the arrival of Jean Meadmore and his colleagues from the French consulate. Most of the American contingent had left the capital.

Holt had sent a message to London via the Cable & Wireless Company (the legation didn't have its own wireless station) asking for instructions, but he didn't expect a reply until Wednesday at the earliest. The latest information suggested the marauding North Koreans would reach the capital by nightfall on Tuesday.

On Monday evening the group gathered to decide on a plan of action. Holt told his colleagues that strictly speaking, according to the terms of his mission, he should follow the South Korean Government, to which he was accredited, wherever they went. But of course they had already fled en masse, telling no one of their destination, so he felt free from any such obligation. All his instincts urged him to remain; he felt it was both his diplomatic and moral duty. Paul Garbler, a young American naval intelligence officer, recalls him picking up a sword that he kept over his mantelpiece, brandishing it and saying: 'I'm not leaving; this is my legation and British soil. If I have to, I'll fight them with my sword.'

Britain was a non-belligerent in the war so its representatives were, at least in theory, under no threat. Blake and Owen were mindful of their brief to act as a 'listening post' in the event of invasion, so they too had no intention of deserting.

Most of Tuesday was spent in nervous anticipation as the sound of gunfire grew ever closer. There were loud explosions and flashes of fire from the direction of the river, and Blake and his colleagues learned later in the day that the road and railway bridges had been blown up. Even if they had wanted to escape, there was now no way out. Blake and Owen spent several hours journeying to and fro from the American Embassy, laying in stores – principally quantities of food and petrol – that the departing diplomats had left behind.

On Wednesday, 28 June, the sound of the fighting died down and an eerie silence descended on the city. The servants who hurried back and forth from the compound with scraps of information reported that Seoul was now in the hands of the invaders. Indeed, a large contingent of troops had taken over the broadcasting station directly overlooking the legation.

In the evening, while waiting for the inevitable knock on the door, the party settled down for dinner in Captain Holt's house. The meal had the feel of a Last Supper and for Blake, who saw Biblical parallels in most situations, there was a further analogy waiting to be drawn: an act of gross betrayal was about to take place back home in the corridors of Whitehall.

On the previous day, Tuesday, 27 June, the Labour Cabinet had convened in Downing Street. Once the lesser matters of possible subsidies for beleaguered trawlermen and aid for similarly struggling hill farmers had been dealt with, the bulk of the meeting was naturally concerned with the crisis in Korea. The Prime Minister, Clement Attlee, and Foreign Secretary, Ernest Bevin, had been forewarned that later that day President Truman would say 'centrally-directed Communist imperialism had passed beyond subversion in seeking to conquer independent nations and was now resorting to armed aggression and war'. This made them nervous, as recorded in the Downing Street minutes.

Attlee and his colleagues had no desire to depict the aggression by the North Koreans as part of a wider Communist conspiracy in the region. Simply put, they didn't want to say or do anything that would draw the Chinese and the Soviets further into the equation at this stage. They even worried that America's inflammatory words might provoke China to attack the British Crown colony of Hong Kong. Nonetheless, despite the Cabinet's concerns, they swung behind America's resolutions at the United Nations. The first one, Security Council Resolution 82, issued on the day of the invasion, simply condemned it. Then, later that day, Resolution 83 was published. This was a call to arms, recommending that member states provide military assistance to the Republic of Korea.

Blake and his colleagues had, of course, been too busy with their own survival prospects to follow the latest political developments. More practically, the Cable & Wireless Company had evacuated the city the day before so they couldn't communicate with their government back home. It was, therefore, with some consternation that they listened to the BBC news and discovered precisely what part Britain was to play. Attlee had told a subdued chamber in the House of Commons: 'We have decided to support the United States action in Korea by immediately placing our naval forces in Japanese waters at the disposal of the United States authorities to operate on behalf of the Security Council in support of South Korea.'

Winston Churchill, leader of the Opposition, vowed that his party would give Attlee 'any support he needs in what seems to be our inescapable duty'. He asked the Prime Minister if the British naval force would 'make a substantial contribution relative to the American forces which are there'. Attlee replied: 'Yes, Sir. I think our forces are almost the same as those the United States have there.'

Blake and his British colleagues were not safe after all: 'What we heard was a great shock and surprise,' he recalled. 'We had been caught. Instead of being neutrals, as we thought, we were now belligerents in enemy territory . . . I did not blame SIS for what had gone wrong. I am certain that the British Government had not intended to join in the war but had been drawn into it by the United States. In fact, I don't think that the Americans originally planned to get involved either, but General MacArthur pushed them into it.'

Now that they found themselves behind enemy lines, Blake and Owen decided there was no time to lose and spent the rest of the night burning their codes and secret documents in a corner of the legation garden, hoping all the while that the smoke wouldn't attract the attention of the North Korean troops outside.

The following morning, the bell rang and the British contingent went to the gate to meet a delegation from the conquering army – a North Korean officer and two of his men. The soldiers were disarmingly polite; the only demand they made was that the Union Flag should be lowered as it might attract the wrong sort of attention from aircraft.

For the next few days no further visits followed and by Sunday – a week after the invasion – Blake and the others were feeling a shade more optimistic about their prospects. Shut away from the world, they had no real sense of how the invaders were behaving, but what reports they did receive indicated no widespread marauding or retribution. Their guarded optimism, however, was swept away around 6 p.m. on Sunday, 2 July. This time, three jeeps full of armed soldiers drove through the gates of the legation and made their way up to the main house. The British contingent was told to assemble in the courtyard and despite protests from Captain Holt, were ordered into lorries and driven off to the Police Headquarters in Seoul. They were promised they didn't need to take any clothes or provisions as they would only be detained for twenty minutes.

Upon arrival, they faced detailed questioning, with the English-speaking interrogator appearing dissatisfied by their replies. A series of dramatic events then began to unfold. 'While I was sitting at a narrow desk opposite the officer who was questioning me, somebody in a room below fired off a rifle,' Blake recalled. 'The bullet passed through the floor and the desk at which we were sitting, shattering the inkpot that was standing between us and covering us with ink, then whizzed past our foreheads and disappeared in to the ceiling.'

No sooner had Blake recovered his composure than he witnessed a sickening sequence of incidents at the other end of the room. Two South Korean policemen were in the middle of being interrogated when their inquisitor decided to take a break and left his desk to smoke a cigarette. The policemen, who already bore the scars of severe beatings, managed to get to their feet and made for the second-floor window. There, with defiant screams, they threw themselves out, hoping to kill themselves and end their torture. A few minutes later Blake watched in horror as the men were dragged back to the room, bleeding profusely, their faces completely misshapen by scars and bruises, limbs torn and mangled. They were put back in their chairs. The interrogator put out his cigarette, turned to them and resumed questioning as if nothing had happened.

Meanwhile Captain Holt asserted vehemently that the treatment meted out to him and his staff was contrary to international law and demanded to be allowed to communicate with his government. His protestations were in vain.

Around midnight, he and his companions were given a sparse meal of rice packed tight into a ball. Shortly afterwards, the British and French contingent, together with a couple of American businessmen who had stayed behind, were bundled into the back of a lorry and driven out of the city, accompanied by guards with bayonets. Their nerves weren't helped by the excitable behaviour of the 'little major' in charge of them who, along the way, persisted in practising with his newly issued Russian pistol, firing off volleys of indiscriminate shots into the darkness.

After about an hour the vehicle stopped in a small valley in the surrounding hills. The captives were ordered out of the jeep and made to stand in a line. They had little doubt as to what was to happen next: 'We all had the same thought. We'd been taken to this remote spot to be summarily executed. After all we had heard about the Communists, this seemed to us the only explanation which fitted the circumstances,' Blake recalled. 'Even the reserve barrel of petrol we took as confirmation. It was to be used to burn our bodies afterwards.'

As he would do constantly in the coming months, Commissioner Herbert Lord of the Salvation Army, attempted to rally spirits. 'We nodded at each other, and we thought we might as well go happily. I said a short prayer.'

Minutes passed and nothing happened. Then, after about an hour, a lorry drove up with two North Korean officers on board and the journey resumed. They had been reprieved, but the danger was far from over.

It was a treacherous and frightening trip, 120 miles across the Parallel along bomb-cratered roads up to Pyongyang. The hostages gazed around them at abandoned trucks riddled with large-calibre bullet holes, and passed burnt-out villages where survivors wandered around dressed in rags and the stench of rotting corpses was overwhelming.

They halted frequently while their captors checked on the possible presence of American B-26 aircraft in the area; the planes from the US Far East Air Force were busy sweeping the skies of North Korean aircraft. Eventually in the early evening, exhausted and hungry, the hostages reached their destination – two abandoned schoolhouses five miles out of Pyongyang that served as the main foreign civilian internee camp in North Korea.

During the first two weeks of July, fresh groups of prisoners arrived at the old schoolhouse to join Blake and his colleagues. Eventually there were around seventy in all, a disparate collection of diplomats, missionaries, journalists and others, of all nationalities – British, American, French, German, Austrian, Australian, Russian, Turkish, Swiss and Irish – and all ages, including small children and the elderly. At first they entertained hopes that they were being gathered in one place as a prelude to some sort of prisoner exchange arranged through the International Red Cross – even the pitiless Japanese had approved some Red Cross involvement in the Second World War – but it quickly became apparent that the North Koreans had no intention of allowing any such swap.

The prisoners were locked into five rooms off a long corridor, forbidden to communicate with anyone beyond their own four walls, and punished if they talked too loudly. The regime was a harsh one. They were only allowed to leave their rooms under supervision to go to the lavatory. Buckets of water were placed in a corridor and members of each room had to queue to wash in the mornings. They were desperately hungry all the time as the food was little more than a starvation diet, consisting merely of a small cupful of rice a day and a bowl of 'soup' – hot water flavoured with leek or cabbage. Just occasionally, some unripe apples or plums would be added to the menu. The main distraction was found in fighting off the army of insects that invaded their cells. 'What we suffered most from were mosquitoes, fleas and lice, and we became experts at picking the lice off each other,' recalled Blake.

Spirits were raised at the end of July with the arrival of Philip Deane, the fearless, ever-optimistic correspondent of *The London Observer*. Wearing his arm in a sling and leaning on a stick, he nonetheless sported a big smile and flashed the famous Churchill victory sign, whispering to fellow captives that the Black Watch, one of Britain's elite fighting units, was on its way to the country.

The Greek-born journalist had just experienced an extraordinary few weeks, even by his standards. What he had witnessed on the frontline at Yongdong was sheer carnage, the gallant General William F. Dean and five thousand troops from the 24th Infantry Division attempting to stem the Red tide from the North: 'A flood tide of Communist soldiers, well led, Russian-equipped, confident and victorious, faced by mere kids of seventeen and eighteen, who have gone straight from school into the Army and only a few weeks ago were still enjoying their first tentative experiments in manhood in the heady role of occupiers of Japan.'

Deane watched GIs dying under sniper fire alongside him, and had tried to drive a group of soldiers to the safety of UN lines before being ambushed and captured. Bleeding copiously from his untreated wounds, he was made to walk over a hundred miles in five days, traipsing mountain and country paths until he and his fellow prisoners reached Communist Army Headquarters near Suwon. Taken to Pyongyang, he was accused of being a spy. Having convinced his captors he was merely a journalist, they urged him to make a broadcast condemning the 'American atrocities' and the United States 'unjustified intervention in a civil war – contrary to the United Nations charter'. Deane didn't break, however, and so it was, a week later, that he found himself in the old schoolhouse with Blake and the other prisoners.

With his natural good humour and cocky yet careful attitude towards authority, he immediately lifted their spirits, teasing and provoking their captors yet never quite overstepping the boundaries of rebellion.

Two months of monotonous captivity went by. Then, on the evening of Tuesday, 5 September, Blake and his fellow prisoners were hastily assembled and told to hand in their blankets and food bowls and be ready to leave the schoolhouse in just half an hour. A short, fat Korean colonel, whom they dubbed the 'Panjandrum', addressed them in words of bogus reassurance: 'Life for you is becoming too difficult and dangerous, with these rascally Americans raining bombs on women and children, and especially on schools. So we are sending you to a nice place in the mountains where you will have peace and comfort.'

The seventy prisoners were first escorted to Pyongyang jail, where they remained for a couple of hours, from time to time glimpsing 'wretched-looking convicts and grim-faced warders'. Then two trucks arrived and took them to the railway station. They were heading far north to a town called Manpo on the Yalu River, which forms the border between Korea and Manchuria. Accompanying them on the trip – and for further journeys in the next few months – would be more than 700 American prisoners of war.

As Larry Zellers, the Methodist minister, stared out of the window of his carriage, he saw long lines of haggard-looking young GIs marching past to board the train further on down the platform. It was a sight that profoundly shocked him: 'I couldn't believe what I was seeing. These ragged, dirty, hollow-eyed men did not look like any American soldiers that I had ever seen . . . the North Koreans had provided no special consideration for the wounded. Some of the more badly injured prisoners were half-carried by companions; others limped along as best they could.'

The soldiers were all survivors from the 19th, 21st and 34th regiments of the 24th Infantry Division, the first to engage the North Korean Army at the Battles of Osan and Taejon, where they were subject to humiliating defeat. Many of these men were physically and mentally spent. After capture in July, they had been marched to Seoul, where they were interrogated and many of them tortured, taunted by their Korean captors who said that they were 'bandits', not prisoners of war, and thus liable to receive a shot in the back of the head at any moment. By the time they boarded the train for Manpo – corralled in the open coal trucks, while Blake and his fellow prisoners were put in the only passenger coach – a good number of them were suffering from dysentery, dehydrated through lack of food and water.

Lying cramped together, the stench of body odour and the rotting flesh of the wounded compounded the GIs' misery. Four died during the six days it took for the train and its large human cargo to make it to Manpo; two of whom, after much pleading, were allowed proper Catholic burials. The other bodies were just discarded near the tracks.

At one point in the journey Blake and Holt managed to engage the highest-ranking Korean officer in conversation, and as a result this 'very polished, well-educated' colonel called the group together. If they were expecting words of explanation, of any comfort whatsoever, they were quickly disabused. He launched into a ferocious attack on the American nation, ending with a withering assessment: 'The American soldier is the worst and most cowardly in the world. In fact, one soldier of our army is the equal of ten American soldiers . . . I think I might be able to handle eight myself.'

All the while the prisoners could hear the roar of approaching planes over the mountains and the crackle of their guns; the danger of being strafed by F-51 fighters with their six 50-calibre machine guns was ever present. There was also evidence of large-scale traffic moving towards the battlefront, as the freight trains that passed in the night were often long and had two engines to haul them. Tanks, artillery and lorries were clearly visible on the flat cars or in the open trucks.

On the afternoon of Monday, 11 September, the party finally reached their destination. They discovered Manpo, an industrial town with several large lumber mills, also to be a place of great natural beauty. The River Yalu meandered through its narrow valleys on its long journey towards the Yellow Sea, while away to the north of the town, as far as the eye could see, were the imposing Manchurian mountains.

The GIs were placed in cramped barracks close to the railway station while the civilian prisoners were taken along a road that followed the river west and, after two miles, they reached their destination. Their new home was a former Japanese quarantine station for immigrants arriving from Manchuria. It proved to be a totally different environment from the harsh regime at Pyongyang. Here, they were allowed to do their own cooking and the daily food ration was plentiful, including rice, vegetables, cooking oil and dried fish. They were given meat three times a week, and sugar too.

'From time to time we were given the choice between a kilogram of apples or a small tobacco ration,' Blake recalled. 'Korean apples are delicious and I chose them in preference to the tobacco. Since then I have never smoked again.'

The days were warm and bright, and nearly every afternoon there was an excursion to the Yalu River. A guard would escort them half a mile down the road and then through fields to the water's edge. There, they could wash their clothes, bathe in the river and bask in the sun. Judging by the standards of the neighbouring villagers, they were living in the lap of luxury.

More good news soon arrived, delivered by a brave 15-year-old Korean schoolboy, who risked the wrath of the guards to deliver updates on the war's progress. They learned of General MacArthur's daring amphibious assault on the strategically important city of Incheon on 15 September, the subsequent retreat of the North Korean Army to Seoul, and then the recapture of the capital by UN forces on 27 September.

Blake and his colleagues began to excitedly calculate how long it would be before the UN advance reached Manpo. 'Sweepstakes were started. Plans were made about freedom, about the gifts that we would buy for our relatives. That first telegram was mentally written and rewritten,' recalled Deane.

Blake and Deane's friendship grew in this more invigorating period. Deane was particularly impressed by what he had quickly identified as Blake's 'characteristic ability to shed worry'.

Larry Zellers, too, grasped the opportunity to get to know Blake better although, he didn't know then the exact nature of the other man's job, accepting the story that the 'diplomat' had recently entered British Government service and risen quickly in rank. Zellers recalled that Blake was interested in learning about the history of the American Southwest: 'He occasionally showed some antagonism for the US government and its involvement in the Korean War, but never toward our American group. He seemed to feel that we were being held prisoner only because America had sent troops to fight for what he considered the very corrupt regime of Syngman Rhee in South Korea.'

There were, however, aspects of Blake's character and behaviour that he found unsettling. An occasional arrogance was one, exhibited when Zellers asked him to translate from French what had gone on in a conference between the British and French groups: 'Blake answered with a question that was also a putdown: "Larry, don't you know French?" I told him I did not but that I could struggle along in Spanish. He did not consider my remark worthy of comment.'

Zellers also found Blake reluctant to open up about his adopted country: 'One thing that bothered me was his unwillingness to share his knowledge about life and events in England. I was very interested in England and had been all my life, but he told me very little. He was always friendly, but when he wanted to leave, he would simply walk away, and at other times he didn't want to be bothered.'

The month in the old quarantine quarters at Manpo had been as comfortable an experience as the prisoners could have expected. Nourishing food, medical attention, decent enough accommodation and a relatively relaxed regime had raised their spirits. Added to that was the expectation that the conquering American forces would soon arrive to free them. All that optimism started to fade, however, when on Saturday, 7 October, they were given the alarming news that they were to be moved. The group of detainees weren't to know it, but they were being evacuated – as were the American POWs near the railway station – to make way for more important guests: Chinese troops from Manchuria were about to enter the war.

They were told to take themselves, along with their blankets, cooking utensils and food supplies, to a point on the river bank a couple of miles upstream. There they would wait until boats arrived to transport them to their next destination. The boats never came, and the party was forced to camp out in lashing rain. After two nights in the open, trucks finally appeared to take them to the village of Kosang, fifteen miles away, where they were put in another school building. After only a week in this camp, the group – now re-joined by the 700 or so American POWs – was moved on again, this time forced to march over mountain paths to a remote mining hamlet, Jui-am-nee. Here they were housed in rows and rows of large, derelict huts.

Meanwhile over the hills came small groups of retreating North Korean soldiers, wounded, dispirited and hostile. The detainees thought they could sense the war drawing to a climax, and they had been told by some of the local people that the UN forces were just twenty-five miles away to the South. So near, yet so far from freedom.

In this chaotic environment, the British and French internees got together and worked out a plan whereby a small group of them would – with the help of two of the Korean guards – attempt to reach the American lines and initiate a rescue. A party consisting of Blake, Holt, Deane, and the French trio of Charles Martel (Embassy Chancellor), Maurice Chanteloup (correspondent for the French Press Agency) and Jean Meadmore set out on the morning of Wednesday, 25 October, accompanied by their two Korean captors. They walked all that day, avoiding houses and villages, and rested overnight in a small valley. After resuming their journey the next morning, they travelled for a couple of hours before they reached a mountain pass, where they encountered three Korean soldiers coming the other way.

The two sets of soldiers sat down to a long conversation. For Blake and his companions, the outcome was a dispiriting one: 'When our guards rejoined us we at once noticed a change in their demeanour.

They told us that the situation had changed completely in the last twenty-four hours and that the Chinese volunteers had come to the rescue of the North Korean Army and were now engaged in heavy fighting . . . it was now too dangerous, indeed impossible, to get through to the American lines and there was nothing for it but to return to the camp. Freedom had seemed so near and had now receded indefinitely.'

The dejected group trudged back to the camp and the colleagues they had left behind in Jui-am-nee. The next day, 28 October, they were ordered to return to their old refuge in Manpo. Now the situation was clear – they witnessed Chinese soldiers pouring past by the thousand, complete with artillery, automatics and brand new Molotov lorries. 'Those, perhaps, were our worst moments,' recalled Deane.

The party spent the night in a Presbyterian church near the main road before resuming the trek to Manpo. Three miles from the town, they were diverted from the main road and taken across fields to a burnt out house near a sawmill. A fire was built and maintained most of the night, but even so it offered little protection against the harsh wind that blew across the Yalu River. During the night a Korean officer came and kicked it out.

Conditions were far more severe for the 700 GIs who had been made to camp in an open cornfield, half a mile away. In an attempt to ward off the bitter wind, they collected into groups of five and made for hollowed-out shelters – nothing more than shallow holes – on the lee side of a slope. There, they huddled down together in an effort to share body heat. Others found odds and ends of wood or scrub, apparently, as the civilian captives saw a few small fires glowing fitfully.

Meanwhile Blake had been pondering what had happened to his escape party a couple of days earlier. Had the guides told them the truth about their conversation with the Korean soldiers? Had they simply become apprehensive and backed out? Could the American lines really be that far away? Realising the desperate situation they were now in, he decided to make another escape attempt.

* * *

That day, Monday, 30 October, Blake canvassed opinion among a number of his fellow prisoners. One of those he asked to join him, 17-year-old Sagid Salahutdin, declined to do so, preferring to stay with his large family. After some deliberation, Jean Meadmore also decided against: 'I said no, I haven't got the guts to do it, and it's doomed to failure. You'll be caught and shot as a spy.'

So, alone, Blake headed off into the hills after nightfall, once the guards had settled down in front of the campfire. He calculated that the American lines lay fifty miles or so to the South, and his strategy was to walk mainly at night, avoiding roads and villages, and fortify himself with maize and berries. He had only been walking for two hours, and was about to descend into a valley through a cornfield when he heard a bolt click, and a torch shone in his face. A young North Korean soldier stepped out with a rifle and screamed something at him – presumably asking who he was and where he was going: 'I told him I was a Russian. He evidently did not believe me or, if he did, felt I should establish my identity to his superiors for he ordered me to follow him.'

After a short while they arrived at what looked like the entrance to a cave, where a group of ten North Korean soldiers were seated around a fire. The captain of the company began to question him, in Korean, and at first – through a mixture of a few words and a lot of hand gestures – Blake tried to keep up the pretence that he was Russian. When asked to produce his papers, he realised his story wouldn't stand up and so he admitted to being a British diplomat who had escaped from a camp near Manpo. He was eventually told to go and sit against the wall of the cave, where he remained, closely watched, for the rest of the night. Tired and depressed that his efforts to flee had failed so soon, he could only guess what awaited him in the morning.

At breakfast time the soldiers washed in a nearby stream and then ate, all the while observing their prisoner with great interest, guffaws of laughter intermittently bursting forth as they assessed this rare specimen of a white man. Blake was given a meal of pork soup and rice and a packet of cigarettes, before the questioning resumed. Now the mood of the captain and his senior colleagues took a turn for the worse, and they shouted at him, accusing him of being a spy and telling him he would be shot. Eventually a new officer arrived, a major, and he and two soldiers accompanied Blake on the two-hour walk back to Manpo. His life was very much in the balance, he felt.

Once back at the camp, his fellow inmates, men, women and children, were instructed to form a circle, and he was made to stand on a wooden box in the middle. At best, the scene seemed like a classroom lecture for a miscreant pupil; at worst, it had all the trappings of a show trial. The major who had brought him to the camp spoke for twenty minutes, haranguing Blake for his escape attempt, while Commissioner Lord, alongside him, translated for the benefit of the group.

At the end, there was huge relief: 'He ended up with the warning that if I ever tried to escape again I would be shot there and then and so would anybody who tried to emulate me.'

Blake's admonisher that morning would, as events unfolded, become known to them all as 'The Tiger'. One of the GIs later explained the nickname: 'He was mean and he loved killing.'

The 'Death March' was about to begin.

8

Death March

Some of the missionaries had encountered The Tiger in the early weeks of the war when, in his crisp white jail-governor's uniform, he had interviewed them in their solitary confinement in Chunchon. Now he was clad in the blue of the North Korean security police. An Australian priest, Father Philip Crosbie, described The Tiger as a tall, lithe man, wearing knee breeches and a tight-fitting jacket: 'When he walked, he leaned forward a little. His features were regular, but protruding teeth gave him a perpetual grimace. His bright eyes were keen and restless.'

On the afternoon of Tuesday, 31 October, there was a sense of grim foreboding among the captives as they were brought together to hear The Tiger's plan for their future. To the East, in the cornfield, they could see the American POWs lining up and preparing to move. 'You see,' The Tiger said, pointing to his military epaulette, 'I have the authority. Everyone must march. No one must be left behind. You must discard at once everything that can be used as a weapon. After all, you are my enemy, and I must consider that you might try to do me harm.'

After those words, he proceeded to inspect the line of prisoners, stopping in front of Father Paul Villemot, an 82-year-old French priest, who was leaning heavily on his wooden cane. 'That can be used as a weapon. Throw that away,' The Tiger told the sick old man. He then proceeded to mock the missionaries in the group. 'Suppose you were the engineer on a train and the locomotive broke down. What would you do? Would you kneel down and pray that it would run? Or would you get an expert who knew about such things to repair it? In this country we know what we would do. We don't need you religious people anymore: you are parasites. There are things in this world that need repairing; we know what to do about it.'

Once The Tiger had finished his speech, Commissioner Lord made desperate entreaties on behalf of the older members of the group, who were clearly in no state for a long march. He relayed Father Villemot's bleak assessment of his chances: 'If I have to march, I will die.' The Tiger's response was brief, matter-of-fact and all the more chilling for it: 'Then let them march till they die.' And with that, he gave the direction to move out of the camp.

The Tiger had orders to transport his group of 800 prisoners as quickly as possible to the north-eastern town of Chunggangjin, some 120 miles away. It was all too evident he was prepared to use any methods at his disposal to achieve this objective with no regard for human life or suffering. As the prisoners started to assemble, they heard an unmistakable burst of machine gun fire from the field where the POWs had been corralled. Six sick soldiers were the first victims of what they would soon realise was The Tiger's ruthless policy of abandoning the enfeebled and the ill.

The march began – a long, slow, straggling, pathetic-looking column of men, women and children, with the GIs at the front and the civilians following. To the sound of '*ballee, ballee, ballee*' (quick, quick, quick) constantly barked in their ears by the guards, they struggled on, weak, hungry, already chilled to the bone and now facing an arctic wind blowing in from the North.

'It was to be the darkest and most dramatic period in our captivity,' Blake recalled. 'We walked all day through wild mountain country, stopping at night in fields or deserted villages, where we sometimes found only burnt-out shells instead of houses.'

The group covered about six miles before being ordered off the road by The Tiger just before midnight, to spend the night in an open field. He was angry because his meticulous schedule had already been disrupted: on day one he had planned to cover sixteen miles.

At daybreak the next morning, after a derisory meal of boiled corn, they were off again, heading towards the distant snow-capped mountains of the Kosan Pass, with The Tiger setting an even more gruelling pace. He split the group of 800 into fourteen sections, instructing the American officers assigned to 'command' each one to keep their charges moving, and to make sure they kept a distance from the section in front.

That sort of discipline proved impossible to maintain, with GIs collapsing by the roadside and the older civilians stuttering along painfully. After two hours, an enraged Tiger halted the column and ordered the officers in charge of each section to gather round. He then explained through his interpreter, Commissioner Lord, that he would shoot the five officers whose sections had collapsed into disorder. Lord proceeded to beg for the lives of the young Americans, pleading that they had acted in good faith and his decision was unjust. The Tiger reconsidered: 'Then I will shoot the man from whose section most men were allowed to fall out. Who is he?'

That man was 34-year-old Lieutenant Cordus H. Thornton of Longview, Texas, who stepped forward, whispering to Commissioner Lord as he did so: 'Save me if you can, Sir.'

Just then a group of haggard and exhausted North Korean soldiers, in retreat from the frontline, passed by, and The Tiger decided to recruit them as his 'jury' in Lieutenant Thornton's 'trial'. Larry Zellers heard The Tiger ask the soldiers: 'What is to be done to a man who disobeys the lawful order of an officer in the Korean People's Army?'

'Shoot him!' they all shouted.

'There, you have had your trial,' The Tiger mockingly told Thornton.

'In Texas, Sir, we would call that a lynching,' the American replied contemptuously.

A weeping Commissioner Lord sank to his knees and started to beg for Lieutenant Thornton's life, only to have the gun waved in his face before being pushed brusquely away.

The Tiger began to prepare for the execution. He asked Thornton if he wanted to be blindfolded. On receiving an affirmative reply, he instructed one of his guards to tie a handkerchief round the American's head. A small towel was then used to bind his arms behind his back.

'You see,' The Tiger said, pointing once again to the epaulettes on his shoulder, 'I have the authority to do this.' Pausing for a moment, The Tiger pushed up the back of Thornton's fur hat. Zellers continued to gaze in horror at the unfolding scene: 'I had seen too much already; my eyes snapped shut just before The Tiger fired his pistol into the back of Thornton's head.'

In the terrifying moments that followed, there was no flicker of movement nor a word spoken. Then The Tiger barked out: 'Bury him!' A tall, fair-headed prisoner of war (POW) stepped forward and, gazing around at the group of horror-stricken fellow prisoners, pleaded: 'Won't some of you come down to help me?' Sergeant Henry (Hank) Leerkamp of Company L, 34th Infantry Regiment, 24th Division, from Chester, Missouri, was Thornton's close colleague. He clambered down the steep slope to a level spot some fifteen feet below the road, and started to dig away at the stones with his bare hands. Someone threw down a crude shovel, and then others came down to help him. They dug a shallow grave, laid Thornton's body in it, and covered it as best they could with large rocks. Once more the prisoners fell into line, and the march resumed.

The meagre food the captives were given once a day (twice, if they were lucky) was almost always a ball of half-cooked maize, which was difficult to digest but even more so for the older ones who had lost their teeth.

The threat of being hit from the air was ever present. 'Sometimes our column was attacked by American fighters which, sweeping down low, machine gunned us so that we had to scatter hastily in ditches and fields,' Blake recalled.

No one, POWs and civilians alike, was dressed for the cold, all having been captured in the summer. The civilians had been issued with thin blankets that afforded hardly any extra protection; some of them also followed the example of Russian prisoners, stuffing their clothes with straw and tying a rope round their trouser legs at the ankles. The GIs had only their fatigues, lightweight coats and the fur hats they had managed to pick up in an abandoned warehouse at Jui-am-nee.

The toughest of men would have been hard pushed to survive in these circumstances and most of these regular American troops were not of the calibre of the battle-hardened veterans who had swept all before them in the Second World War. Physically unready for warfare after months of soft occupation duty in Japan, a good many of the young soldiers were simply not mentally attuned to deal with the ordeal facing them.

It might seem perverse, but these experiences did not breed enmity towards Communism in Blake, nor sympathy for the Americans. In fact, as he watched their suffering at close quarters, his prejudices about the American way of life only grew stronger. Looking back much later, he would reflect harshly: 'Very soon they became thoroughly demoralised. They refused to obey their own officers and degenerated into a cursing, fighting group of rabble. They were totally unprepared, both physically and morally, for the hardships they had to endure and early on many of them just gave up hope and lost the will to live.' He contrasted the GIs unfavourably with his own civilian colleagues, 'who suffered as much, although some of them were men and women in their fifties and sixties, and even some in their seventies. They survived the ordeal much better and I ascribe this not only to a greater physical resistance, but above all to a tighter mental fibre.'

What Blake failed to acknowledge was that in the course of the enforced march, the POWs would be driven on without mercy almost to the end, and none that fell were spared; whereas in the midst of the brutality afflicted on the civilians, there were at least occasional acts of leniency.

On Wednesday, 1 November, the day of Lieutenant Thornton's murder, all the captives, GIs and civilians alike, fought to survive while camped out in a field and open to the elements. By morning, ten POWs had perished, having either frozen to death or simply given up on life. Eight more were so ill and weak they were in no fit state to march. The Tiger ordered everyone on their way, and remained behind briefly to talk to the headman of the village. Commissioner Lord, by his side as ever to translate if necessary, heard him say: 'Bury the eighteen, and don't leave any mounds.'

As well as being cruel, The Tiger was also deceptive. He knew the US Army might well capture this territory one day, and he wanted no evidence left of his war crimes. The other ploy used to cover his tracks after the execution of Lieutenant Thornton was to order all the soldiers' dog tags to be handed over to the guards. This, he knew, would make identification of bodies all the more difficult.

'Don't worry,' he had told the prisoners earlier that morning. 'The wounded and the ill will be carried by oxcarts. Those who are unable to travel will be taken to People's Hospitals.' It became all too clear, before long, that 'People's Hospitals' was a euphemism for execution, and the promise of transport proved illusory. Everybody had to walk, with The Tiger insistent on an even faster pace. At the front, any GIs who were lagging were beaten with rifle butts, while at the back, the elderly nuns were suffering terribly.

Mother Beatrix had served the poor of Korea for fifty years. Now the 76-year-old Frenchwoman, provincial superior for the St Paul of Chartres congregation, was falling badly behind as the march progressed. Her constant companion, Mother Eugenie, had almost worn herself out trying to support her, but continued to stay by her side and urge her forward. The old nun struggled on for a mile or so, but then sank down by the roadside. Guards surrounded the two women and tried to harry them along. They pushed Mother Eugenie to one side, and then prodded Mother Beatrix in an attempt to make her get up and walk. Mother Eugenie begged the guards to show mercy, to help her friend, but they tore her arms away from Mother Beatrix and angrily told her to move on and rejoin the column.

'Go, my Sister, go,' were the last words a weeping Mother Eugenie heard from Mother Beatrix as she reluctantly set out to catch the group. A few minutes later a shot rang out. Execution was the price paid for exhaustion.

That night The Tiger instructed Commissioner Lord, while holding a pistol to his head, to sign Mother Beatrix's death certificate with the verdict 'from heart failure'. It was not the first time, and it would not be the last, when Lord was made to falsify such a document.

As the prisoners crossed the Kosan Mountain pass the next day in a biting blizzard, more and more GIs dropped out of the line. An ever increasing number of shots sounded as the guards despatched the worst of the 'feeble, tottering skeletons' to the 'People's Hospitals'. Many desperate soldiers simply sat by the side of the road and looked to their own comrades to put them out of their misery. 'Will someone please hit me on the head with a rock?' Larry Zellers heard one American soldier say, not for the last time.

Blake himself at this stage was suffering from dysentery, while his companions, Vyvyan Holt and Norman Owen, were in even worse shape, starting to develop the symptoms of pneumonia. In the midst of his own illness and distress, Blake looked upon the executions of the GIs with a certain detachment. Years later, he had adapted a brutal rationale for the killings: 'As far as the shooting of the stragglers was concerned, it seemed pretty merciless, but if they'd been left behind they would have died of hunger and cold in any case. So, in a way, shooting them might have been considered an act of mercy.'

Once they had reached the top of the mountain, The Tiger, apparently satisfied that a major objective had been achieved, began to relax the pressure, at least on the civilian detainees. Commissioner Lord and Monsignor Thomas Quinlan argued successfully for transportation for the very weak and, later that day, a bus and a truck arrived, on which the children, women, old men and five very sick POWs were driven away.

On Tuesday evening, with journey's end in sight, The Tiger sat down with Commissioner Lord, Major John Dunn, senior officer with the POWs, and Dr Ernst Kisch to complete the cover-up of his crimes. Along with the absence of burial mounds, the removal of dog tags and the falsification of Mother Beatrix's death certificate, he now asked the three men to draw up a list of all those who had died or been killed. After the name of each person, in a column marked 'Cause of Death', he told Dr Kisch he should enter the explanation as 'enteritis'. The doctor was then forced to sign the false document. For Kisch, there was nothing new in this obligatory collusion. The Austrian had been forced to make similar declarations by the Nazis, in the Buchenwald and Dachau concentration camps. Enteritis, a relatively mild form of inflammation of the intestines, is rarely fatal to anyone except weak babies.

Finally, on Wednesday, 8 November, the column arrived in the town of Chunggangjin. They had been walking for nine days, travelled more than a hundred miles, and lost a hundred men and women along the way, lives sacrificed to the maniacal Tiger and his compliant henchmen.

After a week's respite in another deserted schoolhouse, the captives were ordered to march once more. Chunggangjin had been peppered by F-51 Mustang fighter aircraft firing machine guns and rockets, and The Tiger wanted his charges out of harm's way. This time their journey was much shorter – five miles to the deserted village of Hanjang-Ni.

If the journey from Manpo to Chunggangjin had been the Death March, the prisoners' accommodation at Hanjang-Ni would prove to be a Death Camp. The Carmelite nun Mother Mechtilde was the first to die there on 18 November, followed by Bishop Patrick Byrne on

25 November, Father Charles Hunt on 26 November, Mother Thérèse and Monsieur Alfred Matti on 30 November, Father Frank Canavan on 6 December, Sergei Leonoff (an old White Russian in his seventies) on 9 December, Bill Evans on 12 December, Father Joseph Cadars on 18 December and Father Joseph Bulteau on 6 January.

'It was difficult to bury the dead because the ground was frozen and we had no tools,' Blake recalled. 'All we could do was cover the bodies with snow and stones.'

The prisoners were granted a degree of self-sufficiency and, within strict limits, allowed to cook their own food, draw their own water and keep the fires going. Tiger and his men refused to allow the fires in daylight hours, fearful that the smoke drifting from the chimneys would alert American aircraft.

The food ration continued to be miserly, consisting of 600 grams of millet per person per day – 'bird seed' was what the captives called it, as it ranked lowest in the scale of grains – plus a vegetable portion of one desultory frozen head of cabbage for about thirty-five people. More often than not they made soup from bean paste, water and cabbage. During the entire winter they received a tiny piece of meat just three or four times, and fish twice. By now, Blake had recovered from the dysentery contracted on the Death March, which was just as well, as he needed as much strength as he could muster to nurse his colleagues, Holt and Owen, who were close to death. The two Britons had by now succumbed to pneumonia as well as dysentery, with their temperatures rising to 106.7°F.

The Tiger suddenly grew worried at the potential consequences of their deaths and sent the camp's in-house 'doctor', a Korean medical student, on a five-mile trek to bring back penicillin and sulphapyridine tablets. He was nearly too late to administer the medicine. 'The medical student came in and they [Holt and Owen] were completely delirious,' remembered Deane. 'Owen was certain there were ambulances outside ready to take him home, and he fought me time and again to get out of the room. At other times both the sick imagined there were stacks of chicken sandwiches in the room. They accused me of stealing their share.'

Vyvyan Holt believed he was going to die: 'If it were not for George Blake and Philip Deane, I would not have survived even the last leg of the Death March. They nursed me and Consul Owen and gave us their rations, although they were themselves sick and hungry.'

The British and French contingent, together with Deane, was crammed in a room no more than nine by nine foot. Deane was impressed by Blake's stoicism and resolve, none more so than on Tuesday, 5 December, when the two of them were on water-carrying duty.

This was a perilous business. It involved two hours' carrying after breakfast and another one after lunch, and the biting wind felt as if it had penetrated to the very marrow of the bones. The men had to bring the water from a well two hundred yards away, in a twenty-five gallon drum carried between two of them, slung on a pole. The mouth of the well would slowly ice up until a bucket could hardly fit through its opening; the well rope would be frozen solid and invariably stuck to their hands. On that day Blake and Deane were asked to fetch four drums of water rather than the usual three and they promptly refused, saying they were just too exhausted. As Dean recalled: 'The guard ordered George Blake and me to kneel down in the snow. He accused us of not carrying the amount of water laid down in regulations. We replied that this was not so. The guard said he would teach us not to lie, and he beat us with the butt of his rifle, kicked us and slapped us. George Blake, who got the worst of it, smiled throughout the ordeal, his left eyebrow cocked ironically at the guard, his Elizabethan beard aggressively thrust forward.'

The other prisoners were summoned to watch this punishment meted out, and warned that they would be treated in similar fashion if they disobeyed orders. Blake and Deane were made to remain, hands behind their back, crouched in the snow, for over an hour.

For Blake, the positive, philosophical side of a fatalistic approach to life served him well in this period. It enabled him to cope when all the evidence, all reason, might have led him to give up.

What Blake had, many of the GIs lacked, however, and they fell into despair. Still on starvation diets, many now chose to sleep for eighteen hours out of twenty-four; it was a means of preserving energy, but also a way for those who had dysentery to avoid the dreaded fifty-foot walk to a lean-to communal latrine, which afforded precious little shelter from the biting December winds and temperatures of -40 to -60°F. That walk alone was the cause of many deaths. For those in the lowest spirits, starvation seemed an easy way out; they had seen their colleagues float into a coma and never wake up, and it seemed a peaceful way to go. Some simply stopped eating.

The soldiers who struggled on resorted to all kinds of selfish, thoughtless behaviour. There were those who worked in the cookhouse, who stole their comrades' food. Others, in relatively good health, kept the sick away from the stove. Some left others alone to die because they were unpleasant to be around, being dirty and unable to make it to the latrine. There were even those who stole clothes from their skeletal comrades even as they lay dying. The thin veneer of civilised behaviour was torn away: in The Tiger's world, they lived on the edge.

While Blake and his fellow prisoners at Hanjang-Ni were preoccupied with an elemental life and death struggle in the winter of 1950–51, during which 200 people died, outside the camp gates the intervention of the Chinese had irrevocably altered the course of the war.

After his tactical triumph at Incheon and subsequent rout of the North Korean forces, General Douglas MacArthur, Commander-in-Chief of the United Nations forces, was transfixed by the prospect of total victory in the shape of a united Korea. At a meeting at Wake Island on 15 October, the General assured President Truman there was little chance of Chinese intervention in Korea. In the unlikely event that Mao decided to send in his troops, MacArthur told the President, then UN air strikes would render them ineffective long before they reached the battlefield. Yet, on that very weekend, the first men of the massed armies of the Chinese Communist forces – the Chinese People's Volunteers (CPV) – were stealthily entering Korea over the Yalu bridges at Antung and Manpojin, concealed by rugged terrain, weather and smoke from forest fires.

In the course of the next six weeks, General Peng Dehuai and his army of 300,000 first crushed South Korean opposition and then forced the US-led UN forces into a humiliating retreat, all the way back to the 38th parallel and beyond. Dehuai combined all-out attack with clever tactical retreat to mountain hideouts, and MacArthur and his generals were completely outmanoeuvred. A national humiliation was underway.

December 1950 was the nadir of the US-led United Nations campaign in Korea and things looked desperate, until Lieutenant-General Matthew Ridgway replaced Eighth Army commander Walton Walker, killed in an accident in his jeep on 23 December, and slowly but surely, the tide began to turn. Ridgway, a celebrated airborne commander in the Second World War, quickly set about re-establishing discipline and raising morale. Unlike MacArthur, he bought into the political strategy of holding the line and fighting a limited war. He wanted to take back territory, but not at the expense of large casualties, and was happy to fight a war of attrition.

It started to pay dividends in early February. Ridgway had been forced to abandon Seoul, but as his troops retreated, he stretched the Communist supply lines to their very limit. In the coming month, he led a series of successful, limited attacks by UN forces – the colourfully named Operations Killer, Ripper and Rugged. After they had recaptured Seoul and the front began to coalesce roughly around the old demarcation line, the 38th parallel, expectations were raised that peace negotiations would open soon. Back in the camp at Hanjang-Ni, greater stability in the war led to a corresponding improvement in living conditions for Blake and the other captives.

Food was more plentiful and ill treatment rare; life altogether felt not quite so desperate.

On 2 February 1951, the group of British and French diplomats and journalists was taken aside from the others, and addressed by an elderly Korean army officer, who informed them political conditions had changed and they were being moved elsewhere. Blake, Deane and the others were first taken by bus back towards Manpo. They spent a night in a town through which they had passed during the Death March, receiving, by the standards to which they were accustomed, an evening meal of stunning proportions – overflowing bowls of white rice and soya bean soup, accompanied by pepper and soya sauce.

The next day they walked into Manpo and witnessed the severe damage UN planes had done to the frontier town. In the centre the large concrete railway bridge stood intact, virtually the only structure to have survived. Everywhere else lay the wreckage of scores of homes, shops, factories, and schools. Now and then a ruin would poke up defiantly and incongruously amid the rubble.

On Monday, 5 February, the party was made to walk three miles north on the ice of the Yalu River until they reached a small hamlet called Moo Yong Nee. There, a farmhouse had been requisitioned for them. When they arrived at the doorstep, its occupants were in the process of moving out into the already over-crowded home of a neighbour. The old woman of the house, despite her eviction, smiled and welcomed them into her home. For Blake and his colleagues, this would prove to be journey's end as far as Korea was concerned. As they settled down to life in the farmhouse, they no longer faced the extraordinary physical privations suffered at the hands of The Tiger in Hanjang-Ni. From now on, the pressure would not be on their bodies but their minds.

9

Stalin's New Recruit

In the Communist Eastern Bloc, the Stalin Peace Prize – or to give it its full, characteristically verbose title, the International Stalin Prize for Strengthening Peace Among Peoples – was belatedly established as a rival to the West's Nobel Peace Prize. In 1951 and 1952, among the recipients of this dubious award were two Britons, Dr Hewlett Johnson, the Dean of Canterbury, and Dr Monica Felton, journalist, writer, town planner and one time Chairman of the Stevenage Development Corporation. Korean and Chinese propagandists were keen for Blake and the other prisoners at Hanjang-Ni to have access to the thoughts of these two luminaries of the 'Peace Movement', so copious magazines with pictures of them and articles by both were widely distributed.

After Felton visited North Korea as part of an international women's delegation in 1951, her criticisms of the United Nations mission would become increasingly vitriolic. She would go to the extreme of likening the UN prisoner-of-war camps to concentration camps in Nazi Germany. She also claimed that whole North Korean families, men, women and children, who had been imprisoned for days without food and water, had then been shot, burnt to death and even buried alive. Tape recordings of her conversations with American Air Force officers 'confessing' their part in 'a crime against the peace-loving people of the world' were also played in the camps.

Among the more outlandish claims of Dr Johnson – 'The Red Dean' as he was known, for his slavish devotion to the Communist Party and, in particular, Stalin – was that the United States was waging a deliberate policy of germ warfare on the North Korean people. His pamphlet on the subject, *I Appeal*, was distributed among the captives.

Blake and his colleagues had now been in captivity for eight months. The propaganda material flowing from these two colourful characters was just a first, small step, a taster of the attempts at political indoctrination that both the Chinese and the Russians would gradually make on them once they were settled in Moo Yong Nee.

This was the first modern military conflict in which one side attempted to systematically convert prisoners of the other to their own ideology. In April 1951, Padre S.J. Davies and his colleagues in the Gloucestershire Regiment were warned by their captor, a high-ranking Chinese officer: 'You are hirelings of the barbarous Rhee puppet government, but you will be given the chance to learn the truth through study and to correct your mistakes.' Soon, Davies and his fellow prisoners would be put through the Chinese 'Lenient Policy'. This was something of a misnomer: if they refused to undertake 're-education' in Marxism-Leninism, they might face the withdrawal of rations of food and cigarettes, beatings or even solitary confinement. As a Chinese officer famously snarled at one group of prisoners: 'We will keep you here ten, twenty, thirty or even forty years if necessary, until you learn the truth, and if you still won't learn it, we will bury you so deep that you won't even stink.'

Blake, Deane, Holt, Meadmore and the others were a completely different proposition from the ordinary soldiers. These were not just diplomats, intelligence officers, or journalists – all of them had an unusual depth of learning that qualified them as intellectuals.

As they began to accustom themselves to a more benign existence

in the farmhouse, there was an increase in the efforts to lure them
into an ideological conversion. After receiving the outpourings of
Felton and Johnson, they were then given the Communist classics
to help while away the long hours of captivity – Marx's *Das Kapital*,
Lenin's *The State and the Revolution*, Stalin's *Questions of Leninism* as well
as writings from the likes of Engels. In addition, they were supplied
with contemporary Russian magazines and newspapers, in which the
faults of a 'corrupt' Western civilisation were relentlessly analysed
and magnified. One of the books described England as being like
'a pond of stagnant, fetid water where nothing lived, where all was
stifled by the green slime on the surface'. America, recalled Deane,
'was America as seen by one who searched only for horror, soulless-
ness and filth. France, as painted by Ilya Ehrenburg, was a decadent
caricature of her great past.'

This was not like an indoctrination session with an interrogator and
Deane felt this wealth of propaganda material had far more insidious
dangers. 'The absurd and constant assertion began to leave its mark . . .
I felt my thinking processes getting tangled, my critical faculties getting
blunted. I could not think and I was afraid,' Deane remembered. 'It
does not matter what the thought is, its quality is beside the point. If
you cannot think, it frightens you by its immense repetition.'

Relief arrived in an unusual form. In one delivery of books there
was a copy of Robert Louis Stevenson's *Treasure Island* – a mistake,
perhaps, or did the propagandists hope it would be seen as an alle-
gory on capitalist profit? It enabled the captives to leap back into the
straightforward, alluring world of a child's imagination, with good
old-fashioned storytelling featuring adventures with drunken sailors,
pirates, parrots and buried gold. They drew lots to see who would read
it first, and then they all read it over again. 'It made us light-hearted,
so we started dancing lessons,' recalled Deane. 'Those of us who could
dance taught those who couldn't. Music was homemade – singing and
beating a box to keep time.'

Blake enjoyed *Treasure Island* well enough but, unlike Deane, he also found succour in *The State and Revolution* and, in particular, *Das Kapital.*

The captives' living conditions were not comfortable by Western standards. Nevertheless, life at the farmhouse in Moo Yong Nee was far removed from the adversity and constant threat of disease and death at the camp in Hanjang-Ni. The Chinese seemed to have taken a conscious decision not to allow their prisoners to die at the alarming rate of previous months and circumstances for both civilians and POWs alike in all the camps along the Yalu River began to significantly improve. Whether it was because of gathering hopes of a ceasefire that summer and they did not wish to have their reputation sullied by accusations of prisoner neglect, or because they wanted as many converts as possible coming out of their 'political study sessions', remains unclear.

Blake and his colleagues were given padded clothing to see them through the rest of the winter, and the food – although lacking in variety – was a good deal better than the previous starvation rations. The building they lived in had four rooms and a kitchen with a hearth – and the rare luxury of a warm fire. The electricity supply was eventually restored in May.

As winter turned to spring, Blake and Holt would wander out into the field behind the farmhouse and sit on low green mounds in a small family graveyard, where the two of them would read and talk. Holt's eyesight was very poor and had deteriorated further because of malnutrition. Worse, he had lost his glasses while dashing for cover when American fighter columns attacked targets close to the column of prisoners on the Death March. He asked Blake to read to him, and together they embarked on *Das Kapital.* In the weeks that followed, the book provoked much discussion between them as to the merits of a socialist society.

Holt had at one stage considered stepping down from the Foreign Office to pursue a political career, but was unsure as to which party he

would join. Because of his background and upbringing he would have
been a natural candidate for the Conservatives, but Blake inferred
from their dialogue that Holt's sympathies lay more on the left of
British politics. He enjoyed listening to the older man's advanced
and occasionally unorthodox views, and admired his detached and
objective approach to world affairs: 'For example, he believed the
British Empire was in terminal decline, and he was convinced that
humanity was entering a new stage – that of communism. He didn't
welcome it because he was too much of an individualist to enjoy living
in a communist society but he certainly had admiration for what the
Soviets had achieved in Central Asia, in raising the living standards of
those in former colonial territories. He compared that achievement to
what the British did in India.'

Holt's cogent expression of his ideas was inadvertently helping
to dismantle the final barriers in Blake's mind on his road to full
conversion to Communism and, from there, to ultimate betrayal.
But it seemed to Blake that when Holt and other prisoners criticised
Communism, it was always about the form it took, and never about its
real spirit.

In the autumn of 1951 that form was still the dominant figure of
Joseph Stalin, who was starting to ponder a new, dangerous theory
that fitted in well with his increasingly virulent anti-Semitism: that a
group of Jewish doctors was plotting to murder Kremlin leaders. Not a
whisper of this latest expression of his paranoia would be heard by the
outside world for many years. The prevailing view in the West was that
the ailing dictator was a dangerous adversary, but an admirable leader
of his people, despite his flaws. Clues to the real nature of his regime
were still mostly well hidden.

Blake was perturbed by the cult of personality in the Soviet
Union. He later acknowledged that many of the manifestations
of Communism were repellent, and accepted great crimes were
committed in its name:

But these were not an essential part of its creed, which itself represented the noblest aims of humanity and in many respects sought to put into practice the virtues preached by Christianity.

I felt that if a movement was motivated by such aims it was more likely to achieve them than if it had no aims at all, or very vague ones, and that therefore in the long run, in spite of stumbling and backsliding, Communism was likely to establish a more just and humane society than Capitalism.

In this written justification he made for his treachery to the Central Criminal Court at the Old Bailey, nine years later, Blake made it sound, in the semi-religious language he tended to deploy, as if he had embarked on a path of repentance and then sacrifice.

I had become profoundly aware of the frailty of human life and I had reflected much on what I had done with my life up to that point.

I felt that it had lacked aim and had been filled mostly with the pursuit of pleasure and personal ambitions . . . I then decided to devote the rest of my life to what I considered a worthwhile cause, to sacrifice to it not only possibly my life and liberty, but more so my honour and the affection and esteem of my friends and relatives, to live no more for myself but only for this purpose.

His final decision to embrace Communism and then act upon it may well have been taken after reading *Das Kapital* in a cemetery in Korea, but the reality was that this was just the last step on a long journey along the road to treachery, which had begun many years before.

Everything he was about to do he would later justify on the grounds of belief alone, but even the purest of ideological spies have other reasons. Blake's were contempt for the British class system of which, on occasion, he had been a victim, a dislike of the competitive society, virulent anti-Americanism and a deep religious conviction that blended well with Marxism. In addition, a fascination with the secret world had grown in him since childhood, and since his teenage years he had been leading a double life, in one form of intelligence or another, playing a part, deceiving others, living his life – bluntly – as a professional liar.

Besides, what was there to hold him back? The bonds of allegiance to his country had inevitably been weak, despite his father's loyalty and passion for a distant Britain. Blake had spent just three years of his life on English soil, and viewed his nationality with a degree of detachment. In later life he would explain that 'I feel above nationality. I don't approve of national feelings. Loyalty to humanity, loyalty to a human cause, loyalty to religion is higher than loyalty to country.'

And there was something more – a certain quirk of personality – a desire to be in control. 'He was a secret man, it was not easy to know what he was thinking. But I had the strong sense that he liked to exercise power, not just be passive and subservient,' was Jean Meadmore's later assessment. Blake's first wife Gillian would put it even more succinctly: 'I think George liked to be the power behind the scenes. He didn't want power for himself, for his own sake, he didn't want people to say "That's George Blake". He wanted to manipulate the strings and know what was going on.'

Gillian Blake, for her part, believed her husband's ideological switch came some time before Korea: 'I don't think his conversion to communism was really in the camp. It was there before . . . I think it was the result of a mixture of a latent feeling he had always had of wanting to better things, and a lack of the substantial background that people have, of family and schools and all that sort of thing, which makes them able to sink back when they see that sort of thing . . . I don't know, but I don't think that he'd be switched over in camp like that.'

If the conversion had come much earlier, his experiences in the war acted as a catalyst in a mind now fixated against his country and Western aggression: 'I remembered how in Holland, during the war, when I heard at night the heavy drone of RAF planes overhead on their way to bomb Germany, the sound had been like a song to me . . . Now, when I saw the enormous grey hulks of the American bombers sweeping low to drop their deadly load over the small, defenceless, Korean villages huddled against the mountainside, when I saw the villagers, mostly women and children and old people – for the men were all at the front – being machine-gunned as they fled to seek shelter in the fields, I felt nothing but shame and anger.'

Beyond the walls of his farmhouse compound, seismic political and military events were taking place. President Truman and his commanders faced up to the last, great battle for territory in the war – the Chinese 'Fifth Phase' or 'Spring Offensive'. It lasted from 22 April through to 20 May 1951, with three field armies of 700,000 men aiming to encircle and annihilate UN forces in the West. Despite early successes in ferocious battles at Imjin River and Kapyong, the Chinese assault was repulsed by a determined and coordinated rear-guard action by troops under the command of General Ridgway, who had replaced MacArthur in April 1951. The Communists were eventually thrown back with appalling casualties and the UN forces recaptured the 'Kansas-Wyoming Line', just north of the 38th parallel. A long stalemate now developed which would last until the armistice, two years later. Mao, viewing the huge losses his armies had suffered since the beginning of the year, accepted that the UN forces could not be decisively beaten. Stalin too, watching from the sidelines, had come to much the same conclusion.

Low-level peace talks, 'strictly military', with no political content, began between the two delegations at Kaesong on 10 July. Meanwhile in the air, the first 'Jet War' was now underway – the one occasion in the Cold War where American and Soviet military forces regularly engaged each other in battle, with the US Sabres and Russian MIG-15s locked in fierce combat.

In August, Blake and his colleagues' hopes of release were raised when an official from the North Korean Ministry for Foreign Affairs arrived at the farmhouse in Moo Yong Nee. He told them that a message had been received from their families, that they were well and thinking of them. Frustratingly, he had no specific words or details. He then urged the captives to write short messages to their relatives in no more than twenty words and assured them that they would be passed on, via the International Red Cross. Blake tried to cram in as much reassurance about his health and his hopes for a speedy reunion.

For some time the Foreign Office had been making concerted efforts to discover the whereabouts of the captured British nationals and request their release. The quest began in earnest when Sir David Kelly, British Ambassador to Moscow, demanded a meeting with Andrei Gromyko, the Soviet Deputy Minister for Foreign Affairs. Gromyko's manner was evasive. He told Kelly that, in the first instance, the British Government would be advised to approach the North Koreans directly. In February 1951, Ernest Davies, junior minister at the Foreign Office, somewhat overstated his department's progress when he reassured the House of Commons: 'We approached the Chinese Government and the Soviet Government, asking them to use their good offices, and I am glad to say that the Soviet Government are doing so.'

In reality the Soviet Government would make little effort for many months. It did eventually indicate a willingness to play a role as a 'post box', transmitting messages to and from Captain Holt and his group, but the reliability of service was poor. Messages went out from the camp, but there's no evidence that the prisoners actually received any letters from their families.

It is as clear as it reasonably can be that it was in the autumn of 1951 that Blake took the irrevocable step towards which he had been heading, and began actively to betray his country. What remains a matter of contention is how that step was taken – was he actively recruited by the KGB (then known as the MGB), or did he readily *offer* his services, and choose treachery of his own free will? There are two versions of the story.

In Blake's account, he made the first move late one evening when everyone else had gone to bed. He went out to relieve himself in the field behind the farmhouse and, on his way back, he stopped off in the guards' room, where a light was still showing. On opening the door he came across a familiar scene – Commander 'Fatso' giving one of his regular, evening political lectures to a group of colleagues: 'I put my fingers to my lips as I handed him a folded note. He looked at me somewhat surprised, but took it without saying anything. I closed the door and went back to bed.' Blake says he wrote the note in Russian, and addressed it to the Soviet Embassy in Pyongyang. In it, he stated he had 'something important to communicate which they might find of interest'.

For six weeks Blake says he heard nothing. His note, he claims, sent the Soviet officials in the North Korean capital scurrying to confer with their KGB colleagues in Vladivostok, who then swiftly reported back to Moscow. Then a 'young, fair Russian, with pleasant, open features' arrived in Manpo, along with an older man: 'the chief', who was clearly his superior. Blake attaches names to neither of them. His account has him interrogated by the older of the two: 'He was a big, burly man of about forty or forty-five with a pale complexion. What was most remarkable about him was that he was completely bald, so that he looked very like the film actor, Erich von Stroheim, and that, for reasons best known to himself, he wore no socks.'

On that first day, the officer had Blake's note spread out before him on the table and asked him to explain what information he had to offer. Blake told him that he wanted to offer his services to the Soviet authorities. He explained that although ostensibly a diplomat, a vice-consul at the British legation, in reality he was a spy. 'I had no indication that they knew I was an SIS officer,' he recalled. For some time his offer was regarded with the automatic suspicion that all intelligence agencies view 'walk-ins'. As Blake tells it, his interviews with 'the chief' carried on for several months. Finally, he was told his vetting process was over and that he had been accepted as a Soviet agent. When the right time came, they would activate him.

Blake's version of events fits neatly into the legend he created for himself and, though it may well be true, appears to bear the tell-tale signs of a KGB propaganda job: the disillusioned Western intelligence operative, scales lifted from his eyes, brought willingly to the Marxist cause by a mixture of personal experience and ideological conviction. There are those in Russia, however, who have always maintained that Soviet intelligence, in the person of 25-year-old Nikolai Andreyevich Loenko, made the decisive move to bring Blake into the KGB ranks, and there are reliable sources which support that view.

In the early 1950s, Moscow Centre was in need of new recruits within the British establishment after its successful Cambridge spy ring had been broken up. Donald Maclean and Guy Burgess – the former knowing he was about to be brought in for questioning by MI5 – had hurriedly left the country on a boat from Southampton on 25 May 1951, subsequently making their way across Europe to the sanctuary of Moscow. The 'Third Man' in the group, Kim Philby, was incommunicado as growing suspicion mounted over his allegiances. Indeed, during the autumn, MI5 had formally told him that his relationship with Burgess made him a prime suspect for treachery.

A solution for filling these gaps was proffered to the strategists in the Lubyanka by Loenko, an up-and-coming intelligence officer in Vladivostok. Loenko had joined the KGB in 1944, and naturally concentrated his early intelligence work in neighbouring China and North Korea. Despite his youth, his talent was recognised right from the start; he was part of a Soviet delegation that met Kim Il-Sung and his cabinet in 1948, and he would eventually earn the sobriquet, 'Lawrence of the Far East'. Ironically, he would have been one of those Soviet officials that Blake had been tasked to 'turn' when he first arrived in Seoul. In 1951, the boot would be very firmly on the other foot.

Possessed of a rustic charm and a good sense of humour, young Loenko was not cut from the usual cloth of the Soviet apparatchik: his skills also included a facility for languages, including English. Loenko had become aware of the group of British diplomats, journalists and missionaries being shunted around from camp to camp near the Yalu River. He also knew that the Chinese and North Koreans who ran the camps had offered Soviet intelligence operatives like himself unfettered access to the Western prisoners. He suggested to his masters in Moscow that now was the time for an approach.

Loenko arrived in Manpo under the guise of an ordinary army officer, assuming the name of 'Grigori Kuzmich'. One by one, the captives, starting with Captain Holt, were asked to accompany their camp commander, 'Fatso', on the forty-five minute walk from the farmhouse to the small office Loenko had established in one of the few remaining houses in Manpo. Initially, he probed gently about their views on the war, gave them some propaganda material to read, and asked, very politely, if they would sign a statement condemning the conduct of the United Nations.

As Loenko began to win Blake's trust, the SIS officer gradually confided in him his revulsion at the Rhee administration, his opposition to the UN action and, in particular, the brutal American military tactics, his growing disillusionment with capitalist society and newfound enthusiasm, via *The Theory of Communism* and *Das Kapital*, for Marxism. The young intelligence officer showed a keen understanding of Blake's belief system, rooted in his former religious convictions, and offered him an interpretation of the Soviet Union as a country whose goals were not dissimilar to those of Christianity. Paradise on earth instead of paradise in heaven.

Blake may have been ripe for the picking, but it took many meetings over a series of weeks before Loenko felt confident he had his man. Meanwhile the young officer's superiors back in Moscow remained wary of Blake. They suspected the charming, clever Captain Holt of masterminding a ploy against them and grew extremely cautious once they learned of Blake's activities in Hamburg in 1946. He just seemed too good to be true.

Once Blake had, at last, pledged his future to the KGB, he was at great pains to emphasise that he did not want any personal advantages in return for his work; in particular, he made it clear he wanted no money as a reward for his spying on their behalf: 'I was doing it for a cause.' While he remained in captivity, he insisted he should have no privileges of any kind, none that would set him aside from his fellow prisoners. This was not just a matter of principle – any extra benefits he received might well alert the suspicions of his companions at the farmhouse.

He told his interlocutors that he would supply all the information he could on SIS operations directed against the Soviet Union, and indeed, the rest of the world Communist movement: 'My sole aim in all this was to assist in preventing espionage operations from harming the Communist bloc and, more especially, the Soviet Union.' Over the course of the next few months, the KGB men asked Loenko to put Blake to the test: they wanted the Briton to provide them with full details of the structure and organisation of SIS. Of course they already had this information, thanks to Kim Philby and others, which made it an effective way of proving his sincerity. Eventually, the KGB was satisfied it had a bona fide British intelligence officer on its books. In the absence of Burgess and Maclean, and with Philby's usefulness coming to an end, Blake was a welcome addition to the Soviets' roster of moles.

Loenko died in a car crash on 20 September 1976 at the age of fifty. In October 1999 Blake travelled to Vladivostok at the invitation of the Governor, Yevgeny Nazdratenko, and the FSB Head, Major-General Sergei Verevkin-Rahalskogo. Older KGB officers often referred to him as 'Blake's godfather', and Blake made a point of visiting the *Morskoye* cemetery to lay flowers at Loenko's grave.

Whatever the exact truth of Blake's recruitment, his acceptance into the Communist fold proved to be a moment of enormous relief for him, though it was also one of sharp realisation: there was no turning back. He was embarking on a lifelong road of deception and treachery: 'I fully realised I was betraying the trust put in me: I was betraying the allegiance that I owed to Britain, I was betraying my colleagues and friends . . . But I felt it would be wrong to forgo the opportunity of making such a valuable contribution and that was a guilt I should take upon me.'

He slipped effortlessly into this 'atmosphere of illegality'. Albeit now darker and deeper, such shadowlands had been his natural environment ever since he had worked as a courier in the Dutch underground. More than that, though, spying for the Soviet Union gave him his vocation: 'It gave a complete sense to life. Having this very important task put every other problem in my life in perspective. Many of the other problems that concern people – marital problems, day-to-day concerns – they didn't worry me, because they were nothing compared to what I was doing.'

There would no glimmer of an indication in his behaviour as to the change that had taken place. He made sure his fellow captives had no inkling of his very different conversations with Loenko, and he carefully ensured his accounts of discussions with the young officer tallied with theirs.

Another young KGB officer appeared on the scene a few weeks later to aid Loenko – Vasily Alekseevich Dozhdalev, aged thirty, who had just started working out of the London office. Loenko had done all the spadework, but Dozhdalev would ultimately be the one to enjoy a long and fruitful acquaintance with Blake.

In early 1952, the peace talks at Panmunjom looked to be close to securing agreement, but the dispute over the return of prisoners of war remained a major obstacle and the conflict continued – a slow, grinding affair of low-level attrition on the ground.

Back at the farmhouse, in March, Blake and his companions were able to leave the courtyard for the first time in over a year to take supervised walks in the countryside. Little else had changed, however.

Norman Owen kept a diary on the wall and, in the first six months of 1952, there were just fifteen entries: eight of them read 'barber came', while four said 'cigarettes issued'.

In those long, uneventful months when the conversations drifted away from history, philosophy and art, they invariably moved on to food. They had enough to eat now, but remained obsessed by the subject. 'We were also frequently plagued by frustrating food dreams,' Blake recalled. 'We would find ourselves in a pastry shop with all kinds of delicious cakes, or a restaurant with tables piled high with food. All this disappeared just when we had great difficulty making up our minds what we were going to have, and were ready to start eating.'

The relationships with the villagers who came to the farmhouse grew closer. The guards believed servants should be kept in their place and treated the prisoners' cook and her little daughter particularly badly. The woman and her child, a 3-year-old girl named Yong Sukee, were made to take their meals in a draughty, freezing outhouse. As the weather worsened in the winter of 1952, the child grew increasingly unhappy. The captives therefore 'adopted' Yong Sukee, taking her into the house, making her clothes and keeping her warm. 'Owen, an expert father, was in charge during emergencies, when soothing or restraining was needed,' recalled Deane. 'At other times she played with the rest of us, especially with Blake, who was the most patient and who she regarded as her father. She learnt a few words of English, gave us nicknames, and dominated much of our existence.'

Owen's wall chart for the year contained just two more entries in the final five months. The captives had now been together for over two years, and, even in this group of compelling conversationalists, the stories were starting to dry up. Fragmentary news about the war suggested peace was still a long way off and provided little reason for optimism that the monotony would end soon.

It took changes at the top in Washington and Moscow to start to break the deadlock. In November 1952, General Dwight D. Eisenhower, Supreme Commander of the Allied Forces in Europe in

World War II, won the American presidency after a landslide election victory over the Democratic candidate, Adlai Stevenson. Eisenhower made it clear his first priority as President would be to end the war but he was determined not to do so from any position that could be construed as weak. To that end, the successful testing in January of the first surface-to-surface rocket for carrying nuclear weapons – dubbed 'Honest John' – gave the US the upper hand. The Joint Chiefs of Staff noted that 'the timely use of atomic weapons should be considered against military targets affecting operations in Korea'.

Equally crucial for the prospect of peace was the death of Stalin on 5 March 1953. The dictator had continually placed impediments on negotiations, believing the inevitable compromise would damage Communist standing and free the West from the huge burden on its resources that the war had entailed. The first sign that things might be about to change in the camp was when Stalin's picture, which had taken pride of place in the guardroom, quickly disappeared a day or so after the announcement of his death.

On the morning of Friday, 20 March, while the captives were talking their usual morning walk round the courtyard, the British inmates were ushered back into the farmhouse and told to get their belongings together. Soon afterwards, they were in the back of an open lorry and on their way to Pyongyang. They were taking their first steps to freedom, thanks in no small part to the efforts of the new Conservative Deputy Prime Minister and Foreign Secretary, Anthony Eden.

Eden had been 'greatly troubled' by the continued imprisonment of Holt and his party. Ever since coming into office in October 1951, he had tried all manner of means to secure their release, including approaches to more sympathetic Communist powers, all to no avail. One weekend in February he decided to make another attempt through the Soviet Ambassador, Andrei Gromyko. Eden thought he detected indications from the Soviet government that, with the departure of Stalin, they were interested in developing better relations.

'This might be turned to good account, but I was not sanguine,' he reflected. Gromyko was called to the Foreign Office, where Eden charmed and cajoled him in equal measure.

> I gave him an *aide-memoire* setting out the facts and pointed out that these people, who were civilians, had been detained for a very long time.

> Though the Soviet Government had maintained that this was not a matter of direct concern to them, they had been good enough on one or two occasions to transmit messages and I appealed to Mr Gromyko to do what he could to secure the release of these unfortunate people.

At first, Gromyko stuck to the standard position: his Government 'had no responsibility in this matter' and, as far as he knew, nothing had changed. But Eden's argument that he could – and should – exert more pressure on the North Koreans eventually drew a pledge from Gromyko that he would talk to his government in Moscow and see what he could do.

Six weeks later, to Eden's surprise and delight, 'the oracle worked'. The Soviet authorities in Moscow came back with a complete list of the captured British subjects. It was the first time for many months that their existence, let alone their well-being, had been confirmed. Just days later, the Soviet *Chargé d'Affaires*, in the absence of Gromyko, gave Eden's junior minister Selwyn Lloyd an assurance that the prisoners would shortly be freed.

In Pyongyang, the captives were put up in a mountain cave for several days to shelter from American air attacks, which were still taking place several times a day. There, confirmation of their new status came in the form of a sumptuous breakfast served to them by no less than a brigadier. As they tucked into caviar, butter, ham, eggs, spaghetti and petit-beurre biscuits, they reflected on the time when a mere sergeant had beaten them with the butt of a rifle. The VIP treatment continued as they were shaved, given fresh underclothes and newly laundered shirts, and, before long, visited by a tailor, who measured them for suits and overcoats. A cinema operator even appeared with a selection of films for them to watch, including such socialist realist classics as *Knight of the Golden Star*, *Glinka* and *Happy Market*, as well as some delightful sequences of the prima ballerina Galina Ulanova.

The representative of the *Labour Journal*, the *Pravda* of North Korea, came to interview them on the evening of Friday, 7 April, in a final, unsuccessful effort to extract some propaganda value. Diplomats and journalists alike played a straight bat to a barrage of questions.

The following morning they were finally on their way, climbing onto a lorry together with two officers and four soldiers before being driven along the Pyongyang-Antung road to the Chinese frontier.

Deane had been worried that the North Korean customs officers would take away the notes he had made while in captivity, so he had sown the valuable papers into pads, which he then strapped around his calves. As a diversionary tactic, he kept a much larger body of material to which he was not especially attached on plain view in his bag. When the customs men said they were confiscating it, he made a great play of being furious and insisting that it should eventually be posted on to his home in England. The tactic worked, and he crossed the Korean-Manchurian border on 9 April with all his writings intact, ready to be turned into a vivid account of his captivity.

'King Paul of Greece was right,' Blake reminded Deane of a dream the journalist had had, as they finally left Korea after thirty-four months as prisoners. 'You've been freed before the tenth.'

10

Hero

On their first night of freedom in a hotel in the Chinese border town of Antung, Blake and his colleagues celebrated in a communal bath with lusty renditions of hymns and nursery rhymes. The privations of the past three years were forgotten as they revelled in the everyday pleasures of scented soap and freshly laundered towels.

The conditions of luxury continued the next day as their Trans-Manchurian Express train progressed steadily towards the Soviet border. In their special carriage, attentive waiters served them chicken and caviar, and they slept in huge, beautifully decorated cabins. Once they had arrived at Mukden (now Shenyang) and were settled in the best establishment in the city, they were allocated rooms with private bathrooms, and, in the panelled private dining room, the chef offered to cook any kind of food they wanted.

On Monday, 13 April 1953, the party arrived at the Soviet border town of Otpor (now Zabaikalsk). Here, Blake had business to conduct: he was to meet up with a new KGB contact, who would also be on the train that would take his group on the 6,500-mile final leg of their journey, to Moscow. As in Manpo, the meeting was carefully planned so that none of Blake's companions would suspect anything untoward. One by one, the former captives were taken to the customs house at Otpor, where they were met by officials, asked a few cursory questions, and then made to fill in a form. When it was Blake's turn, he was escorted to a small room at the back of the building, where he met his new case officer, Nikolai Borisovich Rodin, an experienced intelligence operative who was just completing his term as KGB *rezident* at the Soviet Embassy in London.

Blake's recollection is that it was a business-like, rather brusque meeting: 'He didn't introduce himself, but simply said that in future we would be working together. Without losing any time he began to discuss plans for our first clandestine meeting.' The two men agreed upon a time and a place in July, in The Hague. The venue was Blake's suggestion. He told Rodin he would feel more confident on home turf, and far better placed to react if anything went wrong. Both would carry a copy of the previous day's *Nieuwe Rotterdamse Courant* under their arm, as a sign that all was well. With that settled, Rodin allowed Blake to rejoin his colleagues. He told him that he would be occupying a compartment three doors along, and that if Blake had the chance to slip away without raising any suspicions, they could talk again. Moreover, he instructed him not to take any risks.

In the event, although Blake and Rodin passed each other in the corridor from time to time, they did not have a further meeting. The week that followed was spent mainly in the restaurant car, where abundant quantities of caviar and vodka were thrust upon the former prisoners. Finally, dazed, overfed and astounded at the turnaround in their fortunes, they arrived in the Soviet capital on Monday, 20 April. They were greeted on arrival at Kazan station by the British Ambassador, Sir Alvary Trench-Gascoigne, and his staff, who later royally entertained them over dinner.

The following morning, an RAF Hastings plane flew them to Gatow airfield in West Berlin. There, they were greeted by Major General Charles Coleman, Commandant of the British Sector in the city;

various embassy staff and other officials, and a large contingent of press correspondents and photographers.

Blake and his colleagues had been instructed to be extremely cautious in their dealings with a naturally eager and curious media. They were told to say as little as possible about the conditions in which they had been kept in North Korea because criticism might endanger the position of other internees yet to be released. The reporters noted that the men were all shabbily dressed, in ill-fitting clothes that had clearly been given to them just before their release. 'All were sunburned and looked relatively well, although the faces of some bore the marks of their suffering,' observed the man from *The Times*.

Among the press corps was none other than Charles Wheeler, Blake's colleague back in Hamburg in the spring of 1946. Now Wheeler was employed by the BBC, as a correspondent for the Corporation's German language service. His encounter with his old colleague that day left him perplexed: 'I went to meet the incoming internees at the airport – it was a good story, obviously. In the midst of this large welcoming party I walked up to George, who had his back to me, and I said, "Hello George". He turned round and saw me, and jumped about a foot in the air and went pale . . . I told him I was now living and working in Berlin, and asked him to come and have a drink with me in the evening. "I shan't have time, I shan't have time," he replied hurriedly, and I was surprised at this, because although we were never close friends, I must have been the only person in Berlin he knew.'

In later years, as events unfolded, Wheeler reflected on Blake's behaviour that day: 'He certainly wasn't pleased to see me. He didn't know I was a journalist – perhaps he thought I was a security man.'

Captain Holt and Bishop Cooper spent the night at Commandant Coleman's residence, whereas Blake and the rest bedded down in the officers' mess at Gatow. The following morning, Wednesday, 22 April, they boarded the De Havilland Hastings aircraft once more for the return to British soil.

Finally, on a glorious spring morning, Blake and his companions touched down at the Abingdon RAF station in Oxfordshire. A Salvation Army band, led by Commissioner John Allan, struck up the well-known doxology 'Praise God From Whom All Blessings Flow' as the internees appeared on the gangway. First down the steps was Holt, quickly followed by Owen, Lord and then Blake. The Pathé News commentary of the event refers to 'George Blake, of the Seoul legation staff', and then – less forgivably – says he was greeted by his wife. In fact, it was his mother Catherine, right at the front of the crowd, who hugged and kissed him the moment he left the steps.

The ragged attire that reporters had noticed at Gatow had been replaced by smarter sets of clothes. Holt's light suit still looked too small for him, but Blake was tidily dressed in light slacks and pull-over, with a dark tie and blazer. The younger man's beard was neatly trimmed in his now-familiar Elizabethan style. The two men, staunch, intimate companions in the camps, stood side by side facing a battery of cameras and a host of questions from the TV and newspapermen.

Holt did most of the talking. Looking gaunt with hollow cheeks, and suffering from a dry cough, he was, as ever, the consummate diplomat: 'It's very nice to be back, and I'm very happy to have been brought back by the RAF, which always gets you out of a jam.' The reporters may have wanted tales of starvation and torture, but Holt remained circumspect: 'Well, we have both pleasant, and unpleasant, memories of our treatment. When the country itself was in difficulties, of course it was not possible for them to treat us with the same consideration as later.'

Blake stonewalled in similar fashion. He shifted from side to side, smiling uncomfortably for the camera, as the reporter conducted a particularly anodyne interview.

Reporter: How did you find the food out there, Mr Blake?
Blake: Well, the food was adequate but very monotonous.
Reporter: It was monotonous, was it?
Blake: Very monotonous.

Reporter:	Anything special? I mean, any odd things they gave you to eat or anything?
Blake:	No, just rice and turnips mainly.
Reporter:	Pretty impressive diet, isn't it?
Blake:	Three times a day.

Commissioner Lord was equally unwilling to condemn his captors: 'We lived in a Korean house and our food was, I think, probably greater in quantity and better in quality than the great majority of ordinary Korean people were getting by then.'

After an official welcome from senior members of the Foreign Office, Blake later received another, quieter approach. He remembered, 'an elegantly dressed, elderly man, whom I had never met before, and who introduced himself as the personal representative of the Chief of the Secret [Intelligence] Service.' This emissary brought greetings from the Chief, an envelope with some money, and an instruction to call at Room 070 in the War Office the following Wednesday.

After saying moving goodbyes with the companions who had shared his bitter experiences over the past thirty-four months, Blake was bundled into his mother's car and was driven off to her home in Reigate. 'That evening,' he remembered, 'we had a quiet supper together in her small but comfortable flat and went to bed early, tired from the many emotions of the day.'

Blake and his party were the first prisoners to return from the Korean War, and fortunate to have made it. Of the more than 700 GIs who had accompanied Blake and the others on the Death March, only 250 survived to make it back to the United States after the final ceasefire in July 1953.

This so-called 'limited' war on the Asian peninsula had wrought terrible havoc, leaving in its wake an estimated four million military and civilian casualties, including 33,600 American, 16,000 UN allied, 415,000 South Korean, and 520,000 North Korean dead. There were also an estimated 900,000 Chinese casualties. Half of Korea's industry had been destroyed and a third of all homes. Moreover, for all the lives lost and the bitter sacrifices made, the century's 'nastiest' conflict had resolved little, if anything. The Cold War continued apace. In his nationwide radio and television address on 26 July, President Eisenhower warned the American people: 'We have won an armistice on a single battlefield, not peace in our world. We may not now relax nor cease our quest.'

Blake's debriefing at the War Office, on 29 April, a week after his triumphant return to England was, with the benefit of hindsight, perfunctory and utterly inadequate. After having his credentials checked by the frock-coated head porter in his gold-braided hat at the front entrance, he made his way into the imposing building, with its seven floors and a thousand rooms, and headed for Room 070 on the ground floor. It was allocated to SIS just as Room 050 along the corridor was available to MI5 (the Security Service) and provided a place to conduct interviews on 'neutral' ground before deciding whether to allow individuals access to Head Office on Broadway.

In the first morning's debriefing, the two interrogators ranged over the circumstances of Blake's initial arrest – his transportation to the prison camp, conditions on the notorious Death March, and then, most critically, his interrogation by his North Korean captors. Blake's answers appeared to satisfy the SIS officers. They were especially gratified that he and his junior, Norman Owen, had managed to destroy all secret documents and codes at the embassy in Seoul before they were led away by soldiers.

The following morning he returned to Room 070 for the second round of questioning and this time, his inquisitors were keen to establish what intelligence material Blake had managed to obtain during his time in captivity, or on his way back to freedom on the Trans-Siberian railway, connecting Russia, China and Korea. They bemoaned the fact that Blake had not thought to bring back a small sample of Siberian soil. Had he done so, they told him, they might have been able to ascertain whether the Russians had carried out any atomic tests in the area. Blake had offered the two men his shoes, in case any soil had remained on the soles, but they told him that would not be necessary.

After just four hours of questioning over two days, Blake's interviewers felt nothing was untoward and their job was done. He was told to report at Head Office on the following Monday.

The laxity of Blake's debriefing seems all the more surprising because, after the defection of Burgess and Maclean, there had been a great deal of pressure, especially from the Americans, for the UK government to tighten up its security and vetting procedures. In October 1951, the Attlee Cabinet accepted the idea of 'positive vetting' in principle and, when Winston Churchill was returned to power, his administration quickly introduced it, in January 1952. The task of the new PV (Positive Vetting) section was not just to stringently evaluate new recruits to SIS, but also to undertake periodical checks on existing members. Blake had spent nearly three years in the hands of the Koreans and the Chinese, with the Russians' interrogators suspected to be never far away. Was four hours of relatively gentle probing really long enough to discover whether or not he was beholden to his former captors?

Sir James 'Jack' Easton, a former Air Commodore in the RAF, was Vice Chief of SIS in that period. 'I don't think at the time that anyone really thought there would have been efforts to turn people [in the camps],' he recalled. 'If it had been an Iron Curtain country it would have different, but we used to regard North Korea as a bit primitive and unsophisticated, if you like, and one wouldn't have suspected them of doing anything.'

On his first day back at Head Office, Blake was ushered straight up to the 'holy of holies', C's office on the fourth floor of the cramped old building with its rabbit warren of corridors and rooms. C, the Chief of the Service, was Major-General John Alexander Sinclair, former Director of Military Intelligence in the Second World War, who had only recently taken up the reins at Broadway. Blake had previously

met Sinclair just once, in August 1948, on the eve of his departure for
Korea. On the strength of that brief meeting he had formed a good
impression of the tall, commanding figure with a pleasant, thoughtful
manner, and known to his staff as 'Sinbad'.

On this occasion, Sinclair listened sympathetically while Blake elab-
orated on some of the more harrowing moments of his time in Korea.
He assured the young officer that he would shortly be found a new
post but that, this time, it would be at home, at Head Office. In the
meantime he was told he could take several months' compassionate
leave in order to put the Korean ordeal behind him.

Jack Easton also felt he should commiserate with the young officer
over his gruelling ordeal, and asked him to come up to his office for
a chat a few days after his formal debriefing. It was the first and only
time he met Blake:

> I remember a bearded young man coming in through the door,
> and I noticed a slight accent in his voice, which made me think he
> didn't sound like someone of British origin.

> It made me have a further discussion about the policy of
> recruiting people like Blake, who I thought might have a doubtful
> background.

> I had always thought – and I had expressed this to my colleagues,
> so this isn't entirely in retrospect – that it wasn't good policy to
> bring in from the 'outside' a person who might make an excellent
> *agent away from the office,* but who should never, if his background
> allegiance to Britain was in any doubt, have been allowed in as a
> member of staff.

Whatever doubts Easton may have harboured about Blake, he did
not act on them. Indeed, he would have been going against the grain
of opinion at Broadway where Blake was fêted as a hero. Here was

a man, even if he was not 'one of their own', who had stoically and courageously withstood the worst the Communists could throw at him.

With compassionate leave to enjoy, Blake spent some of his accumulated salary on a Ford Anglia car and set off on a series of trips around Europe. First, he took his mother, his sister Elizabeth and her new husband on a three-week holiday to Spain. Then the party headed for Holland, where they prepared to spend some time with Aunt Truss in Rotterdam. Blake, however, had more pressing matters to attend to: the time had arrived for that crucial meeting with his Russian handler.

The two men met on the morning of Saturday, 11 July, in the tranquil setting of a small park not far from the classically elegant eighteenth-century mansions that dominated the street of Lann van Meerdervoort, in The Hague. Blake, new to the business of betrayal, was nervous, but the Russian approached the meeting with a degree of sanguinity: he was a veteran of such clandestine encounters, an experienced Cold War operator.

Nikolai Borisovich Rodin, a 45-year-old Muscovite, was better known to SIS by his pseudonym Korovin. He was certain – or as certain as you ever could be in the espionage business – that he had not been followed on the way to the park. His colleagues would often bemoan his lackadaisical approach to tradecraft, borne out of natural arrogance and a certain complacency after years in the job, but on this occasion he had taken the utmost care to ensure that his arrival in the Dutch city had gone unnoticed. The Russian had to be careful: SIS and MI5 had him in their sights because of his years serving under diplomatic cover in London, and his role in the flight of Burgess and Maclean on the SS *Falaise* in 1950. Outward appearance and behaviour may have marked him down as the stereotypical, ruthless Russian *apparatchik*, but behind the imperiousness he could be charming, when required. On this occasion, he knew he needed to be patient and considerate to cement the deal with this new recruit.

Blake was, at least, on territory he knew well, having lived with his

family at the nearby seaside resort of Scheveningen in the 1930s. As
he took his place on the bench beside the KGB officer, families from
the affluent, somewhat sedate neighbourhood in adjoining streets had
yet to emerge in force for the weekend's tasks and pleasures. One or
two customary walkers passed by the two spies and, on the other side
of the square, two young mothers kept watch over their children, who
were playing on the grass. If anyone had cast more than just a cursory
glance towards the two men, they would have noticed that they both
appeared preoccupied by copies of the previous day's edition of the
Nieuwe Rotterdamse Courant, one of Holland's leading daily newspapers.
The headline in black type across the front-page lead story read '*Beria
afgezet en uit de partij gestoten*' – 'Beria deposed and expelled from the
party'.

Putting aside any concerns about the power struggle underway in
Moscow, the KGB officer was keen to establish a *modus operandi* with his
new recruit for their clandestine meetings once they were both back
in London. He also wanted to hear what sort of information Blake
thought he could realistically provide about the counter-espionage
activities of SIS. Rodin was greatly encouraged by Blake's account of
what had happened since April, relieved at how easily his new agent
had survived the debriefing and encouraged by his meeting with C.
It gave him every reason to believe that he now had a committed and
capable mole in place for the long-term. He was especially interested
in one particular piece of information Blake was able to impart.

In the years after the war, with the drawing down of the Iron Curtain,
SIS had found it increasingly difficult to penetrate the Soviet Union
and its satellite states by means of agents on the ground. The focus
had increasingly shifted to more technical methods of intelligence
gathering, in particular the tapping of telephone landlines in Soviet
territory. A new department had been created: Section Y, where the
material obtained could be better stored and where an army of trans-
lators could sit and decipher it. It had been indicated to Blake that a
post for him in Section Y was one of the options likely to be discussed

while he was away on leave. It would put him right at the centre of the Service's newest line of work and he was sure that would suit his KGB masters. Rodin was similarly enthused.

The two men agreed to meet again in early October, by which time Blake would have been back at work for a month and would have been able to assess the possibilities. This time, though, Rodin advised him that their meeting would have to be in London. To convene again in Holland would entail both of them taking two days away from England, which might alert serious suspicion if Rodin was successfully tracked. London might appear the more dangerous terrain, but Rodin knew the capital intimately and was confident he could evade any watchers and set up a secure rendezvous. They fixed the day and the place – Belsize Park underground station. Rodin left the park to make his way back circuitously through the country and on to the ferry bound for England.

Blake also took every precaution on the trip back to his Ford Anglia, walking further down the lengthy Lann van Meerdervoort, past shops, offices and houses, before turning down some side streets to reclaim his vehicle. When leaving the city, he maintained this vigilance deciding not to return to Rotterdam by the motorway route and instead taking a trip down memory lane by taking Delftweg, the road by the canal on which he had cycled many times as a boy.

He was mightily relieved. Doubts about the momentous step he was taking still remained, as they always would. It was the nature of betrayal never to rest easy, always to be dogged by that feeling of guilt, but his path of duplicity was now firmly plotted, and the sense of adventure he had always craved would permanently accompany him in the weeks and months to come.

Later in the summer, Blake invited his fellow captive Jean Meadmore to stay with him in Radlett for a week before the two of them embarked on a journey through the 'Garden of France', the Loire Valley, where they visited the vineyards and toured a selection of the hundreds of stunning *châteaux* that adorn the region. Throughout, he was in good spirits, betraying no sign of the momentous step he had taken in Korea. 'He was the same old George,' remembered Meadmore.

Then, on 1 September, it was back to work for SIS, and the beginning of his traitorous activities for the Soviet foreign intelligence service: 'I still viewed my SIS colleagues as fellow workers but my thought processes now worked on two levels – the level of normal human contact, but also the other, impersonal level, where I was out to frustrate any operations directed against the Soviet Union.'

Blake moved out of the cramped offices of Broadway and across St James's Park into more spacious accommodation in the stately, John Nash-inspired Georgian house at No. 2 Carlton Gardens, just round the corner from the Foreign Secretary at No. 1. The SIS building was the former home of Lord Kitchener and had been seriously damaged in 1940 as a result of a fire caused by an incendiary bomb that fell in the garden, and the house became uninhabitable for several years. When Blake walked in through the imposing green double doors to start work in Section Y, he found faded elegance. Despite the war damage, the 'monumental' interior, with its chandeliered marble entrance hall and majestically curving staircase with wrought-iron gilded banisters remained largely intact and still cast its spell on any visitor.

It was soon clear to Blake that Section Y was the gleaming new weapon in SIS's intelligence-gathering armoury, with a crucial, technical role. It was borne out of necessity because, by the early 1950s, options for gleaning information about the intentions of the enemy had significantly narrowed. Moscow's tight grip on all the territory behind the Iron Curtain made the job of running agents more difficult, while defectors were becoming less frequent. Secret photoreconnaissance flights by high-altitude British and American planes over Soviet satellite countries had started, but were technically hazardous and still felt to be too politically risky. In addition to all this, Moscow had carried out radical reforms of its communications following intelligence gathered in late 1948 from one of its US moles.

William Weisband worked at the heart of America's code-breaking facility as a cipher clerk in the Army Security Agency. Among other things, Weisband had informed his KGB masters about *Venona*, the West's single most important intelligence gathering activity against the Soviet Union. It was the *Venona* intercepts that revealed the network of Soviet atomic spies, some of whom had infiltrated the Manhattan Project. After Weisband's information, Moscow reformed its coding practices and changed its radio-operating procedures to make Western interception more difficult. They made one further alteration which frustrated US and British intelligence: to make their signals more secure, they moved the vast majority from wireless to landline, both above and below ground.

While adopting these defensive measures, Soviet technical experts continued to innovate and explore all manner of new ways to spy on their Western adversaries. Bugging devices of a new, unfamiliar type were found in the American Embassy in Moscow in January and September 1952, which caused great consternation in Downing Street. Churchill, fearful that Britain would be the next target, urged his Defence Minister, Earl Alexander of Tunis: 'Pray take all necessary action with MI5 and "C" and please keep me informed.' Five days later on 14 October, having been briefed in more detail, he wrote again to his minister, saying: 'This is most important. It shows how far the Soviets have got in this complex sphere. Please keep me constantly informed.'

Churchill always took a great interest in intelligence gathering and its methods, and had no hesitation in pursuing whatever means it took to get on level terms with, and ahead of, the enemy. He listened carefully to advice from senior SIS officers, who convinced him that the future of espionage lay in the technical field, and promptly sanctioned the development of offensive bugging equipment for the United Kingdom's own use.

By the time Blake began work in Carlton Gardens, Section Y was a hive of activity, already overcoming the obstacle of the Soviets' move to the landline telephone and telegraph cables. The man behind the

section's burgeoning workload was a bright and creative young intelligence officer named Peter Lunn. He was a slim, quietly spoken man
with a pronounced lisp, whose grey, receding hair made him appear
older than thirty-eight, but there was nothing hesitant about the attitude or approach of a man whose athleticism and courage won him
the captaincy of the British Winter Olympic skiing team in 1936. Blake,
who would remain in his orbit for the next five years, greatly respected
the Old Etonian: 'He was a zealot by nature, as he proved by everything he tackled . . . [he was] an extremely effective, hard-working and
successful intelligence officer.'

In 1949, Lunn had been SIS's Head of Station in Vienna. One
day, while combing through a sheaf of reports from a source in the
Austrian Telegraphs and Telephone Administration, he noted a
number of cables requisitioned by the Soviet Army and, linking their
HQ to important establishments in their zone of occupation, actually
ran through the British and French sectors of the city. He resolved to
tap them, believing it would equip his political and military masters
with crucial information, the sort requested by the likes of US Defence
Secretary General George Marshall, who pleaded around that time:
'I don't care what it takes, all I want is twenty-four hours' notice of a
Soviet attack.' After winning approval from his seniors in Broadway
for his scheme, Lunn recruited a team of experts to build tunnels to
enable him to tap into these underground cables.

This eavesdropping exercise, Operation Conflict, was a huge
success, as were two more that followed – Operation Sugar and
Operation Lord, the latter run from a villa in Vienna's suburbs occupied by a British Army major. Conflict had run its course by the time
Blake arrived in Y section, but the voluminous material it had gathered about Soviet operations throughout Eastern Europe was still
being translated and analysed. Sugar and Lord remained active and
would continue to do so until British and Russian forces left the city in
1955, when Austria finally regained its sovereignty. From the winter of
1953, however, the value of these tapping exercises would be rapidly

diminished – that is, once Blake got hold of their findings and began passing them straight to his Soviet controllers.

The group of characters assembled in No. 2 Carlton Gardens to transcribe, translate, interpret and administer the material pouring in from the Vienna phone taps was eclectic, not to say eccentric.

Head of Section Y was Colonel Tom Gimson, a lifelong Army man, formerly commanding officer of the Irish Guards. In those days, he was just one of a number of senior military figures who were welcomed into SIS when their careers in the Armed Forces drew naturally to a close. Gimson was highly regarded by Blake and his colleagues. Tall, handsome, and always elegantly dressed in a dark pinstripe suit, he was a man of great tact and charm. He particularly needed those qualities when dealing with his diverse, often volatile group of transcribers.

These Russian speakers were drawn from a variety of backgrounds. They might be the bi-lingual descendants of merchants and industrialists who had fled Russia after the 1917 revolution; the daughters of more recent Russian émigrés, often women of high rank, who had married Englishmen; or ex-Polish army officers, former members of their country's intelligence service which during the war had operated from London under SIS control. 'The "crazy Slavs", as we called them, were quite temperamental and the nature of the job – which required great patience, listening to sometimes indistinct passages of speech over and over again – put great strain on them,' recalled one of Blake's Y colleagues. 'Tom was very good at smoothing down feathers that Blake and I might have ruffled among the Slavs. He was a very good man, really excellent in every way.'

The other crucial figure in the office was Gimson's personal assistant, Pamela 'Pam' Peniakoff. A tall, elegant woman, she was the widow of Vladimir Peniakoff, alias 'Popski', the Belgian-born son of Russian parents who formed his own private army in the war to carry out daring commando raids on Rommel's army in the Western Desert. Still a formidable figure, with a sharp but witty tongue, Pam organised the office highly efficiently. 'Tom Gimson, a man of gentle nature himself, was, I think, a little afraid of her,' recalled Blake. 'But she was good fun and together with the three younger secretaries we formed a small working team which got on very well together.'

One of those secretaries was 20-year-old Gillian Forsyth Allan, who had joined SIS shortly after completing a secretarial course in Weybridge, Surrey, close to where she lived. She had been working in Y section for a few months before Blake appeared. Gillian, tall, dark and attractive, came from a conventional, middle-class, Home Counties family. After grammar school, she went to a domestic science college before completing her education at a finishing school in Switzerland.

She immediately observed how Korea had taken its toll on Blake. 'He was in a wild and woolly state when he got back,' she recalled. 'He seemed pretty restless. He found it difficult to settle down, liked to wander round, liked to take his shoes off, hated wearing a collar, went to sleep in the afternoons – all that sort of thing which goes with having been a prisoner. I think he found it all a little alien [in the office] at first.' Gillian and her colleagues, noticing that wearing shoes was a strain, bought Blake a pair of slippers. They also showed similar understanding towards his unusual need for sleep in the daytime.

In Korea, boredom and the need for warmth had led to Blake and his fellow prisoners sleeping for substantial parts of the day. Consequently at work in Carlton Gardens, he found it well-nigh impossible to keep his eyes open after lunch. In the storeroom next to his office, there was a bath covered over by boards. When Blake felt the urge to sleep, he would lock himself in the room, and lie down on the boards with a pile of stationery under his head as a pillow. Gillian or one of the other girls would wake him up half an hour later.

Gillian observed other curious behaviour: 'He had a nervous habit, which I learned he'd had from a child, of twisting off his sleeve buttons while he was talking. You would see him talking at a meeting, and watch as one button after another went into his pocket. It used to infuriate me, but it got much better.'

Despite Blake's odd habits, Gillian warmed to him: 'He was very charming, very nice and very considerate and very easy to work for. He took life very easily, it seemed to me; probably after being in prison for so long he didn't take it as seriously as someone else might have done. He was amusing and entertaining.'

After a few months, Blake asked Gillian out, and they would go for dinner or to the occasional play: 'I liked her a great deal and, as the feeling was mutual, our friendship, gradually and insensibly, developed into a steady relationship.'

It helped the relationship that Gillian's father and older sister also worked for 'The Firm'. Colonel Arthur Allan was a Russian expert and spoke the language fluently. He had served with the British Expeditionary Force in Russia in 1918, fighting to support the Tsarists against the Bolsheviks. Their mutual interest in Russia, allied to Blake's charm, meant that Colonel Allan approved of his daughter's liaison and her suitor became a regular guest at the family home, 'The Warren', in Weybridge.

Blake's private and professional lives were starting to take shape. So, too, was his 'other' life, because he had wasted no time in passing every secret he could lay his hands on to his new Soviet controller.

On a dank, misty evening at the end of October, Sergei Aleksandrovich Kondrashev walked in circumspect fashion through residential streets a few minutes' north of Belsize Park underground station in North London. These were nervous moments for the 30-year-old KGB operative. With only two years experience in the Soviet foreign intelligence directorate, he had been asked to take over the running of one of Moscow Centre's prize assets – *Agent Diomid*, alias George Blake.

The man from Zagorsk had only arrived in London for the first time a couple of weeks earlier. His diplomatic cover was that of First Secretary responsible for cultural relations, which could mean anything from acquiring tickets for VIPs, to arranging the tour of the renowned violinist David Oistrakh. Moscow Centre had made the

decision to make Kondrashev Blake's controller. Nikolai Borisovich
Rodin, the man who had met him in Otpor and then at the follow-up
meeting in The Hague in July, was too well known to British coun-
terintelligence, and KGB bosses were keen to protect their valuable
new source as best they could. Kondrashev, an unknown, was a safer
bet. He had spent the weeks before coming to England poring over
the *Diomid* file, being briefed on British surveillance techniques, and
studying street maps of London. Everything was now in place for the
first meeting with his charge.

    Blake had left Carlton Gardens at 6 p.m. and then headed for the
West End, where he walked through Soho before reaching Oxford
Street. There, he stepped into one of the ubiquitous ABC teashops
– that 'sinister strand in English catering', in the words of George
Orwell – where he was comforted by the sheer ordinariness of his
surroundings. 'I had plenty of time . . . I drank a cup of tea and ate a
cake. It did not taste particularly nice, but then I didn't have much of
an appetite,' was the spy's recollection. 'All the time I was watching to
see if I was being followed, though there was no particular reason why
I should be. I felt in my inside pocket if the folded paper I was going
to hand over was still there.' Blake then left the café and walked three-
quarters of a mile south to Charing Cross underground station. The
precautions continued; he waited until everyone had got on before
catching the train at the last minute. Then, at the next stop – Leicester
Square – he jumped off just as the doors were closing, let two more
trains pass, and finally caught the third, all the while searching around
him for anyone who looked dubious.

    At Belsize Park, as he walked away from the station and left the
crowds behind, the tension eased. 'The further I went, the quieter it
became. A man came slowly out of the fog walking towards me, also
carrying a newspaper in his left hand.' Anyone seeing Blake emerge
slowly from the enveloping gloom and approaching Kondrashev would
have been reminded of a scene from *The Third Man*. Kondrashev
greeted Blake warmly, and they then walked up the near-deserted

street a short distance before Blake handed him the folded piece of paper, which the Russian slipped into his pocket. On it were the first fruits of his betrayal. It contained a preparatory list of all the telephone tapping operations SIS was conducting in Vienna, as well as details of microphones installed in Soviet and Eastern Bloc buildings across Western Europe.

If his meeting with Rodin in The Hague three months earlier had been akin to passing an initiation ceremony, this one, for Blake, felt like the definitive moment of commitment: 'Strangely enough, this gave me a feeling of relief very much like the experience of landing safely after my first parachute jump. An exhilarated feeling of achievement which comes whenever one has overcome fears and apprehensions.'

Blake briefly explained the contents of the paper to Kondrashev as they walked through the streets of Hampstead, before they turned around and headed back towards the main road. For the young Russian spy, there was a growing sense of relief. He had been reassured that Blake was a genuine mole, but it was still possible that his informant was a deliberate plant by SIS, and that the material was 'chicken feed'. Blake's attitude and words convinced the young Russian and, by the end of their encounter, he felt far less anxious. After fifteen to twenty minutes, they parted company after arranging to meet again in a month's time, in another part of London, and also deciding on alternative dates and places in case of emergency.

Blake headed back to the flat in Charleville Mansions, close to Baron's Court tube station, that he shared with his mother. Over a meal and a glass of wine he relaxed and felt the satisfaction of a job well done: 'My mother is a very good cook and this supper remained in my memory, not only because I liked the food, but mostly because the room seemed particularly cosy and secure after the damp, foggy night outside and the dangers of the clandestine meeting I had just lived through.'

He and Kondrashev would continue to meet every three or four weeks, usually close to an underground station in the suburbs. At their next meeting, the Russian provided him with a Minox camera, a bulky device that he nonetheless kept in his back pocket at all times while in the office. It enabled him to work more easily, photographing vital documents rather than attempting to smuggle sheaves of paper out of the building. He would usually wait until lunchtime, lock the door of his office, and then set to work: 'It became automatic. I was almost reduced to a mystical state, when I was the eye and the finger.'

Every three weeks, Y section compiled a lengthy bulletin of its activities, usually amounting to thirty or forty typewritten pages. This paper was graded top security and distributed to the War Office, the Air Ministry, the Joint Intelligence Bureau, the Foreign Office and the CIA in Washington. Blake now made sure a copy also went to the KGB via Kondrashev.

In only their second or third meeting, in early December 1952, Blake handed over a hugely damaging Minox film of a ninety-page report entitled 'Banner 54/1', which contained a compilation of the tapped calls between Austria and Hungary, obtained via the tunnels in Vienna.

Blake's Soviet masters were delighted. He had settled comfortably into the routine of treachery, passing on every document of interest that came across his desk, and though the secrets of the Vienna tunnels were an impressive breakthrough for Moscow Centre, *Agent Diomid* was soon to deliver a far bigger prize.

11

Secrets of the Tunnel

In December 1953, Tom Gimson's office at No. 2 Carlton Gardens was the venue for a four-day conference hosted by SIS with the joint participation of the CIA. Gimson's deputy, George Blake, was the secretary and minute-taker, as intelligence officers and their technical advisers – nine from SIS, five from the CIA – sought to put the finishing touches to an audacious eavesdropping scheme, which surely embodied the spirit of those SOE operations Churchill had so relished in World War Two.

It was codenamed Operation Stopwatch or Gold (the British gave it the former title, the Americans the latter). Its purpose was nothing less than to dig a secret tunnel in a Berlin suburb that would run from the American sector into the Soviet Zone, enabling the Western intelligence agencies to tap the underground cables through which the Soviet military command in Germany communicated with Moscow and all points east. It would clearly build on the work done and lessons learned in Vienna, but this subterranean passage was on an altogether different scale to the short digs from house to street in the Austrian capital.

Ever since 1951 when Peter Lunn and his colleagues decided to share the secrets of their tunnelling exploits, the CIA had been working flat out to develop a scheme that would emulate, and hopefully surpass, that success. The man tasked with overseeing their technical operations was the one who did most of the talking that Friday afternoon in December.

Forty-five-year-old Virginian Frank Byron Rowlett was one of the outstanding code breakers of his generation, spoken of in the same breath as Britain's Alan Turing. A mathematician and chemist by training, in 1930, aged twenty-one, he became the first junior cryptanalyst in the US Army Signal Intelligence Department in Washington. Rowlett was a key member of the team that cracked the Japanese diplomatic code and cipher communications known as 'Purple' in the Second World War, and CIA Director Allen Dulles had eagerly poached him from the rival National Security Agency in 1952 to become chief of Staff D (intelligence intercepts). Rowlett was quiet and softly spoken, a southern country boy at heart, who preferred to work in the background. His calm authority and air of serenity earned him the sobriquet 'Our Father', although the head of CIA station in Berlin, the wisecracking Bill Harvey, would also refer to him teasingly as 'Mountain Boy'.

Among the papers Rowlett had in his possession that day, to which he regularly referred, was one dated 16 September, headlined 'Field Project Outline' and labelled 'TOP SECRET – Security Information Classification'. It was for the eyes of Allen Dulles and a very few others. Essentially it was Rowlett's blueprint for the Berlin tunnel. It did not mention the location by name, but that had already been decided. It would start in Rudow, a rural area of the US Sector southwest of Berlin. The three target cables ran under a ditch on the west side of Schönefelder Chausee in the Soviet Sector in Altglienicke. In his memo, Rowlett explained that the tunnel would need to be some 1,800 feet long, burrowing underneath a heavily patrolled border so that nearly half the length of it would be in Soviet territory. The rewards would be worth the effort: 'It has been established that these cables carry Soviet military, Security Service and diplomatic telephone and telegraph traffic to and from various Soviet headquarters in Germany and in certain instances between those headquarters and Moscow.'

At a jittery moment in the Cold War when the people of Berlin, and the rest of the world, feared a sudden, massive attack by Red Army forces, this was music to Dulles' ears. Now, there would be the opportunity to learn full details of the deployment and strength of the Soviet ground forces, information about their air forces in East Germany and Poland, and perhaps even intelligence of the use of East German uranium for the Soviet atomic bomb. Much, too, might be gleaned on a more personal level by hearing the chatter between the Soviet military elite and their political controllers. Who was up and who was down in the Kremlin hierarchy after the death of Stalin, nine months earlier? Who should the Western leaders really be talking to?

But Rowlett's September memo had thrown up a couple of significant problems. First, how were they to hide such a massive engineering job requiring large amounts of equipment and labour? Several thousand tons of soil would have to be removed and disposed of without alerting suspicion. 'It is reasonable and possible for the US forces in Berlin to construct a number of warehouses within the bounds of the US Sector. Although such constructions will attract attention, the fact remains that knowledge of what transpires within these buildings is a matter not beyond control,' Rowlett had reassured Dulles. One story the CIA was working on to tell the suspicious East Germans was that the warehouses constituted a new US radar station.

Secondly, there was a physical and technical challenge right at the heart of the scheme. 'Upon completion of the passageway,' wrote Rowlett, 'specialists will begin work on the critical and hazardous task of constructing the tap chamber and the opening of the cables. The element of hazard is particularly acute due to the fact that the target cables lie only twenty-eight inches from the surface of the earth.'

Rowlett's right-hand man at the table in Tom Gimson's office that day was Carl Nelson, the CIA's chief communications officer in Germany, and a highly capable electrical engineer. Nelson had previously been stationed in Vienna and was familiar with the work there of Peter Lunn and his team.

On the British side, the three senior officers round the table were George Kennedy Young, Director of Requirements, later to be Vice Chief of the Service; Ian Innes 'Tim' Milne, former head of Section V (counter-espionage); and Stewart Mackenzie, a future Controller of Western Hemisphere operations. Young was SIS's leader at the meeting and the tunnel was a project that entirely suited his adventurous instincts.

He had started his working life as a journalist on *The Glasgow Herald,* but by the end of the Second World War, the Scotsman had switched careers and become an experienced and resourceful military intelligence officer. After a brief return to journalism in Berlin after the war, Young was lured back permanently to intelligence, and SIS. His rise was meteoric. He preceded Peter Lunn as head of the Vienna station before returning to Broadway in 1949 to become head of SIS's economic requirements section (R6). In 1951, he was on the move again, appointed controller of operations in the 'Middle East area'. Here, he was a key figure in the successful Anglo-American plot to instigate a coup to overthrow the Iranian leader Mohammed Mossadeq, who had nationalised the Anglo-Iranian oil company and subsequently severed all diplomatic relations with Britain.

Young felt spies could and should be proactive, and he was in a group of so-called 'robber barons' whose swashbuckling instinct was to take the Cold War to the enemy. As Director of Requirements, however, he accepted that elaborate and expensive attempts to put agents into Soviet territory – places like the Baltic States and Poland – had failed dismally. Moscow Centre knew about all these operations and had wrapped up the vast majority. In his efforts to find high-grade intelligence on Russian intentions and policy-making, the tunnel appealed to his practical, as well as enterprising, side.

Although they had participated in previous meetings, the two main drivers of the whole project were not present, being in Berlin that

day, preoccupied with the task of running their large bases there.
After his triumphs in Vienna, Peter Lunn had a brief posting to Berne
before his move to Berlin in the summer of 1953. His arrival, just as
preparations for the tunnel were gathering pace, was far from coinci-
dental. William King Harvey, his opposite number, had moved in as
Chief of the CIA's Berlin Base six months earlier. He and his operatives
had done much of the early intelligence spadework for the tunnel,
including recruiting agents in the *Ostpost*, the East Berlin post office,
who provided information on the most sensitive cables.

Harvey, who had started his intelligence career at the FBI before
falling foul of the mercurial J. Edgar Hoover, was coarse in manner
and appearance and rather over-dedicated to Martini. He was nonetheless a brilliant field operator and had thrown himself into the tunnel
project with customary gusto – so much so that colleagues would come
to christen it 'Harvey's Hole'.

Blake's minutes of that meeting revealed the potential scale of the
intelligence that the committee believed might accrue from the Berlin
tunnel – and the huge resources needed to process it. 'Cables 151 and
152 are believed to contain 81 Russian speech circuits, of which 19 are
voice-frequency telegraph circuits,' he wrote. 'Using present British
experience as a basis it was estimated that 81 circuits would produce
162 reels a day, each lasting 2.5 hours. The processing of these reels
would require 81 transcribers, 30 collators, 27 cardists, 10 people in
the Signals Section, and 10 Russian typists, making a total of 158.'

Plenty of extra manpower would be required and the committee
did not want to restrict selection to those with a Russian or Slav background. Blake's notes read: 'British personnel who had acquired a
knowledge of Russian in universities had proved, in practice, to be
equally as good at transcribing as native Russians. This would enlarge
the recruiting field and diminish security risk.' It was agreed that the
handling of encrypted material would be divided between the National
Security Agency (NSA) in America and General Communications
Headquarters (GCHQ) in Britain.

This would by no means be the final meeting on the subject of the tunnel. In conclusion, Blake noted: 'The discussions were of an exploratory nature. It was agreed that a further meeting could be held on or about 1 February 1954 at which it will be necessary to come to firm conclusions on the future conduct of the operation.'

As soon as the conference finished that afternoon, Rowlett flew back to Frankfurt, where he brought General Lucian Truscott, the CIA's Chief of Mission in Germany, and Bill Harvey up to date with the latest developments.

After his minutes had been typed up and were ready for limited distribution among CIA and SIS officials, Blake retained the yellow-green carbon copy of the seven-page document for himself. He then arranged for a meeting with Kondrashev. Months before even a sod of earth had been dug from the ground at Altglienicke, the Berlin tunnel was fatally compromised.

On Monday, 18 January 1954 the duties of a cultural attaché came first for Sergei Kondrashev. It was his task to escort Soviet chess grandmasters David Bronstein, Alexander Tolush and Vladimir Alatortsev to the airport for their return flight to Moscow at the end of a politically embarrassing three-week tour of Britain, which had seen them fail to perform at the standard set by the Soviet Chess Federation. They had been vanquished, as it happens, by a British intelligence man – Irish-born Conel Hugh O'Donel Alexander, chief cryptanalyst at GCHQ. Having seen off the grandmasters, Kondrashev spent some hours ensuring he was not under surveillance before boarding a double decker bus.

A couple of stops later Blake joined Kondrashev on the top deck and, knowing he had little time, gave the Russian a brief résumé of the contents of the package he was handing over. Both men felt distinctly nervous. 'I told him in broad outline about the Berlin project and pointed out to him the great secrecy with which the operation was surrounded, and the necessity for taking particular care that any counter-measures the Soviet authorities might take should look natural and not create the suspicion that they were aware of what was afoot,' Blake recalled.

Kondrashev, too, was not his usual, calm self: 'I slipped the envelope into the inside pocket of my jacket. I was very tense. I knew how important this thing was and I felt it was burning into my chest.'

Kondrashev alighted several stops later at a prearranged location, where he was picked up by a fellow resident spy and driven back to Kensington Palace Gardens. As soon as he began to examine Blake's minutes, he realised he had struck gold: 'When I read it in the Embassy I was flabbergasted. This was explosive material. I could not believe my eyes.' He sent a coded cable to Moscow that night, reporting that the meeting with *Diomid* had taken place satisfactorily. Such was the importance of the material that it was despatched immediately via the diplomatic courier, sealed in a special steel case and addressed directly to the Head of the First Chief Directorate (foreign intelligence).

Three weeks later, on 12 February, Kondrashev submitted a fuller report to Moscow Centre under his codename, *Rostov*, summing up the importance of the information Blake had passed on about both the Vienna and proposed Berlin tunnels. His preface to the section about Berlin contained a sentence of monumental understatement: 'The information on a planned intercept operation against internal telephone lines on GDR territory is of interest.'

Interesting it certainly was. As a participant in further SIS and CIA meetings throughout 1954 and into 1955, Blake continued to keep his masters in the Kremlin informed about progress with the tunnel. CIA Director Dulles gave formal approval for the project just two days after the Blake/Kondrashev meeting on the London bus. The warehouse buildings – one for main operations, a kitchen-dining room for staff, and a structure to house three diesel-driven generators – were then erected in the summer. The dig commenced at the end of August.

Bill Harvey was content that the East Germans had no clue as to what was really taking place on the site. A display of fake radar and electronic intelligence gear was mounted on top of the warehouse, helping to fool the Communists into thinking it was signals intercept equipment aimed at the Soviet airport at Schönefeld.

That autumn, the US Army Corps of Engineers began their construction work from under the main operations building. Essentially, the tunnel they were putting together was constructed as a long tube, using hundreds of circular sections of heavy steel plates specifically cast back home in America and tested rigorously in the desert in New Mexico. Only six days into the excavation, however, potential disaster loomed when it was discovered that the water table was much higher than first thought. There was now serious doubt about whether the tunnel could be built at all as it would lie too close to the surface for safety. Harvey and Rowlett were advised a shallower tunnel could be dug, just nine feet below ground rather than sixteen. Work resumed, and the horizontal section of the tunnel was eventually completed on 28 February 1955. It was 1,476 feet in length; 3,100 tons of soil was removed, 125 tons of steel plate and 1,000 cubic yards of grout were used.

Now it was the turn of the British. It was the job of the Royal Engineers to build a vertical shaft from the end of the tunnel to the target cables. This was a tricky task, given the nature of the sandy soil of Berlin, which threatened to collapse everything on top of the diggers. An inventive solution came in the form of a contraption called 'The Mole' – a bottomless steel box, the top of which was made up of a series of sideways cutters interspersed with closable rotating blades. When placed vertically in the tunnel, the soil could then be removed slot by slot before the whole device was levered upwards. That work began on 10 March, and it took eighteen days to reach and expose the cables. Then the British continued with the final, most sensitive part of the whole operation – the tap itself.

The biggest worry now was that the Soviets might notice a slight reduction in power as the tap took place but two jointers from Dollis Hill fashioned what was known in the trade as a 'high-impedance' tap – drawing off as little of the signal as possible – without a hitch in a delicate, painstaking four-hour operation.

The first working tap took place on 11 May; intelligence would flow copiously and continuously for the following eleven months.

Thanks to Blake, of course, the KGB had always known the tunnel was coming. They knew almost exactly to the day when the enemy would start eavesdropping. This gave the chiefs at Moscow Centre a dilemma: if they altered or manipulated the nature of the traffic going through cables 150, 151 and 152, the Americans and British would surely realise before long that something was amiss. Did they want to risk compromising the mole who had brought them the secrets of the tunnel – their eyes and ears at the heart of British intelligence?

In the early months of 1954 there had been much talk of treachery in the corridors and offices of Broadway and Carlton Gardens. With his own traitorous activities now underway, Blake was increasingly anxious. His new unease was first prompted in early April by a high-profile Soviet defection.

Vladimir Petrov was a KGB employee based at the Soviet Embassy in Canberra, Australia, who feared he was about to be recalled to the Soviet Union, where, in all likelihood, he would be 'purged' and shot as an ally of the late but not lamented Security Chief, Lavrentiy Beria. When Petrov's wife, Evdokia, tried to join him, two KGB officials seized her, bundling her onto a plane at Sydney with the intention of taking her back to Moscow. The striking picture of the rough handling of this clearly distressed woman by two Communist 'heavies' travelled all round the world. When the aircraft landed for refuelling at Darwin, officers from the Australian Security Intelligence Organisation (ASIO) were on hand to intercept the kidnapping attempt, and freed Evdokia from the clutches of her KGB abductors.

The problem for Blake – and for Anthony Blunt and Kim Philby,

those other KGB moles still in position in England – was that the
Petrovs had worked in the Lubyanka for years before moving to
Australia. They were familiar with the workings of the KGB in France,
Germany and England, and they knew, even if they did not have the
codenames or any other specific details, that there had been a network
of agents in place in London since the early days of the war.

SIS quickly began to liaise with their counterparts in ASIO, sensing
that the Petrovs might have valuable information about Burgess and
Maclean, and even Kim Philby, then still under suspicion of being
'The Third Man'.

Soon, fresh questions were being asked in the House of Commons.
Foreign Secretary Selwyn Lloyd was understandably cautious in his
response: 'The interrogation is at present in progress, but such information about Messrs Burgess and Maclean which has so far been
elicited is of a limited and general character, and it is not yet certain
whether it is based on Petrov's personal knowledge or on heresay. I will
consider making a further statement in due course.'

Blake had only entered the fray relatively recently, but could the
Petrovs have something on him? 'The Burgess and Maclean affair,
not unnaturally, formed a frequent subject of conversation in SIS and
Foreign Office circles and, frankly speaking, it was a subject I did not
enjoy,' he recalled. 'It was too near the bone and made me feel very
uncomfortable. I tried to avoid it as much as possible.'

Writing in his diary, Housing Minister Harold Macmillan revelled in
the discomfiture of the Soviet Union, but calculated that the episode
might have mixed consequences. The entry for Wednesday, 21 April
read: 'The newspapers are full of the Petrov drama. The account of
how the Russian thugs tried to terrorise her and were disarmed at the
airport by the Australian police is more like a piece of popular fiction
than real life . . . It won't make the Soviet Government any more
tractable at Geneva. I think it will have a good effect at home, where
people tend to forget how horrible Communism really is.'

Blake was, in fact, one of those who made his way to the Swiss city, where high-level talks on securing the future of Korea and ending the war between the French and the Communist Viet Minh in Indochina were taking place. He was not there as an accredited delegate but at the invitation of SIS's Head of Station in Berne, who wanted Blake and his colleagues from Y section to bug the phones of the Soviet and Chinese delegations.

Their mission was a technical success, but it was completely unproductive in terms of the intelligence produced. The conversations of the political leaders were surprisingly discreet on the matters that counted, so the spies were unable to offer British Foreign Secretary Anthony Eden any additional leverage in his negotiations. Instead, the Chinese delegates and Soviet leaders spent most of the time on the phone talking to their wives and children. Blake, listening in to the conversations of Soviet Foreign Minister Molotov, discovered him to be far removed from the stern, obdurate caricature painted of him in the West: 'He discussed with his wife the difficulties which their married daughter had in feeding her new baby, in which matter he sometimes tendered practical advice. He also had long talks with his 6-year-old grandson, listening patiently to his detailed accounts of what he had been doing.'

Despite the lack of useful covert knowledge, Eden concluded that Geneva was, by and large, a success: 'We had stopped an eight-year war and reduced international tension at a point of instant danger to world peace.' But he and his fellow diplomats had also stored up trouble for the future. Vietnam was granted its independence and elections promised within two years; but in a worrying echo of Korea, the country was divided in two – this time at the seventeenth parallel, with a Communist regime (Democratic Republic of Vietnam) in the North led by Ho Chi Minh, and the southern 'nation' (Republic of Vietnam) led by the Catholic Ngo Ding Diem. When Ngo – supported by Eisenhower – refused to authorise the agreed-upon elections to reunify Vietnam in 1956, his decision led to a resumption of the war. This time, the Americans took the place of the French – and their involvement would prove to be a political, military and humanitarian disaster which continues to trouble the American conscience to this very day.

As the interest over the Petrov case diminished and the hunt for the truth about Burgess and Maclean and 'The Third Man' died down for the moment, George Blake's double life continued. For relaxation he attended a weekly evening Arabic language class at London University. A male colleague from Y section had also joined the course, and after the lecture finished the two would have coffee together in a snack bar near Russell Square, or go back to Charleville Mansions, where Blake's mother would cook them dinner.

His personal life, meanwhile, was dominated by his relationship with Gillian, which was now developing apace: 'After my absence in Geneva, it became clear we were both in love and that the natural thing for us to do was to get married.' Natural perhaps, but Blake, living a most abnormal kind of existence, now found himself faced with a crucial dilemma. The unselfish option would have been to break off the relationship, however much hurt that might cause. The odds on his eventual discovery were high. Irrespective of the stresses and strains that his double life would put on a marriage, the ultimate unmasking, when it came, would have devastating emotional and social consequences for Gillian.

Blake agonised over what course of action to take: 'I made some feeble attempts to put her off by telling her that I was half-Jewish and that her father, who was the kind of Englishman who had little time for Jews, blacks and dagos, would not like this.' But Blake's antecedents did not remotely concern Gillian:

> He told me all about his background, that his father wasn't English, all the 'off-putting' side, as much as to say 'Do you still want to marry me?' It didn't bother me . . . My parents liked George very much. He was very charming and got on very well

Early in the afternoon of Tuesday 14 May 1940 the pilots of the Luftwaffe began raining down their bombs on Rotterdam. *Mary Evans/Sueddeutsche Zeitung Photo*

The aftermath of the attack: the city was reduced to smoking rubble, with 900 dead and 80,000 made homeless. *Gamma-Keystone via Getty Images*

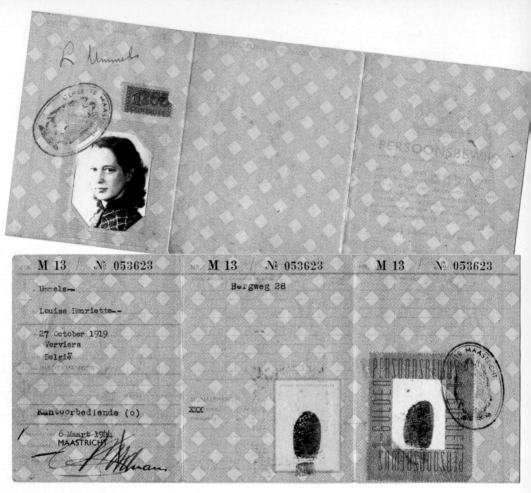

The false identity card of 23-year-old Greetje de Bie, the resistance worker who escorted Blake to safety in Belgium. Her picture was superimposed on the card, which once belonged to 22-year-old Louise Henriette Ummels. *Courtesy of Leo Van Ewijk*

RMS *Empress of Australia* – the ocean liner turned troop ship that brought Blake to Britain in January 1943. *TopFoto.co.uk*

SIS headquarters at 54 Broadway, Westminster: 'a dingy building, a warren of wooden partitions and frosted windows.'

City of Westminster Archives Centre

Iris Peake, SIS secretary and later Lady-in-Waiting to Princess Margaret. She and Blake formed a close attachment in The Hague in 1945. *Courtesy of Country Life*

Gillian Blake, leaving the divorce court in March 1967.

Getty Images

A Seoul resident walks through his shattered city. Over three months in 1950 the South Korean capital was the scene of fierce fighting.

© Bettmann/CORBIS

The freed Korean captives at Berlin airport in April 1953. *Left to right:* Blake, Bishop Alfred Cooper, Commissioner Herbert Lord, Norman Owen and Monsignor Thomas Quinlan.

CORBIS

A delighted Catherine Blake with her son after their reunion at RAF Abingdon on 22 April 1953. *Getty Images*

Blake celebrates his freedom with family and friends after thirty months in captivity. *Mirrorpix*

Charles Wheeler, who handed over command of a Royal Navy intelligence unit to Blake in Hamburg in 1946. He later became the outstanding foreign correspondent of his generation. *BBC Photo Library*

An aerial view of Berlin in the early 1950s. In the centre is the Gedächtniskirche (Kaiser Wilhelm Memorial Church), wrecked by an Allied bombing raid in 1943. For Berliners, its shattered appearance served as a memorial to the dead and a warning of the futility of war. *Popperfoto/Getty Images*

When Blake arrived in Berlin in 1955, six years before the Wall went up, there was still plenty of movement between East and West. But the conquering powers guarded their individual sectors jealously.
Time & Life Pictures/Getty Images

The Berlin Tunnel was 'discovered' by East German guards on 22 April 1956 – eleven months after the CIA and SIS began their eavesdropping operation. Blake had told the KGB about its existence at the planning stage.

Getty Images

The Soviets were determined to extract maximum propaganda value from the tunnel. Here officers show journalists the work of the West's 'nest of spies'.

Getty Images

Lord Parker of Waddington, the Lord Chief Justice *(centre)*, who was the judge at Blake's trial in May 1961. He is flanked by Lord Goddard *(left)*, his predecessor in office, and Lord Evershed, Master of the Rolls.
© *Illustrated London News Ltd/Mary Evans*

below left: Attorney General Sir Reginald Manningham-Buller QC, prosecuting counsel at Blake's trial. © *Illustrated London News Ltd/Mary Evans*

below right: Jeremy Hutchinson QC, Blake's barrister. His stirring fifty-three-minute speech of mitigation was delivered behind closed doors. © *Illustrated London News Ltd/Mary Evans*

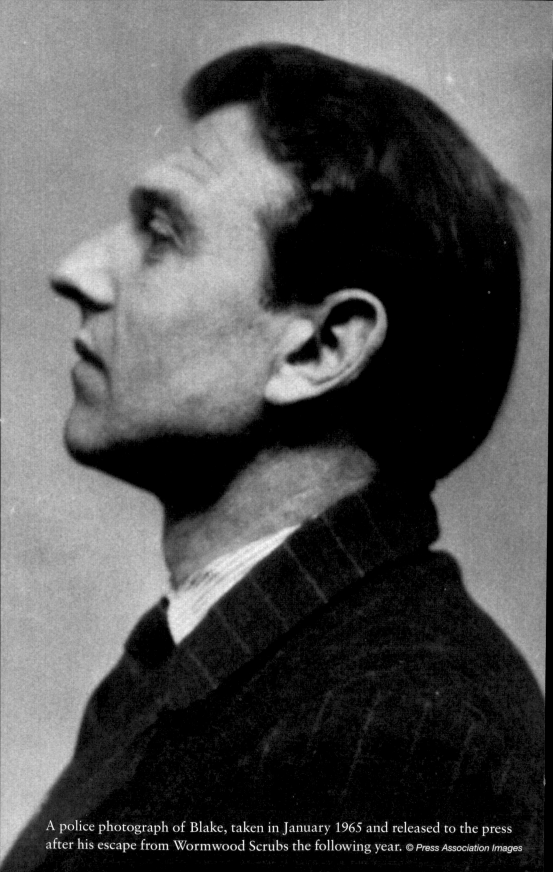

A police photograph of Blake, taken in January 1965 and released to the press after his escape from Wormwood Scrubs the following year. © *Press Association Images*

right: Pat Pottle, inveterate anti-nuclear campaigner, under arrest in 1961. The following year he would meet Blake in Wormwood Scrubs. *Getty Images*

above: Michael and Anne Randle in 1962. Four years later, they would hide Blake in their Commer van and drive him to freedom beyond the Iron Curtain. *Getty Images*

Sean Bourke, the unpredictable Irishman who devised and executed Blake's daring escape from Wormwood Scrubs. *Getty Images*

The home-made rope ladder, with knitting needles for rungs. The flower pot was one of Bourke's diversionary props, giving the impression that he was merely a visitor to Hammersmith Hospital opposite the jail.

The National Archives UK

The climax of Blake's jailbreak saw him scale the twenty-foot outer wall of the Scrubs, before jumping down into Artillery Road. *The National Archives UK*

below left: The cast-iron bars on the window of the landing in 'D' Hall were broken two days before Blake's escape. *The National Archives UK*

below right: The getaway car: a 'two tone' 1955 Humber Hawk. Police discovered it just a few days after the breakout. *CORBIS*

Blake and his mother Catherine relaxing on holiday in the Carpathian Mountains in September 1967. *Popperfoto/Getty Images*

Donald Maclean was Blake's closest friend in Moscow, a man he revered. Here Maclean *(left)* is pictured at the funeral of another of the Cambridge spies, Guy Burgess, in the summer of 1963. *© AP/Press Association Images*

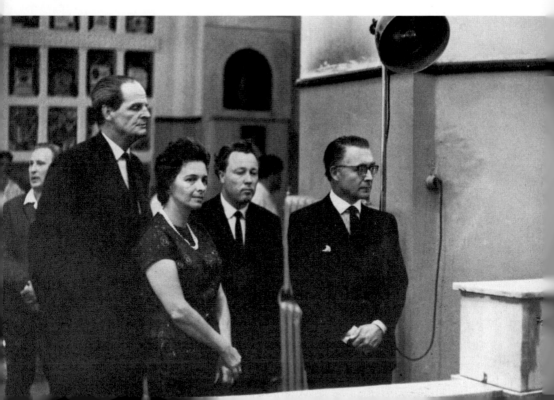

Blake and Kim Philby didn't meet until the spring of 1970. They (and their wives) were good friends – until the two men fell out over a series of photographs Philby's son released to Western newspapers. *Associated Newspapers/Rex Features*

Pat Pottle and Michael Randle outside the Old Bailey in June 1991 after their remarkable acquittal. © *Press Association Images*

Colonel George Blake
in 2001 – a traitor
to Britain, but by then
firmly established
in the hierarchy
of Moscow's
greatest agents.

with my father. I had brought George home and they had seen a
lot of him, but thought it was nothing in particular.

So I think [at first] they were rather alarmed, actually to find out it
was something after all – so was I, actually. But they never tried to
dissuade me at all. My mother suggested that perhaps I was a little
young but she was fond of George too. My father had no objections
at all.

With no obstacles in his way to seize upon, Blake squared his
conscience through moral contortionism: 'I was really in no different
position from a soldier during the war who got married before he was
sent to the front, and consoled myself that it would all work out in the
end, and nothing terrible would happen to me.'

The wedding happened in something of a hurry. In August,
Blake was told he was being posted to Berlin in the November. So
the couple became engaged in September and set the big day for
Saturday, 23 October. The marriage certificate lists the occupations
of both bride and groom as 'Government Official (Foreign Office)'.
The witnesses were Gillian's father (another 'Government Official'
– Foreign Office) and Blake's mother Catherine. The bride wore
traditional white, while Blake looked somewhat uncomfortable in a
morning suit. The Allan family, from Weybridge and beyond, filled
the aisles comfortably on their side. Apart from his mother, Blake's
sisters Adele and Elizabeth (with her husband) were present, as were
his uncle Anthony Beijderwellen and his wife from Holland, and his
old mentor in SIS, Commander Douglas Child.

'We were married in church because I wanted it,' Gillian recalled. 'I
wouldn't have been happy if we hadn't. Then I was very conventional
like that. I went to church when I could, but George was not a church-
goer in the religious sense. He loved services, but he would far rather
go to a Catholic church than anywhere else for the spectacle alone . . .
The best man at the wedding was my brother. This again showed that

besides Jean Meadmore, who was a Catholic and anyway was in New Zealand at the time, he really had no friends, though he knew a lot of people and liked a lot of people. So my brother was really "hauled in", though he and George got on very well.'

The couple spent their honeymoon in the South of France. In the event, the wedding need not have been rushed because Blake's switch to Berlin was delayed for five months. He had been lobbying for a move abroad for some time. To his 'official' employers, the reason he gave was one of ambition, wanting to gain fresh experience at the epicentre of the intelligence war but, in truth, for his real masters he had done all he usefully could from his position in Y section. In any case, the department was being reorganised and an American was to assume Blake's pivotal position as Tom Gimson's deputy.

Kondrashev and his superiors in the Kremlin were entirely content that Blake would be moving to Berlin. There, he would join SIS's biggest station, where the scope for undermining British intelligence would be even greater. The move also suited his personal circumstances; George and Gillian had moved into his mother's flat in Baron's Court after their return from honeymoon, but were yet to find a permanent home of their own.

On the world stage, as Blake prepared to leave for Germany, tensions between East and West remained as great as ever. At the end of March 1953, there was a brief flurry of optimism when Churchill learned that the new Soviet Prime Minister, Marshal Nikolai Bulganin, might be willing to participate in Four Power talks. On 29 March, Churchill told the Queen that he was seriously considering putting off his planned resignation if such face-to-face discussions took place. The following day, however, it became clear through diplomatic chan-nels that Bulganin was not willing to commit to negotiations, and, in any case, President Eisenhower still remained implacably opposed to them. Churchill's resignation went ahead as planned on 5 April. Meanwhile, Bulganin was in fact putting the finishing touches to a treaty called the Warsaw Pact, a mutual defence organisation between the Soviet Union and its seven satellite countries in Eastern Europe. It was a direct if belated response to the West's alliance, NATO, and could only increase the tensions in Berlin and, indeed, the rest of Europe.

It was into this heightened atmosphere that Blake flew on Thursday, 14 April. He was entering the playground of Cold War espionage, and would find there all manner of new opportunities for treachery.

12

Berlin

In Berlin in 1955, it seemed as if everyone was a spy, and the spies were spying for everyone. They all gathered together to practise their trade in this strangest of cities, where the Western sector – the 'Trojan Horse' of democracy – was isolated deep in the Communist heartland, menacingly encircled by 450,000 Red Army troops. At this epicentre of the Cold War, where the clash of ideology and culture was at its sharpest, the perpetual fear that a spark of trouble could lead to a conflagration hung heavy over everyone. It made for an edgy, frantic environment where suspicion, if not full-blown paranoia, was the primary emotion.

Ten years after the devastation wrought by the Russians, Blake observed that the scars were slowly healing, at least on one side of the city. West Berlin was still full of empty spaces where the ruins and rubble – 'Hitler's Mountains' – had been cleared, but starting to fill the gaps where grand, classical buildings had once stood were flat, square, functional office blocks and apartments, a remorseless tide of concrete boxes to some, but vital components of the city's new infrastructure for most.

The Tiergarten, the 600-acre park that had been the lungs of the city, retained a desolate look after its trees were chopped down and lawns dug up in 1945 by a freezing and starving population. But in 1955, the local council had just started to restore it to its former glory and a new generation of trees, shrubs and plants was taking their place.

At the end of the Kurfürstendamm, the Gedachtniskirche, with its steeple snapped off like a rotten stump, remained a potent symbol of the destruction of the city. But up and down the two and a quarter miles of the street, cafés, restaurants, cinemas and theatres throbbed with life as they had done in the 1920s, and to the pleasure seekers in the smart shops who came from the East, 'the shiny treasures in their glass cases, jewellery and handbags and shoes, seemed liked loot from a recent battle'.

This was six years before the Wall sliced through the city, and freedom of movement between East and West was still relatively straightforward. Family and friends on opposite sides of the city could visit each other, students came over to attend schools and universities, and many people crossed the border for concerts and sporting fixtures. It was not all one-way traffic from East to West, either: Berliners from the West took advantage of the extra spending power their currency offered them in the East, and would travel there for less expensive clothes, haircuts and other goods and services.

If the Western sector of Berlin was reaping the rewards of Marshall Aid and the free-market policies of the government of Konrad Adenauer, Blake could see that the Eastern sector remained a grim environment. It had been ruthlessly asset-stripped by the Soviets, who removed factories, rolling stock and generators to replace losses back home. This was still a ruined-looking landscape, with many buildings displaying gutted interiors and lacking roofs. Piles of rubble littered the streets, and the apartment blocks that survived remained pock-marked, with holes drilled by small arms fire evident around the doors and windows. These dismal streets were a world away from the shining shops on the 'Ku-damm'. 'The Russian authorities were well aware of the dangers lurking behind the bright lights of West Berlin,' Blake recalled. 'They therefore discouraged their citizens from crossing the sector boundary in every possible way, though they could not physically prevent them from doing so.'

In the wider battle between East and West, there had been a period of relative calm since the end of the Korean War, though the West's defence alliance, NATO, and the East's newly-created military shield, the Warsaw Pact, both possessed nuclear weapons of an increasingly sophisticated nature, so the prospect of Armageddon never seemed too far away. The nervous politicians and generals were constantly urging their spymasters to gather every last scrap of information that would give them an advantage, should the Cold War suddenly get hot.

An increasing amount of Britain's insight into the intentions of the Soviets was coming through signals and electronics intelligence, but the human variety still had a vital role to play, as long as the spy had suitable terrain on which to operate. Berlin was that ground. On to its streets swarmed both the rich and the poor of the espionage profession, perhaps as many as 10,000 'intelligence gatherers' in all. Professional practitioners from SIS and the CIA toured the streets in their smart Volkswagen cars, making their way to clandestine meetings on street corners, or more discreet assignations in safe flats. Meanwhile, hundreds of amateur, freelance agents loitered around in coffeehouses, clubs and night dives with secrets to sell that might just shed some light on the intentions of those in the Kremlin or Downing Street. The going rate for a scrap of negotiable information could fall to as low as a couple of dollars over whispered conversations in alcoves in cafés, which operated like stock exchanges for secrets. The more resourceful Berliners became double, or even triple agents, incautiously selling their wares to all sides.

Outside, in the alleyways and streets next to homes and offices, even grubbier work was taking place. Operation Tamarisk, for example, was an SIS scheme that involved nothing more than rooting through Communist waste-paper baskets and garbage bins to dig out promising scraps. It even included examining the Red Army's used toilet paper, when the soldiers were forced to employ official documents for that purpose as the Allies had deliberately starved the Soviets of the real thing.

Kidnappings were not uncommon, especially of important East Germans who had defected to the West. It has been estimated that the Stasi (East German state security service) carried out over a hundred of these operations in the 1950s.

Markus Wolf, a bright young officer who was about to head up the Stasi's foreign intelligence arm, the *Hauptverwaltung Aufklärung* (HVA), calculated that as many as eighty secret service agencies with their various branches and front organisations were operating in the city: 'Masquerading as everything from plumbing companies and jam exporters to academic and research bureaux, sat whole groups of case officers recruiting and running their respective agents, who could easily travel between the sectors of Berlin and the two halves of Germany.'

The porous nature of the borders between East and West encouraged the flight of migrants, keen to escape the dour, socialist side of the city for the perceived capitalist Mecca in the West. Those numbers only increased after the ruthless crackdown that followed the June 1953 uprising. By the time George Blake arrived, anywhere from 100,000 to 200,000 migrants were arriving in West Berlin every year.

All of this created opportunities, and dangers, for the CIA, SIS, and the recently formed West German intelligence service, the *Bundesnachrichtendienst* (BND). Those who came over, many of them young and educated, provided these Western intelligence services with vital information about friends and colleagues left behind who worked in the main Government ministries, the Armed Forces, key factories and scientific institutions. The refugees would identify the fiercely anti-Communist among those who stayed and the spies would then coax them over to West Berlin, by letter or courier, and invite them to become agents. The Americans and British had a fair measure of success with this recruitment strategy and a large number of networks were in place in crucial organisations in East Germany.

On the other hand, as Wolf observed, the flow of refugees also worked to the advantage of the GDR, once its own, embryonic intelligence service had found its feet: 'It was not very difficult for our agents to swim along in the stream. They were usually young, convinced Communists, and they laid the cornerstone for many of our later successes.' As well as telling their CIA or SIS interviewer in the camp that they had come over from the West to join relatives, an East German agent's secondary cover story might be that he was trying to conceal his former membership of the Nazi party or the SS, or even that he had made negative comments about government policies and was likely to be severely punished.

SIS commanded a place right at the centre of this vast web of espionage. The ambitious nature of its operation suited the expansive offices it had inherited close to the Olympiastadion, the massive sports arena built by the Nazis for the 1936 Summer Games. SIS had settled to the north-east of the complex and George Blake's office was on the second floor, overlooking the entrance. From his window he commanded a view of the imposing sculptures of two Reich golden eagles perched atop massive concrete pylons in front of his building, beyond which he was able to gaze upon the monumental stadium – a rather imperious position.

SIS did not use its normal diplomatic cover in Berlin. Instead, it operated under the guise of the British Control Commission for Germany, or the Army, both also ensconced at the Olympic Stadium, which meant Blake and his colleagues could blend in more easily among the large personnel of both organisations.

Money was no object. The whole SIS budget was paid for out of continuing occupation costs, shouldered by the German taxpayer. So it was that Berlin Station had a total of around a hundred officers, secretaries and auxiliary staff, in four groups. One dealt with technical operations like the Berlin tunnel, another with scientific intelligence (both sides were then developing the hydrogen bomb) and a third aimed to gather material on the Soviet and East German

Armed Forces. Blake was attached to a fourth group, responsible for collecting political intelligence and attempting to penetrate the Soviet headquarters at Karlshorst, a suburb in the south-east of the city: 'In this framework, I had the special task of trying to establish contact with Russian personnel in East Berlin, and, in particular, with members of the Soviet Intelligence Services with a view to their ultimate recruitment as SIS agents.' Of course he had a head start: as an agent of Soviet intelligence, penetrating Karlshorst required only a knock on the door.

In general SIS officers, the keepers of state secrets, were cautioned against visiting East Berlin, but Blake was provided with a false German identity card which he could present to the passport control at the border if stopped and asked for his papers. It was supposed to give him freedom of movement in his quest to recruit agents but, of course, enabled him to conduct his business with the KGB more easily.

Blake quickly devised a successful routine for meeting his handlers. He would board a U-Bahn (underground) train a couple of stops from the boundary of the British sector, and then get out at the second or third station in East Berlin, more often than not at Spittelmarkt, at the eastern end of Leipziger Strasse. He would then walk for a short distance before a black BMW limousine with drawn curtains would pull up alongside him, whereupon the door would be thrown open. He would jump in and then be driven to a safe flat in the vicinity of the Karlshorst headquarters. There, he would hand over Minox film of the documents he had photographed in the SIS office and, over a light supper and a glass of Tsimlyansk sparkling wine, would explain their significance. After an hour or so, he would be handed some fresh film and then dropped off in the vicinity of a U-Bahn station. A few minutes later, he would be back in West Berlin.

On other occasions, to be completely secure, there would be no human contact. He would merely use the spy's age-old device of the 'dead letter drop' to leave packages at a pre-arranged spot.

Blake found the conditions for plying his trade of treachery much less dangerous, and far more comfortable, in Berlin than in London. He also felt he had much more freedom of action as an agent, which surprised him: 'This seemed to me quite at variance with what I had heard was the common Soviet practice of never taking a decision without express sanction by higher authority . . . I can only explain the departure from this principle . . . by the fact that they felt I was quite capable of judging what was the best course to take in any given situation.'

The experienced Nikolai Rodin travelled to Berlin to introduce Blake to the men who would be his handlers there. His principal new contact was Nikolai Sergeevich Miakotnykh, an experienced intelligence officer in his fifties whose codename was 'Dick'. Blake warmed to him immediately: 'He was a thick-set man with a pale complexion and a friendly twinkle in his eyes behind thick, horn-rimmed spectacles. His manner was quiet and fatherly. In the course of five years of regular monthly meetings, I got to like him a great deal and felt truly sad when, at the end of my term, I had to say goodbye to him.'

The scale of the material Blake amassed for his Soviet controllers during this time is staggering, although at first his mission looked tricky: he shared an office and struggled to find time alone to photograph the documents he wanted. In cases of great urgency, he would be forced to take a risk, sometimes locking the door – a move that would have aroused great suspicion, had he been discovered. But, every six weeks, it was his turn to act as night duty officer. Astonishingly, in an organisation marked by such secrecy and paranoia, he would be left alone in the building, not only with the keys but also the combinations to all the safes. It was during these shifts that he did his most damaging work.

He was ruthlessly efficient: 'I passed a great deal of information on the structure of the Berlin station, on the aims of the Berlin station, on the make-up of the "order of battle" of the Berlin station. I also gave them a lot of information on what the Service wanted to know politically, militarily, economically, about East Germany, about the Soviet Union as a whole. They got a good inside view of how it operated.' But he was wary not to tread in areas that were not his territory: 'Of the [agent] networks, as far as I had access to them I was careful; I made a point never to ask questions, not to concern myself with what was not my business.'

He was also unsentimental. Peter Lunn, the Head of Station, had developed a card index for all the agents SIS employed in Germany. Blake handed over scores of names to his contacts in Karlshorst.

Even Vasily Dozhdalev, who had been one of Blake's case officers in Korea and was now stationed in Berlin, was startled by the detail he supplied: 'I remember this document that showed the staff list and structure of SIS – who, which department, which geographical region they oversaw, and who specifically was in the charge in that department. I remember this document specifically for the following reason, because it contained the surname of who was responsible for intelligence in the Antarctic. So someone wrote in the margins, "Ah, ha. Our man in Antarctic!" That stuck in my memory.'

SIS general policy directives, reports and instructions all went straight to the KGB. These were intelligence documents, but they also gave the Russian strategists a clear idea of the political decision-making in Whitehall that lay behind them. One CIA report would later calculate – after briefings from SIS – that Blake furnished the Soviets with 4,720 pages of documentary material during his eight years of treachery.

Is it possible to identify the true cost of his betrayal? What happened to those agents and other individuals whose identities he so readily handed to the KGB?

In 1955, Erich Mielke, who would later become the feared head of the Stasi, was deputy state security chief to Ernst Wollweber, and responsible for directing *Grosaktionen* (Major Operations) against Western spies then successfully infiltrating government offices, armed forces, factories, and research laboratories. He was struggling to contain the penetration of SIS and CIA agents into East Germany, and may have had good cause to feel grateful to Blake. The KGB, for which both Blake and a mole in the BND, Heinz Felfe, were working, gave Mielke vital assistance in tracking down and neutering many of these spies. This help enabled him to tell the Party's Central Committee in April 1955 that through *Aktion Blitz* (Operation Lightning) 521 agents had been arrested – 188 from the 'American secret service', 105 agents of the 'British secret service' and about 100 agents of the West German service. Then, in *Aktion Wespennest* (Operation Wasps' Nest) in the last three months of 1955, Mielke announced that a further 251 spies had been detained, including some reporting to a CIA scientific intelligence team. If 1955 was the high watermark of his operations, his efforts did not let up in 1956 (679 spies arrested) and 1957 (582).

In many of these cases, Blake's plundering of Lunn's card index was surely crucial. An idea of the extent of the damage that Blake may have inflicted on SIS agents is given in a paper from the counter-intelligence section of the Stasi, published some years later, with names blacked out:

> Blake's work substantially laid the foundations for the liquida-
> tion of networks of British secret service agents in the GDR
> [German Democratic Republic]. So it was possible from 1956
> to 1961 to identify around 100 spies working in the GDR (17 in
> telecommunications).
>
> Among them were dangerous agents, such as [   ] stenogra-
> pher at the GDR Council of Ministers; [   ] Colonel of the NVA
> (National People's Army); [   ] Member of the State Planning
> Commission; [   ] Senior Advisor at the Ministry for heavy
> machinery; [   ] Department head in the Ministry for Trade;
> [   ] Employee in the building committee in Potsdam.

At his trial, it was neither alleged nor proven that Blake was responsible for the deaths of agents. For his part, Blake has always maintained
that he sought specific assurances from his Soviet controllers that no

harm would come to those he betrayed. In April 1961, in his written statement for his defence team, he explained his 'agreement' in a section entitled *Reporting of Names of Agents to Russians*:

> I was very reluctant to do this, but when posted to Berlin in 1955 when my work consisted of controlling agents, I had no good excuse for not passing the names to the Russians. I was by then so involved with the Russian Intelligence Service that I could not avoid this.

> I stipulated however, and repeated this every time I passed a name, that these agents should not be arrested and that the only use the Russians should make of this information was to protect themselves from the activities of these agents by denying them access to information which they, the Russians, thought valuable.

> The Russians agreed to this, but said that if the East Germans independently obtained evidence of the activities of these agents, they could not prevent them taking action.

> In every case when an agent whose name I had passed on was arrested, I raised the matter with the Russian Controllers Officer, and in every case he assured me that the action had been taken by the East Germans on their own evidence and without information having been passed on to them by the Russians.

> I had every reason to believe the sincerity of the Russians in this matter, bearing in mind the attitude they adopted in the matter of the tunnelling operation.

Either Blake was completely naïve in this matter, or entirely cold and calculating. Even if taken at his word, it strains credulity to believe that there would not have been some co-operation between the KGB and the Stasi over his information. At that time, those organisations were led by such ruthless Stalinists as Ivan Serov, known as 'Ivan the Terrible' by the British media for his role in mass deportations and suspected genocide in the Second World War; and Mielke, who had trained in Moscow. It seems implausible that these men would have held back from their usual, brutal approach for Blake's sake. Oleg Kalugin, the KGB's head of foreign counter-intelligence in the 1970s, got to know Blake in later years in Moscow: 'He didn't want to know that many people he betrayed were executed. I think we even discussed this subject at one point, and he wouldn't believe it – he would say, "Well, I was told this would not happen." It did happen; he was not told.'

To justify what he had done, Blake returned to the notion that he was a soldier in an ideological war, where it was kill or be killed, and the battlefield was strewn with casualties: 'I have no conscience because they were in exactly the same circumstances as myself. They were working against their governments, for reasons best known to themselves, and they were doing that work knowingly and willingly, passing information to the other side. They were betrayed – and in the end, I was betrayed. I was in no better position than they were.'

In the heavily redacted prosecution file for Blake's trial in May 1961, SIS Officer B states that he had investigated the cases of a number of agents controlled by the Berlin office from 1955 to 1959, who were in fact 'either arrested by the Russians, or disappeared without trace, or became known to the Russian Intelligence Service as our agents'. Several blacked-out pages follow. His understated concluding summary of the havoc he believed Blake had wrought says simply: 'The disclosure of agents will have resulted in loss of individual liberty.'

How many might have been executed in total is impossible to say, but there are those who claim there is circumstantial evidence to link Blake with the death of a specific individual – a former Communist who had become one of the West's most important friends. Robert Bialek came over to the West in August 1953, his disillusionment with the East German regime of Walter Ulbricht complete after the brutal repression of the East Berlin rising. He was certainly no ordinary defector: he had been first a courageous opponent of the Nazis, then a high-ranking Communist who rose to become Inspector-General in the *Volkspolizei* ('People's Police'), before being finally expelled from the Party in 1952. Charismatic, articulate and a powerful orator, he used all those attributes every Saturday night on a hugely popular BBC German language radio show called *Wir Sprechen Zur Zone* ('We speak to the Zone'), promoting the virtues of life in the West while railing against the deficiencies of the country he had fled.

In the British sector, Bialek worked undercover for the East Bureau of the Social Democratic Party, with the codename Bruno Wallmann. The British authorities took on a duty of care for Bialek, looking after his security by fitting automatic locks to the doors of his flat, steel shutters to the windows and connecting a special alarm system to a British security office. They knew his broadcasts and his writings infuriated the GDR and Soviet high command, and Erich Mielke himself bore a personal grudge towards Bialek dating back to 1948 when the two men drew guns on each other after an argument.

On the evening of 4 February 1956, Bialek made his way to a flat at 21 Jenaer Strasse in the Wilmersdorf district for what he believed was to be an informal birthday party with a fellow refugee from the East, Paul Drzewiecki. In fact he had walked into a trap of Mielke's making. Drzewiecki was an undercover Stasi agent, as was his colleague in the flat, Herbert Hellweg. The two conspirators were aided in their work by a young woman later identified as Drzewiecki's niece. They spiked Bialek's drink. Realising he had been drugged, he staggered to the bathroom in the hall of the building, locking the door behind him. Another tenant arrived, discovered Bialek was unconscious, and unwittingly delivered him back into the arms of his 'friends', who said they would take him to hospital. Instead they threw Bialek into a black limousine, drove him over the border and delivered him to Hohenschönhausen prison. There the trail runs cold, but there are few who doubt that he was tortured and executed by Mielke's men.

The British were mortified by Bialek's kidnapping as it was immediately clear what had happened. The British Commandant Robert Cottrell-Hill wrote to his Soviet counterpart on 8 February, more in hope than expectation, asking him to make inquiries. Questions were asked in both Houses of Parliament. Lord Vansittart urged pressure to be brought to bear on Moscow ahead of the visit of Khrushchev and Bulganin in April. The junior Foreign Office minister, the Marquess of Reading, said they should wait to establish the facts before contemplating any further steps. Lord Vansittart replied despondently, though with prescience: 'My Lords, my fear is that we shall never hear anything further.'

Blake has strenuously denied having anything to do with Bialek's kidnapping and, in a court of law, the prosecution would be extremely hard pressed to win a conviction against him. Nonetheless, SIS did know all about Bialek, and the Service was one of the first on the scene after his defection, finding out what he knew and how he might be able to assist it. Although he never became one of its agents, SIS would have been aware of the arrangements for his security and his movements. Blake and Bialek would not necessarily have crossed each other's paths on Platanenalle, where they both lived for a month in the spring of 1955, but it seems inconceivable that Blake would not have taken an interest in this highest of high-profile defectors. Nor is it unlikely that his masters at Karlshorst would have asked him for some information on their target, with the intention of passing it to the Stasi. Charles Wheeler, who knew Bialek and the BBC producers who worked with him, always suspected that intelligence supplied by Blake may have led the defector's kidnappers to him.

Aside from the human casualties of his treachery, and the Berlin tunnel, Blake also betrayed various other technical operations in which SIS and the CIA were engaged. He alerted his Soviet handlers to the eavesdropping on the Yugoslav military mission, and the bugging of their Polish equivalent.

Ted Shackley, the CIA's Chief of Satellite Operations in Berlin, recalled how the agency was keen to listen in when a new man, Władysław Tykocinski, an experienced Polish Foreign Service officer, arrived to take up his post. The opportunity arose because the Polish mission was looking to move to a new building. CIA officers got in touch with Berlin estate agents and brokers to make sure that the Poles were steered towards buying a spacious villa in the Charlottenburg district. Before they could move in, the CIA had bugged it from top to bottom. When Tykocinski settled in, senior politicians paid court, as did Poles who came to East Berlin on business. 'All of them talked, and Tykocinski himself talked the most, making a point of briefing his staff on developments at home and the substance of the cable traffic that was coming in from Moscow. It was a goldmine,' was Shackley's assessment. Then, a few weeks later, a counter-intelligence sweep team were heard looking for, and finding, hidden microphones. The game was up.

Shackley knew there had been a leak and later discovered who was to blame: 'It was Blake who had closed our goldmine. Apparently he had overheard two SIS staffers chatting about it in their Berlin headquarters and had picked up just enough of their conversation to enable him to tell his Soviet handler that an operation was in progress against an unidentified Polish installation in West Berlin.'

Blake had clearly performed well for the KGB in Berlin, but he also managed to keep his official employers satisfied at the same time. Running a major Soviet agent, someone in a position of real clout in the political or economic sphere, had proved well nigh impossible for most of his colleagues but, somehow, Blake managed to reel in a top catch. His source in the upper echelons of Soviet government was 'Boris', an economist working for Comecon, the economic organisation that linked all the Communist countries. He also happened to be a senior interpreter at all top-level Soviet negotiations on economic matters, so he would routinely accompany senior Kremlin personnel and pick up much sensitive political information. Blake recalled SIS's delight: 'They thought he represented a source of great promise and should be carefully cultivated. Though he was not "our man in the Kremlin" yet, there was a good prospect that he might become one.'

Boris was, of course, a plant, put in place by Blake's KGB masters to impress SIS and the CIA and enhance his growing reputation.

The recruitment of Boris was carefully staged. One of Blake's regular agents, Horst Eitner, otherwise known as 'Mickey', had secured a job as an assistant in a clothes shop called Semel on Badstrasse, in the Wedding district of West Berlin. This traditional working-class area lay in the French Sector, close to the sector boundary, and was known as 'Red Wedding' because of its Communist sympathies in the 1920s and 30s. It had been heavily bombed in the war and much of its housing destroyed and, in the wake of that devastation, a business community arose that veered from the vibrant to the seamy, with hard-working local traders being joined by spivs, prostitutes and chancers of every kind in one big, teeming settlement of shops and shacks.

There was dirt on the streets of Wedding, but there was glitter too. It attracted its fair share of visitors from the Soviet sector, looking for attractive items at reasonable prices. One of those who turned up at Semel one day was Boris, who told Mickey he was looking for a fur-lined wind jacket. When Mickey told Blake about this interesting Russian, Blake instructed his agent to buy a good-quality jacket from one of the best men's shops on the Kurfürstendamn and sell it to Boris at half the price. Boris was pleased with his purchase and next showed an interest in buying a Swiss watch for his wife. When Boris said he could not afford the watch (at a deliberately-inflated price set by Mickey), the agent said he could pay by other means. Could Boris supply a dozen pots of caviar, because he knew he had a friend who was interested in buying the delicacy? The deal was struck.

The friend who wanted the caviar was, of course, Blake, and Mickey contrived a meeting between the two men in his flat on Wielandstrasse. There, over liberal amounts of wine and brandy, Boris told Blake about his job, while Blake – who gave his name as de Vries, his wartime resistance pseudonym – explained that he was a Dutch journalist, the correspondent on a newspaper in Berlin. The two men got on well, and Boris readily accepted Blake's invitation to meet again the following week at a nightclub. It was the start of a profitable working relationship that would last for several years.

Boris had been primed to co-operate with this 'Dutch journalist' by the KGB, but – according to Blake – he only realised that the other man was in fact a Soviet agent working in SIS when he picked up a newspaper and read about Blake's trial in 1961. 'Though, ostensibly, the luxury articles which I obtained for him were in exchange for the caviar he continued to bring me, it was well understood between us that what I was really interested in was the information he was in a position to supply,' Blake explained. 'He apparently accepted my explanation that I needed it as background material and my assurance that nothing he told me would ever be published by my newspaper.'

In the way of these counter-intelligence schemes, some of the intelligence Boris supplied to Blake was genuine, in order to build up his credentials as an important recruit back at SIS headquarters in Broadway. Excited by Blake's reports, Whitehall sought ever more detail from this excellent source. They would instruct Blake to ask Boris specific questions on burning questions of the moment and, on nearly every occasion, the 'plant' responded with the required information. Thus the KGB believed fulfilled two objectives. One, to raise the stock of their prize agent in the eyes of his superiors at SIS; the second, through the misleading material Boris fed Blake, to deceive the West about the true state of the Soviet economy and so influence policy-making. It was one of many sources of information that helped to obscure the fundamental truth about the economies of the Eastern Bloc – that they were inherently weak and structurally unsound. Had that been known in the late 1950s, the Cold War might, for good or ill, have ended much sooner than it did.

Horst Eitner, the SIS agent who brought Blake and Boris together, was typical of the cast of colourful characters who threw themselves into the city's espionage world, but for whom loyalty always came with a price tag. He was a major figure in Blake's 'legitimate' spy work during his time in Berlin but, as it turned out, would also have a prominent role to play in his eventual downfall.

Eitner actually began his espionage career with the Gehlen Organisation (forerunners of the BND) in 1951. Reinhard Gehlen, a former general in the German Army and a spymaster for Hitler, was not shy of recruiting ex-Nazis, employing hundreds of them like Eitner, who had emerged from the Allied prison camps after 1945. He was trained at one of Gehlen's spy schools at Bad Worishofen but, as time went on, and as a German who felt resentment at both East and West for the occupation of his country, he increasingly saw Gehlen as a mere appendix of the CIA. More importantly, the payments received for his work were poor and often slow to arrive. Some 'business' friends of his had contacts with SIS, to whom he transferred his allegiance at the end of 1953. There, he was run by two officers, known only to him as 'Peter' and 'Peter 2', before Blake inherited him at the beginning of 1957. Blake resurrected his cover name from his Dutch resistance days, 'Max de Vries', for his dealings with Eitner. What Blake did not know, at the time he first met Eitner, was that 'Mickey' was also working for the Russians.

He had been approached towards the end of 1956, not by the KGB, but by the GRU – Soviet Military Intelligence. From SIS, he received a regular monthly wage of 250DM, which would sometimes rise to 400DM, with bonuses for successful jobs. When the Russians came calling, he asked for 500DM a month and his request was readily accepted. As well as paying more generously, the Soviets proved less demanding than the British: whether his reports were good or bad, he would almost invariably receive his 500DM each month. Eitner had a wife, Brigitte, and three young children to support; he also sent payments to his parents in Cottbus. His flat on Wielandstrasse did not come cheap. In addition, he also had extravagant tastes and an expensive drinking habit.

They were an odd couple, Blake and Eitner. Blake was cool,

calculating, cerebral and restrained in his behaviour; Eitner was an earthy, boisterous extrovert, a carouser and a womaniser. Although each man used the other coldly for his own ends, these polar opposites worked together effectively, and even enjoyed each other's company. 'The reason for the nickname [Mickey] was obvious the moment one saw him,' Blake wrote. 'He bore a strong resemblance to Mickey Mouse. He was small, agile, with bandy legs and large ears. If the expression on his face had been less than cheerful, it might have been called rat-like.'

Just to complicate matters for Blake, Eitner's wife was also doing occasional shifts as a Russian spy, having previously been in trouble with the Soviet authorities for spying on behalf of the CIA. She acted principally as a courier between the GRU and her husband. A pretty, vivacious, highly-strung Polish woman, she was fond of 'Max', who would bring her small presents to cheer her up: 'He was a charming man and very good company. He liked to tell us stories about his time in the British Navy in which, he told us, he'd served as an officer during the war. But Max could be moody, too, you know. One minute he was gay and laughing, and suddenly he would turn very serious and dry up.'

Eitner had no idea Blake was working for the Soviets; but Blake eventually learned of the German's identity as a double agent. His handler, 'Dick', revealed the truth about a year after Blake had started running Eitner: 'I thought the recruitment by them pretty pointless, but as a sister organisation was involved, it was apparently very difficult to do anything about it. On the other hand, it did not seem to matter very much and so it was left at that.'

The partnership endured until April 1959 when Blake finished his tour of duty and another SIS officer, known to Eitner as 'Temple', replaced him, but he had not heard the last of Mickey. An episode on the evening of Sunday, 16 October 1960 would spark off a chain of events that would once more draw them together. The consequences for both would be calamitous.

13

Discovery

At just after 1 p.m. on Sunday, 22 April 1956, East German engineers peered through a hole in the wall they had just dug and were able to take their first look down the length of the Berlin tunnel. They were amazed by what they saw: 'Man, look at this . . . it goes all the way under the street . . . it's fantastic!' Their surprise and appreciation of the sheer technical excellence of the underground listening post was completely genuine, unlike the mock outrage about to be expressed by their political masters in Karlshorst and the Kremlin.

Yevgeny Petrovich Pitovranov, chief of the KGB in Berlin, Ivan Serov, overall Chief of the organisation and Nikita Khrushchev, First Secretary of the Communist Party, had all known about the tunnel and had finally come to a joint decision to stage its discovery on that April weekend.

The tunnel had lasted eleven months and eleven days. For nearly all of that time, this elite group at the very top of the Soviet political and intelligence establishment had been aware of its existence, even before the first sod had been dug from the ground. George Blake, their mole at the heart of the Secret Intelligence Service, had provided them with full details as far back as February 1954.

Khrushchev, under pressure from his critics at home and abroad, was looking for a tough gesture with which to appease the old guard in the Kremlin and retain their support. Abroad, he was irritated that two of his measures for easing Cold War tensions – the withdrawal of troops from Austria, and Soviet recognition of West Germany – had not prompted any reciprocal gestures from the West. The 'discovery' of the Berlin tunnel, and the chance to castigate the underhand West for its 'nest of spies', provided the propaganda coup for which he had been looking.

Blake was warned by Sergei Kondrashev some days in advance that the tunnel was about to be 'blown' but it was still a period of great worry for him: 'I had naturally been watching these developments, which I knew were about to occur, with some anxiety, on the alert for any signs of suspicion on the part of SIS or the CIA that the Soviets might have been forewarned.'

As it happened, the unusually bad spring weather offered the Soviet planners the cover they had been looking for to stage an accidental find. Heavy rains had begun shorting out the long-distance cables, so the Karlshorst signals team had a legitimate reason for descending on Schönefelder Chausee beneath which the taps had been placed.

Meanwhile, Pitovranov, together with General Andrei Grechko (Commander in Chief of Soviet forces in East Germany) and Georgy Pushkin (Soviet Ambassador in East Berlin), began to draw up the equivalent of a modern-day PR plan for Khrushchev on how best to exploit the revelation. They agreed that a strong public protest should be made to the headquarters of the American Army in Europe; their 'German friends' would then be briefed to comment unfavourably on the affair; reporters from West as well as East would be invited to take a good look at the tunnel; and a group of technical experts despatched to study all the equipment. Most interesting of all their recommendations was this final suggestion: 'Regardless of the fact that the tunnel contains British equipment, all accusations in print should be addressed exclusively to the Americans'.

Their reasons were twofold. First, by pinning the blame for the tunnel completely on the Americans they could divert suspicion away from SIS and, most importantly, from Blake. Secondly, on the very day the tunnel was 'discovered', Khrushchev and Bulganin were halfway through a state visit to Britain. They did not want their unruffled progress undermined, or to embarrass their hosts with accusations of spying while there were negotiations over Hungary and the Middle East that might just move in their favour.

Back in Berlin, many in the CIA had assumed the Soviets would not want to advertise the fact that their communications had been so totally compromised. They were surprised when, carrying out Khrushchev's wishes to the letter, Colonel Ivan Kotsyuba, Acting Commandant of the Berlin Garrison, called a press conference on Monday, 23 April, to inform the world of this 'blatant act of imperialist aggression'. The Soviets accused the US of tapping 'important underground long-distance telephone lines' linking Berlin with other nations. They conducted official tours of the tunnel, sending carefully chosen delegations of workers from East Germany to gaze on this 'damning evidence' of the CIA's use of West Berlin as an espionage base against the 'peace-loving East'.

The Eastern side of the tunnel took on a carnival-like atmosphere. A snack bar was set up and an estimated 90,000 East Berliners toured the 'capitalist warmongers' expensive subterranean listening post'.

The KGB story, as told in the East German press, depicted heroic Soviet technicians surprising the hapless Americans, forcing them to abandon their earphones and recorders and flee humiliatingly down the tunnel. In reality, a senior American officer on site had a smart idea to halt the advancing Soviets: a 50-calibre machine gun was brought into the tunnel and set up on a tripod. When the Americans heard the Soviets coming, the slide was pulled back on the gun, making a very loud, unmistakable noise that echoed around the enclosed space. The intruders promptly turned on their heels and disappeared back into the East.

In the West, there was no sense of ignominy about the tunnel's discovery; instead the operation generally amused and delighted the public. American newspapers marvelled that the CIA was capable of such a remarkable clandestine manoeuvre, and revelled in the fact that US intelligence was now competing on level terms with the Soviets, long acknowledged as masters in such matters. For *Time* magazine it was the 'Wonderful Tunnel'. The *Boston Globe* confessed it would never have believed that American intelligence agents, thought to be stumbling neophytes, could be 'that smart'.

Despite Khrushchev's aims, America, and specifically the CIA, emerged as the real winner in the propaganda battle. Only eight years old, the agency was still viewed with scepticism in Washington, where not everyone had been convinced about its usefulness, or that it spent its money wisely. The obvious technical ingenuity of the project silenced the critics but what, really, was the practical benefit of this 6.7 million dollar project? For five years afterwards the CIA was utterly convinced that the Berlin tunnel had been a 'unique source of current intelligence of a kind and quality that had not been available since 1948'. They believed it to be their best insight into Soviet intentions in Europe.

When the truth emerged about Blake's betrayal, they were forced to question that assumption. The KGB had known about the tunnel all along, and the voluminous intelligence the CIA believed it had gathered about the Soviet Army, Soviet intelligence, the Soviet atom bomb programme, and all the personalities in the Soviet political and military hierarchy could no longer be trusted. Was it laced with deliberate disinformation? Though later analysis on both sides would suggest not, it was impossible to be sure.

Joe Evans, a CIA officer based in London who analysed a lot of the tunnel material, noted: 'In a disinformation campaign, literally thousands of Soviets in East Germany would have had to know *something* about this operation, and to know the KGB had an inside source. That would have left George Blake's security in tatters.' Some years later, Blake's handler, Sergei Kondrashev, endorsed Evans's view and officially dismissed the disinformation theory: 'It would have been impossible. Why? Because with such huge amounts of material going through different lines – diplomatic, military, GDR lines and others – to insert a page or two of disinformation into such a huge amount of material, well, just a simple analysis using simple methods would show that the disinformation contradicts the huge bulk of real material. So it wasn't done.'

With this, Kondrashev revealed another startling piece of information – that the KGB had even kept the secret of the tunnel from its *own side,* its military counterparts the GRU and the Red Army, the main users of the cables being tapped. This extraordinary piece of subterfuge in the Lubyanka was intended to protect their precious asset. 'We didn't tell the military about the existence of George Blake. We simply couldn't betray our secret to anyone,' said Kondrashev. 'He was too important for us. You realise that at the time, George Blake was of course one of the most important sources at the heart of the British Secret Service. He was crucial for us.' Unless and until the Soviet archives throw up fresh information, the astounding conclusion must remain that the KGB were ready to let the West listen into Red Army communications in order to protect Blake. Nothing better illustrates his importance to the KGB than this remarkable action – or inaction.

There is one other, completely speculative yet fascinating theory about why the KGB did not exploit their knowledge about the tunnel: could it have been because they *wanted* the listeners-in to know what the Soviet policymakers were thinking and doing? Did the KGB actually want the West to realise *no* attack was planned on them? Could it have been one of the very first calculated acts of *détente?* Post-Stalin, this was a period when policymakers in the Kremlin were thinking far more of accommodation with the West. It's an unlikely scenario, perhaps, but the Berlin tunnel has thrown up so many surprises over the years that this theory is not beyond the realms of possibility.

As to the value of the 443,000 fully transcribed conversations, which led to 1,740 intelligence reports, Joe Evans and David Murphy had no doubt. Examples from both officers illustrate the major advantages the tunnel information could offer to their political masters.

At the Twentieth Party Congress in Moscow in February 1956, Khrushchev denounced Stalin and the cult of personality, and discussed the regime's previous crimes and misdeeds in his famous 'secret speech'. It was an extraordinary turn of events. 'Delegates to the Congress were buzzing about the speech for days afterwards. We heard some of that on the tapped cables, and so thanks to the Berlin tunnel we were the very first to report news of the speech to Western intelligence – and then to the Western world,' recalled Joe Evans.

Further scoops were put to use in May 1959 when Christian Herter, Eisenhower's new Secretary of State, sat down for face-to-face talks in Geneva with his Soviet counterpart, Andrei Gromkyo. They were attending a Foreign Ministers' conference on the status of Berlin and the future of Germany. One of the themes in the run-up to the conference was – yet again – the accusation by the Soviets that the West was misusing West Berlin for intelligence and subversion purposes. It was a diplomatic card the Russians played very strongly. Herter came equipped for the meeting with Gromkyo with a comprehensive memorandum, courtesy of the CIA and the long-closed Berlin tunnel. Murphy described their encounter: 'Gromyko was invited to the villa, and he sat there for two hours while the Secretary of State read him, word by word, every single thing from this memorandum about East German and Soviet intelligence operations in East Berlin. We had completely turned the tables on the Soviets. It was the first time we had used counter-intelligence material in this way, and we were able to do it because the tunnel had provided it to us.'

In the aftermath of the discovery of the tunnel, all attention naturally focused on the CIA's role. There was no suggestion that the British had even known about it, let alone participated. SIS's Head of Station, Peter Lunn, was a consummate spy who was loathe to discuss his work except when absolutely necessary, but he felt piqued that SIS's contribution was going unnoticed, especially now that the plaudits were starting to roll in for the Americans. The least he could do was make sure his own staff were aware of the part the British had played in this great Cold War episode. 'As soon as the news broke in the press, he assembled the whole staff of the Berlin station, from the highest to the lowest, and told the whole story from its inception to its untimely end,' recalled Blake. 'He made it quite clear that this had been essentially an SIS idea and his own to boot. American participation had been limited to providing most of the money and facilities.'

A few months later when the report of the joint SIS/CIA investigation into the discovery of the tunnel was published internally Blake breathed a sigh of relief. The verdict it reached was that the cause had been purely technical, and there had been no leak from within the services.

In the summer of 1955, while holidaying on the shores of Lake Garda, Blake struck up a curious conversation with his wife. 'George showed me a London newspaper reporting Mrs Maclean's flight to Russia to join her husband Donald, who had absconded from the Foreign Office with Guy Burgess the year before,' Gillian recalled. 'And George then asked me, "How would you feel, darling, if I went to Russia? What would you do?"' She did not dwell on it at the time, regarding it as no more than a question put in jest. Years later, it took on a whole new meaning, and she then remembered other conversations she had had with her husband about his political views: 'I knew at the time he was a communist, from the forceful way he would talk about it, and he would show the full cause of communism, not the way it was put into practice, but the idea of it. He liked that idea. I knew that very well, but I never dreamed he would put it into practice.'

Blake often toyed with his wife in political discussions, amused at what her reactions might be. Perhaps it was a way of relieving the strain of his double life, obliquely confessing his treachery in the sure knowledge that Gillian would never join all the dots together. 'Sometimes he would talk of Khrushchev with admiration. He would say what an astute man he thought he was, usually over some diplomatic point. "How clever of him to put the West into such a position," George would say. He would say this to me, not to anybody else. Then he would watch my reaction.'

Blake's reading tastes were unashamedly highbrow, without affectation. Once he had finished perusing his daily copy of the *Manchester Guardian* he would dip into his growing collection of mainly Russian and French language books. Philosophy, history and theology were his principal interests, with Baruch Spinoza and Edward Gibbon among his favourite writers. He rarely ventured into fiction but, if he did, it would usually be to revisit writers such as Dostoyevsky from his time at Cambridge. Another rare exception was *Not By Bread Alone* by Vladimir Dudintsev, the story of an engineer whose invention to produce pipes more efficiently is opposed every step of the way by narrow-minded, Stalinist bureaucrats, which seemed to capture the mood of change in Khrushchev's Russia.

For much of his time in Berlin, Blake's other life, of the normal family variety, ticked along happily enough. His flat at 26 Platanenallee in Charlottenburg, just a five-minute Volkswagen drive from the Olympic Stadium, was certainly spacious, if a little staid-looking with its austere, institutional furniture. The Blakes brightened it up with new covers and curtains, adorning the walls with pictures and prints collected from galleries in Berlin. Wedding presents of china, glass and silver helped them entertain properly from time to time, and they gave one big party a year, for sixty people.

They also liked to go out in the evening and explore the lively West Berlin nightlife. Berlin had become a centre for jazz, especially in the American Zone, where the likes of Miles Davis and Chet Baker would perform. Money was no real object and expensive establishments like the Ritz, Maison de France, Kopflers and Rollenhagen were regular haunts. Just as often a table on the pavement at Hotel

Kempinski, whiling away the evening with a bottle of wine, would suit them perfectly well.

Gillian built a busy social life around the army and intelligence 'community'. She would go to the Officers' Club quite often to play tennis, and went riding and sailing with the other wives. Blake himself learned to ride, but his real passion was swimming, which he was able to indulge in one of several magnificent pools at the Olympic Stadium.

The Blakes were a handsome couple, sociable and well liked by their contemporaries. One Army officer recalled: 'Blake was a delightful, charming man who turned up at all the parties, used the Officers' Club – which was a social centre – and everybody knew him.'

Both George and Gillian loved to travel. Lake Garda was a favourite spot, where they would water-ski. They drove their Ford Anglia through Italy, finishing up at Venice, went skiing at St Anton in Austria, and also visited Dubrovnik in Yugoslavia. 'We had tremendous "leaves" and didn't save any money at all, which didn't worry me,' said Gillian. 'George would organise it all – he had much more initiative in everything.'

This apparently carefree, young married life inevitably slowed down when their first child, Anthony, was born in the Military Hospital in Berlin in 1957. The Blakes drove back to England via Holland to have him christened at St Michael's Church, Chester Square, close to where Gillian's parents were living.

Blake seemed content to let Gillian make nearly all the decisions about Anthony's future – and that of James, who would follow in 1959: 'I was pressing for an education policy, and my point was that, as we would be travelling around and going abroad continually, it would be far better to give them a boarding school education. George rather fobbed it off, saying "Oh, well, in ten years' time we'll all be going to state schools anyway, and what's wrong with that?" But he didn't push the issue, and to keep me happy he let me put Anthony – and then James – down for Rugby, where my brother had been.'

Despite all outward appearances, Blake was starting to feel the enormous pressure of his double life, particularly now with the birth of his first child. He wondered if there was any way out of the web in which he had become entangled: 'This contradiction in my life became even greater and an increasing strain on me. Here I was, building with one hand a happy family life with its roots firmly attached to this country, and with the other hand I was pulling the foundations from underneath it so that it might crumble any moment.' His high-minded idealism, his secret dedication to the Soviet cause remained, but the will to sustain his treachery was faltering.

In the autumn of 1958, an exit strategy presented itself. His superiors in Broadway suggested he should leave Berlin the following spring, spend a short time in London, and then go to the Lebanon to learn Arabic at MECAS (the Middle East Centre for Arabic Studies), a language school in Shemlan for diplomats, businessmen and intelligence officers. Blake was delighted at the prospect: 'I saw in this an opportunity to bring the work to an early end, and it would give me the opportunity to think of a permanent way out, possibly by trying to get, through my knowledge of Arabic, a good job in an oil company.'

It was in good spirits that he returned to England with his wife and child in April 1959. He was out of the Berlin shadowlands, free of the perpetual stress and responsibility of dealing with the likes of Horst Eitner and Boris, free of juggling his two lives ever more precariously. Gillian, too, welcomed the move: 'We didn't mind staying out there quite so long, but we were both happy to come home when we were eventually posted.' With much relief, Blake resumed work in Broadway on 12 April, on a junior desk dealing with Lebanon and Jordan, where he could gradually ready himself for his posting to MECAS in the autumn.

Within weeks, all hopes of extracting himself from his duplicitous existence had been dashed. The obstacle came in the shape of Robert Dawson, who had been Head of one of SIS's sub-stations in Berlin, and was most impressed by Blake's work there. The avuncular Dawson, who had run a happy ship in Berlin, was back in London and had taken over a department called Directorate of Production 4 (DP 4), dealing in Russian affairs. He wanted to recruit the best and the brightest, and asked for Blake, who was desperately disappointed. Though he protested as far as he felt able, Dawson was adamant he needed him and ultimately had his way. Blake did, however, manage to extract the concession from the personnel department that the appointment was only temporary and that he would be on his way to the Lebanon in October 1960.

On 15 June, after just two months immersing himself happily in the Middle East, Blake was back on the same old beat, concentrating once more on intelligence operations against the Soviet Union, but this time on home soil. An example of the kind of work he undertook was recorded by one of his targets.

One day in the winter of 1959, a 23-year-old undergraduate was in his rooms at Merton College, Oxford, studying for what he hoped would be a First Class degree in Oriental Studies, when there was a knock on the door. The student was Oliver Miles and the man he ushered into his living room introduced himself as George Amis. Miles had been expecting the visit, as Amis had rung some days earlier to ask if he might stop by. It quickly became evident to Miles what Amis's business was, although the other man never spelled it out in so many words.

> He said he was from the Ministry of Defence, and that his job was to keep an eye on Russian students in British universities and make sure they weren't getting up to anything they shouldn't be getting up to.

> He went on, 'I understand you know some of the Russians who are here as undergraduates. Would you be willing to keep track of what they're doing, and contact the authorities if you think they're up to anything suspicious?'

Miles realised Amis must know all about his background. He had learned Russian during his National Service in the Navy and when he came up to Oxford in 1956, got involved in various Russian-related activities, including travelling to Moscow on an exchange visit in 1958. 'Although at the time I was convinced of the wickedness of the Soviet system, I told Amis I was not terribly keen on becoming an unpaid spy,' Miles recalled. 'This was my final year reading very difficult subjects, Arabic and Turkish, and I was concentrating all my energies on that, so there wasn't a lot I felt I could do for him. He was very sympathetic and left me alone.'

Amis, however, continued to contact Miles from time to time while he was still at Oxford: 'I told him I was hoping to pursue a career in the Foreign Office. He asked if I'd be interested in having my name put forward for a "sister service". I said I'd heard about that, but I really wanted to get through the front door rather than the back, so to speak, and we left it at that.'

'George Amis' was, of course, Blake. He had tried and failed to recruit a young man who would go on to become one of Britain's leading diplomats, his posts including Ambassador to Libya, Ambassador to Luxembourg, and Ambassador to Greece. Their paths would soon cross again, in Shemlan in October, where they were both on secondment – one from the Foreign Office, the other from SIS – to improve their Arabic. Even years later, the long shadow of Blake's treachery would also fall on Miles: he was refused a post in Moscow purely and simply because of these few passing encounters with Blake.

Students, dons, businessmen, scientists, people in the world of art – Blake attempted to recruit anyone who, in one way or another, was in direct contact with Soviet citizens. In the late 1950s this could be achieved more easily than the image of a world divided by the Iron Curtain might suggest. This was the era of Khrushchev's 'peaceful co-existence' with the West, when contacts with the Eastern Bloc countries opened up a little and there was a flow, or at least a trickle, of visitors back and forth between Britain and the Soviet Union.

There had previously been a clear rule that SIS should not carry out intelligence on British soil as that had always been the preserve of the Security Service, MI5. Such strict territorialism was abandoned in order to exploit the opportunities available in the more relaxed environment. SIS could now run agents at home.

Blake's immediate boss was Arthur Temple 'Dicky' Franks, a gifted, energetic intelligence officer who, twenty years later, would rise to the very top of SIS as Chief. As Blake recalled: 'His trim figure had something boyish and, with his glistening, rimless glasses, slightly too large head and snap reactions, he reminded me irresistibly as the brightest boy in the class.' Franks and a small team worked at recruiting agents within large companies and newspapers, cultivating the chairmen and managing directors of such firms in particular.

One of Blake's more interesting tasks was the setting up of the Anglo-Russian Interpretation Agency, which had offices in Queen's House, off Leicester Square. It was entirely an SIS front organisation. Two 'White' Russians, with established links to SIS, were its directors, and the whole of the staff worked for the Service. 'In this way,' Blake recalled, 'SIS was able, in time, to have its agents attached, in the guise of interpreters, to almost every Soviet visitor of interest and send them to the Soviet Union with British delegations of every kind.' Blake betrayed them, of course, passing the full details of the front to two of his oldest case officers who were now back in London – Vasily Dozhdalev, whom he had met in Korea, and Nikolai Rodin, the 'old hand' he had first met in Otpor.

Blake relished the company of the younger man, who would remain a good friend in future years: 'He had a much more cheerful disposition and looked typically English so that if he didn't open his mouth, nobody would have dreamt of taking him as a foreigner.' For his part, Dozhdalev was delighted to be working in London again. 'A superb city from the point of view of intelligence,' he reckoned. 'It is a haystack where a person is like a needle. And you will never find him there.'

As they strolled through the quiet streets of the city's northern suburbs, Blake was also able to inform Dozhdalev of other, shadier SIS activities in London, such as the proposed bugging of the Moscow Narodny Bank in Moorgate: 'It was at its planning stage. George told us what people SIS had selected to install the technology and so on, so we have plenty of time to prepare for it and, by using various means, quietly prevent them from implementing it.' Not that all the clerks and managers in the Moscow Narodny Bank were bona fide bank officials. There was usually a spy or two among them, and a number of its employees were thrown out of the country in 1971 as part of Prime Minister Edward Heath's mass expulsion of over a hundred agents.

The darker arts of espionage within SIS were left to the Special Political Action Section (SPA). Set up in 1953, the short-lived SPA specialised in 'black' propaganda: influencing elections, even occasionally helping to overthrow leaders, as in Operation Boot that removed the Iranian leader, Mohammad Mossadeq. This was retribution for Mossadeq's nationalisation of the country's oil industry, under British control since 1913. SPA was known within Broadway as the 'jolly fun tricks department'. Among those tricks, Blake was able to tell the KGB about Operation Lyautey, a scheme designed by SPA to gather political and personal information on Soviet officials with a view to blackmailing them. It was always intended as a long-term operation, hence the decision by some wag in Broadway to name it after the great French Marshall Hubert Lyautey, who once asked his gardener to plant a tree for shade. The gardener objected, saying that it would not reach maturity for a hundred years, to which the Marshall replied: 'In that case, there is no time to lose. Plant it this afternoon.'

After living with her parents in Chester Row for a short while on their return from Berlin, the Blakes moved out into the suburbs, to Bickley in Kent. There, they took a top-floor flat in Lauriston House, on Bickley Park Road, a large mansion that for many years had been the home of Lewis Wigram of the well-known shipping and brewing family.

In the morning, Blake's routine was to read the papers in bed, shave, and sit down to breakfast at 8.30. He would leave the house half an hour later, allowing plenty of time to catch the 9.17 from Bickley station to Victoria. At the age of thirty-seven, to any casual onlooker, Blake would have appeared the archetypal commuting civil servant, minus bowler hat, which he disdained to wear despite Gillian's prompting. Invariably he would be dressed in a 'dark grey, heavy flannel suit, with a soft collar (he couldn't wear stiff ones – again, a legacy of Korea)' and carrying an umbrella. He would get to his new offices at Artillery Mansions, Victoria Street, by 10 a.m. For the return journey, the 6.24 would get him home just after 7 p.m. For his KGB work, he might occasionally take the earlier train, the 6.18, which took him into Bromley South station. There, or in a nearby street, he might have a brief encounter with Dozhdalev, handing over some film from his Minox camera under cover of a folded newspaper. He would then pick up the next train to Bickley, perhaps arriving home just after 7.30.

The couple's second son, James, was born soon after their return from Germany. 'George loved playing with the children. In London he didn't get back in time in the evening to see them – they were too small,' recalled Gillian. 'But he loved taking Anthony, when he was old enough, on little expeditions. They would go up on the train to Victoria, with nothing particular to do. They would go up to town and do something and come back down, because Anthony loved to go on trains.' When Anthony was a little older, encouraged by his father, he started to develop a love of churches. He was drawn to the sound of the bells and the music of Bach. Father and son would go on little expeditions to the prettier churches in Kent.

After the disappointment of being denied a posting in the Middle East, Blake had adjusted to his temporary grounding in London. His home life was fulfilling and he was settled enough at work, so he was content to bide his time. This mood of well-being was abruptly shattered in November 1959, when his boss in DP 4, Robert Dawson, requested that he stay in the section for a further three years. Blake was distraught: 'I refused to stay, and said that if he insisted I would resign from the Service. When the Personnel Department realised how strongly I felt about this they agreed to abide by their original promise, to let me go to the Lebanon in September 1960.'

When Blake eventually informed Rodin and Dozhdalev about his move to this Cold War backwater, he was somewhat economical with the truth: 'In reporting my new appointment to the Russians I did not say it was my own choice that I'd been sent to the Lebanon, but that this was a decision of the Service, which it would be unwise to go against. The Russians were naturally anxious that I should stay in the position I was in, in London.'

Lebanon would offer a vital respite, but Blake, in his darker moments, had a sense of foreboding. Reckoning was surely close at hand. He or his KGB colleagues might slip up and fail to evade surveillance, and there was always the risk of being unmasked by a Soviet defector. In that eventuality, what should he do? Would the KGB want him to confess or deny? Would they want him to stand up in court and denounce the subversive activities of the Western intelligence services against the Soviet Union? One summer evening as they were walking along a quiet street in Croydon, he sought guidance on this matter from Rodin. To his surprise, his controller was completely unwilling to talk about it: 'He argued that if I did everything right and made no mistakes, nothing could go wrong. The very fact of discussing the subject was already an admission of defeat.' Suitably chastened, Blake resolved to suppress his anxieties.

He flew out to Beirut with his family on Saturday, 17 September 1960, glad to be away from the complex, murky, compromised world of espionage, and looking forward to academic life.

14

The Unmasking

At around 5.30 p.m. on Wednesday, 4 January 1961, a call was put through to the emergency telephone number at the CIA's Operations Base in Berlin. The caller, who did not identify himself, told the switchboard operator that he was ringing on behalf of Mr Kowalski. He informed her that his client would be arriving at the agreed meeting place – the American Consulate on Clayallee – in half an hour's time. He also asked the telephonist to tell the reception committee that Mrs Kowalski would be accompanying her husband, and that particular consideration should be given to her. This was the moment that CIA counter-intelligence officers had been anticipating for over two and a half years. They were finally about to come face-to-face with their brilliant source within Soviet Bloc intelligence, the man who had signed his first, anonymous letter to them back in April 1958 as *Heckenschütze* (Sniper).

Sniper had already told them much from his position embedded deep in the heart of Soviet intelligence, and the CIA had also briefed their MI5 and SIS colleagues in London about him, not least because he had revealed that there were two KGB moles within British intelligence.

Managing a defector like this, especially in such a high-profile case, was a hugely nerve-wracking affair, fraught with peril. In this instance the dangers were increased because Sniper was not on home territory. He had contrived an operational mission to Berlin from Warsaw where, as a 'stranger', despite his lofty status, any surveillance would be far more difficult to evade. Sniper also suspected that he was being watched more closely than usual. The KGB believed there was a 'pig' (traitor) in the organisation, more likely than not in Polish intelligence, and had asked Sniper, of all people, to investigate, but that did not mean they were not also investigating him.

Tense but full of anticipation, David Murphy, head of the CIA's Berlin station, and his new deputy, John Dimmer, started to enact the plan they had prepared several days earlier. Military police guarded the Consulate as unobtrusively as possible. Inside, microphones and recorders had been carefully installed in the room where the first introductions would be made. A safe house, to which Sniper would then be taken prior to his flight from the country, had been readied; a car was parked near the front entrance of the consulate. Murphy had selected a Polish-speaking officer to drive the vehicle, so he could pick up any interesting snippets of conversation between Sniper and his wife.

At 6.06 p.m. a West Berlin taxi pulled up outside the front door of the consulate. A burly, barrel-chested man with a large flourish of a moustache, somewhat like a nineteenth-century cavalry officer, stepped out with a small bag in his hand. A slim woman, also carrying a bag, accompanied him. The couple were quickly ushered into the building and taken down the corridor to the consular office. There, they were told they would be offered asylum in the United States, but only if they clearly identified themselves and agreed to be debriefed by the authorities. Sniper then revealed that the woman with him was not his wife but his mistress – a 31-year-old East Berliner named Irmgard Margareta Kampf. Having received guarantees that Irmgard would be treated well, she left the room, and Sniper proceeded to identify himself fully to the CIA.

He was not called 'Kowalski'. In fact he was 38-year-old Lieutenant Colonel Michał Goleniewski and had, until January 1958, been deputy chief of Polish counter-intelligence. As he laid out his credentials, the depth and breadth of his intelligence work, for friend and foe, became apparent. At that time, Goleniewski still held a senior position in the Polish Intelligence Service, as head of its scientific and technical section. Unofficially, he was also the KGB's source within Polish intelligence, supposedly keeping tabs on any incompetence or deviance from the Moscow line. As Goleniewski talked, the American officers in the room breathed a collective sigh of relief. It was clear that this was indeed Sniper and that he was 'the real deal'.

The CIA's plan had been to escort the couple to a safe house for a few hours, then to proceed to Wiesbaden Air Base for the trip back to America at 10 p.m., but Goleniewski and Kampf were physically exhausted and emotionally shattered, and it was thought best to delay the trip until 7 a.m. the following morning. Goleniewski assured his handlers that colleagues would not start to miss him until the evening of 5 January, a full day later.

At Wiesbaden the next morning, Murphy and Dimmer handed Goleniewski over to the care of Howard Edgar Roman, a 44-year-old officer and a good friend of Director Allen Dulles, who had been studying the Sniper information since it first started flowing in 1958.

Once they had touched down on American soil and the debriefings began, it became clear that the Soviets were running a small army of moles, with sources in West Germany, Sweden, Israel, Denmark, France and America. One was Israel Beer, close confidante of Prime-Minister David Ben-Gurion; another was Irvin Scarbeck, a US State Department official, blackmailed after Polish agents took compromising pictures of him with his mistress in Warsaw; a third was Colonel Stig Wennerström, the Swedish air attaché in Washington, but also a general in the KGB. Then there was Heinz Felfe, the counter-intelligence chief of the BND, who had been exposing West Germany's agents in the Eastern Bloc for more than a decade. Finally, there were the British moles.

In April 1959, a little less than two years before he first began to debrief Goleniewski, Howard Roman flew to London. There, in the fourth-floor conference room in Broadway, he addressed a group of SIS and MI5 officers, telling his startled audience: 'Sniper says the Russians have got two very important spies in Britain; one in British Intelligence, the other somewhere in the Navy.' LAMBDA 2 (the Navy 'mole') would be more difficult to track down, Roman informed them. Sniper's intelligence was that this individual had worked in Warsaw in 1952 and had been blackmailed into espionage after Polish State Security uncovered his activities in the black market. On LAMBDA 1, however, Sniper had provided more specific clues.

The mole in British Intelligence had seen, and then passed on to the KGB, three identifiable SIS documents. One was a section on Poland from 'R6', the annual report circulated to all SIS stations, summarising the intelligence gained by the Service, country by country, region by region. The second was an excerpt from 'RB', another SIS annual survey sent to all stations abroad, outlining the latest scientific and technical research and operations. The third was the 'Watch List' for Poland, which detailed those Polish nationals who SIS thought worth approaching to recruit. These documents narrowed the hunt down to SIS employees in Berlin and Warsaw. The task was obvious – draw up a list of those officers at the two stations who had access to all three documents, and then begin to eliminate them one by one.

That list comprised just ten officers but an inquiry led by Terence Lecky, Head of SIS's counter-intelligence branch, failed to pin the disclosure on any of them. Indeed, according to Peter Wright, MI5's chief scientific adviser, who attended Roman's briefing that day in April, Lecky came up with a completely different explanation for the breach. 'The records of all ten were investigated, and all were exonerated, including George Blake,' Wright recalled many years later. 'Blake, MI5 and MI6 concluded, could not possibly be a spy. The best explanation for the leak, in the absence of any credible human candidate, was a burglary at an MI6 station safe in Brussels, which had taken place two years before.' Wright's own relentless, obsessive investigation into the penetration of Britain by Soviet intelligence led him down one or two rocky paths of conspiracy theory, but he remains a good source on the workings of British intelligence, and there is no reason to doubt his memory on this case.

In April 1960, when all of the Berlin and Warsaw staff had been cleared, SIS officially informed the CIA that the burglary was the source of Sniper's LAMBDA 1. The case remained closed for six months, but Blake was by no means out of the woods, and anyway, Goloniewski was not the only threat at hand. In a bar in Berlin, on the evening of 15 October, an apparently harmless celebration drink was unravelling in a way that would have far-reaching consequences for Blake.

Horst Eitner ('Mickey'), his wife Brigitte and a couple of friends had decided to hold a party to mark the fifth anniversary of Brigitte's release from a labour camp in Siberia. It was a typical night's carousing for the Eitners: they and their drinking partners downed bottles of liqueur, brandy and prosecco before continuing about town, first at the nearby Künstler Café bar, and later at the Bierquelle pub on Schlüterstrasse. By midnight the party was becoming progressively more inebriated. The Eitners were a volatile couple at the best of times, frequently arguing and fighting with each other, the disputes usually fuelled by alcohol. More often than not their rows would fizzle out and a heartfelt reconciliation would follow, until the next session. This occasion was different: Brigitte was angered by the attention the naturally flirtatious Horst was paying to her girlfriend, and something snapped.

First, she tried to ring 'Temple', their SIS contact who had taken over from Blake. When she failed to reach him, she walked into the nearest police station in Charlottenburg and blithely informed the officer on duty that her husband was spying for the Russians. She would later say this was merely carrying out a plan she had been thinking about for some time: she was tired of her husband's spy work and constantly urging him to get a normal job. The bitter memories of

Siberia, together with the alcohol, and yet another of Horst's perceived infidelities, had just provided the spur.

Her husband was arrested immediately, at 6 a.m., while still in the Bierquelle.

In the early days of the interrogation that followed, he admitted that he had done some espionage work, but claimed it was only for the Gehlen organisation. During separate questioning, however, Brigitte told the police a very different story and, gradually, Horst was forced to confess to his work for both SIS and the KGB. The German authorities established that he had tape-recorded conversations in his flat with British agents, had photographed them with a small camera, and had then handed over the recordings and photographs to the Russians. As details of his work as a double agent began to emerge, so SIS officers joined the investigation. They could verify Eitner's claim that he was a British agent but, more importantly, needed to know which secrets he had betrayed to the Russians and who else, if anyone, was involved in his treachery.

The first interrogation the Service conducted with Eitner took place a week after his arrest. Further sessions followed early in January 1961, and then a third series towards the end of March. The officers could never be sure of what he was telling them as truth, lies and fantasy all came tumbling out in equal measure. Eitner tried to play the patriot card: he had never done anything to harm Germany, he was merely fighting the enemies occupying his country. He told his questioners Germany was too much in thrall to the Americans; at the same time, he denied being a Communist. On another day, he said that he was relieved to have been arrested because his briefs would have gone on getting bigger and more wide-ranging and he could have done great damage – especially to the English.

Eventually, there came a claim that made his questioners prick up their ears: Eitner said he wanted to make a statement that could lead them to another person who had links to the KGB. A year or so earlier, he told his interrogators, a Russian intelligence officer had told him they knew of one leading agent working for them who had a vital role in the English Secret Service. That, combined with Eitner's account of his relationship with the man he knew only as 'Max de Vries', led the SIS officers to wonder about George Blake's activities in Berlin. They were all too aware of his reputation as a successful agent-runner, but if what Eitner was telling them about 'Max' was anywhere near the truth, then Blake's methods were, at best unorthodox, and at worst, dangerous. Either way, after many hours interrogating Eitner, it was now time to get some answers from his handler.

At about the same time, in January and February 1961, SIS officers on the Soviet desk back in Broadway, having pored over new evidence from Goleniewski in great detail, were now all but certain of the identity of LAMBDA 1. The trail led them back to George Blake and so to the Lebanon.

The small village of Shemlan, situated twenty miles from Beirut, stands 2,500 feet above sea level and commands breathtaking views. The city is displayed below like a shimmering carpet, the Lebanese coastline stretches out languidly to the West, and the crystal-clear, infinite blue waters of the Mediterranean lie beyond. Life has not always been quite so tranquil in Shemlan, a Christian Maronite community right on the border of the homeland of the Druze, its fierce religious and political rival. The director's office at the Middle East Centre for Arabic Studies (MECAS) was blown up during the Suez crisis, fortunately without the director in it. Early in July 1958, during the Lebanese Civil War, Kemal Jumblatt's Druze forces attacked the village and MECAS students were forced to evacuate, at first to the neighbouring village of Souk El Gharb, and then to Beirut.

By the time George Blake arrived to join the forty or so others on the Arabic course at MECAS, all was calm. In the autumn of 1960, the inhabitants lived in low, white terraced houses spread out along the winding road heading up towards Mount Lebanon. Village life centred around the grocery store and the butcher's shop, and a bar with a few rough tables and chairs where the locals would sit in time-honoured fashion in the cool of the evening, sipping their *arak* and nibbling on a plate of *mezze*. Resentment over Suez and the perceived British rejection of the Arab cause bubbled up occasionally in some quarters, but by and large, in the halcyon seclusion of the hillside, there was little to bother the students.

The legend that MECAS, sponsored and run by the Foreign Office, was a 'School for Spies', went right back to its earliest days in Jerusalem. One of its joint founders, Brigadier Clayton, had been Head of Intelligence in Cairo, while the Principal Instructor, Major Aubrey Eban, was a British army officer who went on to become Foreign Minister of Israel. The mutterings among the Arabs continued off and on, and Blake was certainly not the only spy ever to pass through the school's doors, but joining him that autumn was the usual mix of diplomats, businessmen, linguists and Oxbridge graduates, all there to immerse themselves in this extremely practical, exceedingly tough language course.

The Blakes were given a large apartment on the top floor of a house built against the mountainside, just outside the village. They had no garden, but red geraniums grew against the wall of the house, and there were some flourishing tomatoes left by the previous occupant. At the start Gillian found the move stressful: 'The first four months of life in Beirut were absolute hell, because I was pregnant and I felt miserable. But I settled down and it became a wonderful time, a terrific time, and we were frightfully happy there. I liked being out of the running, I liked being out of the town and having a relaxed lifestyle.' She hired a 'live-in' maid, a local girl called Khadijh, to help look after Anthony, now four, and James (Jamie), not yet two. 'I even had time to take the occasional Arabic lesson myself, although I was not gifted in that respect like George. For the first time in my life I was rather well organised.'

Blake's course was designed to last eighteen months, the first half providing students with a sound working knowledge of written

and spoken Arabic, the second preparing them for the Civil Service
Higher Interpretership Exam. A spirit of healthy competition existed,
with regular tests, and taxing exams at the end of each term.

Blake relished the challenges, but took one day a week off to give
his mind a complete rest, when he and Gillian and the children would
invariably picnic by some beautiful ruins in the mountains, or find a
sheltered cove along the rocky coast. Often Louis Wesseling, his best
friend on the course, and his wife and two young children, would
accompany them. Wesseling, a 32-year-old Dutchman, had previously
worked for Shell in East Africa, but now the oil company wanted him in
the Middle East. He talked a lot about politics and current affairs, and
quickly became aware that his new friend was part of the intelligence
community: 'These things were known between us, if never actually
acknowledged. As for his politics, he was clearly a man of the left. He
never hid his distaste for what he saw as the crass commercialism of
firms like mine. I was particularly struck by his criticism of the Royal
Family. He disliked the pomp and circumstance and injustice of public
life; he said the present Queen would be the last one in the line.'

On one occasion, Wesseling had a curious conversation with Blake
that, in hindsight, took on a greater significance:

> There was at the time the discovery of a British naval officer [Henry
> Houghton] passing secrets to the Russians. George discussed that
> case at length with me, and he told me, 'You know, this is really,
> really small beer'. I said, 'Well, for Christ's sake, it's not so small,
> betraying your country in that way.'
>
> But he merely said, 'No, those sorts of people are paid, and the
> *real* spies are those who are not paid and do it for conviction.' Of
> course at the time, I had no idea he was referring to himself.

In Wesseling's view, Blake had few equals on the Arabic course:
'He was the best student, probably because of his blood, his father,

but also because he was very intelligent – he was the star of the class. He was admired by the younger students for his ability, but also for his strong, original opinions on most matters.' Not everyone shared Wesseling's high opinion of Blake, though. John Coles – later Sir John, Private Secretary to Mrs Thatcher and Head of the Diplomatic Service – thought him 'a dull swot': 'He was always walking about with those word cards, checking the English on the front with the Arabic on the back. He answered questions with a broad smile, but did not have anything very interesting to say.' Coles did recall a group outing, which gave a surprising glimpse of Blake's true state of mind:

> We had formed a dining club called, I think, 'The Mountain' . . . the normally punctilious Blake had turned up very late for one of our dinners, probably because he was seeing some agent some-where in the city. We further remembered going on to the Casino Du Liban and playing roulette.

> Blake had bet on single numbers. More, he had won a pile on one number and immediately put all the proceeds on another number. It takes a real gambler to do that. And that of course is the point. We were watching someone who was engaged in a lifetime gamble and got his excitement from living on the edge. But it had not struck us so at the time.

Blake may have been away from operational work, immersed in study, but the KGB remained eager to stay in touch with their prize. Soon after his arrival in Lebanon, he made contact with the organisa-tion's Head of Station in Beirut, Pavel Yefimovich Nedosekin. There was little information Blake could pass on, but the two men decided to meet once every two months regardless, and Nedosekin gave him a telephone number on which he could be reached in the event of an emergency.

What Blake did not know was that SIS was equally keen to keep an eye on him. All the while, a couple of his fellow students – who were really British agents – were doing their level best to monitor his movements. They were placed there in Beirut because, back in the summer of 1960, although Terence Lecky had provisionally cleared him in the mole hunt, doubts persisted. Lecky and his colleagues retained Blake on their shortlist of three as the candidate for the traitor in their midst, and wanted him isolated and kept under surveillance until they could completely prove his innocence – or guilt. So although Blake believed he had won a battle to be sent to Shemlan, the reality was that his employers had eventually been equally keen for him to go there.

Oblivious to the scrutiny, his studies were progressing smoothly. He had passed the tests at the end of the first term with flying colours and, as Easter approached, he was revising hard and hoping for even better results in the second set of exams.

After the Easter break, students were due to head off for month-long placements with Arab families in various parts of the region, where they would have to speak the language daily and would hopefully build up their confidence and expertise. With Gillian expecting their third child, the Blakes had to come up with a different plan: George would spend his placement with a Lebanese family in the nearby village of Souk El Gharb, and it was agreed that his mother would come out and look after the boys while Gillian was in hospital.

Seemingly free of the intrigues of London and Berlin, indulging his passion for languages, and soon to be a father again, perhaps, for the first time since his posting to Korea, Blake began to appreciate a modicum of peace.

Back in Broadway, what had once been mere doubts about Blake were hardening into near certainty: SIS's most respected Soviet specialist, having studied the evidence provided by Goleniewski and Eitner, was now ready to confront the man he was '90 per cent sure' was the traitor. Blake's nemesis would be Harold Taplin Shergold, known to colleagues and friends as 'Shergy', an intelligence officer of a retiring disposition, but possessing an outstanding intellect, great drive and complete moral integrity.

Shergold, born in 1915, was educated at St Edmund Hall, Oxford, and Corpus Christi College, Cambridge, before becoming a schoolmaster at Cheltenham Grammar School. When war broke out, he joined the Hampshire Regiment, but quickly switched to the intelligence corps. He eventually joined the Combined Service Interrogation Centre, based in Rome, from where he was attached to the Eighth Army in North Africa and Italy. So obviously effective were his skills that he was put in charge of all interrogations from the Battle of El Alamein in Egypt to Cassino in Italy. Shergold chose to join SIS in 1949, and, as the pace of the Cold War quickened, was posted to Germany, where he earned a reputation for running agents with calmness, persistence and authority. In 1954, he was brought back to Head Office to manage agent networks in the Baltic States.

Of no great height, slim, with open features and a high forehead, Shergold's 'bright eyes and compressed vitality suggested intelligence, competence and tight restraint'. He was revered by his colleagues in Broadway. 'In the office he seemed to be utterly reliable. You *believed* what he said, you listened to his every word. He was a real leader of the very best sort,' said an SIS officer who was one of Shergold's protégés in the 1960s. 'He led because of what he was, he was "all of a piece". He could be very tough – but he was also very loyal to his staff.'

Shergold was a very private man, rigidly separating work from personal life. He was never in danger of breaching the intelligence officer's dictum that 'a secret is for life'. Few photographs of him exist; he was to be particularly irritated – and only reluctantly acquiesced – in April 1961 when his CIA colleagues persuaded him to pose with them and the defector Oleg Penkovsky for a picture. Few colleagues knew his wife Bevis, who was an Olympic discus thrower and shot putter at the 1948 London games; nor did they know of Shergy's lifelong charity work for Guide Dogs for the Blind. When he died in December 2000, not a single newspaper ran an obituary.

Goleniewski's other British mole, LAMBDA 2, had already been unmasked by MI5 as Harry Houghton, a clerical officer at the Underwater Weapons Establishment in Portland. Houghton, a heavy drinker and black marketeer, was recruited by Polish intelligence while on the staff of the British Naval Attaché in Warsaw in 1952. Back home, he was in an office where sensitive documents about submarine warfare regularly landed on his desk. He started to routinely pass these secrets on to Polish spies, who in turn passed them on to the Soviets. Houghton also recruited his girlfriend, Ethel Gee, a filing clerk at the base, to help with his spying. The MI5 investigators on their trail stumbled on a much bigger enterprise – in fact they uncovered a whole spy ring.

Their surveillance established that Houghton and Gee were regularly in touch with a businessman called Gordon Lonsdale, who leased jukebox machines, and an antiquarian bookseller named Peter Kroger, and his wife Helen. Lonsdale and the Krogers were revealed to be 'illegals', Soviet spies who had been living in England under deep cover for several years. Lonsdale was in fact Konon Trofimovich Molody, the son of two Soviet scientists, who was selected as a potential foreign intelligence officer from childhood. He had established his fictional identity in Canada, where he obtained a passport in the name of a 'dead double'. Peter and Helen Kroger were in reality Morris and Ethel Cohen, longstanding American KGB illegal agents. At the Old Bailey on 22 March, Molody was given a twenty-five-year sentence, the Cohens twenty years, and Houghton and Gee were each sentenced to fifteen years.

Now it was SIS's turn to trap LAMBDA 1, and by the time of the Portland Spy Ring trial, Shergold felt he had assembled all the pieces of the jigsaw. The Golenieswki material had all been re-evaluated, and documents known to have fallen into KGB hands painstakingly cross-checked and cross-referenced with every report that had landed on the desks of SIS officers in Berlin during the period 1955–59. There was one common denominator – one man who appeared to have had access to them all. Then there was the Eitner evidence. One clue, above all others, persuaded Shergold of Blake's treachery: why had the microphones and recorders in Horst and Brigitte's flat only been installed after Blake had left Berlin? Surely it was because the KGB had no need to listen covertly to his conversations: he was already one of them.

Easter was approaching. Dick White, the Chief, who had been closely briefed on Shergold's findings, was worried that any delay might risk the possibility of an internal leak. The Lebanon was not a secure place for an interrogation and so he wanted Blake brought back to London as quickly as possible. Letters were despatched to Nicholas Elliott, the SIS Chief of Station in Beirut, disclosing that Blake was a suspected Soviet mole and urging the officer to tell him that he should return to London immediately, on the pretext of discussing a future posting. The second letter was for Elliott to hand personally to Blake.

When the letters arrived, Elliott was shaken by the revelation. Like many other senior figures in SIS, he had regarded Blake as a most promising officer. Nonetheless, he quickly got to work, contriving an apparently random encounter with the suspected traitor at which he could relay the request from Broadway. That meeting took place on the evening of Saturday, 25 March.

Earlier that day, Elliott's secretary, a friend and former work colleague of Gillian's, went to the hospital in Beirut where the Blakes' youngest son, Jamie, was being treated after catching pneumonia. The boy was out of danger, but his mother was sleeping in the hospital with him, while Blake was visiting. The secretary told the couple she was going to see the production of *Charley's Aunt* by the local British drama group that evening. She had a spare ticket and wondered whether Blake would like to accompany her? Blake was reluctant at first, pleading pressure of work – his end-of-term exams were just a few days away – but Gillian persuaded him that it would be good to take a break from his studies, so he eventually acceded.

Blake and the secretary enjoyed the first act, and then decided to go to the bar during the interval. There, they encountered Nicholas Elliott and his wife Elizabeth. 'In the course of conversation, Elliott drew me aside and said he was glad I happened to be there as this had saved him a trip up the mountain to see me,' recalled Blake. 'He had received a letter from Head Office with instructions for me to return to London for a few days' consultation in connection with a new appointment. It suggested that I should travel on Easter Monday so as to be available in London early on Tuesday morning.'

At home that night, Blake's thoughts were awhirl. Elliott's news was disconcerting, indeed deeply worrying. Why was he being contacted like this now, when he was in the middle of intensive study? Could not a meeting about his next appointment, which was some way off, wait until July when he was back in London after his holidays? He had been called back hastily to London before for consultations and courses – perhaps this was no different to any of those previous summonses? The more Blake pondered the message, the less he was reassured and his mind turned to a potential escape plan. He had a valid visa for Syria, and as soon as his son was well enough to leave hospital in a couple of days' time, he would be able to drive his wife and children over the border to Damascus. There, he would receive sanctuary from his Soviet masters. It would mean, however, explaining to Gillian what he had done and, anyway, what if he was running away on a mere hunch? Words from Proverbs 28 came to him: was this not a case of 'the wicked flee when no man pursueth'?

By the following morning, Blake's worries had subsided a little. Nonetheless, he felt the need to elicit Moscow Centre's views on whether he was in jeopardy, and so rang Nedosekin's emergency number. The two men arranged to rendezvous that evening on a beach not far from Beirut. At their meeting, Nedosekin attempted to calm Blake's fears, promising he would contact KGB headquarters and relay their views the following day. In their second encounter, the Soviet officer told Blake that Moscow saw no cause for concern. The KGB's enquiries had failed to reveal a leak: Blake should return to London, as requested. Blake was relieved: 'This was exactly the news I wanted to hear. The moment of truth had been put off. I would not have to confess to my wife that I was a Soviet agent.'

He then embarked on two days of exams. When the results were announced on Thursday, 30 March, he finished fourth overall. That evening, winding down after the various tensions of the last few days, he was persuaded to join a stag party in one of Beirut's more expensive restaurants, followed by a session at the Casino du Liban. He won well, but then lost everything in a single throw.

The next day, at the start of the Easter weekend, he called on Nicholas Elliott at the British Embassy to collect some money for his airfare, and took charge of the letter from Broadway. He found nothing in it to worry him. However, there was to be one last jolt to his system: on parting, Elliott asked whether he would like to be booked into the St Ermin's Hotel, just opposite head office in Broadway, for the duration of his visit. Blake replied that he would be staying at his mother's home in Radlett, as usual. Elliott persisted, suggesting it would be more convenient to stay at the hotel. 'For a moment a shadow of a doubt passed my mind but it passed away again,' Blake recalled.

His final day in Lebanon, Easter Sunday, 2 April, was a memorable one. The Blakes headed off by car for a trip to Byblos, which, with its Crusader citadel, Phoenician ramparts and Bronze Age temples was reputed to be the oldest continuously inhabited town in the world. After a picnic by the side of the desert under a fig tree, they drove back through colourful, festive Maronite villages where the locals were out in force in their best clothes, celebrating the holy day. That evening, the Blakes were invited to dinner by fellow student, Alan Rothnie, already an established diplomat, and his wife Anne. A bottle of champagne was opened to celebrate Blake's new appointment.

Next morning, Easter Monday, 3 April, Gillian accompanied her husband to the airport for an early flight. Blake promised to be back in

Shemlan on Saturday in time for Anthony's fifth birthday party.

He touched down at Heathrow to a sullen, wet day in London in sharp contrast to the endless blue skies and warmth of the Lebanon. With much to look forward to, he remained in good spirits. At her flat in Shenley Hill, Radlett, he told his mother about Jamie's illness, Gillian's pregnancy, and their plans for Anthony's birthday party at the weekend. Mother and son stayed up talking until after midnight.

A few hours later, the dismantling of this happy family life would begin.

15

Confession

The SIS officers gathered at Head Office in Broadway on that Tuesday, 4 April 1961, had been pondering the trickiest of matters: how best to interrogate a colleague they now believed was a traitor.

The Chief, Dick White, was determined to learn the lessons of the Philby débâcle in 1951, when a haphazard, episodic 'trial' of sorts had brought no results and no conviction. Nor did he think it appropriate in this case for an outsider like Jim Skardon – the skilful MI5 interrogator who had broken Klaus Fuchs, the physicist who gave the Soviets secrets of America's atomic bomb – to be let loose on Blake. Instead, he decided to assemble an SIS 'tribunal' led by Harold Shergold, with support from his close colleague on the Soviet desk, Terence Lecky, and Ben Johnson, a former police officer who had experience in interviewing defectors. White was banking, above all, on Shergy's calm authority and doggedness to extract the truth from Blake.

Blake arrived at the office of SIS's personnel department on Petty France, a short walk from Head Office, just before 10 a.m. He was met, as he had expected, by Ian Critchett, Deputy Head of the department. He was not, however, anticipating that Critchett would be accompanied by Shergold. After cordial greetings, Shergold asked Blake if he would come with him first, as there were a few matters that had cropped up about his time in Berlin that needed to be ironed out.

Then, instead of heading towards Broadway, Blake was surprised to be led through St James's Park, across The Mall, and up the flight of stone steps by Duke of York's Column that led to Carlton Gardens. They were heading for familiar ground – No. 2, where he had worked in Y section. It was here that he had sat round a table helping to formulate plans for the Berlin tunnel, and where, more happily, he had first met Gillian. As he followed Shergold into the spacious committee room commanding a panoramic view of the stylish Nash terrace below, he sensed that he was no longer in friendly territory.

Lecky and Johnson rose to greet him, and then Shergold got down to work. It quickly became evident to Blake that this conversation was not going to be about a few minor 'housekeeping' problems as he had been led to believe. The questioning, always courteous yet firmly probing, concerned vital operational matters from his time in Berlin – 'Boris', the Eitners, the tape recorders in Mickey's flat, and much else besides.

'Shergold asked me why I thought the Soviets had wanted to install microphones only after I had left and another officer had taken over. To this I could only reply that I did not have the faintest idea,' Blake recalled.

It was clear, Shergold told him, that 'Boris' was a mere KGB plant. How could Blake explain that? 'I agreed that the evidence pointed that way, but as to why, well, all I could say was that Mickey had been a convenient link for this purpose.'

Similar questions followed over the next few hours. When lunchtime arrived, and with it a much-needed break, Blake's uncertain position was further underlined when nobody suggested going to eat together. Instead, pariah-like, he headed out alone to a favourite Italian restaurant in Soho, and anxiously considered his fate.

The afternoon's session only deepened his unease. Shergold moved the conversation on from Berlin to Poland, displaying on the table all the SIS documents that had fallen into the hands of the Polish Intelligence Service. Access to these papers had been highly restricted but Blake had been on the distribution list in every case. Was there anything he could tell them about that? 'I said I couldn't, and that their guess was as good as mine . . . it was clear to me that they must have a source in the Polish Intelligence Service at a pretty high level.' As the afternoon went on, the inquisition – for that is what it had become – reached its logical conclusion. Blake was bluntly accused of working for the KGB. 'This I flatly denied. At six o'clock we broke up and they asked me to come back the following morning at 10 a.m. On the way back to Radlett, I kept turning over in my mind all that had been said that day. Of one thing I was no longer in any doubt – SIS knew that I was working for the Soviets. Otherwise such a grave accusation would never have been levelled at me.'

By now, the reason for the interrogation taking place in Carlton Gardens was clear to him: they had wanted to record the conversation, and it was a far more suitable place to set up the necessary equipment than the cramped offices in Broadway.

That evening, Blake kept up the agonising pretence that all was well. Over dinner with his mother he continued blithely to discuss plans for the weekend in Shemlan. As he reflected on the day's events, he concluded: 'I was in deep trouble, but I thought I could still save myself.'

Day two of the interrogation again focused on the Polish documents and the likelihood that they had been photographed and passed on to the Soviets by someone in the Berlin station. Shergold led the way again, piling up small pieces of additional evidence, accumulating them into a substantial case. Once more, Blake was accused, quite straightforwardly, of being a Soviet agent. 'It wasn't hostile,' Blake recalled, 'but it was persistent. I continued to pretend I knew no more than they did. Somehow, I still hoped to get out of it.'

At lunchtime Blake took his mind off the interrogation for a while with a walk over to Gamages, a department store at Holborn. In the 'People's Popular Emporium', he ordered a mosquito net his wife had requested, ensuring it would be delivered in time for his weekend journey to Lebanon, though he felt ever more pessimistic about his chances of being able to deliver it in person.

That afternoon, Shergold was interested in exploring any ideological motives Blake may have had for his treachery. When and how did his loyalty to Marxism and the Soviet Union begin? How had it taken such firm root? Blake managed to survive this line of questioning and, at the end of the day, returned once more to the flat in Radlett in utter turmoil: 'These were, without doubt, the most difficult hours of my life. Knowing that I was in serious danger, that, whatever happened, life would never be the same for any of us, I had to pretend to my mother that all was well.'

On Thursday, 6 April, day three of the interrogation, Shergold decided to adopt a different technique. He had come round to the view that Blake was as much an emotional traitor as a professional one, and what was needed was something to spark his sense of moral indignation. 'Whether by luck or by planning, they hit upon the right psychological approach,' Blake recalled. What they said to him was this: 'We know that you worked for the Soviets, but we understand why. While you were their prisoner in Korea, you were tortured and made to confess that you were a British intelligence officer. From then on, you were blackmailed and had no choice but to collaborate with them.'

After hours of relentless questioning, met throughout by a solid brick wall of answers, Shergold, Lecky and Johnson were astonished by Blake's reply.

> When they put the case in this light, something happened which went against all the dictates of elementary common sense and the instinct of self-preservation. All I can say is that it was a gut reaction.

> Suddenly I felt an upsurge of indignation and wanted my interrogators and everyone else to know that I had acted out of conviction, out of a belief in Communism, and not under duress or for financial gain.

> This feeling was so strong that without thinking what I was doing I burst out 'No, nobody tortured me! No, nobody blackmailed me! I myself approached the Soviets and offered my services to them of my own accord.'

Blake's account of his interrogation was first told in his autobiography in 1990 but, years earlier, in 1964, when discussing this pivotal moment while in Wormwood Scrubs prison, he gave a slightly different explanation for his outburst. In that account, there was no ideological outrage, but rather a curious, inverted moral reasoning. Fellow prisoner Kenneth de Courcy recalled Blake's words: 'If I denied what I'd done, I would have had to live with a lie on my lips, and I couldn't have tolerated myself for doing that.'

Whatever the impulse behind its collapse, the wall suddenly came crashing down. Shergold and his team had won a confession, or at least the beginning of one. Then, after the hours of pent-up tension, Blake began to unburden himself in extraordinary fashion: 'I explained, in great detail, why I did it and what I had done. Their attitude didn't change, they continued to be polite, even friendly.'

A confession to an SIS tribunal was one thing but if Blake was to be prosecuted, statements made to police that could be submitted to a regular court of law would be necessary. Special Branch officers Detective Superintendent Louis Gale and Detective Chief Inspector Ferguson Smith arrived on the scene. They told him that there was evidence that he had committed an offence or offences against the Official Secrets Act, and they cautioned him. Blake told them he wanted to make a statement and, over the course of the afternoon, proceeded to confess his treachery. It was 8 p.m. before he told

Gale and Smith that he wanted to stop. They agreed to resume the following day.

A chauffeur-driven car took Blake back to Radlett. He had been given strict instructions not to tell his mother, who had no idea her son was a Soviet agent, anything about what had taken place. He told her only that the trip to Beirut would have to be postponed as he had been asked to leave London for a few days to attend an important conference.

If there was a fleeting moment when he considered trying to escape, perhaps to reach the sanctuary of the Soviet Embassy, he quickly dismissed the idea: 'It would have been impossible. I was already sure I was being followed. I felt the game was up.'

The next morning, Friday, 7 April, he was back at Carlton Gardens. Gale and Smith arrived at 3.15 p.m. to finish off his statement, which was finally completed by 6 p.m. In the course of the conversation, he also admitted to being in contact with a Soviet intelligence officer in Beirut in November 1960. Gale produced five photographs of Soviet officials in the Lebanon and asked him to pick the right man. Blake pointed to Nedosekin.

Dick White and his colleagues were in a dilemma. Blake's unequivocal confession, welcome though it was, had been unexpected. Despite his statement to the police, they felt there was still much more they could extract from him, as he seemed in the mood to reveal anything and everything about his years as a KGB mole. As a result, instead of locking him up in a prison cell straightaway, Blake was driven under police escort to a small village in Hampshire, where Shergold and his wife Bevis had a cottage. Joining him on the journey were Ben Johnson and John Quine, Head of R5, the counter-espionage section of SIS which worked closely with MI5. It was a highly unusual way of treating a self-confessed traitor. Although Blake was being subjected to prolonged interrogation, to an outsider it might have looked like a weekend party among friends.

Special Branch officers ringed the house and every time Blake went

for one of his numerous walks with Quine or Shergold, a police car
followed slowly behind. At night, Quine shared a bedroom with Blake,
listening sympathetically as the confessor poured out his worries
about his family's future. Above all, they wanted to understand the
motivation for what he had done. It was a strange weekend, as Blake
remembered: 'I particularly remember one afternoon which I spent
in the kitchen making pancakes with the old grandmother. I am something of a specialist in this, and when it was suggested we should eat
pancakes, I offered to make them.'

Throughout, as Shergold, Lecky and Quine learned of the full extent
of Blake's activities, they relayed their discoveries back to Broadway. In
turn the Service liaised with Government ministers – including Edward
Heath, the Lord Privy Seal, whose brief covered the intelligence
services – to formulate a plan of action. They were in uncharted territory. The old ploy of offering a traitor immunity from prosecution in
exchange for full disclosure of his crimes surely did not apply: Blake
was willingly, it appeared, offering up all his secrets. On the other hand,
charging and prosecuting him in open court would have the disadvantage of exposing the Service to public attention and possible ridicule.
Moreover, if Blake underwent a change of heart and decided to retract
his confession, then that exposure could be exponentially disastrous.

Blake himself was contemplating a far worse fate: 'I thought I might
well be got rid of, even though it wasn't British practice to assassinate
people.'

He was driven back to London on Sunday afternoon and taken to
an SIS safe house in Vicarage Road, East Sheen. Here, it appeared
to him that his future was finally decided. 'There had been frequent
conversations in the house over the weekend, conducted in another
room so I couldn't hear what was being said,' he recalled. 'Then, in the
course of Sunday night, while we were having supper in the kitchen,
there was another telephone call. From the reaction of my colleagues I
could see they weren't best pleased with that; they had expected something different.'

A decision had now been made. At just after 7 a.m. on Monday, 10 April, Detective Superintendent Gale and Detective Chief Inspector Smith arrived at Vicarage Road. This time, they told Blake they were arresting him on a charge under Section One of the Official Secrets Act, 1911. He was driven to New Scotland Yard, where he was formally charged and cautioned, and then on to Bow Street Court, where the Chief Metropolitan Magistrate, Sir Robert Blundell, had organised a special hearing in circumstances of exceptional secrecy.

This was a closed hearing to which none of the usual court reporters had been invited. No official notice was posted afterwards and, apart from the Magistrate's clerk, Blake and the Special Branch officers, no one witnessed the proceedings. It was as if they had never happened. In a matter of ten minutes, Blake was remanded in custody for a week. He was then taken immediately to Brixton prison, where he was put in a room in the hospital wing.

In the following days, his mood ranged from cautious optimism to utter despair. In his bleakest moments – even if he now realised that assassination was a far-fetched idea – he still wondered if he might face execution: 'I believed that the maximum sentence for the offences I'd committed was fourteen years. On the other hand, I didn't exclude the possibility – because I didn't know so much about British law – of there being somewhere on the books an old law, dating back to the Middle Ages, which had never been abrogated, which would enable them to sentence me to death.'

While Blake spent his first night in jail, back in Shemlan, steps were being taken to inform his unsuspecting wife. 'April 10 had been a lovely day, and although it was only 8.30 p.m., I had dozed off in my armchair,' Gillian recalled. 'Having helped Khadijh get Anthony and Jamie to bed, I was pretty tired. I was expecting my third child in six weeks' time. Funnily enough, I had felt extremely restless all day. In fact, I was thinking of going down to Beirut to do some shopping, just for something to do.' Instead, she received an unexpected visit from a couple called the Everitts, representatives of the British Embassy, who told her to stay in as a 'Foreign Office official' would be coming to see her that evening. She was surprised, but heartened, as she had heard no news from Blake since his departure for London a week before.

That evening she opened the door to John Quine, whom she had never met but knew was a close colleague of Blake's. She thanked him for taking the trouble to come, but could sense embarrassment in his halting reply. So she poured them both a drink and sat down to listen to what he had to say: 'First of all he asked me if I knew anything at all about what had happened, and quickly discovered I didn't. Then he began to unveil a story of treason and duplicity that left me horror-struck. Horror at what had happened to our life, horror at what George had done to my country and to the Office. Horror – but not disbelief.'

Despite the shock of learning that her husband was a Soviet spy, she did not doubt what she was being told: 'Clearly it was hard to believe, but I didn't think for a moment that they'd made a mistake. I didn't think, "They must have got hold of the wrong man, or this can't be true" – even though, of course, I had no idea he was working for the Russians. As I thought back to George's background, and to the six and a half years of our very happy married life, it all seemed to fit in somehow.'

Quine searched the house for evidence that could help the prosecution, and he found Blake's diaries for 1946 to 1960 – the only years missing being the period when he was in Korea. The Everitts returned to pick him up at 11.15 p.m. Both they and Quine offered to stay the night but Gillian declined the offer: 'I was just longing for them to go, and in the end everybody went off. I took some sleeping pills, which had a wonderfully tranquillising effect and made me feel quite out of this world, though I felt a bit like that anyway. But I didn't sleep much.'

Next day, she started to pack up and get the children ready for a hasty return to London. Rather than risk being cornered by the press at her parents' home in London, it was felt she should instead stay with friends in the country. John Quine and one of her friends from the Embassy, who was an old schoolmate, accompanied her on the journey home.

Meanwhile, at MECAS, word had begun to spread that Blake was facing some sort of charges of treachery – to the consternation of his fellow pupils. 'The younger students in particular looked up to him and held him in great esteem. So they all got together to write a letter, a petition, to the Foreign Office, saying there must have been a mistake and George was innocent,' recalled Louis Wesseling. 'They took it to Alan Rothnie. To be quite honest, I don't know if it was ever sent – but it was certainly written.'

In Brixton prison, Blake's spirits were lifted by hearing the extraordinary news on the radio that Yuri Alexeyevitch Gagarin, the young Soviet cosmonaut, had become the first human being in space after his Vostok 1 craft completed an orbit of the Earth on 12 April. The *Daily Mirror* called it 'The Greatest Story of Our Lifetime'. The carpenter's boy from the small Russian village of Klushino had spent 89 minutes travelling in his capsule above Africa and South America. 'It was a great boost to my morale . . . I experienced it as a confirmation that I had not laboured in vain, that I had helped those who were in the vanguard of progress, who were opening up new horizons and leading mankind to a happier future. I felt then that it showed Soviet society was ahead,' Blake recalled.

Meanwhile, in Whitehall and the Inns of Court, careful preparations were being made for his trial – for how, exactly, the Establishment should present the case to the outside world. The strategy they settled on was, in short, to cover up as much as possible.

On Saturday, 15 April, Edward Heath chaired a meeting of Foreign Office and other government officials to come up with a plan of action for handling the media. They considered two options initially: first, to claim – or rather pretend – that Blake was a temporary but genuine member of the Foreign Service; or, secondly, to admit right from the start that he was not actually a Foreign Office employee and so imply that he was a spy. The former was swiftly ruled out, as 'it would produce another Burgess and Maclean case with incalculable effects on the Foreign Service'. Unfortunately, the alternative was also rejected. Heath and Dick White believed that it 'would produce immediate grave repercussions in the Lebanon and perhaps elsewhere in the Middle East, and would also destroy the valuable protection deriving from our traditional refusal to comment on intelligence matters'. Finally, they decided that government press offices would merely be instructed 'to be as non-committal as possible'.

The notes of this meeting also show that a decision to try Blake *in camera* had already been taken in principle by that weekend.

To reinforce the Government's approach, the D-Notice system was put into action. Launched in 1912 as a supposedly voluntary code that asked news editors not to publish or broadcast items that might endanger national security, in reality it had the force of law as few newspapers dared to ignore it. The D-Notice Secretary in 1961 – as he had been since 1945 – was the amiable 74-year-old Rear-Admiral Sir George Thomson. No stranger to espionage stories, in the preceding two decades he had blocked quite a few, although he had also allowed one or two through, usually if he believed they could flush out some information that would be of benefit to the intelligence services. On the whole, he maintained a very friendly relationship with most newspaper editors and so, when he sent out a notice to them on 1 May (pointedly ignoring the Communist *Daily Worker*), he could be assured of their co-operation.

The notice explained that 'Blake is an employee of MI6 [SIS], and therefore comes under 'D' Notice dated 27.4.1956, requesting you not to disclose the identities and activities of employees of MI5 and MI6, nor any mention of the association between MI6 and the Foreign Office'. Just in case that proved insufficiently persuasive, Thomson went on: 'In addition, for your personal and confidential information, there is special reason for requesting your co-operation in this case in that the lives of MI6 employees are still in danger'.

All SIS employees had by then been informed that there was a mole in the organisation. A coded telegram had been sent out to every station around the world, the first part reading 'THE FOLLOWING NAME IS A TRAITOR'. After deciphering, the second part spelled out the letters G-E-O-R-G-E-B-L-A-K-E.

The news came as a huge shock to the Service and, like the students at MECAS, many of Blake's former colleagues at Broadway simply could not accept it. 'I'm having difficulty persuading some of the staff that he's a traitor,' White told senior colleagues at the time.

Over at 'The Fort' – Fort Monckton, SIS's principal training centre on the south coast at Gosport, in Hampshire – all work was abandoned after an emotional meeting. The Head of Training called all the recruits together. They were told that their futures were uncertain, and that he now had to tell them something he never in his life thought he would have to say: there was a traitor in the ranks. He had been unmasked, and his name was George Blake. The recruits watched as he promptly broke down and wept.

Blake's solicitor was Albert Edward Cox, known to all as 'Bill', from the firm Claude Hornby & Cox in Great Marlborough Street, which had built a reputation for specialist criminal work, particularly the more glamorous society cases. Cox's tall figure was a familiar one around the central London criminal courts. He had contracted the debilitating disease spondylolysis shortly after joining the Scottish Regiment in the war, damaging his vertebrae and giving him a distinctive stoop.

Blake's barrister was Jeremy Hutchinson QC, who had only taken silk a couple of months earlier. The previous October, he had been a member of the defence team that successfully defended Penguin Books on a charge of breaking the Obscene Publications Act over the publication of the full, unexpurgated version of *Lady Chatterley's Lover.* Hutchinson and Blake, who had both served in the Royal Naval Volunteer Reserve during the war, hit it off immediately. 'I was enormously taken by him. He had great charm,' recalled Hutchinson.

What he emphasised to me were two things. One was the behaviour of the Americans on the 'Death March'. He felt they were so spineless, and so corrupt, and so third-rate in every way, and he took terribly against them. They were wimps, you know, in his view.

The other was Marx. He read *Das Kapital* from cover to cover and he said it was a remarkable book and completely convincing. He said, 'I had a lot of time to think, and it seemed to me a basis for a better world.' I think he was completely genuine – that was the impression I got. I didn't feel he was trying to justify himself in any way.

Communism was a religion, and remains a religion, and he had that kind of mind, and became obsessed by something that was idealistic. That's what gave me my enthusiasm for doing this case; it wasn't a squalid money arrangement with the Russians, and it wasn't a sexual thing like old Vassall [the 1962 Admiralty spy]. I accepted it was a true conversion and he had that kind of mind that would be 100 per cent committed, and that his spying was based on this absolute religious conversion.

On Tuesday, 18 April, Blake was back in Bow Street Magistrates Court, again in front of Sir Robert Blundell, and again in conditions of complete secrecy. This time, however, the press were fed the bare bones of the hearing and, for the first time, the case of George Blake entered the public domain: 'Secrets Charge in Guarded Court' was the headline on the third page of the *Daily Mirror*.

Six days later, Blake made his third and final appearance in Bow Street, this time to be sent for trial at the Old Bailey. Under the front-page headline 'A Secret Trial At The Old Bailey', the *Mirror* reported that Blake – described as a 'government official' – would be the first defendant since the war to have his case heard entirely in private. After the 95-minute hearing, the paper pinned up outside the court revealed that Blake faced three charges under Section One of the Official Secrets Act: one allegedly committed between April 1955 and April 1959; the second between April and June 1959; and the third between June 1959 and September 1960. It was stated, through his solicitor, that he reserved his defence.

Bill Cox visited Blake in Brixton jail the following day and then, on Thursday, 26 April, he went to Chester Row to meet Gillian and her mother. He asked Blake's wife if she could think of any as yet unspoken motive for her husband behaving as he had. She did not answer immediately but, on 1 May, Gillian sent a letter to Cox thanking him for his visit and offering her thoughts on her husband's relationship with Iris Peake, and how this might have affected his mood as he set off for Korea. She told Cox she believed that the end of the affair with Iris – who was now Lady-in-Waiting to Princess Margaret – had added to Blake's 'restless state of mind' as he left for his SIS posting in Seoul.

On Tuesday, 2 May, Gillian came up from Sussex to pay her first visit to Brixton jail, together with her mother-in-law and John Quine. It was only from his visitors that Blake learned his trial at the Old Bailey would take place the following day: 'Nobody had told me, and I was quite unprepared. On the other hand, I reflected, what was there to be prepared about? Whether I would be found guilty or not guilty? That had been settled by my confession. That left only the sentence.'

'It was very emotional and he was heartbroken by it all for my sake,' Gillian remembered. 'It was no different seeing him there, somehow. I didn't reproach him at all.'

The stage was now set for Blake's trial in London's Central Criminal Court, the Old Bailey. He would be following in the footsteps of a number of other spies who had stepped into the dock of the famous No. 1 Court since the war, notably Klaus Fuchs, similarly charged under the Official Secrets Act.

Fuchs, who gave away the Allies' atom bomb plans, had feared the worst. 'What will happen to me,' he asked his counsel, Derek Curtis Bennett, 'will I be executed?' Bennett, astounded by his client's naiveté, had patiently explained that the maximum penalty the judge could hand down for violation of the Act was fourteen years.

Jeremy Hutchinson reassured his client in exactly the same way. Nonetheless, Blake spent the night before the trial in a state of anxiety and uncertainty: 'I didn't know what my fate was going to be. I was torn between hope and despair.'

16

Trial

A little less than an hour before the trial was due to begin on 3 May 1961, Jeremy Hutchinson walked down the steps to the waiting room beneath No. 1 Court at the Old Bailey, with a final request for his client.

He knew that the task he faced – to persuade the judge, Lord Parker of Waddington, the Lord Chief Justice, to show leniency – was an extremely difficult one which would be made a little easier if the defendant would offer some contrition. 'He said it would help, in his mitigation, if I would say I was sorry,' recalled Blake. 'But there was no possibility of me showing remorse for my actions. I told him it would be dishonest, because if I hadn't been caught, I would still be carrying on with my activities.'

It was a disappointment, but when Hutchinson stepped into the courtroom to set out his papers, he suddenly had a much more serious issue to grapple with. The Attorney General, Sir Reginald Manningham-Buller, prosecuting for the Crown, told Hutchinson that he now proposed to deal with the whole case in open court, not *in camera*, as previously agreed. In those circumstances, Hutchinson would be prevented from referring to a long list of subjects upon which his argument depended – first and foremost, Manningham-Buller wanted no mention of the existence of SIS, nor that Blake had been an officer of the Service.

Hutchinson was taken aback by this last-minute request: 'I had no idea they wanted it held in public. Of course, in principle, I would have liked an open trial. But the conditions they laid down would have meant I didn't have the freedom to tell George's side of the story. I conferred with him, and reluctantly – despite the disadvantage that the outside world would not hear a word of mitigation, however constrained – we decided it would be better if it was held *in camera* so I had complete freedom in my address to the judge.'

Manningham-Buller was a formidable adversary for the new young QC. He had built a reputation as an able and hardworking law officer, his ability noted by Churchill, who had, to the surprise of many, appointed him Solicitor General in 1951. In the years that followed, he had proven himself a tough and effective debater in the Commons, and a formidable opponent in the courtroom, though his abrasive style endeared him to few. The sobriquet *Spectator* columnist Bernard Levin bestowed upon him – 'Sir Reginald Bullying-Manner' – stuck.

For Hutchinson, the encounter with the Attorney General was to be a bruising one: 'I demanded to see – counsel to counsel – the actual evidence that this man [Blake] had caused the deaths of large numbers of people as a result of them being named by him to the Russians . . . I heard no evidence, nor did I see evidence of any of these terrible things that were supposed to have happened. I was simply told what the Lord Chief Justice was told; evidence of – maybe – places and names, potential damage, changes of procedure and so on, resulting from Blake's activities, but never any *hard* evidence that lives had been lost.' Hutchinson's new status as a QC made him nervous about creating a fuss: 'I was bullied into submission over this. If I'd been ten years more senior I might have been tougher, I might have even gone public about it.'

Manningham-Buller's right-hand man that day was a recent adversary of Hutchinson's from the *Lady Chatterley's Lover* obscenity trial. Mervyn Griffith-Jones QC had led that failed prosecution, revealing the extent to which he was out of touch with modern times by wondering, during his opening statement, whether this was a novel 'you would even wish your wife or servants to read'.

Hutchinson might also have had cause for concern over the judge. On the face of it, Parker was a welcome change from his irascible and domineering predecessor, Lord Goddard, who had always made his decidedly conservative political and social views quite plain. By contrast, Parker appeared to be unassuming and tolerant, at least in the early months of his tenure. Himself the son of a famous judge, he gained a double first in science at Cambridge, and initially contemplated a career as a geologist before settling for the Law. Such was his reputation that scores of convicted offenders appealed to his court hoping for reduced sentences. Parker quickly dashed those hopes – in fact, more often than not, he and his colleagues increased the punishment. In a series of speeches in North America and Britain, he proposed harsher sentences – criticising the 'indiscriminate commuting of death sentences' – and also showed himself to be a keen advocate of corporal punishment.

Society was slowly changing, but deference was still very much the order of the day in 1961, and that did not just mean *to* the ruling class – the 'Establishment' – but also *within it*, by one group of 'Old Boys' to another. Judicial independence from government was unusual and Parker was not about to buck the trend. In a speech to the organisation Justice in 1960, he made it very clear where he stood: 'The courts must recognise that national policy requires a measure of administrative freedom,' he told his audience. 'They have a positive duty to be the handmaiden of administration, rather than its governor.' In other words, to enact state power, rather than protect citizens from it.

So, with a rough and ruthless prosecutor – the Government's representative in court – and an illiberal judge, both in undoubted, if unstated harmony, Hutchinson faced a seemingly insurmountable challenge.

Blake stepped into the dock of No. 1 Court just before 10.30 a.m. and as his gaze swept round the courtroom, he spotted some familiar faces in the public gallery – the Chief, Sir Dick White, John Quine, and other SIS colleagues. Also present were Roger Hollis, the Head of MI5, and Sir Theobald Mathew, Director of Public Prosecutions. Small details lodged in his memory: 'One thing that disappointed me was that the judge had a small wig on, much smaller than I expected. And I was puzzled as to why, instead of sitting in the middle of the dais, he was sitting on the left of it.' What also struck him was the stark contrast in physical appearance between the two principal lawyers: 'I liked very much my intellectual, ascetic-looking counsel, who compared very favourably to the Attorney General, to whom I remember taking an intense dislike. I thought he looked very gross, with red, wobbling cheeks and bulging eyes, over-indulgent looking.'

The Clerk of the Court, Leslie Boyd, read out the five charges. It was now clear that each related to a different period of Blake's employment with SIS, but the same charge applied to all five periods: 'that for a purpose prejudicial to the safety or interests of the State, you communicated to another person information which might have been directly or indirectly useful to the enemy'. To each charge, the Clerk asked Blake if he pleaded guilty or not guilty. To each one, Blake replied simply: 'Guilty.' Then Manningham-Buller got down to business.

The prosecutor's task seemed straightforward enough; after all, as he told the court right from the start, Blake's confession had been 'complete and detailed'. But he had no intention of quoting from it: 'Its contents – except for very short passages to which I propose to refer – must remain secret.' The same cloak of concealment extended to Blake's job description. 'He has been employed in the Government's service, both in this country and overseas,' was all Manningham-Buller would say.

What he was prepared to reveal from Blake's confession was the chronology of his ideological switch: 'In his statement, Blake says that more than ten years ago his philosophical and political views underwent a change, and in the autumn of 1951 he held the strong conviction that the Communist system was the better one and deserved to triumph. To quote his own words, he resolved to join the Communist side in establishing what he believed to be, on balance, a more just society.'

The court heard that, for the preceding nine and a half years, Blake had been working as an agent for the Russians, delivering a wealth of information to them. Manningham-Buller again reiterated that he was unable to publicly reveal the nature of that information but emphasised that, in his confession, Blake had admitted passing to the KGB officers any interesting official document he could lay his hands on.

> He had access to information of very great importance. Although he held responsible positions, his employment fortunately did not give him any access to information or documents relating to secret weapons or any nuclear or atomic energy, but it is the case that he has done most serious damage to the interests of this country.

Then Manningham-Buller made his case for handing Blake the stiffest of sentences. Referring to the recent Portland Spy Ring trial – in which he had also prosecuted, and over which Lord Justice Parker had presided – he commented: 'That was a grave case but that this is an even graver case is, in my submission, clearly shown by the confession made by the accused.' Gordon Lonsdale, the mastermind of that espionage group, had been handed a twenty-five-year sentence – might Blake be given more?

Manningham-Buller's address had taken just eight minutes.

Then, referring to his conversations with Hutchinson about holding the case *in camera*, Manningham-Buller invited Parker to move into closed session so that 'matters may be referred to which would be prejudicial to the National Safety'. The judge replied: 'Mr Attorney, Mr Hutchinson, I have a very strong dislike, I think we all have, of hearing anything *in camera*, but you are satisfied, are you, it would be better?' In restrained language, Hutchinson's response nonetheless showed the frustration he felt at this course of action having been forced on him at the very last moment: 'That is the choice I have had to make in the last ten minutes. I had no idea until then that these proceedings were going to be held in public. Having had a word with my client, he wishes, despite the disadvantages in many ways to him, that I should have complete freedom in addressing your Lordship on all matters.'

It was 10.40 a.m. when Parker ordered the court to be cleared of press and public, and Jeremy Hutchinson stood up to deliver his speech of mitigation. It would last fifty minutes and tell a compelling story of a flawed man's life in a turbulent period of history – an eloquent *apologia* for Blake's actions. Until now, more than fifty years on, what Hutchinson said has remained unknown to anyone who was not in the courtroom during that hour.

First of all came recognition of the scale of his client's crimes: 'It is perfectly clear, of course, that any man who pleads guilty to an offence of this kind must be looked at by any court, indeed by any Englishman, with distaste, and therefore I cannot claim any sympathy from your Lordship, but I do ask some patience and some understanding.' Hutchinson also wanted to establish from the start that this should not be any kind of 'show trial'.

> My Lord, whatever else this is, this is not a political trial, and it is not a propaganda trial, and it is not a move in a Cold War. The offences of course, in this matter, are inextricably bound up with politics, but that does not make it a political trial.

> We here in modern days have never had trials in order to bring comfort to our allies or fear to our enemies, but here in this court your Lordship is trying an individual for the crime which he has committed. I know your Lordship will bear in mind, as well as the offence, the offender.

Hutchinson then began to lead Parker through the story of Blake's life, from his childhood in Rotterdam, through his time in Egypt, his family's escape to England, and his internment in a German camp. He paused to reflect on Blake's role as a courier in the Dutch resistance: 'It needs no words of mine to say what he saw as a boy of that age, running messages, running the gauntlet, seeing men die in front of him during that time in Holland.' He moved on, through Blake's spirited flight through occupied Europe, then his voyage to England, his adopted country that he saw properly for the first time at the age of 20.

The first reference to the real nature of Blake's job came soon afterwards. After recounting how he had left the Navy following the unfortunate experience on midget submarines, he told the court that Blake was 'put into the Intelligence Service as Dutch speaking, and then went back to Holland in that job. In 1946/47 he was transferred permanently to the Intelligence, and was then sent after the end of hostilities to Germany.'

In recounting Blake's seven months at Cambridge, Hutchinson emphasised that the switch to the other side had not yet taken place: 'However anti-Fascist he was, and however much pro-Russian propaganda he had been subjected to in the war, his view was firmly and strongly anti-Communist. He had had a conservative, moral, religious upbringing. He belonged to the Calvinist faith and from 13 to 16 he formed a firm intention of joining the Church, which your Lordship may think is relevant when we move on a bit in his life.' But at Cambridge his views about Russia did begin to alter: 'He learnt for the first time about the better side – and it was a revelation – of Russian culture and literature. He learnt the Russian language and this was the first time in his life when he had had a period of contemplation and thought at all.'

Hutchinson urged Parker to consider that on the eve of his posting to Korea, Blake's life had been almost wholly forged in the furnace of war and upheaval: 'I know your Lordship will realise that this young man, with no attachment to this country by birth, [or] by growing up, by tradition, by education, when others more fortunate than him had all these things in peace and quiet, was either in Egypt, or running messages for the underground, involving himself in war, deprivation, murder and suchlike, from the age of 16 onwards.'

Then he described the occasion in Korea when Blake, Holt and their fellow captives were driven out of Seoul and taken up into the mountains in a jeep, and made clear that this was a life-changing moment for his client.

> They were told to get out. This man, being 28, and having been through all that he had been through, knew – or thought he knew – this was when he was going to be shot, as other people had been.

> Most people, I suppose, have faced a moment when they think they're going to die, and they have no doubt done what he did, which was to review his life.

> He came to the conclusion then – he asked himself – 'Why am I going to die? What am I dying for?' He had seen the brutality of one side, but he had also seen for the past year in the regime of Syngman Rhee, notorious for its utter corruption and cruelty, exactly the same methods being used on the other side . . .

> My Lord, in addition to that, he had also seen for the first time in his life poverty of a kind which we in this country know nothing of, which made a profound impression on his mind.

> At that moment, when he stood outside the jeep, he realised he had done nothing with his life. There was no reason for him to continue to live. If he was going to die, he had nothing to show for it at all. From then on, he was determined, should he escape, if this matter ever arose again he would give a different answer.

Hutchinson said that the conversion, when it came, followed

Blake's reading of Marx to Vyvyan Holt in the camp at Moo Yong Nee: 'Gradually he came to the conclusion that here was a theory, a way of life, which seemed to him to bring hope for the future . . . Your Lordship will appreciate his Calvinist background; there may have been some echo here, in this strict morality, which is to be found in Marx. That is what the effect of this reading was on him.'

The QC's most difficult task was explaining why Blake, having found a new belief system which was at odds with his work, had not resigned from SIS. Being a Communist was not illegal, after all. Hutchinson conceded that Blake's aim had been 'the total disruption of the Intelligence Service' but stressed that the secrets his client gave away did not cause the country any 'military damage'. He argued that Blake's actions had been essentially defensive – to protect the interests of the Soviet Union.

Hutchinson again repeated Blake's claim that he had been given a guarantee from the Russians that none of the agents whose names he had passed to them would be put in mortal danger: 'They would be neutralised in their usefulness, but they would not be physically harmed. That is what he was told, that is what he believed, and it appears on the depositions that only two persons were arrested. It is agreed that never has this man received one penny piece for what he did. When he was in prison in Korea he received no advantages. He was released no earlier than anyone else, and was treated the same as everyone else. He has received no benefit from what he has done.'

In 1958, Hutchinson told the court, Blake had wanted to put an end to his treachery: 'He assures me when the time came and he had finished his course in Arabic, he was going to resign his job and get himself a job in an oil company, and finally rid himself of the course he had taken.'

As Hutchinson neared the end of his speech, he reminded Parker that his predecessor, Lord Goddard, had only imposed a fourteen-year sentence on Klaus Fuchs, the atom bomb spy. Fuchs' information, he argued, was the opposite of that passed by Blake: 'It was information of the most vital kind directly affecting the safety and security of this country.'

As his final gambit, Hutchinson appealed to Parker's more merciful instincts by urging him to uphold the values and practices of democracy – in sharp contrast to those of Communism: 'I suppose however logical, however clever, however moral, however watertight the theory may be on which another country's form of government is based, here in this country there are qualities which will never, and could never, be found if this man was now facing a judge in the country which he has seen fit to support. Among those I hope I can mention those of humanity and understanding.'

It was an eloquent, persuasive address. Hutchinson had clearly identified many of the contributory factors that led Blake, right from his teenage years, on the path to treachery. His central thesis – that it was only in the desolation and despair of captivity that Blake had turned to Communism as an alternative 'theory of life' – was altogether too simplistic, but Hutchinson was sure of it, and a high-minded conversion was always a better defence, and had more chance of convincing a judge, than any other concoction of motives.

There was then a final interchange between Hutchinson and Parker, which seemed to indicate the course the judge might take in his sentencing. 'This court will not sentence a man for becoming converted to a genuine belief in a system which he thought better,' Parker brusquely told the QC. 'The real trouble, and I would like you to deal with it further, if you will, the real trouble is that you should stay on and retain your service in the Government in order to betray your country.'

Hutchinson did his best, but he was clearly fighting a losing battle: 'My client was convinced he had to swallow the disagreeable and unpleasant and appalling deceit, which in a sense was part of his training, in order that he should be able to make a contribution which he thought was vital to this cause. As I say again, he was convinced throughout [that] the contribution he was making was to completely upset the Intelligence Service in this way. He was therefore preventing harm being done to this country rather than – this is how he convinced himself – than bringing harm to this country.'

At this point Manningham-Buller fired a firm riposte: 'I don't accept the position that the defendant has not given positive information to the other side. I think it appears from the depositions that he clearly has.'

It was now 11.30 a.m. Parker adjourned the court while the shutters were removed and the public was allowed back in to hear the sentence.

Blake was optimistic: 'Hutchinson spoke very well and movingly. I felt sure that his words would make an impact on the judge and all those who heard him.'

The Clerk, Leslie Boyd, addressed the defendant in the customary way: 'Prisoner at the Bar, you stand accused of felony. Have you anything to say why the Court should not give you judgement according to law?' Blake replied: 'No, Sir.'

Lord Justice Parker then began his summing-up: 'Your full written confession reveals that for some nine years you have been working continually as an agent and spy for a foreign power. Moreover, the information communicated, although not of a scientific nature, was clearly of the utmost importance to that power and has rendered much of the country's efforts completely useless.' And while Parker accepted that Blake had not been motivated by greed, but because of his conversion to a genuine belief in the Communist system, the judge reiterated the point that Blake ought to have resigned rather than betray his country.

In conclusion, he told Blake: 'You are not yet 39 years of age. You must know and appreciate the gravity of the offence to which you have pleaded guilty. As I have said, your case is one of the worst that can be envisaged in times of peace.'

Just for a moment, though, Parker's next words suggested that Blake might escape with a relatively lenient sentence: 'For a single offence of this kind the highest penalty laid down is fourteen years' imprisonment . . .' But it was a flickering moment of hope, almost immediately snuffed out.

Not only did Parker hand down fourteen-year jail terms for all five of the charges, he went further, stipulating that three of those sentences were to be served consecutively. When the final judgement was pronounced – forty-two years behind bars – it was so unbelievable that several onlookers emitted audible surprise. Blake himself was left in something of a daze. In that moment, his punishment had no real meaning for him.

Two prison officers led him down to a cell below the court. It was small, dirty and damp, and the walls were covered in graffiti. Some of the messages were obscene, but most conveyed messages of hope, anger and despair from previous occupants. While Blake sat there, a doctor arrived from Brixton jail, ready to administer sedatives for shock.

On the journey to Wormwood Scrubs, he could read that evening's lead story on the passing billboards and hear the cries of the newspaper vendors. His trial had wiped the London dock strike and the civil war in the Congo clean off the front pages.

The same afternoon, Bill Cox wrote to Gillian Blake: 'I can only say how desperately sorry I am about it, and assure you that not only did Jeremy Hutchinson do all that could be done, but in my opinion he conducted the matter beautifully to the point where I anticipated a comparatively light sentence. In the event, everything we had to say was disregarded.'

Gillian reflected later: 'The sentence seems quite senseless. If anyone ever served twenty-eight years he wouldn't be much of a person when he came out. This is equivalent to death, worse than death.'

The newspapers reported that Blake had collapsed after the verdict. Cox wrote to Gillian to reassure her that those stories were untrue: 'I saw him and he seemed to be very much as usual and certainly he did not seem to be suffering from shock.'

In Radlett, Blake's mother refused to despair. Once the grim news had been absorbed, the practical side of her nature reasserted itself. She took out all her son's clothes, folded them neatly and placed them in two large trunks. 'I said to myself – it will be useful to George for the future,' she told friends and family.

Had Lord Justice Parker really acted entirely at his own discretion, or was he directed on his way by outside forces? Jeremy Hutchinson, for one, is sure of the answer: 'I was completely convinced that this was a "political" sentence. Parker was very much a Civil Service kind of judge, a "political" judge. He was an awfully nice man, but not a great representative of the judicial process; he was part of the Establishment and there to do its bidding.'

If that was the case, what was the Establishment's bidding? One story, which emerged later, was that the forty-two years represented one for each agent's life lost due to Blake's treachery. That was certainly the implication of a front-page story in the *Daily Express*, by its well-connected security correspondent, Chapman Pincher, on 20 June. The day before, Pincher had been briefed about the case over lunch by the notoriously indiscreet Labour Deputy Leader, George Brown. Brown had been one of three selected Labour privy counsellors who had been fully informed about the details of Blake's case several weeks earlier. In Pincher's piece, over the headline '40 Agents Betrayed', the silhouettes of that many men rammed home the point.

At the very least, it is curious that the D-Notice Secretary, Rear Admiral Sir George Thomson, who so far had gone to such great lengths to prevent any details of the trial emerging in the national media, should now allow Pincher's article to slip through the net. Was this a Government 'plant', concocted to counter the general bewilderment over the severity of the sentence? Or was there some truth in the tally?

Exactly which agents Blake betrayed and what happened to them as a result of his actions remains secret to this day. A full picture of the damage he caused would be almost impossible to piece together. Certainly no numbers were offered up during his trial, in public or *in camera*.

'I would never put it past Manningham-Buller having a quiet word with Parker before the trial, slipping the words "forty-two" into the conversation. I've no evidence of that, of course, but I would never put it past the activities of the Establishment at that time,' said Hutchinson.

Manningham-Buller is said to have wanted to hit Blake 'with the biggest hammer possible'. But, in truth, he sought the heavy sentence not for his own satisfaction, but because the Prime Minister and his Government willed it. And they, in turn, sanctioned it in large part to mollify the Americans. Blake always felt SIS itself never really wanted to prosecute him: admitting the existence of a mole would cause huge damage to the reputation of the Service, but 'once it had been decided to do so, fourteen years would never be enough. It would not satisfy the Americans, who were raising hell and crying for my blood.'

Macmillan had met the new President for the first time six weeks earlier at the American Naval Base at Key West in Florida. Despite the vast gulf in age and background, the two men struck up an immediate rapport. It might be overstating matters to say that the seasoned Macmillan felt the need to impress Kennedy, but he sensed the raised eyebrows in both the White House and Langley at yet another British spy scandal, and he was determined to show he was rooting out the moles. The young President must have been somewhat baffled when the Prime Minister used the language of the grouse moor to break the news about Blake: 'C's nabbed a wrong 'un,' Macmillan is reported to have told him.

In particular, the CIA was angered by the disclosure that the Berlin tunnel had been compromised – worse, that the KGB knew about it even before digging began. The operation had seemed one of the Agency's greatest triumphs of the Cold War, and medals had been awarded to those most closely connected with its success. 'We in Washington were unhappy about it . . . of course it created extra tension,' recalled Richard Helms, later to become CIA chief. Helms was working for the agency in Berlin during the same period Blake was there.

Many weeks later, when the dust had settled, Dick White travelled to Langley to brief the incoming Director of the CIA on the damage Blake had caused. By then the sentence had been imposed and the stresses in the relationship smoothed out. The CIA trio were impressed with White's account of how Blake had been forensically investigated and interrogated, and the matter was laid to rest.

The day after the trial Macmillan had, in his own words, 'a rather rough passage' in the House of Commons. In his statement, he maintained Blake had been subject to 'a very thorough security vetting' on his return from Korea. 'I would again emphasise that his action was not the result of brainwashing or intimidation while a prisoner,' he told the House. In response, Hugh Gaitskell, the Labour Leader, asked him for an assurance that Blake had been 'positively vetted' before being allowed to join the Government Service. Macmillan's reply drew the sting of criticism and provoked laughter from the House: 'The regulations on employment are complicated on the nationality question. In the old days one had to have two British parents to be a member of the Foreign Service. That would have ruled out both myself and Sir Winston Churchill, had we wished to enter it!'

Meanwhile, Prisoner 455 quickly gave notice that he intended to lodge an appeal against his sentence. In a letter to Bill Cox three days after his trial, Blake told the solicitor he was retaining him as his representative, but that he would not be requesting legal aid. He asked Cox to get in touch with Gillian to discuss ways and means of raising the required money: 'This should be possible, and if necessary, my uncle in Holland could be approached.'

Surprised by the harshness of the sentence, colleagues and friends rallied round. Lady Pethwick-Lawrence of Peaslake, a notable campaigner for peace and women's rights, wrote to Claude Hornby & Cox on 9 May: 'The Blake family are very dear friends of mine and I rate George just about the finest character I know. Deeply religious, he lives by his Calvinist conscience and once he became converted to Communism in Korea, he is the type that would feel impelled to act . . . to me, this appalling sentence appears purely vindictive. I hope you will forgive this letter from an ignorant old woman, but I venture it, because the case is pure heartbreak for me.'

Perhaps even more intriguing was correspondence from two intelligence officers – a married couple who shall be referred to as 'Mr and Mrs B' – who had both worked alongside Blake at SIS. Mr B's letter to Jeremy Hutchinson on 7 May set out criticisms of a practical kind, about the haste with which the authorities had pushed through the case, and how the legal system had trampled over his friend. 'I am greatly disturbed by features of the case that have emerged from the press,' he wrote. 'Little opportunity seems to have been afforded to any who might have been prepared to assist a defence or a plea in mitigation. It was not until April 25 that pictures in the press confirmed for me that the George Blake in question was the George Blake I knew.'

Mr B said he had written to Bill Cox on 29 April offering to give testimony on Blake's behalf but had heard nothing in response. He wondered if Blake's voluntary confession had been made in a 'proud spirit of devotion to Communism, or against some promise or threat from his employers'. He added that two of the five charges related to matters of which he had some knowledge: 'I believe there are strong grounds for denying that these efforts [of the country's intelligence agencies] were rendered useless by Mr Blake's activities.'

When his wife, Mrs B, wrote three weeks later, it was to advance a broader, more philosophical argument about the nature of Cold War espionage. Her experience of intelligence departments, she said, was considerably wider than that of her husband.

I would like to make a point that should be obvious to those in possession of the facts, but who are unfortunately muzzled by the Official Secrets Act.

This is that although Blake has broken the law, morally he has done no worse than those employed by the department for which he worked – many of them nationals of the countries against which they spy.

In short, it seems a monstrous piece of hypocrisy for Blake's department to instigate proceedings against him, when a very large part of their work consists in running George Blakes – albeit probably less successful ones – in hostile countries.

Governments have always taken an ambiguous view of spies. On the one hand, they are criminals, deserving of the harshest penalties; on the other, they are pawns to be traded in a great game where there are fewer moral boundaries. Mrs B was essentially arguing that Blake was now a prisoner of war. 'I realise that this point does not affect Blake's *technical* guilt,' she suggested. 'But surely the extent to which he is *morally* guilty should have some effect on his sentence?'

The Court of Criminal Appeal sat to hear the case on Monday, 19 June, with Mr Justice Hilbery presiding. Hilbery was 77 years old, and a judge in the grand, Victorian manner. Tall and lean with a long, expressionless face, he walked to court each day in his silk hat and morning coat. His book, *Duty and Art in Advocacy* (1946), was presented to every student of Gray's Inn on their call to the Bar. Like Goddard and Parker, however, he now seemed out of touch with a changing world. He regularly advocated more flogging, and objected to the use of new-fangled words such as 'bus'. 'I deprecate the use of these ordinary, perhaps slang phrases,' he said in 1952.

Small wonder, then, that Hutchinson's hopes were not high that day: 'When I knew Hilbery was in charge I felt we had no real chance of getting the sentence reduced. He was an awful man – an acidulated judge, who wasn't going to allow an appeal against the Lord Chief Justice.' But Hutchinson was determined to fight hard on a point of real principle, and of constitutional importance: judges should not be able to ignore a maximum sentence by giving out consecutive jail terms. He told the appeal court that Blake's sentence was 'inordinate, unprecedented and manifestly excessive'. When he asked Hilbery if he could refer to a number of mitigating circumstances in open court, so that press speculation might be halted – and justice be seen to be done – he received a withering reply.

'What difference does it make to him whether it is in public or private?' Hilbery asked. 'We are not concerned with press conjecture. We are solely concerned to administer the Law. We are not here to scotch some rumour; we are here to consider whether this sentence was wrong in principle or "manifestly excessive". What matters is between the Accused and this court.'

Hutchinson reminded the judges of Fuchs's term of just fourteen years. He said Lord Goddard, who had passed sentence on him, was either unaware of the power to pass consecutive sentences, or 'he knew it was wrong in principle to pass such sentences'. Hutchinson went on: 'It was clear he knew what Parliament had ordained, and if he had been able to, he would have passed a longer sentence, but was limited to the sentence imposed by the Act.' In the most resounding passage of his submission, Hutchinson told the court that Blake's sentence was 'so inhumane that it was alien to all the principles on which a civilised country would treat its subjects. No man could survive a sentence of more than twenty years.'

But as he attempted to explain why Blake had chosen to work for Communism by undermining British intelligence from within, Hilbery's interruption must have made clear the futility of his efforts: 'He has not been condemned for having a particular political ideology; he has been condemned for remaining in the service of this country and in a way which is particularly odious, surreptitiously attempting to do this country as much harm as is in his power. He did not go into the open in Hyde Park and preach about it.'

Sir Reginald Manningham-Buller, appearing late in the proceedings to refute Hutchinson's arguments, said no principle had been established that it was wrong to sentence a man to imprisonment for longer than he would serve if he was given a life sentence.

The appeal lasted for three hours, with thirty-seven minutes of it held *in camera*. At the end, just thirteen words put paid to Blake's flickering hopes: 'The application is refused. The court will give reasons at a later date.'

When Hilbery's judgement was published in full a few weeks later, it finished with this stinging justification: 'It is of the highest importance, perhaps particularly at the present time, that such conduct should not only stand condemned, should not only be held in utter abhorrence by all ordinary men and women, but should receive, when brought to justice, the severest possible punishment. This sentence had a threefold purpose. It was intended to be punitive, it was designed and calculated to deter others, and it was meant to be a safeguard to this country.'

It was surely the end of the road. Blake's full and frank confession meant that his value to the Russians in any possible prisoner swap – a feature of the Cold War – was perilously diminished. He was simply not capable, however, of resigning himself to a lifetime behind bars.

17

Prison

In early June, Gillian brought her newly born son to Wormwood Scrubs to see his father for the first time. It was, at first, a joyful, emotional moment for the prisoner. 'George was delighted with Patrick, though he yelled all the time we saw him,' Gillian recalled. 'We were both very pleased it was a boy. We'd had to write to each other about a name, eliminating those we didn't like. We never agreed on names – I rejected all the Biblical ones George suggested. So Patrick was about the only one we were both satisfied with.'

But for Blake, the pleasure in seeing the new baby quickly turned to despair at the prospect of playing no part whatsoever in his life: 'We agreed it would be better if she did not bring the children to visit me . . . these visits, although I would not have wanted to do without them, were a considerable psychological strain on all of us and always left a feeling of great sadness at the thought of the happiness that had been destroyed.'

Blake was at first put in the hospital wing – it was normal practice to monitor prisoners given long sentences for signs of shock. Then, on 27 June, he was designated a 'Star' prisoner, placed on the escape list and moved into C wing.

Inmates on the escape list endured a particularly grim time. For a start, they were marked out by having to wear patches of cloth in different colours on each item of their outer clothing. These clothes, except for a shirt and slippers, had to be placed outside their cell at night, and inside a light burned constantly. They were kept out of cells thought particularly vulnerable, such as those with a ventilating shaft under the floor, and, without notice, they would be moved from cell to cell at irregular intervals.

Undeterred, Blake harboured notions of escape from day one. Indeed, he was almost expected to make the attempt, and the prospect became a running joke with one prison officer, who would ask, 'When's the date, then?' whenever they crossed paths. Blake resolved to lull both the officers and his fellow inmates into the belief that he had no intention of breaking out. If he was seen to be making the best of prison life, they would relax, and, in time, his conditions would be eased.

The ruse worked: to his relief, following monthly reviews by the Governor Tom Hayes, in consultation with the Prison Commissioners, he was removed from the escape list at the beginning of October and placed in a cell of his own in D wing, the block that held serious long-term offenders. He remained, however, a unique prisoner, not to be trusted, and accompanied at all times by a prison officer when out of his cell. A special book was even kept to record his location at any time of the day.

Within these constraints, he started to appreciate the lighter regime of D wing. Let out at 7 a.m., the prisoners here were not locked up again until 8 p.m. In the hours between, there was 'free association' in the hall, television, a film show once a week and an urn of continually boiling water for tea or coffee, bought with earnings from working in the canteen.

Because of the trust placed in a large number of the inmates, and this freedom of movement, Wormwood Scrubs had won a reputation in some sections of the prison community for being something of a soft touch. 'An open prison with a wall round it' was the oft-used description. One hardened criminal who found himself imprisoned there in Blake's time was scathing: 'I was in Parkhurst and Wandsworth. I can tell the difference – this place is easier. The Scrubs is world-famous as a rest camp. There aren't any real criminals here. The ones here have just killed people in temper, or done a bit of thieving.'

Nevertheless, Blake knew that only through strict mental and physical discipline would he survive the all-round rigours of jail. Only by retaining his strength and faculties would he be in a position to take advantage of any opportunities to escape. He began to practise yoga every day in his cell, and being able to stand on his head for fifteen minutes, morning and evening, amused his fellow inmates and bolstered his reputation. As time went by, he would also work on his fitness and body strength by using dumbbells and chest expanders borrowed from younger inmates.

In the autumn of 1961, he began an A-level in Arabic by correspondence, and, the following year, took O-levels in the British Constitution and Russian. He later took an honours degree in Arabic, too. Wormwood Scrubs had an enlightened and enthusiastic 'Tutor Organiser', Pat Sloan, and Blake signed up for several of his classes, including Music and English Literature.

As far as prison labour was concerned, he worked in the canvas shop for the bulk of his time, only transferring to the canteen in February 1966.

The air of serenity that Prisoner 455 carried around with him astonished everyone in Wormwood Scrubs. Invariably polite, unruffled and attentive towards others, he displayed the contemplative calm of a monk.

Blake's standing among the younger prisoners was especially high. On most days, anyone passing cell No. 8 on the ground floor of D wing would hear a gaggle of cockney voices holding spirited conversations in French, or discussing subjects from Parisian newspapers and magazines. The older man's patience and persistence in these classes bore fruit, with a number of his 'pupils' reaching O-level standard. He also helped draft petitions to the Home Office for the semi-literates who wanted their cases reviewed.

As time progressed, Blake's cell took on all the appearance and function of a Cambridge don's tutorial room: book-lined, with an expensive Bokhara rug on the floor, and a medieval print of St Paul on the wall. Visitors would knock on the door to find the 'Professor' at work. 'I may find him alone, standing as he sometimes does, and reading the Koran, which rests on a lectern made for him by one of his pupils,' recalled Gerald Lamarque, serving life for murder. 'Or he may be seated at his table making notes, or again he may be lying on his low bed reading a tale in Arabic from *The Thousand and One Nights*. Whatever he may be doing, if he is alone I am greeted with a charming smile of welcome, an offer to seat myself, and if the time is right, an invitation to take a mug of tea.'

Blake had expected, as a spy and a traitor, to encounter a certain amount of ill feeling 'inside'. Instead, what he had done, combined with his selfless attitude, raised him to a rather exalted status: 'I found myself, because of the length of my sentence and the nature of my crime, belonging to the prison aristocracy. Many people looked upon me as a political prisoner, in spite of the British government's position that no such category exists in Britain.'

Political prisoner he may have been in the eyes of some, but to SIS and MI5 he was a betrayer of government secrets who might yet have more to reveal about his work for the KGB. For the first six months, representatives from the two intelligence agencies made regular visits to the prison. By the time they had finished, SIS had questioned Blake on forty-two separate occasions. MI5, keen to find out as much as they could about the modus operandi of the officers and agents of Soviet intelligence in Britain, were not far behind.

On 20 September 1961, MI5 told the Prison Commissioners their 'intensive interrogation' of Blake would be over by the end of November, and asked if it would be possible to move him to Birmingham Prison.

This move was suggested not on grounds of safe custody, but because they were aware that Peter Kroger (aka Morris Cohen) of the Portland Spy Ring was being moved to Wormwood Scrubs, and MI5 wanted to prevent the two spies being together in the same establishment. The Prison Commissioners argued that Blake should stay in London, pointing out that it would be a considerable hardship for Gillian to have to travel north to visit him. They also told MI5 Blake had 'influential friends who might easily use the move to embarrass the Home Secretary'. In the event, he stayed at Wormwood Scrubs while Kroger was sent to Manchester. It was the first of four occasions when serious thought was given to moving Blake out of London. It never happened, with ultimately fateful consequences.

The whole business of keeping the Soviet spies – Houghton, Lonsdale, the Krogers, John Vassall and Blake – away from one another, in a prison system with a limited number of demonstrably safe, high security jails, taxed the Home Office throughout the early 1960s. A serious breach of security was the association between Blake and Gordon Lonsdale in May 1961 when both were on 'Special Watch' in Wormwood Scrubs. That the two most destructive spies in recent British history should ever have been allowed near each other was unthinkable, but because of a bureaucratic mix-up they found themselves shuffling round the courtyard with just six others during their half hour's daily exercise.

It led to questions in the House of Commons but the authorities put it around that the allegations about Blake and Lonsdale had come from two unreliable sources – one prisoner who was a psychiatric case, and another who had based his statement entirely on hearsay. Nevertheless, Home Secretary Henry Brooke was forced on the defensive, and his reply to the Government's critics was one of a politician's customary equivocation at difficult moments: 'The recollection of those concerned suggests they were kept apart, but I cannot, at the end of three years, prove conclusively one way or another. I certainly can say that even if Blake had any chance to communicate information to Lonsdale in those few weeks when they were in Wormwood Scrubs together, it is highly doubtful whether it would have been of any interest or assistance to the Russians.'

In their brief conversation, we now know that Lonsdale assured Blake they would meet up again in Red Square in October 1967, on the fiftieth anniversary of the Russian Revolution. It must, then, have sounded a fantastical proposition.

The final member of the group of early 1960s KGB agents was William John Christopher Vassall. The son of a clergyman, Vassall was blackmailed by the Russians while working as clerk to the Naval Attaché in Moscow in 1954 because of his homosexuality. He was photographed in various compromising positions at a drunken party, set up specifically to entrap him. Back in England by 1956, Vassall continued to spy for the Russians while holding various sensitive positions in the Navy. When MI5 raided his flat six years later, they found 176 classified Admiralty and NATO documents in the secret drawer of an antique bureau bookcase.

Vassall was sentenced to eighteen years imprisonment in November 1962, and sent to Wormwood Scrubs, where he spent the first nine months on 'Special Watch'. After that he moved to D wing where, at first, he was reluctant to join Blake's circle of friends. However, the two spies met at a classical music class and discovered they had much in common. 'I liked him,' said Vassall. 'He was cultured, with impeccable manners and an open heart, and I admired him for his resignation and the brave face he showed to the world, refusing to be beaten by the system.' The two men also shared a mutual interest in religion, especially liturgical matters. Vassall lent Blake a large volume of the lives of the Catholic saints down the ages; the latter's favourite was St John of the Cross, a Spanish mystic and poet of the sixteenth century.

Blake's fellow spies may have sought his company, but other prisoners continued to trade on his notoriety and make some money. Throughout his time in prison, the Home Office and the Prison Commission were continually fighting off a whole host of stories about Blake in the newspapers. Blake himself grew weary of the coverage. In April 1963, he wrote to Gillian, furious about a story from a former prisoner called Anthony Foley suggesting he was trying to indoctrinate Communism into his fellow inmates: 'You may have heard the rubbish which appeared about me in the *Sketch*. It is of course complete and utter nonsense, and those whose concern it is are treating it as such. Although it is a matter of some indifference to me what the papers write, I must admit that I am not happy at the idea that I am depicted to those who know me as going about the prison like a latter-day John the Baptist.'

While Blake had charmed the vast bulk of the prison officers into the belief that he was knuckling down, reconciled to his fate, not everyone was convinced. In a report from October 1963, one officer described him as a 'dangerous lone wolf'. Then, in November 1965, the Deputy Governor made his views abundantly clear. 'This man must <u>always</u> be under the closest supervision. He is a security risk in every sense of the word, caution <u>always</u>.' In January 1966, when the new Governor, Leslie Newcombe, was asked for the names of security risks who would be safer elsewhere, he offered the Prison Department three names. Blake's was among them.

MI5 agreed with that assessment and, though they completed their interrogations in November 1961, continually fretted about what Blake might be up to, and the messages he was sending to his associates in the world beyond the walls of the Scrubs. As a result, a former Indian police officer, a man who had been MI5's ears and eyes in Britain's rebellious colonies during the 1950s, was Blake's 'watcher' for most of his period in prison.

Now in middle age, A.M. ('Alec') MacDonald had been an adviser for the Security Service in Kenya when the Mau-Mau rebellion was gathering strength. In 1961, however, he was back in Curzon Street working for D Branch, the section responsible for counter-intelligence. From MI5's familiar address – Box No. 500, Parliament Street – he sent out a stream of instructions to the governors at Wormwood Scrubs and the Prison Commissioners.

MacDonald was wary of Blake's desire to pursue his Arabic studies, wishing to scrutinise all the material passing between tutor and pupil. Of greater concern, however, were the letters Blake received from family and friends. In January 1963, MacDonald wrote to the Prison Commission:

> In a recent letter from Mrs BLAKE to her husband she says that she is redecorating the house, and at their next meeting will bring samples of paint and carpet to show him.
>
> She then adds, 'I shall not try to describe other colours as it is boring on paper, but at least we can hold hands when we talk'. These last few words seem strangely out of context and we are wondering whether this is not an attempt to pass a message. From our point of view clandestine communication between the BLAKES might well be very damaging indeed. They are both very intelligent and resourceful people.
>
> I am quite sure that BLAKE's interviews with his wife are indeed closely supervised, but I think it might be helpful if the prison authorities could be particularly asked to keep an eye open for stratagems of this kind.

In May 1964 MI5 officers were called upon to investigate the most extraordinary of all the stories about a Blake escape plot. This one came from a former prisoner in the Scrubs, Old Etonian Sacheverell Stanley Walton ('Sasha') de Houghton, who went to the Governor, Tom Hayes, with a bizarre tale.

Houghton claimed he had been approached by a Russian named Pierre Basinkoff, who told him that the KGB believed Blake was still useful to them. The striking details of the plot could have come from the pages of an Alistair MacLean novel. An ex-prisoner, well versed in the layout of the jail, wearing prison clothing and a 'trusty's' blue armband, would scale the prison wall and drop down into the courtyard. He would then head for the mailbag shop, where Blake would be ready and waiting. A minute or so later, a helicopter would drop into the yard behind the shop, pick up Blake and the ex-prisoner, and fly them to East Germany. No immediate panic would ensue among the prison staff, because the helicopter would have the word 'POLICE' on its sides. The crew in the helicopter would also wear police uniforms.

Despite its fanciful nature, the story was rigorously investigated by MI5, and the Director-General, Roger Hollis, was kept fully briefed. When, on 21 May, he wrote to Sir Charles Cunningham, Permanent Under-Secretary of State at the Home Office, his findings were unsurprising: 'Our conclusion is that Houghton, who has a history of mental instability, is incapable of dissociating fact from fiction . . . he is very much the black sheep of a good family and is a thoroughly mischievous character who, by the Governor's account, would not hesitate to cause any embarrassment to the Government if the opportunity offered itself.'

The reality was that Blake, as yet, had made no serious attempt to escape, though the genesis of his eventual flight can be traced as far back as 1962, when two peace campaigners, Michael Randle and Pat Pottle, were sent to Wormwood Scrubs.

On Saturday, 9 December 1961, the United States Air Force base at Wethersfield in Essex was the scene of what was believed to be the biggest display of force by a Government in peacetime since the General Strike of 1926. The event was the latest demonstration organised by the Committee of 100, a group determined to bring a greater edge to the campaign of non-violent civil disobedience over the issue of nuclear weapons. The climate of protest was a febrile one, and this particular gathering had caused such jitters that it was discussed at Cabinet two days beforehand, when elaborate security measures were agreed. On the day, six and a half miles of barbed wire was stretched around the base and several thousand troops and police officers protected it. It turned out to be something of a damp squib, with the 600 protestors well short of the minimum of 1,500 the organisers reckoned was needed for an effective blockade.

The authorities were not content with the success of their show of overwhelming strength and, after months of trouble from the Campaign for Nuclear Disarmament (CND) and its offshoots, they were in the mood for retribution. They went after the ringleaders and the result was the conviction, in February 1962, of six leading members of the Committee of 100 – Michael Randle, Pat Pottle, Terry Chandler, Ian Dixon, Trevor Hatton and Helen Allegranza. They had faced one charge under the Official Secrets Act of conspiring to enter a prohibited place 'for a purpose prejudicial to the safety and interest of the state', and another for inciting others for the same purpose. The men all received eighteen-month sentences, to be served in Wormwood Scrubs, while Helen Allegranza was sent to Holloway Prison for a year.

Randle, aged twenty-eight, had been at the heart of the anti-nuclear movement for several years. He had been appointed secretary to the founder Bertrand Russell, the venerable philosopher and Nobel Prize winner, at the inaugural meeting of the Committee of 100 in October 1960, but his active opposition to war – let alone nuclear war – had begun as far back as 1951 when he registered as a Conscientious Objector (CO) to military service. In 1956, he began a march from Vienna to Budapest, handing out leaflets expressing support for Hungarian passive resistance to the Soviet occupation, until he was ultimately prevented from entering Hungary by Austrian frontier guards.

Pottle, five years younger, inherited his left-wing views from his Protestant cockney father, a socialist and a trade union official at Morris Motors. Pottle organised his first anti-war demonstration while doing national service at RAF Uxbridge, and later succeeded Randle as secretary of the Committee of 100.

Randle and Pottle first encountered Blake in the Scrubs at a Music

Appreciation class and both felt an instinctive rapport with him. All three men had been charged under the Official Secrets Act, defended by the same QC, Jeremy Hutchinson, and prosecuted by the same Attorney-General, Reginald Manningham-Buller. Moreover, like Blake, they considered themselves to be political prisoners. During the few months in which all three were together, Pottle came to know Blake a little and determined to help him escape.

> It was not that I was in the least sympathetic to the whole business of espionage [but] as Jeremy Hutchinson had said at his trial, it was a sentence which no civilized state would pass on one of its subjects. Forty-two years struck me as a manipulation of the Official Secrets Act, where the maximum sentence was set by Parliament at fourteen years.
>
> The more I thought about it, the more my gut response of wanting to help George was strengthened. I do not claim, however, that at this early stage I carefully weighed up all the political pros and cons. My motive was purely humanitarian. Out of common humanity I was willing, if I could, to help him.

At a music class in late May 1962, Pottle first broached the subject with Blake, in a hurried conversation out of earshot at the back of the classroom. 'If you can think of any way I can help you get out, let me know,' he told him in lowered tones. A few days later Pottle had his response. The two men were sewing mailbags, when Blake gestured to the supervising prison officer that he needed to go to the lavatory. As he left the room, he signalled with his eyes that Pottle should follow him. The two men stood side by side at the urinals. As Blake left, he slipped a small packet into Pottle's hand. At lunchtime, when he had the first, safe opportunity to examine its contents, Pottle was startled by what he found. He pulled out half a bar of chocolate, and hidden inside the wrapper was a note:

> If you feel you can help me on your release, go to the Russian
> Embassy, introduce yourself and say 'I bring you greetings from
> Louise'. [Louise was Blake's emergency KGB codename.]

> Between 10 and 11 o'clock we exercise in the yard outside 'D' Hall.
> If a rope ladder is thrown over the wall at the spot I have marked X
> as near to 10.30 as possible, I will be ready.

Blake had drawn a rough sketch on which was marked the spot
where the ladder should be thrown. The note continued:

> If this is acceptable to them, put the following ad in the personal
> column of the *Sunday Times*. 'LOUISE LONGING TO SEE YOU'.
> If this ad appears, the break will be the following Sunday. If
> they cannot help, place this ad: 'LOUISE SORRY CAN'T KEEP
> APPOINTMENT'. Thank you for your help. Memorise this note,
> then destroy it – G

This excursion into the clandestine world of secret messages, codes
and daring plans took Pottle aback. Apart from the obvious dangers,
he was understandably reluctant to become entangled with the feared
KGB. He planned to discuss his reservations with Blake as soon as his
appeal was finished, but then came the decision to move him from the
Scrubs, so that conversation never took place. Before leaving for an open
prison, however, Pottle did manage to tell Randle about Blake's extraordinary plan. The latter seemed apprehensive: the escape was bold, if
not reckless, and it could have disastrous consequences for the Peace
Movement if Pottle was caught. Both agreed not to become involved.
It would be another three years, long after Randle had left the Scrubs,
before a new man took on the challenge of freeing George Blake.

Sean Alphonsus Bourke arrived at Wormwood Scrubs in December
1961 to serve a seven-year sentence. His crime had been to send a

bomb in a biscuit tin through the post in an unsuccessful attempt to kill Detective Constable Michael Sheldon of Sussex police. The Irishman bore a venomous grudge against the police officer, who he believed had been spreading rumours that he was a homosexual, which he was sure had cost him his job at a youth centre in Crawley.

Bourke was born in Limerick in 1934, the sixth of seven boys whose extended family boasted a colourful collection of poets, drunks, misers, bare-knuckle fighters and general 'wild rovers'. He himself turned out to be a reckless, feckless individual, who embarked on a career as a petty criminal from the age of twelve. He spent three years in a notorious reformatory in Daingean in County Offaly, Ireland, after which he travelled to England, only to land himself in Borstal after being convicted of receiving a stolen wireless set. Thereafter, he drifted from one job to another, on building sites and in factories, usually drinking far too much, until he was imprisoned.

For all his faults, Bourke could also be an immensely charming, witty and intellectually stimulating companion, and extremely loyal to those he liked and trusted.

Bourke was also a self-taught writer, fancying himself in the Irish literary tradition as a Brendan Behan type, and was actually a second cousin of the poet Desmond O'Grady. He undoubtedly had a way with words, editing the prison magazine, *New Horizon*, with some style, and later producing a gripping, painful memoir of his teenage experiences at the hands of the monks in the reformatory. It was the study of literature that drew him together with future fellow conspirators Blake and Randle.

In July 1962, all three had enrolled in the English Literature Diploma class run by the extramural department of London University. Soon, this unlikely trio, the irascible Irishman, the stubborn, idealistic Englishman and the imperturbable Dutchman, were the principal members of a unique political 'salon' that would meet on a Monday in the prison's Education Block. The 'host' of this lively social gathering was another of those remarkable characters who did time in the Scrubs in the 1960s.

Gerald Theodore Lamarque gave himself the pseudonym 'Zeno', after the Stoic philosopher. A petty criminal before the war, he was, from various accounts, a hero during it, becoming a member (under another alias of 'Kenneth Sidney Allerton') of the 21st Independent Parachute Company, who valiantly tried and failed to hold a bridgehead at Arnhem. Lamarque was in prison because he had stabbed and killed the lover of his former girlfriend. As this was deemed a 'crime of passion' he was spared the hangman's rope and instead sentenced to life imprisonment. Even in disgrace he retained the look of a military man with a trim, curly moustache, neatly pressed clothes and erect bearing. He was a gifted writer who would go on to win the Arthur Koestler Award for outstanding artistic work in prison, for his book about his experiences at Arnhem, *The Cauldron*. Lamarque was a trusted 'blue band' (or Leader) in the prison hierarchy, allowed to move freely outside his own wing and to escort other prisoners. He supervised the literature class and would allow it to drift into long debates about politics, representing the right with unorthodox views close to those of Enoch Powell.

Randle enjoyed his intellectual jousting with Blake. He found him an engaging, fascinating conversationalist, and he admired his stoicism in the face of what he considered a vicious and vengeful sentence by the authorities. Throughout his time in the Scrubs he hesitated to broach the subject of Blake's note to Pottle, or the possibility of an escape plan, and, by the time he left in January 1963, regretted not having done so.

With Randle gone, Bourke and Blake were thrown together even more during 1963 and 1964. Bourke continued to be astonished by his friend's self-control and selflessness: 'I always marvelled at the sight of this man without hope giving help and advice and comfort to young fellows in their twenties whose grandchildren would be in Borstal before Blake again saw the light of day as a free man.'

Blake had, in fact, drawn strength from his punishment. Not for a moment would he give up thoughts of freedom, though: 'The sentence was such that it almost became a question of honour to challenge it . . . like a POW, I had a duty to escape.' As time went by, however, hopes that the KGB might be able to help had faded away. He knew he had to rely on his own resources, so he watched and waited, searching for an associate on the inside – someone he could trust never to go to the authorities, someone with 'initiative, courage and the single-mindedness to see the job through'. The more he thought about it, the more certain he was that Sean Bourke fitted the bill.

Blake began to feel that he had little to lose by an escape attempt: that summer, Gillian had met a man she liked while on holiday and was, for the first time, starting to consider divorce. In the summer of 1965 the perfect opportunity arose when Bourke, coming towards the end of his sentence, was due to go before the hostel board. In the autumn, if the interview was successful, Bourke would be released into the outside world by day, returning only at night to sleep in the hostel in the prison grounds – a 'halfway house' on the path to full release a few months down the line.

On Monday, 6 September, as the two men were taking one of their regular walks together in the prison hall, Blake told Bourke he had given up any hope of release through a prisoner exchange. 'I have therefore decided that the time has come for me to leave here . . . er . . . under my own steam, as it were. I am asking you, Sean, to help me escape,' was Bourke's recollection of the request. The Irishman was surprised: 'There had been no warning of this, not the slightest hint in that smiling face over the years.' Blake urged him to take time to think it over, but Bourke said he did not need to.

'Oh?' His face clouded apprehensively. 'What have you decided?'

'I'm your man.'

The interview with the hostel board went well and, at the end of

November, Bourke was released. Over the next couple of weekends, he spent many hours walking every street in the neighbourhood around the prison, building up a detailed knowledge that would be crucial when planning and executing Blake's getaway. Even at this early stage, he had decided that once Blake was over the twenty-foot wall, he would drop down into Artillery Road – now marked on maps as Artillery Lane, and really little more than an alleyway – which was the closest and most secluded place to position the getaway car. The only drawback was that, with Hammersmith Hospital just opposite, the area would be busy at certain times of the day. In particular, they would need to plan around hospital visiting hours.

In the spring of 1966, Bourke, with Blake's encouragement, made a number of fruitless attempts to persuade the spy's family to finance George's escape. It came to a head when he met Blake's mother Catherine and his sister Adele Boswinkle for a meal at the Cumberland Hotel near Marble Arch, during which he set out his stall. Adele, the dominant figure in the family, was singularly unimpressed by what he had to say. She recognised Bourke had her brother's best interests at heart, but thought his plans vague and impractical, and considered him likely to be a shaky executioner of them. In particular, she was perturbed that he seemed to have no clear idea about where to hide George once he was over the wall, and no plan of any sort to spirit him safely out of the country. They decided not to get involved.

To whom could Bourke turn now? The more he thought about it, the more obvious the answer: his fellow alumni from the English Literature Diploma class, who were good friends of Blake, disgusted by his sentence, always prepared to defy authority, and well equipped for such an adventure by dint of their many 'direct actions'. Surely Michael Randle and Pat Pottle would lend a hand?

In mid-May, Randle was studying hard for his final exams for a BA in English at University College, London. He hoped the qualification would provide the launchpad for a teaching career in academia. His first son, Sean, had been born in August 1962, when he was serving his sentence in Wormwood Scrubs, and a second, Gavin, was born in January 1964.

Pat Pottle had seen a hectic few years in the anti-nuclear movement. After his release from jail in January 1963, he had taken up a post as Bertrand Russell's secretary. As Russell's 'emissary' to the Chinese government in 1964, along with Ralph Schoenman, the American left-wing activist and fellow member of the Committee of 100, he had so antagonised his hosts that he had been subjected to a quasi-trial and deported from the country. Chou En-Lai himself was irritated by the activists' behaviour and described the two young men as the 'running dog lickspittles of the American imperialists'.

Despite pressures at work and home, Randle and Pottle barely hesitated before offering their support to Bourke. They were well aware of the Irishman's excitability and bravado, but as they listened to what he was proposing, they became convinced that he had formulated a bold, flexible and viable escape plan.

'I was determined that if I was to get involved with the break it should not fail because of silly and obvious mistakes. If this meant being over-cautious, so be it,' Pottle reflected. 'Clearly he and George had done a lot of preliminary work, including setting up a network of helpers on the inside. What impressed me most was Sean's touch of genius in smuggling in the two-way radios.'

A few weeks earlier Bourke had walked into McDonald's radio and electrical shop in Piccadilly, where he saw a pair of Japanese two-way radios in black leather cases, small enough to fit snugly into a man's inside pocket. They had a range of five miles, but he only needed them to transmit over half a mile at most. By the time he met Randle and Pottle, Bourke had successfully delivered a radio to Blake via the insider who led the team of co-conspirators within the prison. Blake had, in turn, managed to hide it in the prison canteen – basically a cell converted into a shop – to which he had the keys, as he was in charge of stocktaking, bookkeeping and the ordering of new supplies.

After a day's promising experimentation, the two plotters went 'live' with the new sets at 11 p.m. on Sunday, 29 May, with Bourke in his top-floor room in the hostel, while Blake lay in his bed in cell No. 8, the equipment concealed under his blankets. In a lowered voice, Bourke produced the call sequence: 'This is Fox Michael calling Baker Charlie, Come in, please. Over.' Four times he delivered these words before Blake's uncertain voice finally answered: 'Baker Charlie calling Fox Michael. Baker Charlie calling Fox Michael. Can you hear me? Come in, please. Over.' The identifying code that followed made reference to Richard Lovelace, the seventeenth-century metaphysical poet Blake and Bourke had studied together on their literature course. The words were, in the circumstances, singularly appropriate.

> **Bourke:**   Stone walls do not a prison make nor iron bars a cage.
> **Blake:**   Minds innocent and quiet take them for a hermitage.
> **Bourke:**   Richard Lovelace must have been a fool.
> **Blake:**   Or just a dreamer.

The reception appeared perfect, although Bourke's voice came through too loud and Blake had to turn his set down to its lowest volume. Nonetheless, he was ecstatic: 'That first night we talked well into the night. Apart from its immense usefulness, it was a wonderful experience to communicate once again completely freely with someone in the outside world to which Sean, though only fifty yards away in the hostel, to all intents and purposes now belonged.'

The leader of the group in D wing helping with the escape was 29-year-old Philip Anthony Morris. He was serving a six-year term for robbery and aggravation. Despite persistent, generally low-level criminality over the preceding ten years, he was likeable, courageous and fiercely loyal to those he admired and with whom he struck up good friendships. Morris was also a talented banjo player and could often be heard strumming his instrument with a fellow guitarist in a cell on the second floor. His value to Blake and Bourke was immense. As a 'red band', he had freedom of movement outside the wing, and access to the hostel where Bourke was staying, so he could pass messages and parcels between the two. He was also able to store tools that might be needed in the escape in various places in the hostel. He was six foot two with an athletic build, and his experience as a robber gave him various technical skills that would prove invaluable to the escape effort.

At this stage, Randle and Pottle's role was primarily to help find money for the operation, and to advise on logistics. In early July, Randle received £200 from a friend, but after that raising funds became more difficult. 'For those who had never met George he must have appeared as an unknown and sinister figure, convicted of spying for a totalitarian state, and serving a very long prison sentence. Some were also concerned at the possible effect of Pat's and my involvement on the Peace Movement if our role was ever discovered,' Randle recalled. He worried too, that every time he made an approach to a friend, there was a chance that news of it would leak out.

They then had an extraordinary stroke of luck. A young woman named 'Bridget', a family friend of the Randles, had come into a substantial inheritance and wanted to donate it to a worthy case. A staunch socialist, she opposed the idea of inherited wealth and was keen to dispose of her own.

That still left the problem of how to hide Blake before he fled the country. Little detailed thought had been given to this stage of the escape, although the broad idea was for him to fly out of England to Dublin or Shannon in Ireland, on a forged passport obtained from one of Bourke's underworld contacts. From there, he would continue his journey to the Middle East or an Eastern Bloc country. He would need a credible disguise, however, and Randle hit upon a novel idea after reading a review of a book called *Black Like Me* by an American writer, John Howard Griffin. A white reporter from Texas, Griffin took drugs to darken his skin so he could pass as a black man and blend unassumingly into the racially segregated communities of the Deep South. Could Blake be made to pass for an Arab? Randle and Pottle, not without difficulty, managed to purchase the drug required, along with an ultra-violent lamp that was the other vital element in the course of treatment.

Another practical issue was the make-up of the rope ladder that would be thrown over the wall to Blake. There were different views among the team as to whether the rungs of the ladder should be made of rope or wood but, eventually, Anne Randle came up with the clever idea of using size thirteen knitting needles – light, but robust enough to take a man's weight. Bourke went out and rashly bought thirty in a single visit to a haberdashery shop on Old Oak Common Lane, Acton, at the end of August. The woman behind the counter expressed surprise at this bulk buy, and asked if his wife was planning on doing a lot of knitting. 'They're for my pupils at school,' replied Bourke, nonchalantly. 'It's amazing, the abstracts that these young art students can produce from simple things like knitting needles.'

Next, Bourke had to trade in his Humber car for a replacement that could serve as a getaway vehicle. He got to work on this and, before long, reported to Randle and Pottle that he had done the deal, using a false name and address. He assured them that the car was safe, and in a garage being serviced.

Finally, most crucially, there was the issue of the safe house. The idea was that Bourke would leave his job, give up his flat in Perryn Road, and tell everyone he knew, workmates and friends alike, that he was leaving England to return permanently to his native Ireland. In fact, he moved in with Pottle at his flat in Willow Buildings, Hampstead, while he searched for a safe house nearer Wormwood Scrubs. He would rent it under the assumed name of Michael Sigsworth, and give his occupation as a freelance journalist.

After a fortnight, Bourke had still not found a suitable flat. Whether his disguise – a large black beard, spectacles and an English accent – helped or hindered his quest is unclear. He handed in his notice on Friday, 9 October, and moved out of Perryn Road the same day. He then flew to Limerick to spend time with family and friends, but mainly to establish an alibi for the future.

On his return, he renewed his search for a flat and, after registering with a more downmarket agency in Paddington, found one almost immediately, at 28 Highlever Road, barely half a mile from Wormwood Scrubs. He paid the landlady two weeks rent in advance and moved in the following day. It was little more than a bedsit, 12 by 13 foot, with a single bed and gas cooker in the corner. It could only be a temporary refuge, but Randle and Pottle were told it was a self-contained flat, and so assumed it was for the long-term.

It was now Tuesday, 18 October 1966. The date of the escape had been fixed for Saturday, 22 October. Blake was desperate to move quickly, because a spectacular breakout by six prisoners back in June had led to the start of stringent new security measures at the Scrubs. The tall windows at each end of the four blocks were being reinforced with thick steel netting. Those in A and B hall had already been fitted, and workmen had now moved on to C hall. In another week, it would be the turn of D, and his route out would be blocked forever.

On Wednesday, 19 October, Bourke bought a set of clothes for Blake and, the next day, purchased a television for the Highlever Road flat. When his mother visited on Thursday afternoon, she brought Blake some fresh clothing for his scheduled appearance in the divorce court in a few weeks' time. The prison officer sitting in on the meeting noted perceptively that 'the prisoner appeared far happier than one would have expected for a man with his problems'.

That evening Blake and Bourke had a final conversation, using their walkie-talkies, about what was to take place on Saturday evening. Bourke recorded it for Randle and Pottle to hear later. Blake was in Phil Morris's cell on the fourth floor for the briefing, with the light off; Bourke was sitting, as he would be on the night of the escape, in his car on Artillery Road opposite the side gate of Hammersmith Hospital. He had concealed his radio set in a bunch of flowers, so that anyone passing by would think he was visiting a sick friend.

First, Morris explained to Bourke that he had broken the cast-iron bar of the central window in D hall, where Blake was to begin his escape.

He had strapped it back into position as agreed, and also smashed out two panes of glass, using paper and tape to deaden the sound.

Bourke then took over the update, talking Blake through what he had to do, minute by minute, from the second he dropped down into the prison yard to the moment when he turned the lock in the door of the safe house. The Irishman had even planned for his own arrest: 'If you hear an announcement [on TV] that a man is assisting the police with their inquiries, you can take it that man is me. I'll not be assisting them with their inquiries. You'll find on the table in this room an *A to Z* map of London plus an Underground plan to enable you to find where you have to go.'

On Friday evening, 21 October, the plotters gathered in Pat Pottle's flat in Willow Buildings for a final meeting before the escape effort. They spread a map of the area around Wormwood Scrubs on the table and methodically went through the route of the escape, street by street. When they were confident they knew it off by heart, they burned the map and all the other notes they had made. Randle and Pottle demanded assurance from Bourke that he would not carry a weapon during the operation. Bourke agreed, but told them that if anyone tried to stop or arrest him, he had no intention of giving up himself or Blake without a struggle.

After saying their goodbyes, Bourke made his way back via the Underground to Highlever Road. He slept badly, the burden of success uncomfortable on his shoulders: 'There was still time to turn back, but I knew that was now unthinkable. Failure and imprisonment would be infinitely more bearable than the look in the eyes of my friends if I said, "No, I cannot do it."'

The scene was set. Charlie Wilson, the Great Train Robber who was serving thirty years, had scaled the 20-foot wall at Winson Green Prison two years earlier, using a rope ladder and assisted by three highly professional accomplices. Now Blake, serving forty-two years, was attempting an identical ascent, with just one amateur, if enthusiastic, partner in crime on the other side.

18

Breakout

Blake and Bourke had set 6.15 p.m. as Zero Hour. It was the time of day when prisoners were the least policed, enjoying a period of 'free association', watching a film or television show, playing cards, or chatting in the hall. It would be forty-five minutes before they were summoned back to their cells. Outside, darkness would have fallen. The perfect time for a breakout.

Before then there was still much to prepare. Bourke found he had little appetite for his breakfast of sausages and eggs that Saturday morning; he was too nervous, concentrating all the while on the final tasks that needed to be wrapped up before the evening's mission. First, he bought food at the local shops, stocking up for two. On his return to Highlever Road, he put on a clean shirt and his best suit. At 11.30 he strolled down to the florists on Old Oak Common Lane to buy a bunch of chrysanthemums. The flowers would help provide cover for his walkie-talkie, but also performed the secondary function of convincing observers that he was merely a visitor to Hammersmith Hospital, on his way to a sick relative.

Just before midday, he left Highlever Road in his Humber Hawk and drove the one mile to Artillery Road for his final conversation with Blake before the operation took place. After they had talked through the code, Blake assured Bourke that everything was ready at his end. Bourke was relieved. He signed off with a characteristic flourish: 'My friend, in just six hours I shall walk beside you in this world today. Oh, and by the way, it's chops for tea, followed by strawberries and cream. Does that suit? Over.' Blake laughed: 'My mouth is already watering. Over.'

At around half-past four he laid Blake's new clothes out on the bed, along with a London *A to Z*, Michael Randle's telephone number (in code), and some coins and banknotes. He then picked up the rope ladder which he had carefully folded, grabbed coats and hats for himself and Blake, and left the flat. In the hall of the house there was a telephone. Here, Bourke put in a final call to his co-conspirator.

Randle could sense Bourke's apprehension. 'Are you all right?' he asked him.

'Well, my friend, let me put it this way – I've seen better days. But yes, I'm all right, and I'm now on my way.'

'Good luck,' Randle said.

'Thank you,' replied Bourke. 'I'll need it. Goodbye.'

He then walked up Highlever Road, turned left into Barlby Road, down Wood Lane, and then into Du Cane Road for a final reconnaissance of the area around the prison. Fortunately, the sky was overcast and the weather turning to drizzle. Rain would discourage people from loitering in the streets, and it would also reduce visibility within the prison perimeter when Blake made his dash for the wall. As Bourke walked past the prison wall on the opposite pavement, he saw the familiar faces of a couple of warders heading to work, but if they noticed him at all, neither gave him a second glance.

At just after 5 p.m., he walked purposefully back to his car to ready himself for the evening's exploits. Once there, he had time to buy some more chrysanthemums – this time a pot, as the cut flowers had sold out – at the florists where he had become a well-known face in recent weeks. Perhaps too familiar. He placed the pink flowers beside him on the passenger seat, and turned on the car radio for some light music to calm his nerves. Then, after just a few minutes, he switched on the ignition and set off towards Artillery Road.

Inside D wing, just before 3.30, prisoner Derek Madren was making his way down from the fourth landing for tea, the last meal of the day: 'As I got to the last flight of stairs just before I started to come down, another prisoner dashed out of No. 8 cell [Blake's] rather excitedly, looking flushed. He then dashed up the stairs, nearly knocking the cup out of my hand. He said "Sorry", and I continued down.' Madren had unknowingly stumbled upon the Blake 'team' at work.

At about 4.30 p.m., after tea had finished, 210 prisoners from D wing were escorted to the recreation hut for the evening's film. That left only 108 in the hall and in their cells, under the supervision of two officers. It was the quietest time of the week.

One of the few prisoners who knew what was about to take place was Kenneth Hugh De Courcy, otherwise known as 'The Baron'. At fifty-six, he was one of the oldest men in the Scrubs and, in a jail full of characters, perhaps the most exotic of them all. In the 1930s, he had moved in the shadowy passageways of power, his roles including those of publisher, intelligence officer, secretary of the Imperial Policy Group (bent on the appeasement of the fascists), confidant of several Cabinet ministers and unofficial adviser to the Duke of Windsor. In wartime, Stalin himself took umbrage at some of De Courcy's virulent anti-Communist tracts and demanded that the British government take action. After the war, De Courcy, rich but eccentric, seemed to slip permanently into fantasy. He bought a flat in the Empire State building and had his Rolls-Royce waterproofed for underwater driving. When a scheme to build a garden city in Rhodesia failed, he was unable to return a million pounds put up by the investors and resorted to forgery, perjury and fraud. In 1963, he was sentenced to seven years in prison.

Given his extreme right-wing views, it might have been assumed that De Courcy and Blake would have little time for each other but, in fact, the two got on famously, De Courcy particularly appreciating the interest Blake took in his tortuous financial affairs. As a result, when, in May 1966, a covert letter from Bourke to Blake accidentally fell into De Courcy's hands – the Baron was conducting his own secret correspondence via Bourke, and the letters had got mixed up – he became fully aware of the escape plot. He could have given Blake away, and earned rewards for doing so. Instead he told him: 'I won't say a word to anyone. I promise you that. Only, in return, keep me informed how things are going.' De Courcy proved as good as his word. Conspiracies were his lifeblood, and he relished the opportunity to strike a blow at the Establishment that had unjustly – in his eyes – deprived him of his freedom.

At about 5 p.m., he set off for his final meeting with Blake: 'I went down to his cell and said I must say goodbye. He said, "I've now got a bit of an ordeal ahead of me. I'm going downstairs to have a very hot shower." He said he'd like to give me a keepsake, so he handed me his Koran. We shook hands, he put a towel round his neck and walked out of the door.'

As Blake made his way along the landing, Thomas Culling, one of the 'Red' bands, exchanged a few words with him. 'I asked him about some onions because he was in charge of the canteen, and he laughed and said, "Leave it to me."'

After his shower, Blake wandered through into D Hall, where a large group of prisoners were shouting and cheering at the wrestling on television. The programme was not due to finish until 6 p.m. and would thus provide a welcome, noisy distraction during the feat to come. Blake chatted briefly to prison officer William Fletcher at just after 5.30, giving him his opinion that wrestling was a farce and that the bouts were all fixed. He then brewed a cup of tea, and was making his way across the hall when he encountered prisoner Eric Tucker, who was making pancakes. 'That smells good,' he remarked to Tucker, who offered him some. He then went back to his cell. Everything he did had to appear normal and unremarkable.

He knew he had about twenty minutes before the plan was put

into action. While drinking his tea, he read *The Times*, taking in the appalling events at the Welsh village of Aberfan, where a colliery spoil tip had collapsed onto Pantglas Junior School. After a while, he put the paper down and slipped on a pair of gym shoes, placing his walkie-talkie under his sweater, and headed up to Phil Morris's cell on the fourth landing. It was now just after 6 p.m.

It was a few, tense minutes before Bourke called up. He apologised because he had been caught in a traffic jam and asked Blake if he was ready to proceed. 'Yes, I am all ready,' he replied. 'Our mutual friend has kindly agreed to attend to the window for me. He is standing here with the jack in his hand. Can I tell him to go ahead? Over.' Bourke agreed, and Phil Morris strode out of the cell and down to the second-floor landing. He was back in a matter of minutes, the bar on the window having been broken two days earlier and, although temporarily taped up, extremely easy to dislodge this time. Blake immediately reported back to Bourke that both bar and window were now satisfactorily removed. 'What, already?' came back the surprised reply. 'Yes, you can come now, I am ready for you.'

The decisive moment had arrived. Blake shook hands with Morris and said goodbye, tucked the walkie-talkie into his waistband and underneath his sweater, and walked down two sets of stairways to the window on the second-floor landing. As he approached his escape route, the sound of animated conversation came drifting in through the centre hall: the prisoners were returning unexpectedly early from the film show. He needed to get moving.

The two panes of the glass window measured 12 by 18 inches, just large enough for a man of Blake's build to squeeze through. In fact nothing had been left to chance: Blake had made a wooden frame the same size and practised squirming through it in his cell. He would be starting off 22 feet above the ground, and the weather made matters hazardous: 'I slid through the opening in the window and felt with my feet for the roof of the passageway. I carefully let myself down the tiles, slippery from the rain which was pouring down. I got hold of the edge of the gutter, hung on to it, and dropped easily to the ground. I found myself now in a small recess formed by the passageway and the jutting turret at the corner of the hall. Pressed against the wall, it was unlikely that any passing patrol could see me, even if the weather was not driving them to shelter in a porch.'

Blake was now just a 15-yard dash from the prison wall. That night it was being patrolled by two officers but Bourke and Blake had calculated that the patrols passed any given point along the wall roughly every twenty minutes, which allowed plenty of time between one appearance and the next for the escape to be completed. For Blake, everything so far had gone according to plan. But as he waited under cover for the signal to head for the wall, Bourke was having unexpected difficulties on the other side.

He had been about to radio Blake to tell him to run to the wall when a pair of bright headlights turned into Artillery Road, lighting up the whole area. It was a van driven by a patrolman who had come to lock up Wormwood Scrubs Park for the night. All Bourke could do was wait so he radioed Blake to tell him to sit tight and not to worry. Five minutes later, Bourke saw the headlights reappear and watched as the man secured the barrier with padlock and chain. To Bourke's dismay, the van crawled very slowly past his car and came to a halt. The driver got out, mumbled a few words in the direction of the back of the vehicle, and then stood just a few yards away with a large Alsatian dog on a short chain beside him. Bourke, realising his loitering had attracted attention, had no option but to drive away. 'As I turned left into Du Cane Road I felt sure the escape had failed – not just for tonight, but for all time,' he reflected bitterly. 'But what else was there to do? That patrolman must now surely call the police, or at least lie in wait until I came back.'

But his resolve did not waver. When the lights went green at Wood Lane, instead of turning left towards Highlever Road, Bourke turned right and then quickly drove down Westway. A right into Old Oak Common Road, then another right into Du Cane Road again, and he was back at the prison. It was now 6.35 – time was running out.

As Bourke once more turned into Artillery Road, to his relief he saw no sign of the van, though to his horror, another car was parked in its place. It was occupied by a courting couple, who showed no intention of going anywhere quickly: 'I *had* to get rid of them. One way or another, I just *had* to get rid of them. I got out of the car, leaned against the door, and just stood there in the rain staring.' It worked. Perhaps they thought Bourke was a policeman, or a security guard from the hospital. Maybe he was a pervert. In any event, the girl sat up, the man straightened himself out, they exchanged a few words and then the car did a three-point turn before pulling away.

By 6.40, Blake had been standing in the recess of the passageway for twenty minutes, and was feeling desperate: 'I had called repeatedly but got no reply. Had he got into trouble and made a rapid getaway? Or had he got cold feet at the last moment? There was little time left before they would discover I was missing. I began to get visions of Parkhurst.'

Then Bourke's voice came through on the radio: 'Fox Michael calling Baker Charlie. Come in, please. Over.' Huge relief swept through Blake. He replied: 'Baker Charlie to Fox Michael. Receiving you loud and clear. I cannot delay here any longer. They're on their way back from the cinema. I must come out now. No time for explanations. Over.'

Because of the unexpected hitches and delays, it had reached the time of the evening when the final tranche of relatives and friends started to pour in for the last hour's visiting at the hospital. Two more cars pulled into Artillery Road, parking next to the wall. Bourke waited until the occupants had left the vehicles, but realised the road was now unlikely to be completely clear. At 6.55, he heard Blake's voice coming through the radio in a state of great panic: 'Fox Michael! You MUST throw the ladder now, you simply must. There is no more time! Throw it now, Fox Michael! Are you still there? Come in, please.' Bourke responded: 'Fox Michael to Baker Charlie. The ladder is coming over now. No matter what the consequences are, the ladder is coming over now. Over.'

Bourke got out of the car, lifted the boot and took out the rope ladder. He then stepped on to the roof and, gripping the thick rope with his left hand, holding the folded rungs in his right, he prepared to swing. When he made the throw, the ladder successfully flew over the top of the wall, dropping down neatly on the inside with a thud. Bourke leapt down from the car, then jerked the ladder a few yards to the right to ensure that when Blake made his jump, he would not land on the top of the car. Then he waited.

In the sweeping light of the arc lamps, Blake saw the tangle of rope fly over the wall. Stooping low, with his walkie-talkie tucked inside his sweater, he raced over to the wall, grabbed the ladder, and started to climb upwards. The knitting needles had done their job and it was a surprisingly easy ascent: 'In a moment, unseen by the officers in the observation booths at the end of the wall but watched, I am sure, by several pairs of eyes bursting with excitement from the cell windows, I reached the top of the wall.'

At the top, Blake realised that Bourke had overlooked one thing: he had not attached a metal hook to the ladder so that it could be planted on the wall and used to descend on the other side. Instead, he was going to have to make the drop. As Blake peered down with a quizzical expression on his face, he saw Bourke looking anxiously up at him. 'Come on, man, come on,' he shouted. Blake shifted along the wall a few yards to be sure he would not hit the car, and then lowered himself until he was hanging from both hands. He let go.

In the corner of his eye, he saw Bourke make a move underneath as if to try and help break his 20ft fall. Blake, not wanting to injure his rescuer, tried to twist in mid-air to avoid the collision. Bourke stepped aside, but Blake still glanced off him as he dropped, landing badly. His head hit the gravelled road with a thump, and he felt a searing pain in his left arm. Momentarily he was dazed, perhaps even unconscious. Blood poured down his face.

Bourke bent down, grasped Blake under the arms and dragged him along the gravel until he reached the car. As he pushed him onto the back seat, another car drove past with its headlights on. If the occupants had arrived a few moments earlier, they would have witnessed the leap from the wall.

The rope ladder had to be left dangling.

Bourke got behind the wheel, and drove away. Narrowly avoiding a man, woman and girl who stood in the middle of Artillery Road, he turned right into the main flow of traffic on Du Cane Road.

On the back seat, Blake had draped a mackintosh round his shoulders and put a hat on his head. He could sense how tense Bourke was feeling and noticed that the glasses the Irishman was wearing by way of a disguise had steamed up.

Despite slow-moving traffic, Bourke's reduced vision and nerves led to him bumping the Humber Hawk into the car in front at a level crossing. The crash was hardly severe, but the driver nonetheless turned into the kerb to examine the damage, expecting Bourke to do the same. Instead, he slammed his foot on the accelerator and screamed away to the end of the road. He went through a light that was just barely turning green, raced along Wood Lane for a few hundred yards, then turned right into North Pole Road.

Another couple of turns and he was in Highlever Road. Fraught though it was, it had taken no more than six or seven minutes to reach the quiet residential street in North Kensington.

Bourke's nerves, almost shredded by the collision at the level crossing, were now slowly settling. His plan was to drop Blake off at 28 Highlever Road while he went and disposed of the car. He switched off the ignition and turned round to look at Blake: his face was a mess, with blood streaming down from a badly cut forehead. As Blake tried to reach into the pocket of his mackintosh for the keys, he winced in pain, his wrist bent at a sharp angle just above the joint and clearly beginning to swell. Bourke at once abandoned the plan to dump the car and, instead, escorted Blake into the safety of the flat. The ex-prisoner took off his hat and coat and stood in the middle of the room in his grey prison trousers and striped shirt.

'George,' said Bourke, 'I can hardly believe that you're standing in this room. It is going to take me a long time to get used to the idea. It is rather like seeing a double-decker bus on top of Nelson's Column.'

'I cannot believe it myself,' Blake laughed.

Bourke left the flat to buy bottles of brandy and whisky to celebrate. It was 7.20. Inside Wormwood Scrubs, every prisoner would be 'banged-up' and the final roll call of the day was nearing completion.

Blake was discovered missing at around the time Bourke had turned the car into North Pole Road. Upon finding Cell No. 8 empty, Prison Officer William Fletcher immediately called his colleague patrolling the boundary wall and D Wing was scoured for any sign of the escaped prisoner. While that fruitless search took place, the rope ladder was spotted, still dangling over the wall. By 7.35, Noel Whittaker had joined the search party and, when he went outside the prison wall onto Artillery Road, he soon came across a pot of pink chrysanthemums in their green wrapping paper, dumped there by Bourke. Back inside the jail, officers discovered the broken window at the south end of the wing, together with a missing metal bar. In just twenty minutes, it was all too clear how the bird had flown.

At 7.43 p.m., a call was made to Shepherd's Bush Police Station reporting the escape of Britain's most closely guarded criminal. 'This is the Deputy Governor of Wormwood Scrubs. I have just been informed by my Chief that we have lost one of our chaps over the wall. We think it's Blake,' Noel Whittaker explained in agitated tones.

'Blake?' replied Police Constable Stanley Frankling.

'Yes, the one doing forty-two years,' replied Whittaker.

'Can you give a description?' asked the police officer.

'Not at the moment. He's probably in prison grey. He went over the East wall. Look, I'm a bit tucked up at the moment; I'm in the middle of releasing a man. I'll ring you back when I get more information.'

For PC Frankling, it was a surreal moment that interrupted an otherwise commonplace Saturday evening, with its usual reports of

minor burglaries and the odd incident of domestic violence. Putting
his initial astonishment to one side, the police officer was instinctively
cautious about Whittaker's call because he knew that a coded message
– 'Patterson Calling' – was in place for reporting escapes from the
Scrubs, and Whittaker had not used it. At 7.50, PC Child received
confirmation that the report was, indeed, authentic. Frankling then
alerted the Central Information Room at New Scotland Yard.

The manhunt was underway.

While police and dogs flooded into the area around the Scrubs in
pursuit, a detective constable from Shepherd's Bush was in the Gate
Office at the prison with Whittaker searching for an up-to-date photograph of Blake. There was just one, frustratingly out of date, taken
on 2 January 1965. Nonetheless, the picture and its negatives went
off to New Scotland Yard to be duplicated and distributed across the
country. Along with it would come this description of the fugitive: '44
years old, 5'8", proportionate build, oval face, swarthy complexion,
hazel eyes, dress either a prison grey suit or blue overall'.

Detective Inspector Lynch of Special Branch was the 'hands-on'
investigating officer at New Scotland Yard. He began to spread the
search far and wide. By 8.40 p.m., officers covering airports in the
London area had been informed about Blake's escape, along with
those at the cross-channel ferry train at Victoria station. All seaports
manned by Special Branch and Customs Water Guard officers were
informed by 10.25. Lynch was working on the theory that the Russians
had sprung Blake, so police cars were despatched to three embassy resi-
dences in Kensington Palace Gardens and one in West Hill, Highgate,
to question those officials they suspected of being KGB operatives. To
the same end, H.M Customs Water Guard was told to supply details
as quickly as possible on all the Eastern Bloc ships currently berthed
in London docks. Special attention was also paid to airfields, and
anywhere else where light aircraft might conceivably take off.

Harold Wilson, spending the weekend at the Prime Minister's
country residence at Chequers, was informed of the breakout within

an hour. By 9 p.m., he had received preliminary reports from Dick White of SIS and Martin Furnival Jones of MI5, on the implications of the escape for national security.

At 10.25, copies of Blake's photograph were belatedly handed to the duty officer in the Press Bureau at New Scotland Yard, for immediate distribution to all press and TV outlets. Unfortunately, all the Sunday papers had been 'put to bed', bar one – the *News of the World.* The paper's deadline was 10.15 but its editor agreed that no copies should roll from the presses until a special messenger arrived with Blake's photograph.

Even at this very early stage of the inquiry, Special Branch officers worried that time was against them. 'We ran around a bit like headless chickens, trying to work out where we should go,' recalled Wilf Knight. 'We assumed Blake had been sprung by an Eastern Bloc country, because of the organisation and mechanics of doing such a thing, and therefore they must be ready to take him out straightaway.'

Somehow, from somewhere, Special Branch had received an unlikely tip-off that Blake was being spirited away in a harp case carried by a member of an Eastern European orchestra which had just played at the South Bank. Such was the fevered atmosphere that the story was taken seriously. At 2 a.m., as the Czechoslovakian State Orchestra checked in with their own airline to fly out of Britain, they were stopped. '[We] turned them over – men and women, harps, bassoons, cellos, everything. We caused quite a furore diplomatically,' said Knight.

Back at the Scrubs, there were scenes of jubilation as news spread by word of mouth or prisoners listened to radios in their cells. For Gerald Lamarque, the response was unprecedented: 'The excitement in the voices I hear is unbelievable. There must have been nearer a hundred than fifty escapes in the years I have spent here, but I have never known a reaction like this . . . Blake . . . Blake . . . over the wall . . . George . . . had it away. Good old George. Cowboy yells of "Yippee", only once or twice sheer savagery, directed against authority more than in support of Blake's escape. "He's fucked 'em" . . . And then, far away and faintly from the south end of the prison, singing "For He's a Jolly Good Fellow".'

Sharing in the celebrations, with the feeling of a job well done, was Phil Morris: 'It was a great strain, personally, but the atmosphere in the wing itself was electric . . . People were dancing and singing on the landings. The actual prison just ground to a halt for two days. But it was ecstatic, you know, and it couldn't have been a bigger morale booster for people who were under the cosh at the time.'

For Michael Randle, it had been an anxious day, and an increasingly worrying evening. He had expected Bourke to call by 7 p.m. and when, half an hour later, there was still no news, he feared the worst. He had plans to take his wife and her parents out for a meal at the nearby German restaurant, *Schmidt's,* in Tottenham Court Road, and was preparing to set off when the phone finally rang.

'I'm just calling to say that I have been to the party and thrown the bait to our friend, who has taken it hook, line and sinker,' said Bourke, in the coded language he had adopted for these occasions. 'I have him now standing beside me.' Randle was too overcome to reply. He sank back into his chair and curled up in a ball, quivering with emotion and sheer relief. When he recovered sufficiently to congratulate Bourke, he was told that there was one minor problem: Blake's wrist was almost certainly broken, and would need attention from a doctor.

The family meal that followed took on an atmosphere of celebration, even though Randle's in-laws were oblivious to what had happened. While driving back home, they listened to a radio news bulletin that led with the news of Blake's escape. It was a salutary moment. 'The announcement hit me like a blow in the stomach,' was Randle's memory. 'It was like wakening from an exciting but frightening dream to find it was actually happening.'

Back at the house, Randle received two disconcerting phone calls from journalists. Both reporters had made the connection that Randle had been in prison with Blake and asked if he knew anything about the escape. Feeling very uneasy, he denied it, but worried that if journalists could so quickly find a link between them, then so could the police.

At 28 Highlever Road, the mood was one of unconfined elation. Bourke and Blake raised their glasses to drink a toast to each other, the Irishman uttering appropriate words from Antony in Shakespeare's *Julius Caesar*: 'Mischief thou are now afoot – take what course thou wilt.' They then settled back to watch the BBC evening news at 9.45.

The measured tones of newsreader Peter Woods announced the main story: 'High drama in West London tonight. George Blake, the double agent who was serving forty-two years' imprisonment, escaped from Wormwood Scrubs Prison in London this evening.' After details of his crimes and sentence, Woods read out a statement from the Home Office: 'Blake was missed from his cell at seven o'clock, when all the prisoners were locked away for the night. A search was made of the prison grounds but no trace of Blake could be found. He is, therefore, presumed to have escaped.' Woods finished by telling viewers that a careful watch was being maintained at all airports and harbours, and East European embassies were also being kept under observation. He concluded: 'News is still coming in of this dramatic escape, and we will keep you informed.' The delicious incongruity of Woods talking about this extraordinary nationwide manhunt, when here was the subject of it, less than a mile from where the presenter was speaking in Television Centre, was not lost on the two friends.

Euphoria at their success, laced with copious amounts of brandy, had given the evening an unreal, fantastical mood that neither man was eager to break. When they did turn in, Blake found it difficult to sleep, his wrist becoming increasingly painful as the alcohol wore off. Bourke just kept muttering 'Christ, we've done it' as he turned and turned on his mattress on the floor.

Escaping from the Scrubs had, in a sense, been the easy part, though. Fleeing the country would be a far more challenging and complicated affair.

19

Hiding

The criminal underworld had mockingly, though with a degree of grudging respect, nicknamed him 'Whispering Grass'. Shaw Taylor, with his mellifluous voice and amiable manner, had been helping reel in the wrongdoers ever since his programme, *Police Five*, was first broadcast in 1962. When the former actor introduced it as usual at 3 p.m. on Sunday, 23 October, there was little doubt about which crime he most wanted the public's help in solving. 'A few moments ago we received a report from Scotland Yard of a couple of clues about the escape on which they hope *Police Five* viewers might be able to help,' Taylor told his audience.

One of the leads detectives were following up concerned the home-made rope ladder. The knitting needles reinforcing the rungs of the device had been identified as Milward brand, size thirteen, twenty in all. 'Now I wonder if there is a shop somewhere that sold at least ten pairs of size thirteen knitting needles, all in a go?' Taylor asked his viewers. In fact, police would visit a total of 412 establishments in the next few weeks in their search for shopkeeper who might identify Blake's accomplices.

As for the pot of pink chrysanthemums, it had been established that the flowers were fresh, bought on Saturday from a branch of F. Meyers

Ltd. 'Maybe they were used as a marker, maybe they were used as an excuse for hanging about by the wall at that particular time?' mused Taylor.

An offer of help soon came from an unusual quarter. Upon hearing about the spy's escape, Mr J.L. Taylor, Secretary of the *Institute of Psychical Studies* near Bath, had immediately contacted Leslie Newcombe, Governor of Wormwood Scrubs, saying: 'It would be of interest to our research into a process of locating individuals by a method of map divination (akin to water divining by map) if we might include George Blake in our current programme of readings.' Taylor claimed that the Institute's research into 'this use of the earth's electro-magnetic field' had resulted in a 70 per cent success rate. 'Should you feel disposed to give the method a trial,' he wrote, 'and could forward to us the necessary sample (a few hairs from the man's hairbrush, or a well-worn shoe or cap), we would include the sample in our programme of readings and report the result in 48 hours – the time required for testing readings for consistency.' Perhaps unsurprisingly, Scotland Yard declined the offer, and no item of Blake's head or footwear was put in the post.

Meanwhile, more conventional police techniques were reaping few rewards. At Wormwood Scrubs almost all the prisoners had clammed up in the traditional tribal manner, and the widespread respect for Blake made their *omerta* even harder to crack. Nonetheless, whispers about Phil Morris's involvement reached the ears of investigators. In his first interview, Morris claimed he had last seen Blake on Saturday morning, and as for the afternoon, he had either been in his own cell or playing banjo and having a 'sing-song' with others on the second floor. When police came back for a second round of questioning, however, Morris realised they were on to something and was forced into a more aggressive defence:

> Blake never asked any favours. I have no ideas. It's nothing to do
> with me . . . People drop notes in boxes to get you in bother . . .

> I don't know anything about two-way radios. I don't know about
> Sean Bourke having anything to do with it. I'm not in the frame
> and don't know who is. Blake never visited me in my cell. I don't
> remember him having his last visit. I didn't have my light out that
> night . . . I don't take any barrow or tools out.

As detectives started to plough their way through the list of 328
inmates in D wing that Sunday, just a mile away, at 28 Highlever Road,
the subject of their inquiries was in need of urgent medical attention.
A combination of adrenalin and brandy had masked the pain but
when Blake woke up on Sunday morning, his wrist had swollen and he
was in serious discomfort. Bourke left him alone in Highlever Road,
reading the front-page accounts of his escape in the Sunday papers,
and travelled to Randle's home at Torriano Cottages in Kentish Town
to discuss the problem.

Bourke's impatience exhibited itself once more: despite the manifest dangers of identification, he wanted to take Blake to hospital to
have the wrist set. Randle counselled caution, and said he would ring
round his friends and try to find a doctor who could be trusted to do
the job. After a hectic day on the phone, Randle finally found a suitable candidate. Accompanied by 'Matthew' and 'Rachel', the couple
who had suggested him, and in a state of some apprehension, Randle
journeyed by bus to the doctor's home to try and persuade him to
help. The task proved easier than expected. Once it became clear to
the doctor that he would be dealing with Blake, he seemed remarkably unperturbed. Although he made clear his dislike of Communism
and Communists, he told them he had been impressed by what he
had heard about Blake's work for the Dutch resistance, and expressed
sympathy for the effect those wartime experiences might have had on
Blake as a young man.

A major problem remained; the doctor had no plaster at home
with which to make a cast. Fortuitously, Michael Randle had a close
friend who worked in the make-up department at BBC Television

Centre, where they used plaster bandages on actors who played the parts of characters with broken limbs. After another fruitful phone call, Randle and the doctor headed off to Wood Lane to pick up the plaster of Paris. Ten minutes later, at about 8.30 p.m., they arrived at Highlever Road.

Randle was surprised but delighted to see Pat Pottle already there. Blake had been unaware of Pottle's involvement in the conspiracy, and had welcomed his support in the preceding hour or so as an increasingly excitable Bourke had become fixed on the reckless idea of taking him to hospital.

By way of cover, the doctor invoked the Hippocratic Oath, saying to Blake: 'Normally you should go to hospital to have the wrist set. However, I understand that for some reason or other you are allergic to hospitals. Therefore I consider it my duty to help you.' He then warned him that he had not set a broken wrist for ten years, and that to a degree the operation was bound to be makeshift. He recommended an x-ray and further attention as soon as possible.

Over celebratory drinks that night, the plotters decided that Bourke's bedsit was no place to hide out in the long-term. On Tuesday, 25 October, Blake was moved to the home of 'Matthew' and 'Rachel'. It was with some reluctance that they took him in, guaranteeing him the room only until Saturday.

Then he was on the move again, this time with Bourke, who had previously remained at Highlever Road. The new venue looked far more promising – a maisonette in a large house in Nevern Road, Earls Court, in West London, boasting 'high ceilings, sash windows, a splendid marble fireplace, comfortable armchairs and a TV set'. It belonged to John and Marcelle Papworth, a couple who moved in the same radical circles as Randle and Pottle.

John Papworth – gangling, flamboyant and white-haired – had grown up in an East End orphanage, been involved with radical politics and then the Labour Party, but he was, at that time, editing a pioneering environmental magazine. It was he who had agreed to make the apartment available as he and his wife were at their cottage in the Cotswolds that weekend. A week on from the escape and it looked, finally, as if Blake and Bourke had found at least a semi-permanent hideout from where they could plot their way out of the country.

It all went wrong when Marcelle returned on Sunday. Her husband had not informed her about the two new guests and when she discovered one of them was the nation's Most Wanted Man she was horrified. At a further meeting with both of them later in the evening Papworth also expressed dismay at Blake's presence: 'When you said, Michael, that you had two people you wanted me to shelter, I assumed they were American army deserters or something of that kind. I never dreamt for one moment that you were referring to George Blake. This house really is not safe for him and his friend.' He further explained that he had a secretary who worked there during weekdays, and that there were frequent visitors, but nevertheless agreed that Blake and Bourke could stay for just two more days.

The following evening, Monday, 31 October, Randle and the two fugitives were confronted with an astonishing story that propelled them on their way yet again. Papworth came into their bedroom, saying he had something to tell them: 'My wife is undergoing a course of analysis. This requires her to be absolutely frank with her analyst and not to conceal anything from him.' Randle recalled the ensuing conversation:

> We looked at him blankly. 'Are you saying,' George asked, maintaining his composure with a visible effort, 'that she has told him about *us*?'

> 'Yes,' [John] replied. 'Everything. There's no point in it if she isn't completely frank. You must understand, of course, that what she says to him is in the strictest confidence.'

> George had gone very pale (I'm sure I had too!). His voice was thin

and reedy, and he struggled to retain his self-control. 'And what
did the analyst say when she told him?'

'Oh, he said that she was imagining it, and that it was because there
had been so much publicity about the escape of George Blake.'

Unwilling to trust in the sanctity of the analyst's couch, Blake and
Bourke headed straight upstairs to pack their bags.

Already they felt restless following a dramatic front-page story in
the *Evening Standard* a few days earlier announcing 'Blake's Escape
Car Found', followed by further reports that weekend. They said a two-
tone green Humber Hawk had been seen in the vicinity of Wormwood
Scrubs at 6.30 p.m. on the night of Blake's escape, and that detec-
tives had found fibres from a blue prison uniform on one of the seats.
Bourke's connection with the escape had also been made public in a
Daily Mirror report: 'A prisoner at the jail who was allowed out to work
each day has been "gated" while the escape plot is being investigated.
Police are searching for an Irish friend of Blake who was released from
Wormwood Scrubs last August'. Late editions of the evening papers
on Saturday went further and described a '33-year-old man from
Limerick'.

Just as worrying, that same Monday, the *Daily Mirror* indicated that
the police now believed Blake was hiding out in London. The first
theory, the paper said, was that he had already been whisked out of
Britain and was now in the Soviet Union or another Iron Curtain
country, but the second 'strongly backed by Scotland Yard, is that he is
still in London – possibly not far from the jail in Shepherd's Bush . . .
the area has an enormous cosmopolitan area. Whole streets cater for
an army of wandering workmen, who stay a week at a time . . . Blake
could be hiding in any of these.'

This was all too close to the mark, even if Blake and Bourke were
no longer in the Shepherd's Bush area. Michael Randle now began to
think seriously about taking the two men into his own home in Kentish

Town, perhaps building a false partition, a kind of 'priest hole'. Pat Pottle then came to the rescue. His was a bachelor flat in Willow Buildings, Hampstead, and, although small, had three bedrooms. Pottle spent the whole of Tuesday, 1 November bolstering its privacy and security – putting up net curtains and installing sturdy locks in time for Blake's arrival in the evening. When he saw his new hiding-place that night, Blake was delighted. 'You've turned this place into a fortress,' he told Pottle. 'You know, it's the first time I've felt really secure since I escaped.'

It would be another week before Bourke joined them. He had been back in his original hiding place in Highlever Road, keeping his head down except to buy food and papers. He had also been busy at his typewriter, bashing out an early draft of the events of the previous two weeks – indeed the past year – for a book he was putting together about the escape.

Even Bourke, insouciant and impetuous though he was, recognised that to linger too long in West London, when the police were busy accumulating clues about the escape, was reckless. On Tuesday, 8 November, he joined Pottle and Blake in Willow Buildings. Now that they were all finally settled, the conspirators could start work on a plan to get the 'master spy' and the 'Irishman' (as the papers were labelling them) out of the country.

Cranks and crackpot theories abounded during those first, frenzied weeks of the Blake Escape. At times it must have seemed to the police as if Blake had disappeared into The Bermuda Triangle, so little idea did they have of his whereabouts. Wild theories supported by MPs were similarly unhelpful, such as the one put forward by a 'responsible citizen' and reported in a letter from Conservative Keith Joseph to the Labour Home Secretary Roy Jenkins, suggesting that the country was 'ringed by Russian ships for a few days before Blake got away. They could use rubber rafts and land without any fuss.'

In Parliament on Monday, 24 October, two days after Blake's

escape, Ted Heath and the Conservatives had set out to make life as uncomfortable as they could for Jenkins. They had serious questions to raise about the neglect of security in the nation's jails, but they also saw this as their chance to stock up some significant political capital against a promising minister whose successful liberal agenda was anathema to their party. Jenkins hoped an immediate announcement of an independent investigation into prison security to be chaired by Lord Mountbatten, and including the Blake escape in its remit, would quieten his critics. The Tory benches were far from satisfied, pressing instead for a specific inquiry into Blake's breakout. By the end of the debate, still intent on that assurance, they took the unusual step of tabling a censure motion against Jenkins. The debate on the Home Secretary's competence and strategy was set for a week's time.

In the meantime, the Tories had more detailed questions to put on whether Blake's escape had imperilled national security. On Thursday afternoon, 27 October, Heath and his Shadow Foreign Secretary, Sir Alec Douglas Home, met Harold Wilson, Foreign Secretary George Brown, and Jenkins in the Prime Minister's office in the House of Commons. Wilson reassured them SIS and MI5 had carried out exhaustive enquiries and had so far concluded that Blake's disappearance had put no one's life in danger. Moreover, what Blake knew was now five or six years out of date. Of greater concern was whether the Soviets would use Blake as a propaganda tool, by parading him on television, or lauding his arrival in *Pravda*. Even here, though, Wilson told Heath that Sir Dick White, Head of SIS, believed publicity relating to Kim Philby would be more damaging to the national cause than anything regarding Blake.

Wilson, emollient as ever and with his political antenna twitching as always, proposed that rather than listen to him parroting the words of the Chief, why didn't Heath and his colleagues return next Monday – the morning of the censure debate – and hear a briefing from the Head of SIS himself?

The conversation resumed at 10.30 a.m. on Monday, 31 October, with the same group in attendance, along with Dick White. C was a past master in soothing the troubled brows of politicians. He told the gathering he doubted whether the Russians had got Blake. Whereas Gordon Lonsdale had refused to answer any questions during his interrogation, Blake had admitted everything very fully, so his ideological masters had 'no obligation towards him'. White did not rule out the possibility, however, that Blake might have been given some money by the Soviets and 'left to work out his own future'. He told his audience that Blake had had no access to any state secrets since September 1960. On the damage to the working practices of SIS, White conceded that Blake's activities had 'been of considerable danger to us', but said full account had now been taken of all the information to which he had access, and successful counter-intelligence measures had subsequently been put in place.

The politicians left the Prime Minister's room satisfied with what they had heard from Sir Dick. But, of course, they returned to their traditional, warring ways in the Commons chamber that evening for a fractious debate on the Conservative motion that 'This House deplores the refusal of the Secretary of State to set up a specific inquiry to report as a matter of urgency on the escape of George Blake from Wormwood Scrubs'.

In a debate of high drama, Jenkins trounced Heath and Quintin Hogg, the Shadow Home Secretary, by a simple demonstration that everything he had done and not done in dealing with prison security, his Tory predecessors had done and not done to a worse degree. Jenkins went on to explain that, within two hours of the previous Monday's debate, he had met Lord Mountbatten to agree the terms of reference of his inquiry – one of which was that the Blake escape would be a central part of Mountbatten's deliberations. He asked the House to reject 'the trumped-up Motion': 'The Blake case is a most serious matter but it will not be met by that combination of procedural incompetence and petty partisanship which is the constant characteristic of the right Honourable Gentleman's parliamentary style.' At the end, the

Labour backbenchers cheered lustily and waved their order papers in celebration. Dick Crossman described Jenkins' speech as a 'tremendous, annihilating attack, which completely destroyed the Opposition'.

All this political excitement was, however, a sideshow. Blake was still on the loose. There was a sense of despondency in some quarters and Special Branch officers interviewing Blake's mother confided to her that they 'were on a hopeless quest'. They assumed, they told her, that his escape was the outcome of a professional, well financed operation and that her son had fled the country within hours of getting over the wall.

Nothing could have been further from the truth. The amateur gang, holed up in their North London hideout, had still to work out any viable plan for getting their fugitive to safety.

Randle's friends 'Matthew' and 'Rachel' had reconnoitred the area around the Soviet Embassy in Kensington Palace Gardens and believed they had found a sheltered, unprotected spot by the back wall, where Blake could easily be hoisted over. Randle was surprised by the hostility with which Blake rejected the plan: 'George stared at me pale and disbelieving. Sean too looked shocked. "I would be completely and utterly opposed to that!" he said, with more vehemence than I had ever heard him express before.' Blake was convinced that the Soviets would view him as a 'burden and an embarrassment'. His arrival would inevitably cause a major diplomatic incident, and it was entirely possible he would be handed back to the British authorities. He told his friends he had no desire to 'do a Mindszenty', referring to Cardinal Mindszenty, who sought sanctuary in the American Embassy in Budapest during the Soviet invasion of 1956 and was forced to stay there for fifteen years. If that was his only option, he would prefer to be back in his cell in Wormwood Scrubs.

The earlier idea, that of changing Blake's skin colour so he could pass as an Arab, was also ditched. Blake had always been nervous of the possible side effects of taking such large doses of an unpredictable drug like Meladinine and, despite his initial bravado, it had become clear that Bourke lacked underworld contacts who could be relied upon to produce the necessary forged passports.

The conspirators fleetingly considered crossing the English Channel in a small sailing boat and landing the fugitive on a secluded part of the French coast, but the more they pondered the problem, the more apparent it became that the surest way to smuggle Blake to freedom would be by driving him there in a car or a van, concealed for the duration in a container or a secret compartment. A plan to build a false section in the boot of a car was considered, and then discarded. Randle's thoughts instead turned to larger vehicles, like a camper van, and he started scouring catalogues and showrooms for a model that might fit the bill.

Most had a bench seat in the back, with storage cupboards underneath. The hinged seat was designed to fold outwards to make a bed, supported by the open cupboard doors. There was potential here, but the storage space under the bed was surely one of the first places Customs officials would search. Randle came up with the idea of supporting the fold-down bed with drawers, rather than cupboard doors. If the drawers remained open all the time, George could hide in the space *behind them*. Only a highly suspicious official would want to pull out the drawers packed full of clothes. With a £1,000 cheque from their benefactor, 'Bridget', Randle and his friend 'Matthew' selected a type of camper van made by Commer, which had more adaptable fittings than any of the other models. The double doors at the back were valuable too, according to Randle: 'It would make access to the proposed hiding-place at the back of the driver's seat that bit more awkward for any Customs officer to reach.'

Blake welcomed the scheme wholeheartedly but the question of his ultimate destination remained unanswered. He had long favoured Egypt: he had lived there as a boy, he had relatives in Cairo, and he spoke Arabic. He knew, however, that the trip would be too complicated and dangerous, and so set his sights instead on a Communist or neutral European country. For a while, Yugoslavia was top of the list, but was ruled out because there were too many frontiers to cross. Switzerland was considered, but Blake knew from his espionage days that SIS had a close relationship with the country's intelligence service, the *Sûreté*. Eventually, a consensus of opinion formed around East Germany. Blake, who of course knew Berlin and its environs well after his four-year stint there, was enthusiastic. Moreover, he envisaged a route which would save his collaborators from contact with the authorities of a Communist country.

It was clear that Randle would have to be the driver – Pottle had no licence, and Bourke's participation in this enterprise was out of the question. Anne was reluctant for her husband to undertake this onerous and risky trip on his own, so she volunteered to join him. By bringing their two young children, aged four and two, they also thought they might attract less suspicion. To all intents and purposes, they would look as if they were on a family Christmas holiday.

Randle spent much of the next three weeks in the garage that 'Matthew' owned, working with him on the conversion. It proved much trickier than anticipated. Replacing cupboards with drawers was not a straightforward task, and it soon became clear that everything would have to be stripped out and the interior of the Commer van completely redesigned and rebuilt. 'We worked intently, almost feverishly, with a radio in the workshop tuned to a pirate station playing non-stop pop music,' recalled Randle. 'There was still a sufficient sense of urgency to keep the adrenalin flowing, for we knew that neither George nor the rest of us would be out of danger so along as he remained in the country.'

Back in Willow Buildings, Pottle's task was almost as tricky; how to keep Britain's two most wanted men safe and, in particular, how to restrain the restless, volatile Bourke from mischief. Blake, constitutionally self-contained, was content enough with his yoga and a new copy of The Koran, in which he could immerse himself. Bourke, on the other hand, who had for so long been the lead protagonist in this whole conspiracy and made all the major decisions, now found himself consigned to a minor role. He resented it; also the fact that he was confined to the flat all day. On a couple of occasions, the two fugitives allowed in visitors when Pottle was out – once a man from the TV rental company, and another time the landlord's workman came to measure up for replacement windows. Pottle was furious.

What he did not know, which would have enraged him further still, was that Bourke was also venturing out on occasional shopping trips, or taking washing to the launderette in Hampstead High Street. The Irishman relished flirting with danger. 'I had to pass the police station, and I would often pause to read the WANTED notices,' he recalled. 'I was constantly passing policemen on the pavement – they didn't recognise me because they weren't looking for me.'

By the second week of December, the van had been converted and was ready to go. The secret compartment stretched from behind the two larger drawers – there were three in all – to the underneath of the seat immediately behind the driver's. A piece of foam rubber had been placed in it to make Blake's long journey less uncomfortable.

The departure date was fixed, the car ferry tickets bought and the international driving licence and necessary insurance obtained.

Meanwhile, after much soul searching, it had been decided that Bourke would join Blake in the Soviet Union at a later date. The Irishman had wanted to find a way to return home, convinced that once in Ireland the authorities would never extradite him back to Britain. He eventually conceded that it would be wiser if he went missing for a while, allowing the excitement to die down and the trail to run cold. To this end, Randle spent some time in late November forging a passport for him, and an escape route was devised: he would catch the London-Paris train at Victoria at 8.30 p.m. on New Year's Eve, arriving at the Gare du Nord at 8 a.m. on New Year's Day. He would then head for Orly airport and board a plane to West Berlin. After spending a night in West Berlin, he would cross over, through Checkpoint Charlie, at 10 a.m. on Monday, 2 January. By then, Blake would have alerted the

Soviets, and there would be a welcoming party ready for him at Soviet headquarters in Karlshorst. Soon afterwards, he would board a plane for Moscow and he and Blake would be reunited.

The plotters gathered at Pat Pottle's flat at 6.30 p.m. on Saturday, 17 December for a final, valedictory dinner before the Randles and Blake set off for East Germany. Pottle's by now customary fish pie was on the menu, along with liberal amounts of red wine. Knowing he would be cooped up in the secret compartment for as much as nine hours on end, Blake had deliberately drunk very little that day and restrained himself once more. The mood round the table was one of nervous excitement. Blake proposed a toast to the others: 'I found it difficult to find words to express my deep gratitude to these brave and exceptional men and women who put their liberty and happiness at risk to help me.'

At 8.15 p.m. they walked out to the van. Blake lowered himself into his coffin-like compartment, taking with him a rubber hot water bottle for when he needed to relieve himself. The flap was closed, the drawer put in place, and the bed folded down and covered with a mattress. Then they were on their way.

The journey progressed smoothly, if more slowly than Randle had anticipated. The Commer van was built for comfort, not speed, and their progress through South London seemed interminable.

They were just ten miles away from Dover when Anne thought she heard a knocking noise coming from the hideout. Hurrying to make the ferry on time, and unable to hear anything himself, Randle drove on. A few miles further on, they both heard clearly a persistent banging, and pulled in to the side of the road. The children, Sean and Gavin, were moved from the bed to the front of the van and wrapped up in a blanket, before the drawer was pulled back to let Blake out. He crawled out of his hideout looking pale and gasping for breath. Stumbling out of the van, he began to retch, before taking in great gulps of fresh air. The gas-like smell of the hot water bottle had made him feel nauseous, but after a few minutes the colour started to return to his cheeks, and he clambered back into his 'coffin' – minus the water bottle.

The Commer van reached the Dover docks around 11.50 p.m., late for check-in. Fortunately, others had been delayed as well and, after a cursory passport check and no Customs search whatsoever, they were allowed onto the ferry. The most perilous part of the escape was successfully completed: Blake was now out of Britain.

For the crossing, the Randles had to sit upstairs in the lounge with all the other passengers. Below, Blake remained in the hold in his hiding place. Once the ferry had docked at Ostend, Michael drove clear of the city before stopping the van by the roadside. Somewhat fearfully, he and Anne then opened the drawer and peered into the compartment. They had not seen or heard Blake for over eight hours and, given what had happened on the way to Dover, their anxiety stretched to fears that he had been suffocated. Randle recalled the moment vividly: "'George! Are you OK?" There was a shuffling sound from inside the cavity. "I'm fine," he whispered back. "A bit stiff, that's all." "My God, I am glad to see you!" I said as he got out. "Anne and I were giving you up for dead."'

It was agreed, for now, that there was no need for him to return to his hideout. Instead he sat on one of the seats at the back, the children in front unperturbed by the arrival of the new passenger in their midst. Blake was no stranger to them – they knew him as 'Dave' from previous meetings. Perhaps they thought such funny goings-on were a natural part of any holiday.

At around 8.30 a.m., the Commer van passed through Brussels, but they then missed the road to Aachen. Michael stopped to ask for directions and, much to Anne's consternation, Blake interrupted in Flemish. Although more relaxed now safely across the English Channel, she saw no reason to take unnecessary risks.

As they neared Aachen, Blake returned once more to his hiding-place. Passing through the checkpoint into West Germany proved easy

– neither the Belgian nor German officials inspected the van, and gave their passports only a cursory glance. They were through, and soon on the autobahn heading north.

This should have been one of the quickest, smoothest stages of their journey, but the rain began to beat down heavily, and to compound matters, the windscreen wipers stopped working. Michael pulled into a garage to see if he could get them repaired but, once again, Blake's over-eagerness got the better of him, and he insisted on explaining the problem to the mechanics in their own language. It was a Sunday, so there was no way of getting the necessary spares. All the mechanics could do was put back the motor, making it possible to rotate the wipers by hand – a tiring labour which Anne and Blake took in turns.

It stopped raining at around 6 p.m., by which time they were passing Hanover. Michael had by now been driving for twelve hours across unfamiliar terrain in difficult conditions: 'I was overcome by an over-whelming desire to sleep. I bit my lip and concentrated all my energies on fighting drowsiness, but still the car lights in front seemed to sway and I could feel my eyelids drooping.' He had been popping 'uppers' along the way to help ward off fatigue, and took another couple for the crucial leg of the journey towards Helmstedt, the point where the West met the Communist East.

It was just before 8.30 p.m. when they approached the border. Blake was hidden away for the final time, and the Randles' two boys were put back to bed. Passing through the West German checkpoint was a mere formality, with no inspection of the van, no rigorous examination of their passports. The scrutiny they encountered at the East German frontier, however, made for a tense experience. The guard there directed Randle into the customs and immigration shed. After handing him application forms to sign for transit visas, he asked him to open up the vehicle – the first time this had happened on the entire journey.

'The children were in bed at the back, though not asleep as they had only recently been disturbed when we hid George. The guard glanced round, but didn't bother lifting the bed to examine the contents of the drawers. He nodded again, and the examination was over.' Inside, Blake waited in trepidation: 'I held my breath, but a moment later the doors were slammed to again and I heard Michael climbing into the driving seat. Then we were on our way again.'

Although tired, Randle was entitled to feel a sense of elation that the job was now all but done. Instead, as he gazed at the East German border post with its high fences, searchlights and watchtowers manned by guards with machine guns, he began to wonder, somewhat despondently, about the nature of Soviet-controlled Eastern Europe and the future Blake faced. Gone were the pristine autobahns of West Germany, in their place a potholed, poorly maintained road with no hard shoulder. 'There was a tangible sense of having entered an alien and hostile territory,' was Randle's perception.

On he went, now a day and half without sleep. Eventually, at around 11.30 p.m., he crossed the bridge over the River Elbe near Magdeburg, the spot where they had agreed Blake could emerge from his hideout for the final approach to the East German checkpoint near Berlin. Blake crawled out and took his place in the seat behind the driver; the children, exhausted after the day's adventures, were happy to clamber into bed and soon fell asleep. The distant lights of the East German checkpoint near the city rose into view. With about a mile to go, the van drew up and they prepared to part. Blake, feeling very emotional, told Michael and Anne: 'It's fantastic what you two have done. Believe me, I will never forget it or do anything that could put you or your family at risk. We should be celebrating in champagne. One day I hope we may be able to do so.'

Randle stepped down from the vehicle into the road while Blake buttoned up his long overcoat and donned his trilby hat. The two men shook hands for the last time, and then Randle got back inside and drove off towards the checkpoint.

Blake watched the rear lights slowly fade away into the night. He waited a while by the side of the road, giving the van plenty of time to reach the border and clear it, before he himself set off towards it. So it was with a sense of apprehension as well as exhilaration that he began to walk in the direction of the barbed wire and the bright arc lamps.

He knew he faced a difficult task, turning up on foot in the dead of night. The story he was about to tell these young, suspicious border guards was an utterly incredible one. They would take some convincing.

20

Moscow

At around 2 a.m. on the morning of Monday, 19 December, Sergei Kondrashev was taking part in a high-level meeting at the KGB residency in Karlshorst, East Berlin. It was interrupted when the duty officer burst in with a remarkable story to tell.

A man had just turned up at the East Berlin border post demanding to meet a Soviet representative – not just any official, but someone senior from Soviet intelligence. The stranger did not appear to be a German citizen, even though he spoke the language well. He was surprisingly well informed about the security and geography of the area; also most persistent in his entreaties, despite the scepticism of the guards. They had finally been persuaded to summon a young officer from the Soviet command post positioned between the East and West German checkpoints. The stranger then revealed to this officer exactly who he was, and how he had arrived there in the middle of the night: his name was George Blake, and he had just been dropped off by friends on their way to West Berlin. Remarkably, the Soviet officer had not heard of the notorious spy, so the enormity of what he was told was lost on him. But he was sufficiently impressed by the man's calm manner and compelling narrative to decide to alert his seniors back at KGB headquarters.

The intelligence chiefs gathered round the conference table at Karlshorst were instinctively suspicious: it seemed too incredible to be true. Perhaps it was a trick by Western intelligence? Fortunately, there was no one better equipped to discover the truth than Blake's former handler from those days in London a decade ago, who, by sheer chance, happened to be in Berlin on a visit from Moscow.

Kondrashev jumped into a chauffeur-driven car and, after an hour and a half, reached the checkpoint. On arrival, a guard pointed the KGB officer towards the room where the visitor was resting. When Kondrashev walked through the door, a bearded man, dressed casually in jeans, shirt and jumper, put aside his breakfast of sandwiches and coffee and rose to greet him. Despite the growth of facial hair and the passing years, Kondrashev immediately recognised the man with whom he had strolled through the suburbs of London over a decade ago. 'It's him! It's him!' he shouted excitedly, and rushed forward to embrace Blake.

Kondrashev accompanied Blake straight back to Karlshorst, where he was given a comfortable villa in the compound and treated like a conquering hero: 'The comrades seemed especially pleased that I had chosen their city in which to surface. Though I never for a moment thought I would be turned away or not looked after well, I had not expected such a warm welcome.'

Gentle debriefing took place over a succession of convivial lunches and dinner parties and, every day, one of the officials assigned to look after him would take Blake's measurements and head off to West Berlin to buy him a new set of clothes, as his KGB minders wanted him to look and feel at his best for his arrival in the Soviet Union. At this stage, Blake was not allowed to venture far. Security remained exceptionally tight up to the moment, a fortnight later, when a special aircraft flew him to the Soviet capital as the KGB feared Western agents might discover his whereabouts and try and snatch him.

In fact, an MI5 report filed just a few weeks later suggests that Blake's arrival in Germany did not go unnoticed in Western intelligence circles. It read: 'An extremely delicate source had indicated that shortly before Christmas an unnamed man arrived in East Berlin who was considered important enough to be met personally by the Deputy Head of the KGB. This individual possessed only the clothes he stood up in. The possibility that this man was BLAKE clearly cannot be discounted'.

The Intelligence Services received the first concrete proof that Blake was safely abroad and beyond their reach in early April. He sent a series of letters – all postmarked Cairo, 31 March – to his mother Catherine in Hertfordshire, his sister Adele in Bangkok, the daughter of his mother's employer Mrs Christine Rose (just in case Catherine's letter was intercepted), another relative in Holland and finally, to Philip Deane, his old colleague in Korea, who was now living in Canada.

In the letter to his *Allerliefste Mammie* (dearest mother), Blake assured her that everything was fine:

> At long last I am able to write to you to let you know that I am well and in complete safety so that you need not worry about me any more . . . I am sure that you are the first to rejoice that I am a free man again and that soon we shall be able to see each other again . . . I would have written much earlier but in the very special circumstances in which I found myself it was impossible to get in touch with you, longing though I was to do so. Even now, for reasons over which I have no control, I cannot tell you exactly where I am but that will not be for long and soon I shall be able to write more and arrange for us to be together again in freedom so that I can make it up to you, at least in some measure, for all the suffering you have been through because of me . . .

He signed off: 'All love and many kisses, from Poek; PS. Please give a big kiss to Anthony from me on his tenth birthday'.

The Cairo postmark was, of course, a red herring. The KGB had arranged for one of its agents to post the letters from there to throw MI5 and the SIS off the scent. Much wild speculation was generated as a result in the following days and weeks, to the great satisfaction of the Soviet authorities. Back in Moscow, the object of all the confusion was firmly ensconced in a 'safe' flat in the centre of the city.

Another of Blake's old handlers, Vasily Dozhdalev, was assigned to look after him in his first few weeks in the capital, though, in normal circumstances, he would have been considered far too senior to be Blake's minder, commanding as he did his own department at the Lubyanka. 'God forbid that the West would sniff out early on that he was in Moscow, so he was incognito for some time,' said Dozhdalev. The KGB officer took him for a haircut at a barber's shop in Izmailov Square – 'his hair had grown very long while he was in hiding, not the fashion in those days' – and in the evenings he would shepherd his charge on long walks in the park areas around the Boulevard Ring.

The KGB flat was far beyond Blake's expectations. It had four spacious rooms with high ceilings, good-quality mahogany furniture, crystal chandeliers and oriental carpets. A live-in housekeeper, Zinaida, and her daughter, Sofia, kept the place tidy and prepared his meals.

Such was the concern of his masters about the possibility of him being kidnapped or even assassinated by Western agents that Blake was never allowed to stray far – certainly for the first six months or so. He was made to avoid large hotels, restaurants, theatres, anywhere visited frequently by foreigners. He was given a sizeable allowance but little opportunity to spend it. For much of this time he was holed up in the flat, 'leading, in many ways, the same existence as in Hampstead when we were in hiding'.

When he was able to venture out of his comfortable surroundings and into the mix of daily Soviet life, Blake, like many Westerners, struggled to adapt to the strictures of a Communist society. This was the Brezhnev era, a time of stagnation, and Moscow in the mid-1960s was a monochrome place, in both look and character. Old women, mostly clad in black from head to toe, led the long, fractious queues at stalls and shops, where many foodstuffs were in short supply and lacking in quality and variety. Blake observed the rudeness and indifference of the people to one another in public, continually frustrated as they were by the inefficiencies of the State and the great, enveloping blanket of bureaucracy that spread itself over every facet of daily life.

He felt his spell in prison had prepared him well for conditions in Russia: 'In a way, Wormwood Scrubs acted as a kind of airlock which made the transition easier and the rough edges less painful. After prison, it was such a wonderful experience to be able to get up in the morning and dispose of one's day as one thought fit, to go wherever one wished, that it made the lower standard of living and other disadvantages inherent in the Soviet Union much less difficult to accept.' And away from the miserable-looking crowds and the 'cold, ugly and impersonal modern buildings', Blake was entranced by Old Moscow, with its charming backstreets, fine old palaces and churches with golden and blue domes.

But all the while, he retained some lingering hope that, somehow, Gillian and the boys might join him in his new life. Nine months before his escape, she had revealed that she had met a man while on holiday in Cornwall and wished to marry him. Divorce proceedings had been instigated but were adjourned in November 1966 while Blake was still in hiding in Hampstead. On 18 March, news arrived, through the columns of *The Times*, that the divorce had finally been granted in his absence. The newspaper reported that Gillian had been granted a decree nisi because of Blake's 'cruelty'. Mr Justice Orr had made his judgement guided by a case heard in 1956 – quoted by Gillian's counsel – in which it had been ruled that 'conviction of a spouse for treasonable conduct may amount to cruelty or constructive desertion'. Gillian was given custody of Anthony, James and Patrick. Though not unexpected, this caused Blake 'a great deal of grief'. He missed his family enormously but knew full well that, even if it had been possible for her to join him, Gillian would have struggled to settle into Soviet life.

His marriage now formally over, the other key friendship in his life was also beginning to deteriorate. Blake and Bourke, by now sharing the same flat, had begun to quarrel.

The British Embassy, a striking pre-Revolution mansion that once belonged to a wealthy sugar merchant, was located in one of the most commanding locations in the whole of Moscow. It stood on the Maurice Thorez Embankment – named after the long-time French Communist Party leader – and looked directly across the River Moskva to the golden domes of the Kremlin. At 5.20 p.m. on Monday, 4 September 1967, just as the Embassy was preparing to close its doors for the day, a scruffy, unshaven man, 'looking like someone coming in straight off work', arrived at the front gate and asked the guard if he could speak to an official. He had a story to tell, he said, adding elliptically: 'I am the man you're looking for.' The guard ushered him into the waiting room of the mansion building and went to summon the most senior diplomats he could find.

Bourke had clearly put on weight after nine months of being wined and dined by the KGB, but he had lost none of his beguiling charm. In his report of the incident to the Foreign Office, Anthony Williams noted that he had a 'squarish face, dark curly hair and a ruddy complexion . . . he speaks English with a soft, pleasant Southern Irish brogue and is clearly not unintelligent.' The men who arrived to conduct the interview were First Secretary Peter Maxey, his colleague Brian Fall and the Consul, Leslie Sturmey.

Bourke had come to them to ask for refuge in the Embassy – asylum, effectively – and, after that, he wanted their help in obtaining the necessary documentation to leave the Soviet Union. Without equivocation, he confessed to having planned, engineered and carried out Blake's escape. He did not reveal all the details, merely assuring them with characteristic bravado that it had been 'child's play to get out of

Wormwood Scrubs in those days'. He emphasised that there had been no involvement by the KGB, and that, indeed, the Soviets had known nothing of Blake's flight until their arrival in East Berlin. He explained his motives – that he felt Blake's sentence was inhumane, and that Blake had persuaded him that he was not guilty of treason and had not betrayed a large number of British agents to the KGB.

To have Britain's second most wanted man sitting opposite them, confessing his guilt, was one thing, but the diplomats listened in amazement as Bourke then span a dubious story of how Blake had turned against him, and was now plotting murder. Bourke explained that he had become disillusioned with exile in Russia – he was 'a fish out of water' – and had gone to Blake and told him that he felt the time had come to return to the United Kingdom and 'face the music'. Blake's immediate, startled response had been that it would be best if the Irishman remained in the Soviet Union for a lengthy period – say, five years – before making his return but that he would talk to 'Stan', their KGB colleague, and put the request on his behalf.

That conversation between Blake and 'Stan' had taken place just three days before Bourke turned up at the Embassy. Williams' dramatic second-hand account of it to his Foreign Office masters read as follows:

> The KGB officer arrived and Blake took him off in the corridor leaving Bourke on his own in the living room in order, as he understood it, to persuade the KGB officer to let Bourke go. Bourke, according to his account, was suspicious and listened at the door. In this position, he heard Blake asking that Bourke should *not* be allowed to go, and with some alarm he noticed a significant emphasis, in particular on something to the effect that 'If he gives trouble you will have to give thought to what other steps you might have to take'. It was this latter comment which particularly prompted Bourke to seek assistance in repatriation.

Bourke gave the diplomats a sample of his handwriting to establish his identity, even though they were by now convinced that he was who he claimed to be. Nonetheless, he was destined to go away disappointed. He was an Irish citizen and the Embassy would first have to contact Dublin to see if it was possible to issue him with a fresh passport, which would take at least a week. As for asylum, that was out of the question. As Bourke rose to leave, he told Sturmey, with some melodrama: 'I must now face the music. If you don't see me again, I would like you to pass it on – that I done it myself.'

While Bourke was having his interview Embassy officials had noticed an increase in the number of Soviet militiamen in the vicinity. After the Irishman left the premises by the eastern gate, he was observed being stopped by soldiers and asked to produce his papers. Some short time after this, having apparently satisfied them, he was seen walking west-wards. That was the last the British Embassy saw or heard from Bourke.

In his concluding remarks on this curious episode, Anthony Williams observed: 'If Bourke's appearance yesterday was KGB engineered, and the aim to embarrass the Embassy, it failed. On the whole, my feeling is that Bourke's approach to us was a genuine if naïve attempt to escape from a situation which looked ominous to him . . . the motive is of a one with the old lag who returns to prison as the safest and warmest place he knows.'

By that stage Bourke was patently disenchanted with life in Moscow, despite all the comforts that had come his way as the man whose heroic actions had recovered one of the KGB's greatest assets. He had landed on Saturday, 7 January, just over a fortnight after Blake's arrival, his own faultless escape having taken him via Paris, Berlin, through Checkpoint Charlie, and eventually into the protective arms of the Soviets. In the ensuing months his minders did all they could to keep him happy, supplying him with good food, drink and the company of attractive women. To occupy his restless mind, they found him a job as an English translator for Progress Publishers.

Bourke, however, missed the freedom and the familiarity of London and Dublin life. When he was not writing, he had liked nothing better than to take up a chair in the corner of a pub, a whiskey in his hand, and regale an appreciative audience with stories of his exploits; there was no equivalent outlet in this drab city. The ubiquitous, shabby little kiosks on most street corners were a poor substitute for a good pub, even though their customers had a similar capacity for drink as he did. 'The Russians don't drink themselves under a table – they drink themselves under a snow bank,' was how he derisively described the street scene on a winter's day.

In Moscow, his substantial allowance of three hundred roubles a month (£30 a week) enabled him to dine out at the best establishments, but nearly always in a carefully controlled fashion, and often in the company of Blake and their KGB minders. When he evaded the attentions of his watchers and ventured into local restaurants, he discovered they all had identical printed menus, and the unappetising fare comprised two basic dishes – a kind of Beef Stroganoff, and a scrawny fried chicken. The gregarious Irishman, like Blake, found ordinary Muscovites distant, even unfriendly. He observed many of them playing chess on miniature boards – everywhere it seemed, even on buses. They kept their heads down, not necessarily by inclination, but out of anxiety at being seen engaging with a foreigner.

When he and Blake had been forced together for that month in Pat Pottle's flat, they had tolerated each other because of what they had been through and achieved together, and because of the anticipation of the endgame. To Bourke, it now felt as if he was imprisoned in a different way, and the man sharing this particular 'cell' was someone with whom he had very little in common. More than that, he began to perceive, rightly or wrongly, with some bitterness, that Blake had merely used him to make his escape, and was now quite prepared to discard him.

Gone was the ever-ready smile, the patient and understanding disposition, the willingness to listen and sympathise. Blake was now sullen, intolerant, arrogant and pompous. The George Blake we had all known in Wormwood Scrubs had been a completely false image, deliberately and calculatingly projected for his own long-term benefit. In Moscow, Blake had suddenly, dramatically, reverted to type.

Over time, Bourke's disillusionment with his old friend knew no bounds. Now he was 'the vainest man I had ever met in my life . . . more than vain, a complete narcissist, unashamedly in love with his own image . . . he had great delusions of grandeur and loved to strut about the flat in his crimson dressing gown, a glass of champagne held delicately between his fingers.'

By contrast with Bourke's revulsion and scorn, Blake's own reflection on the parting of the ways was less personal, and more magnanimous:

> Sean had neither the ideological commitment to Soviet society nor the imperative need to adapt to it which I had. I knew I would have to spend a great part, and possibly all of my life in this country, and was intent therefore from the outset on looking on the positive side of things and making the best of it . . . Sean's approach was not unnaturally quite the opposite.

> He had been reluctant to come here in the first place and wanted to leave again as soon as possible. He was determined from the start not to like it here and latched on to everything negative, which could confirm him in his intention. For this I could not and did not blame him.

Blake was constantly mindful of protecting the identities of the Randles and Pat Pottle, and, to that end, did his best to persuade Bourke to stay in Moscow for as long as he could bear it: 'This he strongly resented and he never forgave me for not taking his side.'

After the visit to the British Embassy, Bourke spent several days sleeping rough in Izmailovsky Park before he returned to their flat.

Given his state of mind and his approach to the British government, his KGB minders thought it prudent to remove both him and Blake from Moscow. The warring odd couple therefore embarked on a Grand Tour of the Soviet Union, starting off in Leningrad before moving on to Vilnius (Lithuania), Odessa (Ukraine), Sochi (on the Black Sea coast), Yerevan (Armenia), Tashkent and other towns in Uzbekistan, before returning to the capital.

Bourke's mood calmed somewhat after this month away. An MI5 source reported seeing him in a Moscow theatre just before Christmas, looking 'fairly prosperous and happy'. It improved further the following year when he started a relationship with a young university language student called Larisa. He met her on one of his frequent sojourns in the Warsaw Hotel, where he was made to stay when Blake's mother arrived to take up residence with her son in the flat. Later on he was allocated an apartment of his own. By this point his relationship with Blake had healed to the extent that they would meet regularly once or twice a week for a meal and a discussion.

In the autumn of 1967, however, with the help of his twin brother, Kevin, Bourke finally obtained a one-month visa to enable him to travel back to Ireland. Once there, he would begin a legal battle against the British authorities' attempts to extradite him to stand trial for his part in the Blake escape. He would also finish work on his book about the whole saga, which he had long seen as his ticket to fame and fortune. He had attempted to smuggle a portion of the manuscript out of Moscow in August – via his brother – but the authorities had thwarted him and confiscated it on the way to the airport.

On Tuesday, 22 October, when Bourke landed at Amsterdam en route to Dublin, the press was out in force, eager to hear the full story from the inside. He made sure they had it, chapter and verse.

Bourke's departure coincided with significant changes to Blake's own situation. His mother's lengthy visits were a source of great comfort, but because of security considerations, he remained socially rather isolated. For instance, it would be nearly two years before he could visit the Bolshoi Theatre, because of fears that a foreigner would spot him and report his presence to Western agencies. But by the autumn of 1968, however, he was beginning to settle into his new life. In particular, he had started a relationship with Ida, a woman thirteen years his junior, who he had met in the spring while on a cruise on the River Volga.

Ida had studied mathematics and physics as a student but, like Blake, she was a good linguist, and at that time she was working as a French translator at Moscow's Central Mathematical Economic Institute (TsEMI), located in a former mansion house in the Neskuchny Gardens, the oldest and one of the grandest parks in the city. She was an effervescent type with a love of the outdoor life – a swimmer, skier and long distance walker – and so not unlike Gillian. Blake eventually married her in 1969 and was introduced to her wide circle of friends, which helped bind him more fully into Russian life.

For some time after his arrival in late 1966, he had been extensively debriefed by the KGB. He also wrote essays and papers about the workings of SIS, but there was only so much analysis he could usefully provide, and he soon hankered for more challenging work. Early in 1969, he was given a position as a Dutch translator at the same publishing house that had briefly employed Bourke. He regarded the job as far from stimulating and, anyway, most of it was carried out in isolation at his flat, when he really craved company, particularly of the intellectual kind.

The scale of the KGB's infiltration of SIS during the 1940s and 50s meant that Blake had joined an extended family of expat British spies and traitors in Moscow, and it was through such a route that he was to be saved from boredom. However, the fortunes of the three members of the Cambridge Five spy ring had been mixed. Guy Burgess, who had arrived with Donald Maclean in 1951 died of liver disease in August 1963, aged only 52, long before Blake's arrival. By temperament and lifestyle he was never suited to the Communist way of life, and he missed Britain badly – the pubs, the intellectual badinage, the ease of casual homosexual encounters. He refused point blank to learn the language and thus assimilate himself properly into Soviet life.

Maclean was quite different and had approached his exile in Moscow with a fierce determination to reshape himself to the needs of an alien environment. Like Burgess, he had been a heavy drinker, a near alcoholic in Cairo, but over time he gave up drink almost entirely, only on rare occasions pouring himself a glass of Scotch. He steadily mastered the Russian language, being able to read and write it fluently after just four years. As well as belonging to the Communist Party, he was also determined as far as possible to live the life of any ordinary member, and so foreswore many of the luxuries he was entitled to as an *apparatchik* – the luxury *dacha* and the official car.

He was no unthinking convert, however, and among the highest quarters of the party, Maclean's views were regarded as unorthodox and unwelcome. He held the old men of the Brezhnev regime in contempt, often criticising the Arms Race as wasteful and damaging to the economy, and also lamenting the lack of political freedom. Indeed, he was friendly with a number of leading dissidents and, when they were jailed, even donated part of his salary to help their families. Yet this did not prevent Maclean from gaining a senior position at one of Moscow's leading think tanks, the Institute of World Economy and International Relations, known as IMEMO. Here he established himself as one of the preeminent experts on British foreign affairs, even writing a short book entitled *British Foreign Policy Since Suez: 1956–1968*, which was also published in the United Kingdom.

It was Maclean who found Blake a job at IMEMO, freeing him from his dull translation duties. Blake soon fell under the spell of a man whom he felt to be a kindred spirit: 'There was a strong Calvinistic streak in him, inherited from his Scottish ancestors and this gave us something in common.' But it seemed much more than a mutual liking for each other's company and shared intellectual interests.

Maclean was only nine years older, but became something of a father figure. Visitors to Blake's flat or *dacha* in later years would be struck by two photographs on the table by the side of his chair in the sitting room: one of his mother, the other of Maclean.

When Maclean died in 1983, as a mark of the esteem in which he held Blake, he bequeathed to the younger man his vast library of books, including a collection of Trollope, Macaulay's *History of England*, Morley's *Life of Gladstone*, and the memoirs of various Prime Ministers, including Macmillan and Eden. He also left him something else – his old tweed flat-cap, its inner lining frayed and stained. For many years afterwards, Blake wore it.

Blake always thought Maclean only spied 'out of a sense of duty' but believed Kim Philby, the third member of the Cambridge Five, saw espionage more as a vocation, while also relishing the adrenalin rush from intrigue, and the heady sense of hidden power. Perhaps surprisingly, it was not until the spring of 1970 that Blake and Philby finally met. They had both worked at Broadway during the war, albeit on different floors and in very different roles, and both had been in Beirut in 1960 and 1961: Blake at MECAS, Philby reporting for *The Economist* after being forced out of the Service amid suspicions over his loyalty. Nonetheless, it was not until they were each invited to a lunch party given in their honour by the KGB hierarchy that they eventually sat down together.

Philby had been in poor shape for some time. After the breakdown of his relationship with Donald Maclean's wife, Melinda, in 1968, he had resumed drinking heavily, and lived a bored, empty kind of existence, drifting between his Moscow apartment and a holiday home by the Black Sea. He had coped better than Burgess with the constraints of Soviet life, although, like him, he did not bother to try and learn the language. Unlike Maclean, he appreciated the trappings of the elite and enjoyed being shown some deference as an intelligence officer of standing. He claimed – not always convincingly – that he did not miss England, 'except for some friends, Colman's mustard and Lea

& Perrins Worcester sauce', but on most days endeavoured to keep in touch through *The Times* and the BBC World Service.

In July 1970, Blake and his wife were responsible, quite by chance, for introducing Philby to Rufina Ivanova Pukhova, a Russian-Polish woman more than twenty years his junior, who became his fourth wife later that year. The Blakes had managed to get tickets for a performance of a touring American ice show at the Luzhniki Sports Complex. Ida invited Rufina along – she was a friend and colleague at the same institute – and it seems the original idea was to pair her off with Philby's visiting son, Tommy. When they all convened at his flat later that night after the show, the older Philby seemed much taken with Rufina. The Blakes were keen to matchmake: 'My wife and I thought a friendship with an attractive woman would relieve his loneliness and make him drink less, and so decided to encourage further meetings.' A few weeks later they invited Philby and Rufina on a driving holiday to Yaroslavl, a beautiful city of churches and theatres on the Volga, built to the design of Empress Catherine the Great in the late eighteenth century, during which the romance became more serious. The Blakes were among a small group of family and friends present at Philby's registry office wedding in December.

The Blakes and the Philbys maintained their friendship for several years, but the two spies were to fall out in spectacular fashion late in 1975. Over a weekend at Blake's *dacha*, Philby's eldest son, John, had taken a series of photographs which Blake had been reassured would be kept private, but one, a shot of the two men and their wives having lunch, quickly found its way into the *Observer* magazine. Blake was wounded by this breach of trust, and incensed by the ensuing publicity in the British press.

His anger was only compounded by a simmering, suppressed resentment that Philby and Anthony Blunt had, compared to him, been treated so leniently by the British establishment. He always suspected that Nicholas Elliott, the SIS officer who had given him the order to return to London from Shemlan, had also been sent out to Beirut, two

years later, to warn Philby not to return. These suspicions betray the
feeling of inferiority that had troubled Blake since first joining SIS: 'It
was probably because I was of foreign origin, and I could more easily
be made an example of. They also didn't want yet another spy scandal.
They were members of the Establishment and I was not.'

Despite the rift, when Philby died in May 1988, Blake attended
his funeral, held with full military honours at the Kuntsevo cemetery
in Moscow.

On Sunday, 15 February 1970, just over three years after his arrival in
Moscow, Blake was finally permitted to step in from the shadows and
take his place in the spotlight. *Izvestia*, the mouthpiece of the Soviet
government, published the first of a two-part interview with the spy,
with the second part following two days later. In it, he recounted his life
story and provided much detail on the workings of SIS and some of his
own operations for the KGB. The first article took the reader through
his life from boyhood in Rotterdam, resistance work in the war, escape
through Europe to Britain – 'London welcomed Blake rather coldly;
strict interrogations followed' – and his early days in SIS. The second
would furrow more brows at Broadway as it detailed various bugging
operations Blake claimed SIS's Y section had carried out in a number
of European capitals. He also went into rather indulgent detail about
the Berlin tunnel.

The KGB was clearly determined to sow mischief among their
Western opponents. Blake described 'how the intelligence agencies
work against one another', claiming that SIS and the CIA were spying
on France, Sweden, West Germany and Japan. In particular, he said,
British intelligence was 'constantly and actively engaged in studying
the work of French intelligence and counter-intelligence agencies'.
While he was in Berlin, he claimed, the Service had maintained a card
index of French agents for 'the purpose of determining which of them
could be used by SIS'. He also claimed that the SIS station in Paris
was actively spying on its host country, seeking information on the

French military, as well as the country's atomic energy programme, and he explained how SIS routinely placed agents in the BBC, and in companies that sent representatives to Socialist countries.

As well as hailing the achievements of their agent and embarrassing the British, there was also an announcement: the 'selfless work' of Mr George Blake had been rewarded by two of the highest state medals – the Order of Lenin and the Order of the Red Banner.

With the political and intelligence establishment looking favourably on him, the restrictions on Blake's life gradually lifted. The KGB remained nervous about allowing prize assets like Blake and Philby to travel, still fearing they might flee back to England and deal a propaganda blow to the Kremlin, but carefully controlled holidays in countries like East Germany and Hungary could be arranged, and so it was that Blake's minders finally gave in to his requests for a vacation abroad. They sent him to the Baltic island resort of Usedom in East Germany, where the KGB's sister service, the Stasi, had a retreat.

Blake made four or five trips to the German Democratic Republic in the 1970s and 1980s, usually at the request of Markus Wolf, head of the foreign intelligence section of the Stasi, who invited him to lecture trainee agents and help instil a 'sense of belonging and tradition within the Communist espionage community'. The two of them enjoyed each other's company, being of a similar age and sharing the same intellectual interests, and the German particularly appreciated Blake's 'British habit of understatement'. Yet the German spymaster – dubbed 'The Man Without A Face' because he guarded his identity from Western intelligence for so many years – found Blake very reticent in discussing the seedy aspects of the espionage business: 'It struck me that Blake suffered terribly under his reputation as a callous agent and wanted to be regarded as an idealist. Despite his commitment to the Soviet cause, I also had the feeling that he refused to accept that he really was the traitor his country considered him to be.'

Hero or traitor, life was looking brighter for Blake. A son, Misha, was born in the spring of 1971, and the family had by then acquired a pleasant *dacha* in a KGB compound an hour out of Moscow. His work at IMEMO was becoming more stimulating and he was assuming the role of the institute's Middle East expert.

In the early 1980s, his fervent and long-maintained hope that he would be reconciled with his first family also looked as if it might be realised. Blake's mother had continued to see Gillian and her grandsons in England and Holland, so George had not gone without news or photographs of the boys. When they reached their early teens, Gillian told Anthony, James and Patrick the full truth about their father and in 1983 his middle son, James, then aged 24, expressed a wish to see him. A meeting was arranged in East Germany, where the young man and his grandmother travelled, joining Blake, Ida and Misha, who were holidaying at a resort on the Baltic coast.

Blake was apprehensive – not only had he abandoned his son, but now the boy knew he was a traitor: 'It was a complete gamble how we would take to each other for he did not remember me, of course, as he had been only two when I disappeared from his life.' He recounted his whole life story, leaving nothing out, and hoped that his son would understand what had led him to act as he did. He sensed James's disapproval, but also a certain understanding of his motives: 'It constituted in no way a barrier between us . . . we got on extremely well.'

After this success, his two other sons – Anthony, aged 28, and Patrick, 23 – followed in James's wake and came to Moscow twelve months later. This time, the ice took longer to break, but the thaw set in when Anthony noticed that his younger brother had inherited some of Blake's mannerisms, despite never having met him.

Gillian had allowed the boys to make up their own minds about their absent father, to her considerable credit: 'My wife had never spoken to them about me in any disparaging terms [and] my mother had always discussed me in a normal way.' Moreover, both boys were committed Christians and Blake felt this also gave them something in common.

The early 1980s were a time of change in the Soviet Union, and of a limited degree of optimism. The grey old men in the Kremlin – Leonid Brezhnev, Yuri Andropov and Konstantin Chernenko – disappeared into history's backrooms to be replaced by Mikhail Gorbachev and his efforts to dismantle lingering Stalinist values and structures: this was the era of *glasnost* (openness) and *perestroika* (restructuring). Blake shed no tears for the outgoing regime. Although deeply committed to Communism, he agreed with Gorbachev that the system had to be developed in a democratic way. For Blake, the whole Soviet experience had to be re-assessed, even the hitherto sacrosanct status of Lenin.

Possibly the new spirit of openness lay behind Blake's first ever television appearance in April 1988, on the late night chat show, *Before and After Midnight.* At the commencement of the twelve-minute interview he was introduced as 'an outstanding Soviet secret serviceman . . . an honorary member of the state security service who has been awarded the Orders of Lenin and the Combat Red Banner'. At the age of 65, he appeared relaxed, wearing a grey suit, open-necked shirt and cravat. Speaking in fluent, slightly accented Russian, his answers betrayed none of the Stalinist hyperbole of his newspaper interview seventeen years previously, when he had claimed he betrayed Britain to help in 'exposing and interfering with imperialist aggression and subversion'. Instead, in easy, conversational mode, he admitted to the watching audience that adjustment to life in the Soviet Union had not been easy, with 'a different country, different traditions and even a different society'. He offered few details about his new family or his work, apart from saying: 'My life has been amazingly good, beyond my expectations.'

Of his escape from Wormwood Scrubs, he remarked: 'I was very lucky in that there were some good people who sympathised with me, people inside and outside jail, and who were ready to help me.' As ever, he conscientiously avoided any comment that might expose his friends back in England, but by now, the tide was coming in for Michael Randle and Pat Pottle. Before very long, Blake would be forced to reveal the part they had played in securing his freedom – and make a stand on their behalf.

21
Endgame

Thirty years after he had stood in the dock charged with betraying Britain to her Cold War enemy, George Blake was once again back in the Old Bailey's famous No. 1 Court. This time, however, the man who had once been the anxious defendant of May 1961, awaiting the Crown's punishment for crimes 'akin to treason', was a relaxed witness for the defence. Now there was no wooden seat amidst a sea of suspicious eyes, but the solitary comfort of an armchair in his Moscow flat. The sober suit and tie had been replaced by the navy blue blazer and knotted silk scarf. A bald head and neatly trimmed beard succeeded the clean-shaven, tanned face and longish brown hair.

Blake's 'virtual' presence at the Old Bailey on Tuesday, 25 June 1991, came towards the end of the trial of Michael Randle and Pot Pottle, who had finally been charged with helping him to escape from Wormwood Scrubs, and then conspiring with Sean Bourke to harbour him and prevent his arrest.

As his voice echoed around the historic courtroom to a spellbound packed gallery. The three-minute video recording ran on three screens at points North, East and West of the oak-panelled room, so that everyone would have a clear view of the star turn. Flanked by

Randle and Pottle's lawyers, Blake read slowly and deliberately from his text.

Back in 1961, the court had determinedly and deferentially avoided any mention that a secret organisation (SIS) was fighting a clandestine war against the Soviets, so there was delicious irony in the opening remarks of the former 'foreign office official'. This time, everyone would know the unvarnished truth. 'I was a member of the British Secret Intelligence Service from August 1944 until the date of my trial in May 1961,' Blake told Mr Justice Alliott and his court. 'I was engaged in secret, subversive operations directed against the Soviet Union, the socialist countries and world Communism. It was my task to attempt the recruitment of Soviet citizens, and in particular members of the Soviet intelligence services and those of other socialist countries.'

Yet again, however, he was determined to challenge the general perception of the human cost of his treachery: 'It was said that my actions led to the deaths of British and other agents. I can confirm that at my trial it was never alleged that in working for both the British Secret Intelligence Service and the Soviet Intelligence Service, I was ever responsible for the death of agents. However, I do not deny that I disclosed the identity of a number of agents to the Soviet authorities.'

He then devoted the rest of his statement to refuting suggestions that the KGB had been involved in his escape, or that Randle and Pottle had received any financial reward for their efforts: 'There was never any doubt in my mind that they acted as they did out of purely humanitarian concern, and specifically because of the length of my sentence. I say this as they repeatedly commented on the harshness of the sentence.'

Blake concluded his remarks by saying he was 'deeply grateful' to the two defendants for 'having enabled me to lead a normal life over the last twenty-four years'.

To trace the origins of Blake's second court appearance at the Old Bailey, you have to go back to January 1970 when MI5 received an advance copy of Sean Bourke's book, *The Springing of George Blake*.

* * *

Bourke had been determined to chronicle his leading role in Blake's escape, almost from day one of its inception. He wanted to write a detailed book about the daring operation that would bring him acclaim as a writer and substantial financial reward.

In the course of the mission in 1966, Blake, Randle and Pottle had been perplexed and at times angered by what looked like careless, sometimes reckless behaviour by Bourke. His mistakes, it seemed, were giving the police far more clues than was necessary. Some of Bourke's decisions were merely slipshod, but others were deliberately made to lead police on a chase after him, so that the world would clearly know that the Irishman was responsible for this audacious plan. The pursuit would add extra colour to the book.

This goes some way to explaining why he failed to sell the Humber Hawk registered in his name before the escape; why, just four days after he had sprung Blake, he phoned the police to tell them of the car's whereabouts; why he left Randle to go looking for it, knowing the police were also trying to find it; and why he left potentially incriminatory letters, photographs, his typewriter and the walkie-talkie sets in the bedsit at Highlever Road.

All the while, he was also surreptitiously photographing scenes in Wormwood Scrubs, keeping recordings of his conversations with Blake, and retaining all correspondence related to the plot. He was building up a full record of events for when he eventually put pen to paper.

When Randle confronted Bourke about his reckless actions on visiting him not long after his return to Limerick, his co-conspirator merely replied enigmatically: 'Well, you see I am not the simple, uncomplicated Irishman that some people imagine.'

After he had successfully fought extradition to Britain in the High Court in Dublin in January 1969, he settled down to complete his colourful account of the Blake escape.

When MI5 read their advance copy, they swiftly forwarded it to Chief Inspector Rollo Watts, the Special Branch officer who had been fruitlessly hunting Blake and his collaborators for the past four years. Watts knew immediately that the book was Bourke's own work, not that of a ghost-writer: 'Bourke has always considered himself to have a flair as a writer, and the style and phraseology is typical of the articles he wrote when editor of the prison magazine, *New Horizon,* and of the many long letters to his brother and others of which we have copies.'

Watts, who described the account as '99 per cent' authentic, took a particular interest in pages 211 and 246. The former referred to Bourke's first accomplice as 'Michael Reynolds' – a man aged about 30, slight in build, pale-faced, and married to Anne, with two children aged four and two and a half. The latter described his other co-conspirator, 'Pat Porter' – a friend of 'Michael Reynolds', two years younger, single, with a flat in Hampstead. It did not take Watts long to join up the dots. 'A very probable identification thus comes to light in the form of Michael Joseph Randle, very well known to Special Branch for his militant activities with the Committee of 100,' he wrote in his report to MI5. From there, he had no difficulty in identifying Pottle.

While Randle and Pottle read the published book with mounting anxiety, fearing a knock on the door at any moment, Chief Inspector Watts took soundings among his police and security service colleagues. On 28 April he spoke to an MI5 officer who consequently filed this intriguing report: 'Chief Inspector Watts added that the Special Branch decision at present was to take no steps to interview or attempt to prosecute the RANDLES or POTTLE. It was considered that to do so might be persecution – a big fish had got away, so they were taking it out on the little fish. It was considered, however, that it had been necessary to investigate their suspicions and place them on record.'

To this day it has never been clear who took the final decision not to go after the two men. The official line was that the decision had been taken by the police, and by the police alone; the Director of Public Prosecutions had not been consulted, and the Home Office had played no part. At the very least, however, their lack of enthusiasm to tackle the 'little fish' makes it clear that the authorities never had any intention of prosecuting Blake's accomplices. The escape and subsequent manhunt had made them look foolish, and a full airing of their failings in trial at the Old Bailey would have done little to enhance their reputation.

So there the matter lay for seventeen years. Then, in September 1987, a train of events was set in motion that would eventually lead to Randle, Pottle and Blake's appearance at the Old Bailey. First, the writer and former intelligence officer H. Montgomery Hyde published a book entitled *George Blake – Superspy*, which provided more clues to the identity of Bourke's accomplices. This was followed by a *Sunday Times* story on 4 October, under the headline 'Soviet Spy Was Sprung by CND Men', and this time the two men were properly 'outed'.

The following week, Randle and Pottle released what amounted to a holding statement to the *Guardian*, neither confirming nor denying the claims made by Hyde and the *Sunday Times*, but pointing out inaccuracies in both. It was not a sustainable stance. The following days and weeks saw a wave of speculation. The *Sunday Times* even carried an erroneous story that the actress Vanessa Redgrave, known for her sympathy to left-wing causes, was 'Bridget', the mysterious woman whose bequest had funded most of the escape operation.

In the New Year, the two men sat down to consider their options. They had always wanted to keep their story secret, but now the genie was well and truly out of the bottle. Also, they were concerned about the damage the publicity was doing to the Peace Movement, with continuing suggestions that they were pawns, willing or otherwise, in a KGB operation. They decided to put the record straight and write a book that would give a full account of their motives and actions.

Meanwhile there were developments in Parliament. In a speech on 19 December, the Conservative MP for Colne Valley, Graham Riddick, demanded the two men be prosecuted, accusing them of 'the most appallingly treacherous behaviour'. He then put down an Early Day Motion on the House of Commons Order Paper urging the Director of Public Prosecutions to 'institute criminal proceedings forthwith against these two men', and also demanding that they should receive no royalties from their forthcoming book. He gathered 111 signatures from Tory MPs. The parliamentary pressure was all too much for Sir Allan Green, Director of Public Prosecutions, to ignore, and he ordered a somewhat reluctant Metropolitan Police to look at the case again.

In the meantime, further pre-publicity for the book, by way of a Thames TV documentary, *The Blake Escape*, on 26 April, in which Randle and Pottle clearly explained their roles on camera for the first time, only increased the likelihood of prosecution.

On 3 May, at Gerald Road police station in south-west London, Randle and Pottle were formally arrested by Special Branch. It did not come as a surprise. After they had been questioned, they were put in the cells for several hours and later that day their homes were searched.

The Blake Escape was published in June, and charges against the two men finally laid on 10 July. In the course of the next two years, they fought an unsuccessful battle in the High Court to have the case dismissed.

By the time Randle and Pottle finally stood in the dock at the Old Bailey on Monday, 17 June 1991, it was thought they had created history: it was the longest gap – nearly twenty-five years – between an alleged offence and the subsequent criminal trial.

Blake's video statement was shown on the penultimate day, turning the case into a front-page story. For Randle, this was important: 'Not only could we now be sure that the trial and its outcome would be widely known and discussed, but we could be confident that the humanitarian motives for our actions – which George stressed in his statement – would be well publicised.'

Nonetheless, they feared the worst. Despite conducting their own defence in remarkably effective fashion, the judge told the jury to ignore Randle's argument that they had a 'defence of necessity' – that sometimes it was right to disobey the letter of the law for a greater good. The only issue, Mr Justice Alliott said, was whether they had helped Blake escape and spirited him out of the country.

Nonetheless, in their eloquent closing speeches, Randle and Pottle persisted in asking the jury to ignore their offences and concentrate on the 'natural justice' of their case. Pottle waspishly condemned the forty-two-year sentence the 'Establishment' had inflicted on Blake, while treating the Cambridge Five with relative leniency. He argued that Blake had been the victim of snobbery, if not racism: 'What did George do that set him apart from other spies uncovered at that time? He was not British, was he? Not of the old school, not one of us. Deep down he was a foreigner and half-Jewish to boot.' He concluded by quoting Bertrand Russell: 'Remember your humanity and forget the rest.' It was an impassioned, witty, beguiling piece of oratory.

Randle could not compete with that on dramatic impact. Instead, he persuasively delved back into British history, to the great moments when blows for freedom were struck. He referred to the 1688 Bill of Rights, 'one of the great documents of liberty in this country', and its prohibition of 'cruel and unusual punishments': 'George was sentenced to forty-two years' imprisonment and was not even allowed privacy during prison visits. If this is not a cruel and unusual punishment, what is?' He also knew the value of levity and recounted the story of the trial of two Quakers in 1670. On that occasion, the judge had directed the jury to find the men guilty and when they refused to do so, he locked them up overnight 'without meat, fire or other accommodation; they had not so much as a chamber pot, though desired'. 'Now I'm not suggesting that if you bring in a Not Guilty verdict his lordship is going to lock you up . . .' Randle concluded, to widespread laughter among the jury members.

He finished by reminding them of the relatively recent Clive Ponting case, when the jury acquitted the civil servant 'whistle-blower' of offences under the Official Secrets Act, despite a strong direction otherwise from the judge: 'The lamp of freedom shone more brightly that day, and a dangerous shift towards arbitrary power was avoided. I appeal to you today to keep that lamp burnished and shining, and to allow considerations of humanity and commonsense to guide your judgement.'

In his closing remarks, Mr Justice Alliott once again reminded the jury to concentrate on the evidence and the facts of the case. On the defence of necessity, he told them sharply: 'You must loyally honour my ruling on the law, whatever view you have formed of the defendants.'

Three hours later, the jury emerged. They had ignored his strictures and returned verdicts of Not Guilty to resounding cheers from the public gallery.

The press were less impressed. 'Crazy Verdict' was the headline in the *Daily Express* the next day, and no doubt there were those who agreed with the paper's writer: 'Yesterday's decision mocks the idea of national security. It mocks the law itself. Above all, it mocks our complacent faith in the jury system.' If somewhat odd, the analogy offered by the *Telegraph* was no less disparaging: 'The acquittal suggests a frivolous preference for moral gesture over moral reality that resembles the animal rights activism that frees mink from captivity to roam and destroy at will.'

In Moscow, the relief and joy were palpable. Blake had vowed that if his friends were imprisoned he would turn himself over to the British in exchange for their release. Whether the Home Secretary would have countenanced such an extraordinary offer was moot. 'It's incredible,' Blake told the *Guardian*. 'I'm absolutely delighted. It almost makes me cry.'

At the time of Randle and Pottle's trial, Blake had already embarked on his own, lengthy legal battle with the British authorities over the publication of his autobiography in the United Kingdom. *No Other Choice* – the original title was *The Georgian Enigma* – immediately sparked off a series of high-level discussions in Whitehall, with civil servants consulting widely to assess whether it breached national security, or was likely to cause any material damage to SIS. The answer to both questions was no, according to a memo the Cabinet Secretary, Sir Robin Butler, sent to Prime Minister Margaret Thatcher's Principal Private Secretary, Andrew Turnbull, on 13 September 1987. Butler argued that there was therefore little point in trying to stop publication of the book, but did make a case for trying to prevent Blake from making money from the enterprise, and a six-year legal battle over the royalties began.

SIS itself had been wary of engaging in a public dispute with Blake over the contents of his book. Senior officers in the Service who read *No Other Choice* could find no revelations serious enough to warrant them challenging Blake and exposing the organisation to public glare, and, anyway, they had seen the way MI5 had been dragged onto the front pages two years earlier by the controversy over *Spycatcher*, the memoirs of former officer Peter Wright. At the conclusion of that long, drawn-out case, the Law Lords did decide that Wright's book had constituted a serious breach of the confidentiality owed to the Crown by an intelligence officer. More pertinently, however, they ruled that the media was free to publish extracts because the damage to national security had already been done by the book's publication abroad. The whole affair had been a mess, and both the Government and MI5 had come out of it badly.

At the same time, forward-thinking officers like the new SIS Chief, Sir Colin McColl, realised that in the new post Cold War landscape, they needed to open the doors just a little and let some light shine on the workings of the Service. The fiction – prevalent in Blake's day – that a few mysterious figures in some small corner of the Foreign Office were carrying out the nation's vital clandestine work, had become an absurdity. The Secret Intelligence Service had, for some time, no longer been secret in the minds of the public. In 1994, the Intelligence Services Act placed the Service's operations on a statutory footing. The opening words of this new legislation highlighted the pretence under which the Service had been labouring for the previous eighty-five years: 'There shall *continue* [author's emphasis] to be a Secret Intelligence Service under the authority of the Secretary of State.'

Blake's quest for his book royalties appeared to be over when he lost a decisive, final battle in the House of Lords in July 2000. The British legal system had defeated him, but he was not finished. Next, he lodged a claim in the European Court of Human Rights in Strasbourg in 2001.

Five years later, a panel of seven judges finally delivered a verdict, unanimously deciding that Blake's human rights had been violated because of the number of hold-ups to his case, despite the fact that some of the delay had been caused by his attempts to win legal aid to pay for his lawyers. The United Kingdom government was ordered to pay Blake £3,500 in damages for the 'distress and frustration from the protracted length of the proceedings', plus £2,100 costs and expenses.

'Britain must pay traitor for breaching his human rights' proclaimed the *Telegraph* the next day. 'MI6 double agent Blake wins damages from Government' was the less judgemental headline in the *Guardian*. Contacted by a *Daily Mail* reporter to be told about the decision, Blake responded in courteous fashion: 'Oh, that's very nice. Thank you for letting me know. I didn't expect anything.'

Forty-five years on, he had finally concluded his courtroom business with the British Government.

The rootlessness that characterised much of George Blake's life reached its apogee in December 1991. 'I am once again living in another country, only this time without having actually moved,' he wrote, three days after the Soviet Union was formally dissolved. He had betrayed one country for another, only to see the latter disappear, having abandoned the very cause that had won him over.

By then, all the old Communist regimes in Eastern Europe had been discredited and removed from power. Blake and other adherents of Soviet ideology had to ask themselves some searching questions. Could they still believe in the teachings of Marx and Lenin and did they cling to the idea that one day, however far in the future, Communism would still overwhelm and supersede capitalism? Blake freely conceded that the dream of a fully functioning Communist society in his lifetime was over. He believed the mistake had been to try and instil it by force, discipline and terror: 'I would be blind not to see that the experiment has failed. Nobody can seriously claim that we are advancing towards Communism. In fact my wife, who is just back from a visit to Holland, says that the Dutch are closer to a real Communist society – a place of justice, equality and peace.'

In that moment, he seemed to accept that a social democracy with a mixed economy would be the best way forward for the faltering new Russia. He blamed the collapse of the Soviet Union on its over-centralisation.

> Unlike the capitalist countries, literally everything was controlled by the central government, from which type of intercontinental missiles should be built to how many buttons there should be on the fly of a pair of trousers.

> Every decision was taken in Moscow, and it is humanly impossible for one man – or ten men – to run a country of this size efficiently if every request has to travel all the way to the capital, then right up to the top of the Kremlin, then back out again to the furtherest parts of the empire.

Yet out of the ruins of the Soviet Union, Blake believed one very substantial benefit had been realised.

> The most important thing is that the threat of nuclear war has at last been removed. In all our woes, this is something we tend to forget and should, on the contrary, often bring to mind and be thankful for.

In 1991, he was fond of comparing favourably the way Russia dealt with the loss of her empire with the efforts of Britain and France. Britain, he said, suffered conflicts in Cyprus, Aden, Kenya and Rhodesia, as well as ill-advisedly maintaining its long resistance to Indian independence. France's record, too, was poor, with its long and bloody war in Algeria and several coup d'états. 'Here,' he said, 'this enormous, closely-knit empire has disintegrated without any bloodshed or concerted attempts to hold it together.'

Blake spoke too soon. Russia's brutal war in Chechnya and clash with Georgia in 2008, among other conflicts, would give the lie to his theory.

Yet despite everything that happened, he remains convinced there is an instinctive yearning for Communism, but that we, as human beings, have to improve before we can fit the model. In 1992 he observed: 'It's the highest form of society, but the people who build it must have the highest moral qualities . . . they must really love their neighbours as themselves. Therein lies the crux. Neither in this country, nor anywhere else, have people at the end of the twentieth century grown to the moral stature required to build a Communist society.'

By 2010, his views were not much altered. After a quick jab at the country he reviles the most – 'The American empire will disappear because everyone who lives by the sword dies by the sword' – he told *Izvestia* he still had not abandoned his belief in Communism: 'I understand now that the Soviet project was doomed. The problem was not the Russians but human nature. Humankind was not sufficiently moral to build such a society. One day – and it may take thousands of years – I believe that the majority of governments will voluntarily choose the Communist model. Without violence, revolution or terror. Maybe it sounds like a Utopia, but I believe in it.'

In 2007, Blake was awarded his latest medal, the Order of Friendship, at gala celebrations for his eighty-fifth birthday. At the ceremony, Sergei Ivanov from the SVR – the successor to the KGB's foreign intelligence department – told the audience: 'It is thanks to Blake that the Soviet Union avoided very serious military and political damage which the United States and Britain could have inflicted on it.' The timing of the award served notice that the habits of the Cold War die hard. In Britain Oleg Gordievsky, one of the most senior KGB defectors to the West, had recently been named a Companion of the Most Distinguished Order of St Michael and St George (CMG). To seasoned espionage watchers, Blake's award seemed like old-fashioned tit for tat.

Four years later, Georgy Ivanovich, as his Russian family and friends now know Blake, had a minor role in a flattering 'docudrama' of his own life, broadcast on late night Russian television. It was called *The Choice of Agent Blake*, and the 88-year-old former 'scout' (as the Russians prefer to call their spies) featured as a narrator towards the end of the 100-minute film. With a young German actor, Marcus Kunze, playing the part of Blake, it starts with a scene set in Wormwood Scrubs in May 1961. A police photographer snaps the obligatory front and side 'mug shots' of the new inmate, before the prison officer barks out the words: 'Prisoner Blake – out for a walk!' A door is unlocked and the hero led away. The film, which has the feel of a Hollywood B-movie, certainly moves along at pace, and the detail in the scenes of Blake's escape from Wormwood Scrubs is commendably authentic.

Colonel Blake is now cast as the Grand Old Man of Russian espionage. The film, made with others to commemorate the ninetieth anniversary of the creation of the foreign intelligence service, is an illustration of the high esteem in which he is still held. He is among the most revered Russian agents, alongside men such as Richard Sorge, the German Communist who spied for the Soviet Union in the Second World War; Rudolf Abel, who worked for the KGB in America; and his SIS colleague, Kim Philby. The accession to power of Vladimir Putin, a former KGB man, has surely safeguarded his heroic status.

Invariably every year on his birthday, 11 November, Blake is interviewed by Russian television and a selected newspaper, and asked for his views on the current geopolitical situation. In 2012, to mark his ninetieth birthday, the *Zvezda* TV channel, run by the Russian Ministry of Defence, broadcast an hour-long documentary entitled *The Two Lives of George Blake*. *Rossisskaya Gazeta*, the official government newspaper, also chipped in with a rare interview with the spy. After regaling his readers with stories of sipping Martinis in Moscow with Kim Philby, he asserted: 'I am a happy person, a very lucky person, exceptionally lucky. These days in Moscow have been the calmest years of my life. When I worked in the West, the danger of exposure always hung over me. Here, I feel myself free.'

On this auspicious occasion, there was also the most fulsome of tributes from President Putin. 'You rightfully belong to the constellation of strong and courageous people,' he wrote in a telegram to Blake. 'You and your colleagues made an enormous contribution to the preservation of peace, to security, and to strategic parity. This is not visible to the eyes of outsiders, but very important work deserves the very highest acknowledgment and respect.'

These days Blake has retreated from Moscow and spends all his time in his *dacha* in the middle of a pine forest, an hour from the capital. Virtually blind, he can no longer read from that vast collection of books Donald Maclean left him. Otherwise, he is in good enough health for a man of ninety, and still goes for long walks in the woods with his wife, Ida. He relishes the odd glass of vodka, and is particularly proud of his recipe for mulled wine.

Whatever motives first drove his loyalties to switch, once they had done so, Blake was a calculating, conscientious and quite unrepentant traitor. Whenever he has been asked why he betrayed Britain, he has never wavered from the script. He says he spied for Moscow because he had developed an unshakeable belief that Communism was the best way forward for mankind.

Nonetheless, the values and precepts of his Calvinist upbringing still cling to him, especially a belief in predestination. When looking for an explanation of his life, Blake turns, as ever, to the Bible. In the Book of Romans, the apostle Paul says: 'Nay but, O Man, who art thou that repliest against God? Shall the thing formed say to him that formed it, Why hast thou made me thus? Hath not the potter power over the clay, of the same lump to make one lump to honour, and another unto dishonour?' He maintains he has been formed in the way he is – whether by God, or someone or something else – and it is not for him to question why. He does concede, however, that his has been a strange path.

> I would say that I have been an unusual vessel, in that I have been fashioned both to shame and to honour.

Sources

Across the various broadcast and print interviews he has given, George Blake's own account of his life and times has generally been very consistent. Most of those intended for Western audiences took place around the time his autobiography was published in 1990. I have drawn liberally on that book, *No Other Choice*, in recounting certain major episodes.

Equally as important – if not more so – are two other fresh sources of information. First, there are the hours of interviews Blake recorded with Tom Bower for the BBC *Inside Story* documentary, 'The Confession', most of which did not make it on to television. These provided considerable detail on Blake's motivations and actions as an agent of the KGB, as well as valuable reflections on other characters in his professional and private life.

The second new source is a batch of papers lodged with the legal team that represented him at his trial in May 1961, which now reside in the Department of Documents at the Imperial War Museum. They include a fascinating, eighteen-page handwritten paper Blake wrote while on remand in Brixton jail – essentially the story of his life, for the benefit of his lawyers. This treatise provides the best explanation for why he turned to Communism. Among many other crucial insights, it explains how he eventually wanted to give up the spying game and seek a new, safer career in the oil industry. The collection also includes various letters – from Blake himself, from his former wife Gillian (including the one mentioning Iris Peake), and from the two SIS colleagues I have called Mr and Mrs B. Most significant of all, however, is the full transcript of Blake's trial. The fifty-three-minute speech of mitigation by his counsel, Jeremy Hutchinson, which was heard *in camera*, can now be read here for the first time.

When quoting Blake in the foregoing pages, I have not always been specific about which particular source has been used, although where I think it is significant, I have provided such details. For example, I should mention that Blake's story about walking past the beggar one night in Seoul – 'like the story of the priest and the Levite in the Bible' – comes from the essay he wrote for his lawyers. The quote right at the very end of the book comes from the documentary, *The Confession*.

A couple of chapters – those covering his flight to England and his SIS interrogation – have relied largely on Blake's own account. Somewhere in the vaults of SIS there is a recording of Blake's inquisition which has been played to new recruits to the Service over the years but which was not made available to me. Had it been so, there might have been a different emphasis to that chapter, but such has been the uniformity with which Blake has recounted those few dramatic days to all manner of people that I do not doubt the essential facts of his narrative.

I should mention one other Blake interview that proved particularly helpful – Phillip Knightley's in the *Sunday Times*, in autumn 1990. Knightley and his 'Insight' team are experts in this field and produced possibly the best book ever written on the Cambridge Spies, *The Philby Conspiracy*, which contains a masterly introduction by John Le Carré.

Another key source, which provided a detailed insight into Blake's life, was the lengthy series of interviews his wife Gillian gave to the *Sunday Telegraph* in December 1961. They were published over three weekends, but I have learned more by reading the full, unedited transcripts in the papers of Michael Wolff, the freelance journalist who conducted them. These are lodged in the Churchill Archives Centre in Cambridge, to which I am grateful for its permission to quote excerpts.

I must highlight three other valuable sources. One is a file, housed at the Ministry of Justice, containing statements from SIS and Special Branch officers (heavily redacted, but illuminating nonetheless) for Blake's trial in 1961. The second is a voluminous set of Home Office papers, released under a Freedom of Information request in 2008, which is essentially the official record of Blake's incarceration and includes letters from the prison authorities, MI5, and Blake himself. The third is a Metropolitan Police dossier featuring the full reports of the investigation into Blake's escape, including prisoner statements.

Among all the books I read during my research, those of Michael Randle and Sean Bourke were invaluable in helping me piece together the story of the plot to spring Blake from jail. As for his time in Korea, I was well served by the vivid accounts of his fellow captives Larry Zellers, Philip Crosbie and Philip Deane. Three other books were invaluable in informing and guiding my thoughts on different aspects of Blake's story – *The Meaning of Treason* by Rebecca West, *The Korean War* by Max Hastings, and *MI6 and the Machinery of Spying* by Philip H.J. Davies.

Principal Source Material

The Bower Tapes – from interviews for BBC Inside Story's *The Confession*.
Gillian Blake interviews – Churchill Archives Centre, the Papers of Michael Wolff WLFF 1 (1/1).
Blake Papers at Department of Documents, Imperial War Museum.
CRIM 1/3650 (Ministry of Justice – Blake trial statements).
National Archives – Police reports into Blake escape (HO 278/7).
National Archives – Police inquiry into Blake, including prisoner statements (MEPO 2/10736 and 10737).
Federal Commissioner for the Stasi Files – Blake's 100 agents 'liquidated' (MFS – HA11 Counter-intelligence division Nr. 3469).
CIA History Staff/Center for the Study of Intelligence – Documents on the Intelligence War in Berlin, 1946–1961 (Berlin Tunnel documents).

'The Blake Escape – The Men Who Sprang a Superspy' (an episode of
    Thames TV's *This Week*), 26 April 1989, for quotes from Phil Morris,
    Richard Helms and Will Knight.

Other Specific Source Material

National Archives – Soviet officials stationed in UK in late 1940s and
    1950s (KV 6/70-73).
National Archives – Royal Patriotic School (KV 4/339).
National Archives – Churchill and bugging (DEFE 13/16 and DEFE
    134/352).
National Archives – 'Plan for Holland' (HS 6/724).
National Archives – JIC 1947 report on Soviet threat (PREM 8/893).
National Archives – Attlee cabinet meeting on Korean invasion (PREM
    8/893).
Nikolai Andreyevich Loenko – *Trud*, 1 December 1998; *Vladivostok News*,
    7 October 1999 and 26 January 2007; *Novgorod Gazetta*, 8 December
    1998; plus additional Russian sources.
Dr Elizabeth Hill – Department of Collections, Imperial War Museum
    (audio interview). Story about her and Guy Burgess from John
    Costello and Oleg Tsaryev's *Deadly Illusions*, reproduced in Geoffrey
    Elliott and Harold Shukman's *Secret Classrooms*.
David Murphy and Sergei Kondrashev discussion – Allied Museum,
    Berlin.
Charles and Hazel Seymour, Richard Helms, Joe Evans, Jean Meadmore,
    Kenneth De Courcy, Charles Wheeler, Sir James Easton, Vasily
    Dozhdalev, Major G.A.Courtice interviews – The Bower Tapes.
Sergei Kondrashev (on Blake's escape) – Courtesy of the Trustees of the
    Liddell Hart Centre for Military Archives.
Wilson, Heath and Dick White meeting re: Blake escape – National
    Archives (PREM 13).
Albert Behar's war records – National Archives (W0 363/364), material
    supplied by *Fourteeneighteen Research* (www.fourteeneighteen.co.uk).
Mountbatten Report on Prison Escapes – National Archives HO 391/5.
Kenneth Cohen – quote from his unpublished memoir, 1982 (courtesy
    of his son Colin).
Maurice Firth – quote and story from Tom Bower's *The Perfect English Spy*,
    plus other private SIS sources.
Iris Peake – information from Dr Emma Dawnay.

Blake childhood quotes (Dina Regoort and Henrik Dentro) – from E.H.
Cookridge's *George Blake – Double Agent*.

Websites

www.cia.gov
www.englandspiel.eu
www.fourteeneighteen.co.uk
www.koreanwarexpow.org/info/tigers
www.rotterdam4045.nl
www.naval-history.net

Books

Aldrich, Richard J. *The Hidden Hand: Britain, America and Cold War Secret Intelligence,* Overlook Press, 2002.

Allbeury, Ted. *Shadow of Shadows,* Panther Books, 1983.

Andrew, Christopher and Oleg Gordievsky. *KGB: The Inside Story of its Foreign Operations from Lenin to Gorbachev,* Sceptre, 1990.

Andrew, Christopher. *The Defence of the Realm: The Authorised History of MI5,* Penguin Books, 2009.

Bagley, Tennent H. *Spy Wars: Moles, Mysteries and Deadly Games,* Yale University Press, 2007.

Blake, George. *No Other Choice,* Jonathan Cape, 1990.

Bourke, Sean. *The Springing of George Blake,* Mayflower Books, 1971.

Bower, Tom. *The Perfect English Spy,* Heinemann, 1995.

Butler, Ewan. *City Divided: Berlin 1955,* Sidgwick and Jackson, 1955.

Catterall, Peter (ed.). *The Macmillan Diaries: Prime Minister and After 1957–1966,* Macmillan, 2011.

Cavendish, Anthony, *Inside Intelligence: The Revelations of an MI6 Officer,* HarperCollins, 1997.

Colville, John. *The Fringes of Power: Downing Street Diaries 1941 – April 1955,* Hodder and Stoughton, 1985.

Cookridge, E.H. *George Blake: Double Agent,* Hodder Paperback, 1970.

Costello, John and Oleg Tsarev. *Deadly Illusions,* Crown, 1993.

Crosbie, Philip. *March Till They Die,* Browne and Nolan, 1955.

Davies, Philip H.J. *MI6 and the Machinery of Spying,* Frank Cass, 2004.

Davies, S.J. *In Spite of Dungeons,* Alan Sutton, 1992.

Dean, William F. *General Dean's Story,* Weidenfeld and Nicolson, 1954.

Deane, Philip. *Captive in Korea*, Hamish Hamilton, 1953.

Donner, Donald. *A Death March and Nightmares*, Trafford Publishing, 2004.

Dorril, Stephen, *MI6: Fifty Years of Special Operations*, Fourth Estate, 2001.

Dourlein, Pieter. *Inside North Pole*, Time-Life Books Inc., 1988.

Eden, Sir Anthony. *Full Circle*, Cassell, 1960.

Elliott, Geoffrey and Harold Shukman. *Secret Classrooms: An Untold Story of the Cold War*, Faber and Faber, 2011.

Foot, M.R.D. (ed.). *Holland At War Against Hitler: Anglo-Dutch Relations 1940–1945*, Routledge, 1990.

Foot, M.R.D. and J.M. Langley. *MI9: Escape and Evasion 1939–1945*, The Bodley Head, 1979.

Freeman, David. *The Last Days of Alfred Hitchcock*, Overlook Press, 1984.

Giskes, H.J. *London Calling North Pole*, Bantam, 1982.

Glees, Anthony. *The Secrets of the Service*, Carroll and Graf, 1987.

Haslam, Jonathan. *Russia's Cold War*, Yale University Press, 2011.

Hastings, Max. *The Korean War*, Pan Books, 2010.

Helms, Richard (with William Hood). *A Look Over My Shoulder: A Life in the CIA*, Ballantine Books, 2003.

Hood, William. *Mole*, W.W. Norton, 1982.

Hunt, R.N. Carew. *The Theory and Practice of Communism*, Pelican Books, 1964.

Hyde, H. Montgomery. *George Blake: Superspy*, Constable, 1987.

Jeffery, Keith. *MI6: The History of the Secret Intelligence Service 1909–1949*, Bloomsbury, 2011.

Knopp, Guido. *Top Spione*, New American Library, 1997.

Macmillan, Harold. *At the End of the Day: 1961–63*, Macmillan, 1973.

Maddrell, Paul. *Spying on Science: Western Intelligence in Divided Germany 1945–51*, Oxford University Press, 2006.

Madsen, Chris. *The Royal Navy and German Naval Disarmament 1942–1947*, Frank Cass, 1998.

Malkasian, Carter. *The Korean War 1950–1953*, Osprey Publishing, 2001.

Marks, Leo. *Between Silk and Cyanide: A Codemaker's War 1941–1945*, HarperCollins, 1999.

Martin, David C. *Wilderness of Mirrors*, Lyons Press, 1980.

McEwan, Ian. *The Innocent*, Vintage, 2005.

Ministry of Defence. *Treatment of British Prisoners of War in Korea*, HMSO, 1955.

Modin, Yuri. *My Five Cambridge Friends*, Headline, 1994.

Moran, Lord. *Churchill: The Struggle for Survival 1945–60*, Carroll and Graf, 2006.

Murphy, David, Sergei Kondrashev and George Bailey. *Battleground Berlin: CIA vs. KGB in the Cold War*, Yale University Press, 1997.

Page, Bruce, David Leitch and Phillip Knightley. *The Philby Conspiracy*, Ballantine Books, 1981.

Perrault, Gilles. *A Man Apart: The Life of Henri Curiel*, Zed Books Ltd., 1987.

Philby, Kim. *My Secret War*, Arrow Books, 2003.

Philby, Rufina. *The Private Life of Kim Philby: The Moscow Years*, St Ermin's Press, 1999.

Pincher, Chapman. *Traitors*, Penguin Books, 1988.

Randle, Michael and Pat Pottle. *The Blake Escape*, Harrap Books, 1990.

Rankin, Nicholas. *Ian Fleming's Commandos: The Story of 30 Assault Unit in WW2*, Faber and Faber, 2011.

Sampson, Anthony. *Anatomy of Britain*, Hodder and Stoughton, 1962.

Schecter, Jerrold L. and Peter S. Deriabin. *The Spy Who Saved the World*, Macmillan, 1992.

Shackley, Ted. *Spymaster: My Life in the CIA*, Potomac Books, 2005.

Stafford, David. *Spies Beneath Berlin*, John Murray, 2002.

Steury, Donald P. (ed.). *Documents on the Intelligence War in Berlin, 1946 to 1961*, CIA History Staff, 1999.

Sun-Tzu. *The Art of War*, Penguin Books, 2003.

Tempest, Paul (ed.). *The Arabists of Shemlan: MECAS Memoirs 1944–78*, Stacey International, 2006.

Vassall, John. *The Autobiography of a Spy*, Sidgwick and Jackson, 1975.

West, Nigel. *Seven Spies Who Changed The World*, Mandarin, 1991.

West, Rebecca. *The Meaning of Treason*, Penguin Books, 1965.

Wilkinson, Nicholas. *Secrecy and the Media: The Official History of the United Kingdom's D-Notice System*, Routledge, 2009.

Wolf, Markus (with Anne McElvoy). *Memoirs of a Spymaster*, Pimlico, 1997.

Woodward, Leslie. *My Life As A Spy*, Pan Books, 2006.

Wright, Peter (with Paul Greengrass). *Spycatcher: The Candid Autobiography of a Senior Intelligence Officer*, Viking Penguin, 1987.

Zbarsky, Ilya and Samuel Hutchinson. *Lenin's Embalmers*, The Harvill Press, 1998.

Zellers, Larry. *In Enemy Hands: A Prisoner in North Korea*, University Press of Kentucky, 2000.

Zeno, *Life*, Pan Books, 1970.

Index

The abbreviation GB refers to George Blake